Creating Women's Theology

Creating Women's Theology
A Movement Engaging Process Thought

Edited by
MONICA A. COLEMAN
NANCY R. HOWELL
HELENE TALLON RUSSELL

◆PICKWICK *Publications* · Eugene, Oregon

CREATING WOMEN'S THEOLOGY
A Movement Engaging Process Thought

Copyright © 2011 Wipf and Stock Publishers. All rights reserved. Except for brief quotations in critical publications or reviews, no part of this book may be reproduced in any manner without prior written permission from the publisher. Write: Permissions, Wipf and Stock Publishers, 199 W. 8th Ave., Suite 3, Eugene, OR 97401.

Pickwick Publications
An Imprint of Wipf and Stock Publishers
199 W. 8th Ave., Suite 3
Eugene, OR 97401

www.wipfandstock.com

ISBN 13: 978-1-61097-177-5

Cataloging-in-Publication data:

Creating women's theology : a movement engaging process thought / edited by Monica A. Coleman, Nancy R. Howell, and Helene Tallon Russell.

xviii + 256 pp.; 22 cm.—Includes bibliographical references and index.

ISBN 13: 978-1-61097-177-5

1. Feminist theology. 2. Womanist theology. 3. Process theology. I. Coleman, Monica A., 1974–. II. Howell, Nancy R., 1953–. III. Russell, Helene Tallon. IV. Title.

BL458 C70 2011

Manufactured in the USA

Permissions

"Androgynous Life" by Valerie Saiving in *Feminism and Process Thought*, edited by Sheila Davaney, © 1981 Edwin Mellen Press. Reprinted by permission of Edwin Mellen Press.

Pages 2–5; 49–61 from *God—Christ—Church* by Marjorie Hewitt Suchocki, copyright © 1989 Crossroad Publishing Company. Reprinted by permission of Crossroad Publishing Company.

Pages 68–71 from *Sexism and God-Talk* by Rosemary Radford Ruether. Copyright © 1983, 1993 Beacon Press. Reprinted by permission of Beacon Press, Boston.

Pages 240–53 from *Gaia & God* by Rosemary Radford Ruether. Copyright © 1992 Rosemary Radford Ruether. Reprinted by permission of HarperCollins Publishers.

Pages 316–26 from "The Sin of Hiding: A Feminist Critique of Reinhold Niebuhr's Account of the Sin of Pride," from *Soundings: An Interdisciplinary Journal* by Susan (Dunfree) Nelson. Copyright © Fall 1982. Reprinted by permission of *Soundings*.

Pages 7–15; 26–27; 248–52 from *From a Broken Web* by Catherine Keller. Copyright © 1986 Beacon Press. Reprinted by permission of Beacon Press, Boston.

Pages 39–47 from *Journeys by Heart* by Rita Nakashima Brock. Copyright © 1991, 1998. Permission granted by the author.

Pages 47–55 & 141–50 from *The Body of God* by Sallie McFague, copyright © 1993 Fortress Press. Used by permission of Augsburg Fortress Publishers.

Pages 148–63; 165–69 from *Dancing with God* by Karen Baker-Fletcher © 2006 Karen Baker Fletcher. Reprinted by permission of Chalice Press.

Pages 179–91 from "The Importance of Being Chimpanzee" from *Theology and Science* by Nancy R. Howell. Copyright © October 2003. Reprinted by permission of *Theology and Science*.

Pages 33–53 from *God, Creation and All That Jazz* by Ann Pederson © 2000 Ann Pederson. Reprinted by permission of Chalice Press.

Pages 289–91, 299–311 from "Reconstructing Divine Power: Holocaust Jewish Theology, Feminism, and Process Philosophy" in *Women and Gender in Jewish Philosophy* edited by Hava Tirosh-Samuelson, copyright © 2004 Indiana University Press. Reprinted with permission of Indiana University Press.

Pages 197–210; 230–36 from *She Who Changes* by Carol P. Christ, copyright © 2003 Carol P. Christ. Reproduced by permission of Palgrave Macmillan.

Pages 107–23 from *Making a Way Out of No Way* by Monica A. Coleman, copyright © 2008 Fortress Press. Used by permission of Augsburg Fortress Publishers.

Dedicated to
John B. Cobb Jr. and Marjorie Hewitt Suchocki,
who encourage women's theological creativity

Contents

Permissions

Acknowledgments • xi

Foreword—Marjorie Hewitt Suchocki • *xiii*

Introduction—Monica A. Coleman, Nancy R. Howell, and Helene Tallon Russell • *xvii*

Part 1: Introduction to the Movement

1. Introduction to Feminist Theology—*Helene Tallon Russell* • 3
2. Introduction to Process Theology—*Monica A. Coleman* • 12
3. Women, Whitehead, and Hartshorne: What Characterizes Process-Relational Women's Worldviews—*Nancy R. Howell* • 20

Part 2: Texts in Women's Process Relational Theologies

4. Experience—*Valerie Saiving* • 31
   from "Androgynous Life: A Feminist Appropriation of Process Thought"
   - COMMENTARY AND STUDY QUESTIONS—HELENE TALLON RUSSELL • 43

5. Methodology/God's Presence—*Marjorie Hewitt Suchocki* • 46
   from *God, Christ, Church: A Practical Guide to Process Theology*
   - COMMENTARY AND STUDY QUESTIONS—JEANYNE B. SLETTOM • 58

6. Rejection of Dualism—*Rosemary Radford Ruether* • 60
   from *Sexism and God-Talk: Toward a Feminist Theology* and *Gaia & God: An Ecofeminist Theology of Earth Healing*
   - COMMENTARY AND STUDY QUESTIONS—KATHLYN BREAZEALE • 71

7. Sin—*Susan L. Nelson* • 74
   from "The Sin of Hiding: A Feminist Critique of Reinhold Niebuhr's Account of the Sin of Pride"
   - COMMENTARY AND STUDY QUESTIONS—NICHOLE TORBIZSKY • 82

8. Self and God: Separation, Sexism, and Self—*Catherine E. Keller* • 85
   from *From a Broken Web: Separation, Sexism, and Self*
   - COMMENTARY AND STUDY QUESTIONS—KRISTA E. HUGHES • 98

9. Christology and Eros—*Rita Nakashima Brock* • 101
   from *Journeys by Heart: A Christology of Erotic Power*
   - COMMENTARY AND STUDY QUESTIONS—MARIT A. TRELSTAD • 110

Contents

10 Ecofeminism and Nature—*Sallie McFague* • 113
    from *The Body of God: An Ecological Theology*
    ⁕ Commentary and Study Questions—*Kirsten Mebust* • 125

11 Holy Spirit and Womanism—*Karen Baker-Fletcher* • 127
    from *Dancing with God: The Trinity from a Womanist Perspective*
    ⁕ Commentary and Study Questions—*Monica A. Coleman* • 142

12 Theological Anthropology—*Nancy R. Howell* • 145
    from "The Importance of Being Chimpanzee"
    ⁕ Commentary and Study Questions—*Ann M. Pederson* • 157

13 Creativity, Christology and Science: A Process of Composition and Improvisation—*Ann M. Pederson* • 160
    from *God, Creation, and All That Jazz: A Process of Composition and Improvisation*
    ⁕ Commentary and Study Questions—*Caryn D. Riswold* • 175

14 Jewish Feminism: Holocaust Jewish Theology, Feminism, and Process Philosophy—*Sandra B. Lubarsky* • 178
    from "Reconstructing Divine Power: Holocaust Jewish Theology, Feminism, and Process Philosophy"
    ⁕ Commentary and Study Questions—*Arlette Poland* • 191

15 Re-Imaging Goddess/God: Re-Imagining the Divine in the World—*Carol P. Christ* • 194
    from *She Who Changes: Re-Imagining the Divine in the World*
    ⁕ Commentary and Study Questions—*Constance Wise* • 210

16 African Traditional Religions and Womanism—*Monica A. Coleman* • 213
    from *Making a Way Out of No Way: A Womanist Theology*
    ⁕ Commentary and Study Questions—*Carolyn Roncolato* • 227

Contributors • 231

Chapter Sources • 235

Bibliography • 237

Index • 253

Acknowledgments

THE EDITORS WISH TO gratefully acknowledge our editorial team at Pickwick Publications and Wipf and Stock Publishers. K. C. Hanson graciously accepted the idea for this anthology in difficult economic times. We felt support for this project from its inception.

We honor and appreciate Marjorie Hewitt Suchocki who hosted a conference on Process and Women's Theologies at Claremont School of Theology in the Spring of 2004 titled "Exploring the Connections: Process-Relational and Women's Theologies." Not only did we all meet in person at this conference, but the desire to immortalize the experience of this conference led us, ultimately, to this project. This conference was the second such gathering. In 1978, Harvard Divinity School and Claremont School of Theology's Center for Process Studies co-sponsored the first symposium to bring together process theology and feminism. We would like to thank Sheila Greeve Davaney who edited the book based on these papers that helped make the case for why process thought and feminism ought to be in dialogue with each other. We are grateful to these scholars whose insights and scholarly intuitions have inspired this new branch of theology. No longer understood as process theology *and* feminism, these two approaches are integrated and integrating the multifaceted elements of theology and theory in the movement's own unique way. Feminist process relational theology has become a movement within theology in its own right.

We give special thanks to all of the contributing feminist process theologians who wrote commentaries. They worked well and quickly in their reflections. The Center for Process Studies was incredibly helpful in compiling the bibliography. Because of the diligent work of Crystal Hughes, the bibliography is updated and expanded as a useful source. The editorial work and formatting by Sonsiris Tamayo greatly assisted in the production of the manuscript. Because of this great community of contributions, the work is stronger and far more rewarding.

Monica A. Coleman gives special thanks to Claremont School of Theology and the Career Enhancement Fellowship for Junior Faculty from the Woodrow Wilson National Fellowship Foundation Office that granted her the resources for the research leave to devote to her part of this project. Vera Bagneris, Becky Dornan and Sansu Woodmancy have been instrumental in assisting with many small (and unforeseen) details in reprinting the previously published work. Finally, words of appreciation go to Michael Datcher, whose support—usually through the sacrifice of time and attention—was so helpful during the final months of this project.

Nancy R. Howell appreciates colleagues and students at Saint Paul School

Acknowledgments

of Theology who have encouraged her teaching and research in process theology. Crystal Hughes deserves another mention for engaging Nancy in weekly conversations about process theology and women's experience during the final months of book preparation, which helped keep focus on the many tasks at hand.

Helene Tallon Russell expresses special appreciation to the Christian Theological Seminary for its generous leave policy and faculty development fund that enabled her to have the time and recourses for research in Claremont for developing and completing this project. She is also thankful to Matthew Upchurch for his editing skills and for the inspiring engagement in conversations about this project.

On a much larger scale, we are all thankful for generations of women scholars and men, such as John Cobb, who formed a community hospitable to the development of women's process relational theologies. We are especially grateful to Marjorie Suchocki for her encouragement and mentoring through this book project and many other projects intertwining process thought, theology, and feminism.

We have embraced a feminist praxis in our collaborative work over distance and time zones. To the extent that this volume reflects our process and commitments, we rejoice.

Foreword

THE PUBLICATION OF THIS volume is particularly significant because 2010 marked the fiftieth anniversary year of Valerie Saiving's 1960 article, "The Human Situation: A Feminine View," in which she suggested that a woman's experience of sin was not quite that of man's. Pride, as described by Reinhold Niebuhr, might well apply to men, she argued, but for women not having enough pride was more likely the problem. Simone de Beauvoir's *The Second Sex* had only been published eleven years earlier, and Betty Friedan's *The Feminine Mystique* was yet to appear. Unlike de Beauvoir's work, Saiving's article took the question of women into the very bastions of patriarchy, Christian theology.

At first there was not much response. But later in the sixties, a Catholic woman named Mary Daly took the issue a further step. Daly had a naïve confidence that once the issue of the inappropriateness of women's subordination in church as well as society was properly raised, the church—agent of salvation that it was—would respond with corrective theology and practice. And so Daly expanded de Beauvoir's argument in her own *The Church and the Second Sex*. The church, of course, considered Daly's book to be rank heresy, but the ripples created by Saiving's article were whipped by Daly's winds to a storm-sized consciousness-raising event. Women began raising the questions: Why is the church patriarchal? What *is* women's experience? What would theology look like if it took women's experience into account? Feminist theology was born.[1]

As women began considering their own experience from a theological perspective, the intensely relational nature of experience began to surface as a dominant category. Patriarchal theology had not ignored relation, for relationality certainly pervades all existence. In Trinitarian development, much theological energy had gone into speculations concerning the intrarelational life of the triune God. But, however inconsistently, relationality was subsumed under the supposedly superior value of immutability.[2] Not so for feminists. And, as it happened, not so for a new form of Christian theology that had preceded feminist theology by only a few decades—process theology, based on the philosophy of Alfred North Whitehead.

Whitehead, influenced by the relational world of quantum physics, developed a complex analysis of the basic

---

1. Feminist theology was not without foremothers in American history—Elizabeth Cady Stanton and her cohorts in the late nineteenth century pioneered revisionist biblical studies on the basis of women's perspective, which of course had theological implications.

2. Charles Hartshorne and William Reese trace alternative approaches to relation throughout the Western tradition in *Philosophers Speak of God* (Chicago: University of Chicago Press, 1953).

structure of existence as essentially dynamic and relational. For Whitehead, all existence—whether animal, vegetable, or mineral, whether human or divine—is necessarily relational. Becoming is the basis of being. To exist is to emerge from feelings received from the past and integrated into a novel unity through a grasp of future possibilities. The immutability so valued by traditional philosophies and theologies is but a chimera, giving way to dynamism, change, relation. Theologians, notably John B. Cobb Jr., began applying Whitehead's philosophical vision to theology. By the 1970s the process vision of a relational world and the feminist vision of a relational world began to converge for key thinkers in both the feminist and process movements.

In 1978 Sheila Greeve Davaney orchestrated a major event in this convergence—the Harvard Divinity School and Claremont Center for Process Studies symposium on feminism and process thought. Papers were given by John B. Cobb Jr., Mary Daly, Sheila Davaney, Jean Lambert, Valerie Saiving, Marjorie Hewitt Suchocki, and Penelope Washburn. Daly's paper was incorporated into her book, *Gyn/Ecology*, and Davaney edited and published the others in *Feminism and Process Thought*. Cobb, Davaney, and Suchocki were process thinkers reaching toward feminist thought, and Daly, Lambert, Saiving, and Washburn were feminists interested in process insights. Daly, of course, would never be bound to any system; her own spiraling cosmogenesis would utilize and then break free of conceptualities other than her own. But the symposium succeeded in establishing the conversation between feminist and process theologians.

While both forms of theology develop from a fundamentally relational view of existence, they do so in very different ways. Process thinkers are guided by the implications of Whitehead's process philosophy. They find his model of the "actual entity" to be enormously fruitful not only for understanding the dynamics of life, but for providing a basis to transform theology and indeed, social structures. Feminist theologians come to many of the same insights expressed by Whitehead and the process school, but they do so by examining the primacy of experience in light of the patriarchal oppression of women. When process and feminist thinking converge, the result is less like the convergence of two rivers coming together to form a third, and more like a spontaneous flow, where two streams of influence touch each other, affect each other, separate for a time, touch again, and sometimes together and sometimes separately continue to enrich theologies in their own distinctive ways.

Thus following the 1978 symposium, feminist insights are woven throughout Suchocki's process theology in the 1982 *God—Christ—Church*,[3] while Rosemary Radford Ruether's 1983 *Sexism and God-Talk* explicitly formulates a feminist relational view of reality. Despite the interweaving, Suchocki is considered a process rather than a feminist theologian, and Ruether a feminist rather than process theologian. In later publications the two theologians are more intentional in naming both feminist and process influences, but the earlier work remains distinctive. Catherine Keller—a Cobb student graduating in the 1980s—most openly draws

---

3. A much revised and expanded version was published in 1989.

equally from feminist and process thought as she begins her publishing career. But even there, feminists are not so apt to notice the process suppositions woven throughout her writing, whereas process theologians clearly identify both process and feminist strands woven together throughout the fabric of her work.

Meanwhile, in the late 1980s and 1990s Cobb students Susan Nelson, Rita Nakashima Brock, and Nancy Howell as well as Catherine Keller publish in both feminist and process theology. In the 90s, Suchocki and Keller took their own turns mentoring women doctoral students who would join the growing school of process feminists—women such as Helene Russell, Monica A. Coleman, Marit Trelstad, Kathlyn Breazeale, Jeanyne Slettom, Mayra Rivera, and Kirsten Mebust.

But I would be remiss to mention only those women directly influenced by the Claremont school of process theology. Two women in particular illustrate a more directly feminist/womanist tradition that also owns the influence of process modes of thought: Sallie McFague and Karen Baker-Fletcher.

McFague began publishing significant feminist books in the 1980s, focusing much of her work on models of God. Her own model, in the 1993 *The Body of God*, is implicitly but not explicitly process. Her 1997 *Super, Natural Christians* names her preference for an organic model in which the world "is characterized by evolutionary change and novelty, structure as well as openness (or law and chance), relationality and interdependence, with individual entities existing only within systems, systems that can be expressed by the models of organism and community."[4] In her 2001 *Life Abundant*, she once again develops a relational feminist theology that is profoundly akin to theologies developed by theologians more explicitly identified as process theologians. Her writings move increasingly toward ecological imperatives, and as they do so, she stresses again and again the panentheistic model from which she works. While not naming process as such, she is as strongly a process thinker as is any writer in the explicitly process field.

Karen Baker-Fletcher comes to her work from a womanist perspective, drawing on the stories and poetry of African American women's experience to reconfigure Christian theology. In many ways, she dances with and around process categories, now naming them and now distancing herself from them as she listens to the music of her life. Like McFague's, her writing in its depths reveals a profoundly relational sensitivity—a process sensitivity—dancing in and through her own distinctive womanist theology.

There are many others, of course, such as Lynne Lorenzen, Ann Pederson, Anne Primavesi, Grace Jantzen, Sandra Lubarsky, and Carol P. Christ. Christ is particularly interesting in that she devoted most of her career and, indeed, her life, to exploring goddess theology. In the 1990s she discovered the writings of Charles Hartshorne, and immediately began utilizing his process philosophy to express her own insights. *She Who Changes: Re-imagining the Divine in the World* tells the story.

---

4. Sallie McFague, *Super, Natural Christians: How We Should Love Nature* (Minneapolis: Fortress, 1997) 20.

Foreword

This present book, edited by Monica A. Coleman, Nancy Howell, and Helene Russell, traces key movements in the dance between process and feminist theologies. In a particularly process way, they present salient articles or chapters from feminist/process thinkers over the past decades, and then pull these "pasts" into the present with responses to the articles, written by young feminist/process theologians. These responses are creative in their own right, written not only in relation to the past, but in relation to a vision of what might yet be possible by an ever-new convergence of process and feminist thinking. In doing so, the authors and editors of this volume richly contribute to the fulfillment of their own vision.

Marjorie Hewitt Suchocki

Introduction

CREATING WOMEN'S THEOLOGY presents the interface between process relational theology and feminist theology. Both of these approaches to theology offer cutting-edge insights into important issues that inspire current theological discourse: the value of experience, the importance of freedom, and the interdependence of humanity, God and all of creation. In the last several decades, scholars entwined strands from these two approaches to produce a textured movement of their own: *process-relational feminist theology*.

This text includes introductions to feminist theologies and process theology, their intersection, and excerpts of groundbreaking texts and ideas in the movement. We have three hopes in offering this text. First and foremost we seek to expose new generations of undergraduate, seminary and other students to the movement's methods and insights, and we hope, to engage them in the continuing conversation. Second, we are gathering the beginnings of this integrative school of thought to take account of how we have come to this new way of approaching theology. And third, we seek to inspire new possibilities for progressing in process and relational women's theology.

The book is divided into three primary sections. Part 1 consists of three chapters, each introducing one of the following three areas: feminist theology, process theology, and the intersection of feminist and process theologies. We provide basic introductions to orient new readers and reframe the significant themes for advanced scholars. There are several fine introductory books on feminist theologies and process theologies. We shape our introductions to emphasize the themes that are important to the process-relational feminist theological movement. We imagine this book serving as an informative introduction to feminist theology, to process theology and to this third integrated field of process-relational feminist theology.

The second section of the book is comprised of chapters that contain three elements: a selection of passages excerpted from previously published work; a short commentary on this excerpt; and a list of discussion questions. First, all of the excerpted essays are examples of how women theologians interweave their feminist commitments with a process relational view of God and the world. We selected these texts primarily with two criteria in mind. The first concern was to identify the key texts that characterize ideas with "staying power," by which we mean they are women's ways of speaking process theology and they inform and inspire women who continue to articulate creative forms of theology. Selecting these excerpts was no easy task. There were many interesting works we could not include. We chose

Introduction

these selections based on their influence upon the movement as a whole. Second, we wanted to reflect a wide variety of key themes and perspectives that characterize process relational women's theology. We also wanted to show writings addressing topics within process thought, Christian theological categories and various religious traditions. The texts presented here illustrate key themes in this movement, and we hope that they whet the appetite of scholars unfamiliar with this movement and encourage further analysis for those scholars already so engaged.

Each chapter also includes a commentary by another process relational feminist theologian who interprets the meaning and significance of the excerpt and who traces the influence of the excerpt on theology by women in dialogue with process theology. The commentary also reflects on how the themes of the excerpt may shape the further development of the field. We intentionally invited theologians who studied with the author of the selected work or were strongly influenced by the excerpted work. This process highlights the communal and relational nature and development of women's process-relational theology, reflecting the feminist praxis of both our commitments and the movement itself. Lastly, each chapter ends with study questions that allow for guided investigation through the text presented in the chapter.

We are honored by Marjorie Hewitt Suchocki's foreword that gives an historical overview of the progress of the movement and its significant ideas to date, as well as a call toward its continued creative advance. Suchocki has been and continues to be a leader in women's process theological work in her own research, activism and mentorship. Finally, we conclude with an extensive bibliography of published articles, essays, and books in process-relational feminist theology.

Monica A. Coleman
Nancy R. Howell
Helene Tallon Russell

PART ONE

Introduction to the Movement

1 Introduction to Feminist Theology

HELENE TALLON RUSSELL

THIS INTRODUCTION WILL DESCRIBE the ways that Christian feminist theology[1] seeks to re-vision and reconstruct Christian theology by focusing on three important questions: who does theology; how to do theology; and what does theology tell us? These three questions loosely correlate with three primary contributions of feminist theology to the field of theology in general. The first and perhaps most important claim of feminist theology is the centrality of experience, especially women's experience. It is taken as a source and resource for theology. This answers the question, *who is doing theology?* The second issue relates to critical hermeneutics, the criteria by which texts and claims are evaluated and appropriated. This answers, how do feminists and women do theology differently? *How are texts read and used?* The third section of this introduction examines an example of the content that flows from these first two claims. Attending to the experience of women who have been ignored and silenced coupled with employing a critical reading of authoritative sources leads to women writing about alternative theological claims and concerns. I will use the doctrine of sin as an example of this. What are the contributions of feminist theology to the content of theology? *What are feminist theologians saying about sin and other concerns of theology?*

THE *F* WORD

The term *feminist* is itself a sticky wicket. It is thought that Hubertine Auclert is the first person to have used the term in 1882 to indicate women who were fighting for our political rights.[2] It is an ambiguous term because it has a history, a reputation and many negative connotations that are difficult to overcome. The term and those associated with it have been derided on both the conservative and the more radical sides of the discourse. Popular notions about feminists are laden with negative connotations ranging from man-haters, to prudish women who have to be in control

---

1. Even though feminist theology is present in many religious traditions as well as posttraditional spiritual communities, this introduction will focus on Christian Theology for the sake of expediency and because Christianity and Judaism reflect the dominant religious traditions in North American discourse, out of which most women who call themselves process theologians have grown. Note that process theology and the movement of women who are influenced by it are open to the diversity of religion which will be reprised below.

2. Anderson and Zinsser, *A History of Their Own: Women in Europe from Prehistory to the Present*, vol. 2 (New York: Harper & Row, 1988).

all the time. There is a noted phenomenon found today in which young women deny that they are a "*feminist* but . . ." The sentence is usually followed by claims that are part of definitions of feminism. For example, I am not a feminist but I expect equal pay. However, recently there have been campaigns by women to change the image of "feminist" with the popular T shirts and images of a variety of women proclaiming, "this is what a feminist looks like" with even President Obama getting on the band wagon.[3]

And so it looks as though the term could be redeemed or rescued, yet there is another important concern. The term has at times been associated with a movement that is primarily composed of white women. Other terminology such as womanist (African American women's theology), or *mujerista* (Latin American women's liberation theology) have arisen to describe the distinctive religious experiences of particular racial-ethnic minorities. Yet even those terms are not perfect and have been questioned.[4] I would like to reclaim the term feminist and assert that a feminist or a woman seeking liberation can be of any ethnic origin or race, any class, any religion, any sexual orientation, en-abled in any way, etc. Toward being as inclusive as possible I will use a few different nomenclatures, such as *women's liberation theology* and *feminist theology* to denote an approach to theology that is of, for, and by *any* women who are seeking liberation from patriarchal norms and phallocentric discourse.

Feminism is an unusual discipline. In addition to being an academic field, filled with theory and criticism, hermeneutics and constructive thought, it is also a social/political movement concerned with equal rights, eliminating misogyny in cultural and social values, and otherwise improving women's lives. It constructs and offers a vision of inclusivity, diversity, and well-being, in which the world is more friendly to women, ethnic minorities, gays and lesbians, all socio-economic classes, animals, and the earth herself. The current wave of feminism has its fore-sisters in both the first wave of suffragettes near the turn of the twentieth century and the second wave of feminism which began in 1960s and 1970s which focused on equal rights and other issues that affect the quality of women's lives, such as equal pay, maternity leaves, sexuality, etc. This movement has had widespread impact on women by effecting changes in the internal and external lives of women, especially in women's ways of understanding our own subjectivity.

More than most other disciplines, feminism is built upon an experiential transformation of consciousness. It begins not as an objective field of study like philosophy or history, nor is it limited to theoretical knowledge. Rather it is usually propagated by persons who have had some sort of awakening or a transformation of consciousness. Women do not start out being feminists; we become feminists through a realization of a countercultural worldview. This realization, this awakening, often occurs in dialogue with other women who share common experiences and perspectives.

---

3. See Goodman and Smeal, "This is What a Feminist Looks Like," *Democracy Now*, online: http://www.democracynow.org/2009/1/27/ms_magazine_on_barack_obama_this/.

4. See Coleman, "Must I Be a Womanist?" *Journal of Feminist Studies in Religion* 22 (2006) 85–96.

The consciousness-raising phenomenon moves beyond the minimal self-consciousness of being a woman, and toward an awareness of two important claims. We become aware that as women our importance, function and even our very being have been devalued in the normative western discourse, tradition, and culture. Our feelings, thoughts, beliefs and values have not been included and acknowledged as part of the common discourse. As we become aware that the embedded assumptions which we have taken to be true are actually biased and not accurate representations of the world, their power over our internal beliefs fades. At the same time that women learn a critical posture toward the current discourse, we also learn to discover and develop our own values, ideas, thoughts, and ways of being in the world, society and with ourselves. The process continues to spiral toward greater self awareness.

At least this is the way it is supposed to happen. However, since the dominant worldview has been constructed out of male-centered experience, by men, for men, and benefited men over women, this bias can and does without a doubt influence our experience and our interpretation of events, encounters, feelings, relationships, ideas and experiences. Our experiences occur within social/political/cultural/discursive contexts. These contexts influence the nature, form, and quality and quantity of our experiences.

EXPERIENCE

Unlike many other disciplines, feminism is explicitly and acutely experiential. This realization, which is fundamental for feminist consciousness, arises out of certain types of shared and personal experience. Nelle Morton spoke of *hearing each other into speech* and Mary Daly writes of the necessity of a "profound alteration of consciousness and behavior—that is of the context in which words are spoken."[5] All of this requires participation and not merely thinking. Experience then is a primary epistemological source for feminist thought.

Experience is important on the front end for engaging in feminism, but also it is important methodologically for feminist theology. It is a primary source and resource for feminist theology. Valerie Saiving makes this claim clearly in her ground breaking essay "The Human Situation: A Feminine View."[6] Here she shatters the common embedded assumption that men's experience include women's experience—that a man can fully represent a woman. She continues to develop this notion in her lecture on the interface of process thought and feminist theology in the essay that is reprinted in this volume.

Women are certainly not the first group to utilize experience as a source of religious knowledge and truth. Many would argue that to some extent all religious knowledge is based on experience consciously or unconsciously. Nor are women even the first to consciously highlight experience as a source of theological truth.[7] Women's liberation theology however, is one of the first theological schools

---

5. Daly, *Beyond God the Father: Toward a Philosophy of Women's Liberation*, 2nd ed. (Boston: Beacon, 1985) xix.

6. Valerie Saiving, "The Human Situation: A Feminine View," in *WomenSpirit Rising*, eds. Carol P. Christ and Judith Plaskow (New York: Harper & Row, 1979) 25–42.

7. John Wesley, William James, and Frederick Schleiermacher explicitly speak of experience as a theological source.

to highlight women's experience as significantly distinctive. This distinctness has led to alternative theological viewpoints and new contributions to religious knowledge created out of the experience of women and other under-represented groups.

The notion that women's experience is somehow completely different from men's experience is wrong-headed. Further, not all women share the same experience about everything. While one may assert that many women have experiences in common, no two women are the same. Yet as a group women's experiences have been excluded, repressed, or otherwise not adequately represented in Western philosophical and theological theories. This shared context itself gives a common flavor to some of women's experience especially as it relates to the formative experiences of liberation and becoming more fully oneself and more fully participating in the world.

Experience is a complex topic. I will begin with a brief analysis of this complexity. There are three different issues to be distinguished and addressed. First is the priority ascribed to experience as an epistemological source. In other words, experience is a means by which one knows what one knows. This sense of the phenomenon of experience as a medium and form for all types of knowledge is about the immediacy of the moment—one's experience right now and right here. Experience, used in this way, is part of one's interpretive framework.

Second in addition to the immediate form, experience can also be understood as the content of past experiences. The results of one's past encounters, practices, experiments lead one to think, feel and ascribe value to various claims, events and concerns. These experiences and interpretation of experiences (because all experience is interpreted) could be recent or long ago; they could be one's own experiences, or experiences others have shared or one has read about or witnessed. Over time they become codified as history and tradition. Then we can reflect upon them and their significance, effects, and implications. One means of analysis and evaluation of experience is to judge the fruits of the experience. For example did the experience make one a better person? Did it teach skills or impart wisdom? Did it enable more compassion or sensitivity? Did it show a person what not to do? Has it imparted greater self-knowledge? Or knowledge and bonding with others?

Third, experience is noteworthy in feminist theology because most of the Western philosophical and theological tradition and scripture has reflected the experience, situations, and concerns of the men in power. Women's voices have not been heard. Women's experiences, perspectives, and concerns have not been addressed. This is problematic for women because we are excluded from both the constructive procedures of theology as well as the claims theology makes. It is also problematic for theology because it leaves theology as a half discipline. Theology itself is less rich, diverse and deep. One remedy that is practiced by all types of liberation theologies is to give priority to those who have been marginalized. The experiences, needs, and questions of the poor and under-represented are highlighted. In this approach women's concerns for theology would be encouraged and given increased attention. And women would be encouraged to write constructive theology. Another remedy is a redactionist one like Jewish feminist Judith Plaskow.[8] She surmises that even though women's concerns and responses to the covenant at Sinai are not recorded in the Hebrew Scriptures, we know that women were there and can imagine what feelings and thoughts that they might have had. She bids women to reconstruct the history to include women's stories, even imagined stories, thus rendering visible what has been invisible.

Women's theologies have been careful to highlight the relative and contextual nature of experience. It is different for different persons and different social situations. Experience is always interpreted and always embedded within social, culture, political and personal contexts. These contexts must be taken into account as well. Women's liberation theology focuses on a variety of types of experience and subjects of experience, such as nonverbal means of communication, embodied knowledge, intuition and poetry, movement and dance, stories and novels, images, etc., all of which emerge in communal presence and participation.

Experience is understood to be a primary resource and source for theology. And yet sometimes experience can fool us. One of the weaknesses of women's liberation theology is that it trusts experience. And sometimes it trusts experience naïvely, uncritically and without attention to how to integrate the variety of conflicting claims and implications. Feminist theology sometimes holds up experience uncritically or appeals to experience without effective criteria by which to judge its applicability to communal truth claims.

How can we resist the temptation to retreat into the relativism of "it's true because it is my experience?" How can we avoid the influence of embedded patriarchal norms upon our thinking, beliefs, feelings and experience? Along with encouraging women to listen to women's experience, feminist theology needs to encourage women to continue developing guides for interpreting experience, for understanding its implications, and for the most effective way of utilizing experience. Experience needs to be understood and utilized in feminist theology critically and carefully.

Mary McClintock Fulkerson speaks to this issue and distinguishes between the function of feminist experience in consciousness-raising and the role experience plays in academic feminist theorizing. In the academic disciple of theology and feminist theology, Fulkerson suggests that personal experience alone is inadequate to the complexity and multiplicity of theology. Experience, she writes, "cannot recognize a complex web of signifying processes and the material embeddedness of those processes that makes up the blind side of our thinking."[9]

While women's personal and communal experience is certainly an important source of women's liberation theology, experience can not be the only source and all sources, even, especially experience, must be understood as interpreted and thus contextual and only an approximation of its source. We can not know our own experience fully, for we are other and stranger to ourselves.

---

8. Judith Plaskow, *Standing Again at Sinai* (San Francisco: Harper & Row, 1990).

9. Fulkerson, *Changing the Subject: Women's Discourses and Feminist Theology* (Minneapolis: Fortress, 1994) 360.

CRITICAL HERMENEUTICS: INTERPRETING THE BIBLE AND OTHER AUTHORITATIVE TEXTS

Women's liberation theology asks critical questions about accepted norms, beliefs, and practices. These implicit norms are embedded in patriarchal discourse and uphold male experience as the standard experience and promote that which benefits men and those in power. Critical awareness of them leads to the second primary contribution of feminist theology addressed in this essay: practical critical hermeneutics. Many women experience the tradition as ambiguous at best. Texts and theological claims must be appropriately evaluated with special attention given to how they are interpreted and used. This is particularly germane in relation to authoritative texts that have either ignored women or portrayed women as less than fully human. A critical approach to the Bible and the tradition uses practical critical criteria to judge the redemptive quality of biblical and traditional claims.

Rosemary Radford Ruether's critical feminist principle is a paradigmatic example of a feminist critical hermeneutical approach to scripture and tradition. She puts forth a stark and simple criterion for judging whether or not a theological/religious claim is acceptable. Does a particular story or claim or command promote the full humanity of women? "Whatever denies, diminishes, or distorts the full humanity of women is, therefore, appraised as not redemptive."[10] I highlight this principle as a paradigmatic example of a feminist approach to authoritative texts. Other women have set forth similar and more expanded criteria. Katie Cannon, for instance, offers a guiding principle for a critical appropriation of theological claims within the African American women's struggle for human dignity.

Feminist theology demands vigilance in critical awareness and being suspicious of texts and claims. The appropriation of Ricoeur's hermeneutic of suspicion is widespread. Many feminist biblical scholars, such as Elisabeth Schüssler Fiorenza, Renita Weems and Phyllis Trible, employ and adapt this framework for interpreting texts and make use of it by questioning the truth claims being made in the text. Who does the story or the proposition benefit? If the answer is that it benefits the one recounting the events or the ones that are in power, then these claims should be taken with a grain of salt for they might not be so clearly true.

What can feminists who wish to remain part of a mainstream religious community do with the sexist and misogynous passages and stories? What does anyone who remains part of her or his own religious tradition do with the passages and stories that deny, diminish or distort the full humanity of any person or group of people? Feminist critical hermeneutics have influenced theology in general in framing this issue. Many theologians have adopted and adapted this technique for addressing problematic claims and texts as a way that maintains the integrity of both the particular tradition and the justice concerns of the current context in which the text speaks authoritatively. Scholars concerned about this issue, such as Clark Williamson with his focus on ameliorating the anti-Jewishness in parts of the New Testament, have employed Ruether's critical principle and

---

10. Rosemary Radford Ruether, *Sexism and God-Talk* (Boston: Beacon, 1983) 18–19.

other feminist hermeneutical approaches in their own work. The insights of feminist theology are not just for women, but engage any thinker that is concerned about the full humanity and dignity of each person.

WOMEN'S LIBERATION THEOLOGY RE-ENVISIONS THEOLOGICAL DOCTRINES: SIN

As attention has been paid to the theological questions and insights of women along with women's critical concerns in regarding misogynous and problematic claims in sacred texts and traditions, new ways of understanding the content of theology and its doctrines, practices, and values have emerged. New methods lead to alternative conceptualizations. Women read and practice theology in ways that are different from how it has been done in the past. There are many new themes and questions as well as different perspectives on the historically relevant issues.

As an example I will give a brief analysis of women's liberation approach to the conventional formulation of the doctrine of sin. Many women speaking for liberation have challenged the traditional doctrine of sin, suggesting that its traditional formulation ignores women's experience and needs and is biased against women. Valerie Saiving, Judith Plaskow and Sue Nelson[11] (formerly Dunfee) are some of the earliest feminists who criticized the doctrine of sin as formulated by Niebuhr and others, claiming that it reflects the situation, experiences and needs of men but not those of women. Niebuhr develops the main trajectory of the Christian tradition with regards to the doctrine of sin when he names sin as pride. Sin is rebellion against God. It is acting as if one knows better than God and can overcome the limitations God has set upon one.

In Saiving's groundbreaking work on this topic, she sets out the concern clearly when she writes that "there are significant differences between masculine and feminine experience."[12] She makes a direct connection between the fact that women's experience and situation have not been addressed in the main stream of theology, which is seen in the problematic explanation of the doctrine of sin. Since the situation of less than half of the human population has been taken as the norm for all, it is no surprise that the understanding and experience of sin that arises from this way of theologizing is not adequate for all.

Whereas Niebuhr et. al. argued that the fundamental model of sin is pride and rebellion against God, Saiving, Plaskow and Nelson go on to suggest that women's temptations tend more toward hiding from one's abilities and one's transcendence. As Saiving writes that women's sins are better understood as "triviality, distractibility, and diffuseness; lack of an organizing center or focus; dependence on others for one's self-definition; tolerance at the expense of standards of excellence . . . in short, underdevelopment or negation of the Self.[13]"

---

11. Valerie Saiving, "The Human Situation: A Feminine View," 25–42; Sue Dunfee, "The Sin of Hiding: A Feminist Critique of Reinhold Niebuhr's Account of the Sin of Pride," *Soundings* 65 (1982) 316–27; Judith Plaskow, *Sex, Sin, and Grace: Women's Experience and the Theologies of Reinhold Niebuhr and Paul Tillich* (Washington, DC: University Press of America, 1980).

12. Valerie Saiving, "The Human Situation: A Feminine View," 27.

13. Ibid., 37.

A further problem is that naming sin as primarily pride actually propels women into greater sin—sin as it is experienced by women. If I am actually sinning by hiding from myself, not trusting my own conscience and trivializing and negating myself as a child of God, then preaching to me against pride pushes me deeper into the sin.

This also raises another important issue for women's liberation theology—the tendency of patriarchal theology to view itself as speaking for all persons. Part of this penchant for absolutizing is due to faulty assumptions about the universal nature of humankind, and part of it is a narcissistic tendency within patriarchy. It has been assumed that male persons (white men), are the norm by which all others are known and judged. So when Niebuhr speaks out of his experience about the human situation, he assumes that he is speaking for all persons. Feminist theology has demonstrated that he is not. Further women's liberation theologies call into question the claim for any type of absolute. It is not simply a matter of including a few women and persons of color to arrive at a new better absolute universal. Rather, context and particular experience has become significant in the way that everyone ought to do theology. Thus, the very form of the discipline theology is changing in response to women's liberating vision. There may be some characteristics, abilities, situations, and concerns that most people have in common, but how these are interpreted, expressed, and addressed are related to one's context.

Other women have also expressed alternative ways of understanding sin. Womanists Delores Williams and Jacquelyn Grant[14] emphasize the importance of context. Williams develops concepts of sin from historical documents of African American experience, such as ex-slave narratives and slave songs. One assertion she builds upon is the association of sin and suffering—sin is seen as the internalization of the racist defilement of the self. She also expands the notion of sin to include social sin. Wonhee Anne Joh[15] sees a similar tendency from a Korean post colonial perspective to associate sin with *Han*—the suffering caused by oppression. Both the oppression and the suffering as a result of it are expressions of the communal nature of sin.

Carter Heyward follows suit in moving the locus of sin from a lack of personal virtue toward the lack of justice in the society. Marjorie Suchocki shifts the focus of understanding sin away from what the individual does *to God* to how one participates both personally and communally in the violation of the well-being *of creation and God*.[16]

These treatments of the doctrine of sin demonstrate three modes in which women's experience and women's critical approach matters to doing theology. First these women have articulated that their experience of the dominant formulation

---

14. Cf. Delores Williams, "A Womanist Perspective on Sin" in *A Troubling in My Soul: Womanist Perspectives on Evil and Suffering*, ed. Emilie M. Townes (Maryknoll, NY: Orbis, 1993) 130–49; and Jacquelyn Grant, "The Sin of Servanthood," in ibid., 199–218.

15. Wonhee Anne Joh, *The Heart of the Cross: A Postcolonial Christology* (Louisville: Westminster John Knox, 2006).

16. Marjorie Hewitt Suchocki, *The Fall to Violence: Original Sin in Relational Theology* (New York: Continuum, 1999).

of the doctrine of sin is problematic. Further it does not reflect their experience of the divine. And lastly, it does not do justice to their experience of the ways in which sin negatively impacts the connection with the divine in their lives and in the lives around them.

Beyond Christian feminist theology, there are also movements of women seeking liberation in other religious traditions. Some feminist theologians, such as Sandra Lubarsky and Judith Plaskow in their revisioning of Judaism, have had a lifetime of experience in non-Christian religious traditions. Some have integrated elements from various religions with currents of Christianity such as Rita Brock's integration of Buddhism and Christianity in her process feminist thought. Some have chosen to leave their first religious tradition in order to create new more inclusive and liberating religious and spiritual communities, such as Mary Daly. These women often refer to themselves as thealogians, and are important voices in the dialogue of feminist theology. Many women have reprised ancient Goddess traditions and earth-friendly practices and spiritualities such as Wiccan spirituality. Others have looked to uncovering classical, ancient and prehistoric depictions of divinity in feminine form, such as Carol P. Christ's reappropriation of the Greek and Roman mythologies and goddesses.

This introduction has framed feminist theology as offering significant alternative approaches, resources, insights and articulations of theological methods and reformulations of beliefs, practices and values, making significant contributions for both women, and for theology in general.

2 Introduction to Process Theology

MONICA A. COLEMAN

HISTORY

IN THE HISTORY OF Western philosophy, thinkers continuously have debated the following question: What is the most central feature of the world, as we know it? That things are always changing? Or that things are solid and endure? Process thought follows in the tradition of those who emphasize change as the central feature of reality. There are strands of this assertion within Western philosophy as early as the sixth century BCE. Heraclitus (circa 540–475 BCE) best known for his statement, "one cannot step twice into the same river," believed that fire, as a force that transforms all things, embodies the fact that change is fundamental to the workings of the world. This view stood in contrast to Heraclitus's contemporary Parmenides who believed that reality is timeless, unchanging and uniform. Similar debates continue in the philosophies of Plato, Aristotle, Leibniz, Hegel, the American pragmatists, and their contemporaries.

While this sense that change is primary or has priority in the workings of the world appears throughout Western philosophy in different thinkers,[1] its most systematic articulation appears in the twentieth century in the philosophy of Alfred North Whitehead (1861–1947). Born in England, Whitehead began his career as a mathematician and physicist. Within the fields of mathematics, he is best known for his text *Principia Mathematica*, written with Bertrand Russell. He began teaching philosophy at Harvard University in 1924 where he developed his "philosophy of organism" that is commonly called "process philosophy."

Whitehead was greatly influenced by the collapse of Newtonian physics, which describe the physical laws that govern the universe with special emphasis on how particles (ranging from an apple to planets and moons) interact with each other when in motion or at rest. With the rise of Einstein's theory of relativity and the tendency to describe the smallest units of reality as having the characteristics of both particles and waves, Whitehead sought a way to describe the entire world—from the smallest quanta to the complex human—in light of the realization that change and flux appear to be constant even within subatomic particles.

---

1. For process philosophy in Western philosophical history, see Nicholas Rescher, *Process Metaphysics: An Introduction to Process Philosophy*, SUNY Series in Philosophy (Albany: State University of New York Press, 1996).

Whitehead begins articulating his process philosophy in *Science and the Modern World* (1925), with its most in-depth exploration in *Process and Reality* (1929), the published version of his 1927 Gifford Lectures at the University of Edinburgh. Whitehead acknowledges his indebtedness to American philosophers William James, Charles Sanders Pierce and John Dewey. For this reason, and because he developed these ideas while teaching at Harvard, process thought is considered one of America's significant contributions to Western philosophy (along with "pragmatism," where many people locate James, Pierce, and Dewey). Process thinkers also refer to Whitehead's books *Religion in the Making* (1926), *Adventures of Ideas* (1933), *Symbolism* (1927), *Modes of Thought and The Aims of Education* (1929) for his understanding of process thought.

Charles Hartshorne (1897–2000) earned undergraduate and graduate degrees at Harvard University. After two years of teaching in Europe, Hartshorne returned to Harvard for three years as a research fellow, spending one of those years as an assistant to Alfred North Whitehead. There he learned and taught Whitehead's philosophy of organism and found that it had many resonances with ideas he already had been developing under the influence of Pierce's thought. In 1928, Hartshorne assumed a faculty position at the University of Chicago where he taught until 1955. Hartshorne is best known for applying process thought specifically to the field of theology. He referred to his ideas as "neo-classical metaphysics" because he thought that they more accurately represented ancient ideas about God and the world than the more dominant voices in classical Western theology.

Hartshorne's theological work focuses on refuting the idea of God as omnipotent, with *Omnipotence and Other Theological Mistakes* (1983) as his most accessible text. Hartshorne also revived the ontological proof for the existence of God (usually associated with the medieval thinker Anselm of Canterbury). Hartshorne's process theology is developed in the following works published while at the University of Chicago: *Beyond Humanism* (1937), *Man's Vision of God and the Logic of Theism* (1941), *The Divine Relativity* (1948), and *Reality as a Social Process* (1953). Hartshorne is often seen as the founder of the Chicago School of process theology, which includes Henry Nelson Wieman, Bernard Loomer, Schubert Ogden, Daniel Day Williams, Bernard Meland and John B. Cobb Jr.

John B. Cobb Jr. (1925–) studied under Hartshorne at the University of Chicago, and spent most of his academic career at the Claremont School of Theology where he founded what often is referred to as the Claremont School of process thought. Cobb's work is characterized by his integration of process metaphysics with a concern for church and social justice. Cobb's early works *A Christian Natural Theology* (1965) and *Structures of Christian Existence* (1967) utilize process metaphysics to describe core concepts within Christian theology. These works catapulted him to the forefront of contemporary process theology, and initiated the articulation of process perspectives on Christian systematic theological categories. Teaching at Claremont School of Theology from 1958 until his retirement in 1990, Cobb co-founded the journal

Process Studies with Lewis Ford (in 1971) and the Center for Process Studies with David Ray Griffin (in 1973). Holding a joint appointment with the School of Religion at Claremont Graduate University, Cobb mentored many contemporary process theologians into the field.

BASICS OF PROCESS THOUGHT

As a philosophical system, process thought is a speculative metaphysics. As a metaphysics, process thought tries to describe how all of reality works—including God—into a system that is coherent, logical and accurate. As a *speculative* metaphysic, process thought acknowledges that it is always partial and strives to offer its best estimate of how the world works.

The endeavor to maintain accuracy makes process a flexible system that has its base in empiricism. Process metaphysics starts in one field of observation, generalizes in theory, and lands again for observation in another field where the generalization will be tested, adapted and tried again in yet another field. When the model does not fit what we know about reality, we should revise the model to better describe what we know about the world. Thus experience is not only the ground of process metaphysics; it is also the critic of the metaphysics.[2] Because the system welcomes revision as we learn more about the world, process thought is considered an *open* metaphysics.

Depending on one's school of thought, these ideas are variously referred to as "the philosophy of organism,"

---

2. These concerns for empiricism, along with Whitehead's background as a physicist, make process philosophy a ready conversation partner with those who work in the physical and biological sciences.

"neo-classical metaphysics," "postmodern constructive philosophy or theology," and "process thought." This volume will refer to the philosophy and metaphysics as "process thought," and its application within the field of theology as "process theology." In Whitehead's attempt to distinguish his ideas from those of other philosophers, he coined his own terms to the elements of his philosophy. This chapter will use more common language with some reference to Whitehead's terms so that they might be recognized when other authors in this volume use them.

In process theology, everything that happens is a product of the past, what's possible, and what we do with those things. Whether you are a quark, an amoeba, or a person, you undergo this continual process of sorting through these three inputs: what you inherit from the world, what's possible in your context, and what you do about it. Whether you are an atom, a plant, an animal or a human being, you are composed of units of energy that are influenced by the world around it, and available possibilities. Process thinkers refer to these units of energy as "drops of experience" (to use William James's language), "actual occasions," or "actual entities." There are, of course, levels of complexity. Some organisms have a central nervous system that grants them more unity, complexity and harmony. But all aspects of reality have an experience of becoming. Not all entities are conscious of this, but we all experience the world and possibilities with some degree of freedom and with the potential to change.

God offers possibilities to the world, urging us to choose the paths that lead to a vision of the common good. While the principles of God's vision do not change, the way it gets played out on earth depends on what is happening in the world. God takes in, or incorporates, the events of the world into who God is. God then relates those events with God's vision for the common good, searching for the best of what has happened in order to offer those aspects back to us in our next instance of living. In short, our experiences in the world influence who we are and what we do. We then go on to influence those around us. What we do also affects God and how God relates to the world. Process theologians will always refer to God *and* the world. We do not imagine that there is a world without God, or a God without some kind of world.

ELEMENTS OF PROCESS THEOLOGY

Becoming

Process thought refers to the constant change in the world as the process of becoming. We do not just consider our pasts and what the world has to offer us, we actually take them into ourselves. They become a part of who we are. Some process thinkers refer to this as "taking in," "feeling," or "prehending" the world around us. Although there is a vast world around us, we all live within relatively smaller communities. For the most part, just a small part of the entire universe is relevant to our moment-to-moment activities. Thus we are usually referring to the parts of the world that are relevant to us. These are our "actual worlds."

In the process of becoming, we take in what the world has to offer. Generally, that is our past. It could be an immediate past—what happened just two seconds ago—or something from our personal, cultural, environmental or political histories. This is one part of the process of becoming.

We also take in what is possible in each context. This is how we are not destined to repeat the past over and over again. New things appear and surprise us. We often have options to do or feel or be something different than we were in the past. These possibilities are part of what we consider in our individual processes of becoming.

All of these inputs—our pasts and what's possible—represent the multiplicity of the world. In the process of becoming, we draw these things into a unity. That is, we consider them all, we even feel them, and we make a decision. We come to a conclusion about what we will do with all the choices we have. Whitehead referred to this process of sifting and sorting and coming to one decision as the process of "concrescence." It's all part of the process of becoming.

As we each settle on one thing, come to a decision, make a conclusion, or become one thing, we then contribute what we've decided and who we are into the wider world. We all have a level of privacy or solitude in sifting through all the things we have to work with and coming to a conclusion. But as soon as we do that, we become part of the larger world. What we decided and who we are becomes part of the wider world for others to consider when they are in their processes of becoming. We even become part of our own pasts for us to consider in our next moments of becoming. Thus Whitehead describes the basic tenet of this system in these words: "The many become one, and are increased by one."[3]

3. Alfred North Whitehead, *Process and Reality: An Essay in Cosmology*, ed. David Ray Griffin

Most of the time, we aren't aware of this. This is especially true for very small particles. Or for many of the activities we often take for granted—like breathing. Thus, process thinkers say that most of the process of becoming is "pre-conscious." Most process theologians focus on the ways in which human beings are conscious and intentional about the process of becoming.

Whitehead also referred to this activity—that works with multiple sources (the past and what's possible) and can create something new—as "creativity." Many process thinkers maintain this language of "creativity" to discuss a fundamental activity that characterizes the universe. Throughout creation, new things happen.

Relationality

This process of becoming makes the world radically relational. Because we *take in* our past and our future possibilities when we decide what to do in the world, relations are internal. That is, these inputs are more than just data that we consider. These inputs—our past and our possibilities—become part of who we are. Thus, we are not discrete selves that can choose whether or not we want to relate to one another. We do not have relationships, we *are* relationships. We are constituted by our relationships to other people, to our environment, our past, our hopes, our potentials, and our God. There is nothing outside of these relations.

Freedom

The ability to become something new is the cause of our freedom. In our processes

---

and Donald W. Sherburne, corrected edition (New York: Free Press, 1978) 21.

of becoming, we are not bound by the past. We can always choose to go forward in the direction of one of the new possibilities in our contexts. Process thinkers refer to this as "conforming to" or "adopting" what's possible. Because we are influenced by so many factors, process thinkers say that we are "created by" others. But since we are genuinely free to decide what we will do in each moment, we are also "self-creating." Process metaphysics takes seriously the fact that every one has some level of agency. We have some role in deciding what will happen, what we will do and who we become.

Process thinkers understand that context plays a significant role in our processes of becoming. Sometimes we have few possibilities because of a context that we inherited, or because of the decisions and activities of those around us. Sometimes the past can be very influential, and it can appear that it will be a predictor of the future. Yet even within these scenarios, process metaphysics is not a deterministic system. We can always choose to do something new. No one knows what we will do before we do it. Not even God.

God

Variously referred to as "the principle of limitation in the world," "the poet of the world," "the Eros that undergirds the progression of civilization," or "Love," God is the source of novelty in the world. Without God, we would be destined to repeat our pasts over and over again. We would live in a deterministic system. Yet experience shows us that we do not. We can change. We can do something different than we did in previous moments. There are possibilities available to us that do not appear to come from our pasts alone. For process theologians, these possibilities come from God.

Process affirms the omnipresence of God in the traditional sense. Indeed God is everywhere at all times, embracing the world, feeling the world and responding to all aspects of the world. But God's power and knowledge are conceived of differently than in orthodox conceptions of God. Like classical theology, process theologians believe that God embraces the highest form of power. Unlike classical models of God where the highest form of power is an authoritative or coercive power, in process thought, God's power is a persuasive power. God cannot make us do one thing or another. Rather God is said to have an "initial aim." This means that God influences, persuades, lures or "calls" us to embrace the principles of God's vision in every context. Some process theologians have named this aim as the voice of God, the whisper of God, intuition, or God's love for the world.

God has more knowledge than we do because we only have access to our actual worlds. God has access to the entire world and the activities and feelings of the entire world. In that sense, God is always working with more information than we are. However, God does not know what we are going to do before we do it. Process theology takes individual freedom seriously. When we decide what we are going to do, we freely make that decision. Once we act, God then works with what we have offered to God and to the world in order to influence us in the next moment. God does not create out of nothing. God is always working with what the world has to offer. Thus the end is not guaranteed or foreordained. In this sense, process is an open system.

In fact, this is God's process of becoming. Just as we in the world have a process of becoming, so does God. God takes into Godself the events of the world. God feels all of what is happening in the world and that becomes part of who God is. God knows us and knows what happens to us. This is how God rejoices with us and suffers with us. We are a part of who God is. Since there are always new things happening in the world, who God is, God's self is always growing and expanding throughout time. God takes in these experiences and relates them to all that is possible and presents Godself to the world in the initial aim. Thus as God influences the world, God literally becomes a part of every aspect of creation. In other words, divine incarnation is universal. Because of the process of becoming, God is in us, and we are in God. Hartshorne was one of the first process thinkers to note that process theology is a kind of panentheism. God is not identical to the world, but God is not set apart from the world in opposition to what the world is. God is in all, and all is in God.

Process theology describes two aspects of God. Those in the Whiteheadian tradition refer to these as a primordial nature and a consequent nature. Those in the Hartshornean tradition talk about God having both creative love and responsive love. In the consequent or responsive aspect of God, God changes. This is the way process theology talks about God taking in and feeling the experiences of the world. And yet process theology acknowledges that there is a side of God that does not change. In the primordial nature or creative dimension of God, God offers the world possibilities that are relevant for our current context. Many process theologians will refer to this as God's "character." Thus while part of God is contingent on what happens in the world; there is a part of God that is constant. Because process theology affirms these two aspects, or "poles," of God, they will often refer to God as being "dipolar."

Primoridal Vision

The possibilities that God offers to the world are ordered according to a vision that calls us toward principles of beauty, truth, art, adventure, and zest. Many process theologians name this more generally as "the common good." This is God's character and God's benevolence. Process theologians will also refer to this as "the primordial vision." This is how God tries to influence us or call us towards what is good. Some process theologians will say that this is how the kindom of heaven is made available to us in the world.

Process theologians are also known to say that God desires intensity and harmony for the world. That is, God offers possibilities that can lead the world towards experiences that are complex, but that also work well with one another. Sometimes these goals seem conflictual. For example, what is good for the life of a human being eating food, might not be the best thing for the life of the plant or animal that is being consumed. Thus what is good for one aspect of creation, might not be good for another aspect of creation. Process theologians tend not to say that God prefers human beings to animals. Rather, process theologians say that God searches for the greatest common denominator or "the common good."

The Problem of Evil

Process theology is well known for the way that it addresses the traditional problem of evil. The classical question about the problem of evil asks, "If God is all-good and all-powerful, then why is there evil or why do people suffer?" Because process theology does not affirm God's power as an authoritative or coercive power, it offers a response that both supports the freedom and responsibility of creation *and* God's concern for the common good.

To the extent that we use our freedom to diverge from God's call, there is evil in the world. Evil is not an isolated event because of the interdependence of the world. When one of us chooses to operate in a way that is divergent from God's call, it influences all of us. We often do this repeatedly within systems of power and influence, and create greater problems—systemic evils.

But evil is to be combated, and God is involved in this combat. This happens in two ways—within God and through God's activity in the world. When God gathers together the experiences of the world within Godself, God finds the value in everything that happens. Sometimes, there is very little good to work with, but God can find it and preserve it. Since God is eternal, we have a kind of eternal life after death within God.

We also assist God in what process theologians call "creative transformation." When we strive to enact God's ideal vision on earth, we can creatively transform what we have inherited from the world. When we use our freedom in accordance with God's vision, we can negate some aspects of the past that have created evil in the world. God's call offers us the opportunity to overcome evil.

CONCLUSION

Process theological work is as varied as the scholars who employ process thought. Initially, process theologians focused on natural theology, understanding religion—primarily Christianity—through reason and experience (as compared to scriptural texts and other forms of revelation). As time progressed, process theologians applied process thought to various problems in philosophy of religion and different theological categories. Some process theologians have actively engaged biblical texts, issues within spirituality (such as prayer and preaching), politics and social issues like ecological justice. Although most process theological work has been done with Christianity, the metaphysics of process thought can be applied to various religious traditions. That is, because process thought provides a way for understanding how the world works, different religions can be understood with these principles. Thus, many process theologians are interested in religious pluralism, or how various religions interface with one another. There are process theological perspectives on Christianity, Judaism, Islam, Buddhism, goddess religions and African traditional religions, to name a few. Process theology grows increasingly diverse as more scholars pursue their interests in and through process theology.

3
Women, Whitehead, and Hartshorne

What Characterizes Process-Relational Women's Worldviews

NANCY R. HOWELL

WOMEN WHOSE SCHOLARSHIP is influenced by Alfred North Whitehead and Charles Hartshorne are quite diverse in the theological, thealogical, and neo-pagan worldviews they hold and construct.[1] Process-relational thinkers who are feminist are associated with diverse standpoints, identify with a variety of religious perspectives, live in many regions of the world, and name themselves differently in terms of race, ethnicity, and nationality. Consequently any attempt to characterize process-relational thought in women's scholarship is complicated, but if we claim that process-relational feminism qualifies as an identifiable feminist school of thought, then some general trends must be evident. The claim expressed in this chapter is that the most evident characteristic of process-relational feminism is that women construct theology by creative engagement with Whiteheadian and Hartshornean philosophy, but several other trends are generally expressed, ranging from methodological to philosophical, theoretical, and ethical considerations.

Process-relational feminists are distinguished by their engagement with Whitehead's and/or Hartshorne's process philosophies, and this distinction is not without controversy and not without clear differences in approach. Whiteheadian feminists, for example, opt to write in different relationships with the metaphysics, but some feminists, such as Mary Daly, are highly critical of any dependence on male-originated philosophy in the construction of feminist perspectives.[2] Daly's point is well taken, and process-relational feminists must demonstrate why a phi-

---

1. Women who write theology, thealogy, or neo-pagan worldviews may be Christian, Jewish, Wiccan, or multireligious (meaning that they are highly synthetic in their religious identities). Such women may also be white feminist, Black feminist, Asian feminist, womanist, or *mujerista*. Because there is no single term that captures the breadth of women's social and religious locations, readers are asked to keep in mind that words such as *women*, *womanist*, and *feminist* are intended to signal the diversity of perspectives that fall generally under the rubric of *process-relational women's theology*.

2. Daly, *Beyond God the Father: Toward a Philosophy of Women's Liberation* (Boston: Beacon, 1973) 189.

losophy, which may entail elements of patriarchal thought, is appropriate as a dialogue partner for feminist theology. Other feminists are critical of relational approaches to theology because relationality is the stereotypically feminine domain. Process-relational feminist theology may similarly be subject to criticism for elitism and essentialism. Hence, women who are process theologians must take care to demonstrate how the philosophy transforms understanding of relationality without perpetuating generic concepts of the person and of women.

Depending on social location and experience, women engage process thought with a multiplicity of approaches. First, some women unapologetically build theological perspectives highly dependent on Whitehead's technical vocabulary and philosophical cosmology. In such cases, Whitehead's philosophy provides a primary structural source in their theological constructions. For some women, Whitehead offers a philosophical framework to complement more experiential feminist inclinations (and affords a way to respond to criticism that feminist theologies are not scholarly). Second, other women engage Whitehead and/or Hartshorne as informing sources for their theological perspectives. Some women appeal to the more general elements of process philosophy, or even what might be understood as the more metaphorical elements of process thought, and leave aside the more technical nuances of the metaphysics. Whitehead or Hartshorne may function alongside other theological and philosophical influences equally as important and informative for their feminist theological constructions. Third, because open theology is an important conversation partner for process theologians, some women engage Whitehead and Hartshorne through a theological perspective that begins with the Bible as a primary source supporting a dynamic and relational worldview. Finally, some women prefer to identify themselves primarily as process theologians. Such women are not less concerned with women's issues than others, but understand their perspectives as more consonant with process theology than particular feminist or womanist approaches.

If some form of engagement with Whiteheadian and Hartshornean thought typifies women's process-relational theology, what other trends are evident in this theological movement? Both methodological and theological trends are held in common by many women's process-relational theologies. For the sake of clarity, the trends are organized as follows:

METHODOLOGICAL TRENDS

- Process thought as conceptual framework for interpreting women's experience
- Experience as more fundamental than systems
- Particularity as more reflective of reality than universalism
- Praxis or theo-ethical integration as more viable than abstraction
- Relationality and dynamism as postmodern alternatives to modern atomistic and static worldviews
- Organicism as more defensible than classical dualism
- Valuation of nature as contrasted with anthropocentrism

- Openness to dialogue with science as source for theology

THEOLOGICAL TRENDS

- Concepts of the Sacred as alternatives to patriarchal concepts of God
- Availability of process thought as source for diverse theological and religious perspectives
- Engagement with other religious perspectives as dialogue partners

While the methodological and theological characteristics identified may not describe every theology constructed by women in dialogue with process thought, they do reflect the creative synthesis of process thought with women's theological perspectives.

METHODOLOGICAL TRENDS

Process Thought as Conceptual Framework for Interpreting Women's Experience

Autobiographical statements assist in tracking how some women have encountered process thought in light of women's experience. The appeal of the processive-organic worldview for women is based on both conceptual and experiential grounds. For some women, an emerging consciousness about women's issues coincided with discovery of process thought. The serendipitous meeting of feminism and process thought evoked a range of responses. For Valerie Saiving, process thought provided a conceptual framework for interpreting how feminist consciousness was transforming her life, but the role of process thought was limited to its interpretive power because only women's experience and dialogue creates feminist awareness.[3] For Penelope Washbourn, process thought was more generative of her emerging feminist awareness because the worldview facilitated feminist inquiry and fostered integration of her identity in relation to religion.[4] Perhaps a more common trend among women theologians is that process thought fit their experiences in ways that more misogynist, patriarchal, universalizing, or abstract worldviews could not. Process philosophy and theology, while not always unequivocally inclusive, at least, provided a coherent conceptual framework that assisted in exploring questions, testing creative constructions, and expressing women's experience. As the early generations of women scholars teach in universities and graduate schools and participate in scholarly conversations with other women scholars, new communities of women are encouraged to explore women's experience in dialogue with process thought. The persistent narrative is that process thought rings true to women's experiences and provides a more comprehensive conceptuality that accommodates exploration and interpretation of women's experience.

---

3. Valerie C. Saiving, ""Androgynous Life: A Feminist Appropriation of Process Thought" (The Harvard University Dudelian Lecture), in *Feminism and Process Thought: The Harvard Divinity School/Claremont Center for Process Studies Symposium Papers*, ed. Sheila Greeve Davaney, Symposium Series 6 (Lewiston, NY: Mellen, 1981) 12–13.

4. Penelope Washbourn, "The Dynamics of Female Experience: Process Models and Human Values," in *Feminism and Process Thought: The Harvard Divinity School/Claremont Center for Process Studies Symposium Papers*, ed. Sheila Greeve Davaney, Symposium Series 6 (Lewiston, NY: Mellen, 1981) 83.

Experience as More Fundamental Than Systems

While the conceptual ability to interpret women's experience is one methodological reason to engage process theology, a more fundamental reason is that experience is the paradigmatic focus of process cosmology. Process thought dissects and interprets experience as a most fascinating feature of reality. As women look to women's experience as the locus for theological reflection, process thought looks to experience as the locus for reflection on the nature of reality from the complexities of human experience to the spare existence of atoms.

Appeal to experience is central to both process metaphysics and feminist thought, and interestingly both perspectives are critical of worldviews constructed from limited ranges of experience. While women criticize patriarchal worldviews for defending universal systems built from privileged male experience, Whitehead criticized philosophers for defending systems at the cost of dismissing experience. Whitehead's point is that systems of thought are indefensible apart from engagement of all relevant experience. Women who create theology using Whitehead's processive-organic worldview consequently aspire to inclusivity of experience in their theologies. The criterion of comprehensive accounting for experience means that feminist and womanist theologies struggle to include every variety of experience.

Sometimes commitments and criteria are easier to articulate than to achieve. What must be confessed is that the earliest published feminist process-relational theologies were generated by white women, with a few notable exceptions.[5] Similar to other second wave feminists, early Whiteheadian feminists confronted patriarchy with alternative theological constructions that challenged masculine concepts of God and power, as well as androcentric theological anthropologies. Fortunately, the Whiteheadian commitment to inclusivity of experience means that the potential for women's process-relational theologies to construct more nuanced views of women's experience was in the very bones of the philosophical sources. Not only have the formative thinkers crafted more textured views of women's experience over the past few decades, but the community of women scholars and students now reflects a range of women's experiences from diverse social locations—including third wave feminists and international scholars, as well as women who are theologically and racially diverse.

Particularity as More Reflective of Reality Than Universalism

Systems of thought, Whitehead teaches, are weak and irrelevant when constrained by limited experience and by false universalism, but a system that entertains particularities in all their varieties is more attuned to the dynamic and relational character of reality. Women's process-relational theologies suggest a logic based on concrete particularities derived from women's experiences rather than argumentation directed toward abstracted rationality, universalism, and essentialism.

What process-relational feminists synthesize from Whiteheadian and

---

5. One of the notable exceptions is Rita Nakashima Brock.

feminist/womanist thought is awareness that all worldviews are perspectival. While some philosophies, for example, claim to be objectively concerned with matters of fact, process-relational thought acknowledges that expansive varieties of experience must be analyzed of necessity from a particular standpoint. While process-relational scholars reflect on a universe of experiences, they do so with awareness that the subjective perspective of the scholar is applied to the concrete matters of experiential fact. What must be assessed about the perspectival theologies is how well they entertain the breadth of experiences and establish the importance and relationship of concrete facts. Clearly the scope of every scholar's work is characterized by selection of experiences or facts for consideration, and the process of selection always implies the imposition of a particular perspective. In a sense, the scholar's experience shapes the perspective that she takes on a wider range of experiences informing theology, and methodological awareness of the perspective and social location of the theologian is critical.

Women creating process theologies, then, live in the tension generated by naming their own perspectives and experiences while opening their worldviews to experiences of other women, nature, and communities. The intention is not to homogenize diverse women's experiences, but to interpret the real-world connections, creative tensions, and challenging complexity of historical and changing relationships for the sake of proposing more adequate theologies.

Praxis or Theo-ethical Integration as More Viable Than Abstraction

A signature characteristic of womanist and Black feminist thought is the integration of theological and ethical concerns. Because particular ethical concerns arising from the multiple oppressions experienced by African American women generate the urgency inspiring scholarship, their work is most often described as theo-ethical (and not merely theological). White feminist work surely arises from gender oppression, but often their scholarship is distinguished as either theology or ethics in spite of obvious correlations between constructive theology and ethics. Among women who construct theology in dialogue with process thought, theology is mindful of its ethical implications, and perhaps one criterion for assessing the adequacy of their theologies is the ethical perspective evoked by the theology.

Process thought is a meeting place for women's theological reflection because Whitehead's legacy includes the concrete notion that philosophy (metaphysics) and ethics are not separate enterprises. Experience is the integrative center for ethics and theology. Experience is the expression of creativity where thought, feeling, and action coincide in the formative, decisive moments of women's lives. How women name their identities, histories, and struggles and how women encounter each other and God form and inform the becoming, being, and action of women. *Praxis,* so characteristic of liberation theologies, is an ontological feature of process thought where similarly theory, analysis, and action are cyclically and experientially integrated.

Relationality and Dynamism as Postmodern Alternatives to Modern Atomistic and Static Worldviews

A modernist worldview focuses on substances in interpreting reality, and consequently tends to understand substances as atomistic and static. Relationships are limited to external interactions, which have little impact on the nature of individuals. Whiteheadian women, by contrast, are more postmodern in interpreting the world, and their worldviews emphasize relationality and dynamism. The priority of experience explains why Whiteheadian women who are theologians tend to understand interconnections and change as more appropriate interpretations of reality than modernist interpretations that prioritize substances.

First, internal relations in process thought are those forms of connection that describe how experience grows creatively from vast networks and communities, human and non-human. If women understand that relationships are central to our identities because we define ourselves from the influences of the events and relationships we encounter, then we not only have ways of explaining how socially constructed gender, race, and class categories negatively influence our self-perceptions, but we also have ways of explaining why some women enjoy or seek out particular events and relationships that encourage more empowering and enriching ways of understanding women's identities. Rather than rejecting relationality as a stereotypical feminine trait, process-relational women theologians work from a Whiteheadian understanding of relationships to reconstruct relationality and, consequently, self.[6]

Second, the dynamic character of existence further expresses the creative change entailed in experience. In the Whiteheadian worldview, all experience is part of a changing and dynamic world where relational encounters are transformational. Experience is always in process, so that new relationships and events generate new individuals and societies. Dorothee Soelle writes that the Whiteheadian ontology of becoming, rather than being, is compatible with feminist thought because modernist assumptions about substance (being) are replaced by the interpretive concepts of relationality and process (becoming).[7] Change and dynamism point to the transformational character of relationships that change individuals, societies, and ecologies.

Organicism as More Defensible Than Classical Dualism

Many forms of women's theology, philosophy, and ethics argue against oppressive combinations of dualism, hierarchy, and values. Typically the problematic dualism is the opposition of masculine and feminine in systems that value the masculine while subordinating and disvaluing the feminine. Patterns of dichotomizing thought are deconstructed in the process of dismantling patriarchal forms of thought.

Mary Daly was one of the first feminists to credit Whitehead with providing alternatives to the Creator/creature

---

6. The decision to reconstruct rather than to reject relationality as a key category may be one reason why both white feminists and womanists, who value community, are able to engage each other's work well through a common interest in Whiteheadian cosmology.

7. Dorothee Soelle with Shirley A. Cloyes, *To Work and to Love: A Theology of Creation* (Philadelphia: Fortress, 1984) 25.

and human/nature dichotomies, and later women scholars have appreciated the value of process thought in suggesting alternatives to dualism.[8] A methodological trend in women's process-relational theologies is not only the deconstruction of dualism, but also a reconstruction of concepts using Whiteheadian ways of interpreting experience. For example, the subject/object dualism is a corollary to the masculine/feminine duality, but a Whiteheadian way of understanding experience is that all beings who exist are self-creating subjects who are experienced by other subjects as influencing objects in their self-creation. Similarly, body/soul, reason/emotion, body/mind dualisms give way to concepts of the person as psychosomatic whole.

Simply thinking about the integration of old dualisms into newly functioning polarities is only part of the reconstructive project of women's process-relational theology. To be more fully conscious of organic and relational reality means that the complexity of human experience defies simplistic dichotomizing. The world is not simply filled with men and women, but is populated with diverse men and women whose identities are interpreted by race, class, nationality, ability, sexual orientation, and many other culturally defined traits. The postmodern and organic sensibilities of Whiteheadian women generate ways of thinking that attend to how experiential particularity, holism, and complexity defy dualistic fragmentation.

Valuation of Nature as Contrasted with Anthropocentrisms

As the Whiteheadian conceptuality replaces modernism and dualism with process and relationship, what emerges in women's theology is the methodological assumption that humans are not merely connected with nature, but are part of nature. For womanists and feminists, process theology provides an organic worldview conducive to construction of ecofeminist theological positions, which provides a meeting place for women who pursue traditional Christian theological perspectives and women who value the subjectivity and diversity of nature in pantheist thealogy or Wiccan perspectives. Becoming-ontology applies to humans and the rest of nature, so women find kinship with and responsibility for nature in shared subjectivity, as well as shared oppression. Nature is not separate from the cultural and social spheres of oppression in this view, which means that exploitation of nature and oppression of women are connected. Process-relational praxis requires women to attend to wider implications for human community and ecology in their work for justice (inclusive of their critique of white privilege and empire).

Openness to Dialogue with Science as Source for Theology

Ecology and process-relational theology are conjoined in women's theological perspectives because many women presuppose the seamless continuity of humans with nature. The same presupposition creates an environment for reflection on other sciences as methodological sources for theological construction. With feminist

---

8. Daly, *Beyond God the Father*, 189.

philosophers of science as dialogue partners, Whiteheadian women describe methods of science and religion dialogue that remember the concrete social locations and experience that influence both deconstruction and construction of worldviews. Whiteheadian thought not only establishes subjectivity in nature, continuity of humans and nature, cosmic relationality in the universe, and constant change in natural processes, but also advocates for attribution of personhood to animals with central nervous systems. From Whitehead's dialogue with science, women move forward to engage chaos theory, physical cosmology, evolutionary biology, genetics, animal behavior, and cognitive sciences. The engagement with natural sciences follows much earlier attention to the human sciences (for example, psychology and social sciences), so the movement and development of process-relational women's theologies holds together focus on women's experience with expanding awareness of the inorganic and organic experiences described by science. The universe of experience is the subject of women's process-relational theologies.

THEOLOGICAL TRENDS

Concepts of the Sacred as Alternatives to Patriarchal Concepts of God

When few alternatives to patriarchal doctrines of God existed, Whitehead's metaphysics attracted women's attention. Whitehead's God is not a person, but an actual entity, which means that gendered attributes are more subtle or absent. Both Whitehead's and Hartshorne's dipolar theism (the concept that God has two poles devoted to experiencing the world and to envisioning the world's futures one becoming at a time) capture women's theological imaginations as they deconstruct patriarchal theism and reconstruct women-centered concepts of the Sacred. The two aspects of the Sacred in process metaphysics affirm that women, women's communities, and nature are valued and that the Sacred is the source of creative transformation, change, and revolution in individual women's lives, as well as communities and larger societies.

One serendipitous meeting of process thought with feminist thought relates to the concept of love. Women discovered Whitehead's concept of the divine *Eros* at the same time that they were constructing concepts of embodied love, self-love, and divine Love as alternatives to patriarchal and racist theologies. Moving away from hierarchical language for the Sacred, women's theologies tend to emphasize mutuality and reciprocity in relationships with the Sacred. In theistic terms, women's process-relational theologies describe God as one who desires connection with women, nature, and communities. God initiates relationship through contributing an aim toward rich experience for the world and its creatures, while the world and its creatures contribute rich experience, joys, and sorrows to God's experience. Women's process-relational theologies, consequently, name God as Friend, Lover, and Heart.[9]

Perhaps the most dramatic conjunction of process theism and women's theology meets in the revision of power, divine omnipotence. Women's praxis and theo-ethical perspectives require examination of human power dynamics, but real transformation of concepts of power entail

---

9. See, for example, Sallie McFague and Rita Nakashima Brock.

revision of theological concepts of divine power. Women either cite Whitehead's and Hartshorne's revisions of divine omnipotence or join open relational theologians in revising the concept of divine power first through biblical sources and later in dialogue with process thought. Traditional concepts of the absolute and coercive power of God reify concepts of hierarchical, patriarchal power in human relationships. Process theism, on the other hand, speaks more of persuasive or relational power in the Divine. Relational power is power influencing other centers of power. Hartshorne refers to relational power as perfect power because this divine mode of expressing power recognizes the freedom and power of self-creating "becomings" in all experience. The process-relational revision of divine power evokes in women's theologies concepts of the relational and responsive Sacred who changes in the dynamic interplay of the universe of experiences.

Availability of Process Thought as Source for Diverse Theological and Religious Perspectives

Process thought is a theo-ethical meeting place for diverse women. Predominantly Christian, at least in the proportion of publications, women who engage process thought as a source for theology range from liberal and progressive to open and relational perspectives. Out of a Whiteheadian cosmology, women re-invent doctrines and revise theological concepts. Women have engaged process thought in expressing women-centered religious perspectives with Judaism and through Buddhist influences. Women have come to voice about goddess religion, nature religion, and multireligious perspectives in new ways because of engagement with process thought. Opening space for women from diverse social locations to speak from some common methodological and theological assumptions promises to assist in the difficult work of building bridges where women are fragmented by race, class, and other socially constructed historical barriers.

Engagement with Other Religious Perspectives as Dialogue Partners

Finally, women's theological perspectives are shaped by interreligious dialogue. Women's process-relational theologies are shaped by conversation between Buddhist and Christian thought. Post-holocaust theologies are crafted by Christian dialogue with Judaism. The volume of religious experience contributing to women's process-relational theologies includes passage through difficult theological differences, but promises transformative theological construction.

Process-relational women's theology is a diverse and notable movement within women's theological scholarship and within process theology. The chapters of this book provide concrete excerpts from formative thinkers in process-relational women's theology and insightful analyses of the formative excerpts by the larger community of women scholars whose work is informed by process philosophies and theologies. The collaboration represented by this anthology is characteristic of a tradition of supportive relations among women engaged in process thought, and the volume represents a snapshot in time as we acknowledge the formative steps in creating women's theology and the continuing rich potential of the movement to foster innovative theological reflection.

PART TWO

Texts in Women's Process-Relational Theologies

4 Experience

Valerie Saiving

Valerie Saiving earned a PhD from the Divinity School at The University of Chicago in 1963. She was a cofounder of the Department of Religious Studies and of the Women's Studies program at Hobart and William Smith Colleges, where she taught from 1959 to 1987. One of her most influential articles, "The Human Situation: A Feminine View" (1960) called for a broader understanding of the doctrine of sin to include the experience and situation of women as well as men. This essay, the 1977 Dudelian Lecture at Harvard University, was originally published in *Feminism and Process Thought*, edited by Sheila Greeve Davaney in 1981 and is reprinted by permission of The Edwin Mellen Press.

Excerpt from "Androgynous Life: A Feminist Appropriation of Process Thought"

IT IS APPROPRIATE THAT the Dudelian Lecture on Natural Religion be devoted to the mutual relevance of feminism and process philosophy, for these two modes of thought agree, in Whitehead's words, that "we can only deal with things in some sense experienced";[1] both insist that all constructive thought has "its origin in the generalization of particular factors discerned in particular topics of human interest;"[2] and each "refuses to place human experience outside nature."[3] Feminists and process thinkers also agree that what counts as "experience" has been far too narrowly defined in traditional philosophy—that if metaphysical inquiry begins in "subjective experiencing,"[4] it is essential that *every variety* of experience be taken into account:

> experience drunk and experience sober, experience sleeping and experience waking, experience drowsy and experience wide-awake, experience self-conscious and experience self-forgetful, experience intellectual and experience physical, experience religious and experience skeptical, experience anxious and experience carefree, experience anticipatory and experience retrospective, experience happy and experience grieving, experience dominated by emotions and experience under self-restraint, experience in the light and

---

1. Alfred North Whitehead, *Adventures of Ideas* (New York: Macmillan, 1933) 287.
2. Whitehead, *Process and Reality* (New York: Macmillan, 1929) 7.
3. Whitehead, *Adventures of Ideas*, 237.
4. Whitehead, *Process and Reality*, 243.

experience in the dark, experience normal and experience abnormal.⁵

To which feminists now emphatically add: experience female and experience male.

I speak as both a feminist and a Whiteheadian. A brief account of how I arrived at this combined perspective may throw some light on what I have to say.

As a graduate student in theology in the mid-nineteen forties, I was absorbed in the study of process philosophy. At that time, I did not think of myself as a feminist, although I now see that in some ways I was living as though the feminist dream of androgynous life were about to come true. But for the next decade or so I abandoned my study of Whitehead for *Better Homes and Gardens*. During those years I was trying to be a "complete woman," as our culture defined womanhood. In the late fifties, however, a series of events in my personal life awoke in me the first stirrings of feminist consciousness. At the same time I resumed my theological studies. At first these two changes in my life were connected only in an external way: my desire to teach, suddenly freed by a sense of the possibilities now open to me, made it important to complete my graduate work. But it soon became apparent that there was a deeper connection: as I tried to understand the transformation I had experienced, I discovered that process philosophy provided the conceptual framework I needed. Although this framework had been there all along, I had suppressed it, because the androgynous vision embodied in Whitehead's philosophy was fundamentally incompatible with the non-androgynous ideal around which I had been trying to shape my life.

From this personal history I draw two conclusions relevant to any exploration of the relations between feminism and process thought. On the one hand, not even an intimate acquaintance with Whitehead's ideas is capable of *creating* feminist consciousness; such consciousness arises out of certain kinds of life experience, explored in dialogue with other women. On the other hand, feminist consciousness, once awakened, seeks a conceptual framework for self-understanding, and process philosophy may provide such a framework.

This does not mean, in Mary Daly's words, that feminists should let any "prefabricated theory have *authority* over us," for "The essential thing is to hear our *own* experience."⁶ This warning is completely consistent with Whitehead's view that the primary datum for metaphysics "is nothing else than the experiencing subject,"⁷ and that "In order to acquire learning, we must first shake ourselves free of it."⁸ Systematic thought is necessary, but we must not allow ourselves to be seduced into the "dismissal of experience in the interest of system."⁹

But if Whitehead implicitly challenges women resolutely to think out of our own experience, he also reminds us that human experience never comes uninterpreted. At one level, feminists already know this, for to be a feminist is to be aware of the power of cultural images and theories of women to twist our

---

5. Whitehead, *Adventures of Ideas*, 290–91.

6. Mary Daly, *Beyond God the Father: Toward a Philosophy of Women's Liberation* (Boston: Beacon, 1973) 189.

7. Whitehead, *Process and Reality*, 24.

8. Whitehead, *Modes of Thought* (New York: Free Press, 1968) 6.

9. Ibid., 3.

experiences and understanding of ourselves into hurtful and hateful shapes. Yet even as we recognize this fact and struggle to express what we really are and hope for, we become aware that all thinking, including feminist thinking, takes place within a network of unconscious and semiconscious presuppositions about the wider context within which *all* experience occurs. Ultimately, this network constitutes an implicit metaphysics whose premises are embedded in our institutions, in the structure and lexicon of our language, and in the unquestioned deliverances of "common sense." These premises, although not obviously patriarchal, nevertheless shape and are shaped by patriarchal structures and modes of thought. So long as they remain unconscious, they threaten to vitiate our attempts to understand and express our emerging vision. We must, then, bring more fully into consciousness and criticize our unexamined notions about the nature of things. To do this is to engage in metaphysical inquiry.

Perhaps even now a wholly original metaphysics is being constructed on the basis of women's unique experience. But no such metaphysics has yet appeared, and I suspect that there is no Archimedean point at which to begin to create it. In any event, until it does appear, it seems reasonable for feminists to begin with some already existing philosophical scheme, building upon it, criticizing and correcting it, and reconstructing it where necessary in the light of our conversation with each other.

I name this process "feminist appropriation," borrowing a term used by Whitehead to suggest the *creative* way in which an occasion of experience responds to and uses the past from its own perspective and for its own purposes. Feminist appropriation of any philosophical system will be active, critical, and imaginative; it will be open to *new* ways of thinking but will take nothing on authority; and it will insist on testing every hypothesis by reference to the immediate experience of women.

Clearly, most philosophical systems are unsuitable candidates for feminist appropriation, either because they are explicitly sexist, or because they repel criticism based on any special form of experience. However, there are, I suggest, good reasons for thinking that Whitehead's metaphysics might be a creative alternative for appropriation by feminists. Besides the fact that, in principle, it invites a feminist critique, it is noteworthy that a number of feminists have found in Whitehead's writings observations which resonate with women's experience. Most important, however, Whitehead's metaphysics suggests ways of resolving certain problems within feminist thought, not by "indulg[ing] in brilliant feats of explaining away"[10] one or another of the differing points of view, but by helping us to reconceptualize the issues.

One such problem concerns the ideal of androgynous life. For many feminists, androgynous life symbolizes the ultimate goal of the women's movement. The ideal of androgyny begins with the recognition that, out of the whole range of human potentialities, certain traits have been differentially assigned to men and to women, and that all such systems of arbitrary distinctions between the sexes are crippling to women (and ultimately to everyone). Androgyny is a form of life in which every

---

10. Whitehead, *Process and Reality*, 25.

person will be enabled to become a whole human being.

But the ideal of androgynous life is not without serious difficulties from a feminist perspective. It has been observed, for instance, that the concept arises out of and therefore is infected by the very assumption it is meant to deny: namely, that certain characteristics are essentially "feminine" and others essentially "masculine." While this objection needs to be taken seriously, other objections are even more basic. First, it is clear that some proponents of the ideal have failed to recognize the *asymmetrical* relationship between the qualities traditionally ascribed to women and to men. "Femininity" is always defined as oriented to the needs of men (and of children and society conceived as the extensions of men's egos). "Masculinity," in contrast, is never defined primarily as serving the needs of women. Another way of saying this is that the "masculine" is related to the "feminine" in a pattern of dominance and subordination. Given this pattern, the notion that women should acquire "masculine" qualities in addition to their "feminine" traits, and that men should develop their "feminine" side without ceasing to be "masculine," is simply self-contradictory. If masculinity involves domination over women and femininity means subservience to men, then a man who developed his "feminine" potentialities would no longer be masculine, and a woman who developed her "masculine" potentialities would cease to be feminine.

This objection to the ideal of androgyny can be carried a step further. Many feminists want nothing whatever to do with the "masculine" virtues. The qualities ascribed to men, especially in our culture—qualities such as rationality, aggressiveness, objectivity, autonomy, competitiveness, ambition, even courage and boldness in action—have been shaped by the pervasive context of domination. These qualities have therefore taken the form of exploiting and destroying women, other human beings, and our natural environment. Such "masculine" traits are not, from a feminist viewpoint, qualities to be admired in any human being, and they have no place in a feminist vision of the future.

Finally, we need to recognize that the ideal of androgyny has, up to now, been primarily a creation of the male intellect and, like every concept, bears the mark of its origin. When men envisage androgynous life, they do so from the perspective of their own position of actual or symbolic power over women. Thus, unconsciously, but most inevitably, they assume the continuation of their present powers, while imagining the acquisition of "feminine" qualities. No one has stated more incisively the assumptions which permeate the longings of some men for a more androgynous life than Simone de Beauvoir. "No man," she says, "would consent to be a woman, but every man wants women to exist";[11] and: "Man does not wish to be woman; but he dreams of *enfolding within him all that exists,* including therefore this woman, whom he is not."[12] Androgynous life, so conceived, is yet one more example of that imperialistic drive, inculcated as a "masculine" virtue in our society, to possess everything exclusively as one's own.[13]

11. Simone de Beauvoir, *The Second Sex* (New York: Knopf, 1953) 141.

12. Ibid., 172 (my emphasis).

13. This perspective was suggested to me by my colleague, Richard Heaton, Professor of Religious Studies at Hobart and William Smith Colleges.

In this sense, the ideal of androgyny reinforces the status quo instead of providing a vision of liberation.

Still, feminist thinking cannot do without something like the ideal of androgynous life. All feminists agree that sexual stereotypes are false and damaging to women, and that at least some of the qualities ascribed to men, and simultaneously forbidden to and punished in women, need to be fostered in all human beings: for example, the ability to discover who we are and what we want to be; the right to share equally in making decisions which affect us all; the opportunity to develop all our capacities, mental, physical, spiritual; the right to find satisfaction not only in nurturing and supporting others, but in being nurtured and supported in efforts which matter to *us*; the right to be fully equipped—emotionally, intellectually, materially—to stand on our own feet; the power to speak our thoughts and to be really heard by others; the opportunity to act and to make our actions effective. Every feminist, whether or not she accepts androgyny as an appropriate symbol, rejects the arbitrary exclusions and limitations which have distorted women's lives and seeks wholeness for herself and all who are oppressed.

Is it possible to resolve this tension within feminist thought? I suggest that one step toward doing so is to recognize that our difficulty arises, at least in part, from assumptions we have inherited concerning *the basic structure of actuality*—assumptions of which we are not yet fully conscious but which clash with our experience and our visions. These assumptions, which are metaphysical in the last analysis, are partly expressed and partly presupposed in traditional philosophy; they are concretely embedded in our language and institutions; and they are engraved in our deepest feelings. They are not explicitly concerned with sexual distinctions; but the model which they provide is essentially anti-androgynous.

A number of feminists have observed that Western culture throughout its history has been pervaded by a series of mutually exclusive dualisms, or dichotomies, including (for example) creator and creature, humanity and nature, mind and body, reason and emotion, activity and passivity, self and other, subject and object, individuality and relatedness, life and death. Each of these dichotomies has in some way been correlated with the dualism of male and female. Furthermore, all these dichotomies have exhibited a pattern of dominance and subordination. One member of each pair has been seen as more "real," more valuable, or more important than the other and therefore as inherently or ideally in control of its "inferior" opposite. The paradigm of dualism and domination and the linking of these various dualisms with the distinction between male and female have produced the ideologies and social structures which oppress women. It would seem that neither the proximate goal of feminism—the liberation of women to full participation in the life of the human species—nor its final goal—provisionally symbolized as androgynous life—can be achieved apart from the abolition of *all* such dualisms. Androgynous life, then, would be life no longer governed by the paradigm of dichotomy and domination. But this is a negative definition. Is it possible to conceive of androgynous life in positive terms?

Let us examine one aspect of the ideal of androgynous life, to see the difficulties created when we try to conceptualize it in terms of the model provided by traditional thought.

One of the things that androgynous life symbolizes is the dissolution of a cluster of sexual stereotypes which I will designate by the terms "individuality" and "relatedness." In our culture (and in many others), individuality has been assigned to men and relatedness to women. We are taught that men are, or should strive to become, *essentially* self-directing, autonomous, and unique individuals whose needs, interests, and activities are valuable in themselves. In contrast, we learn at our mother's knees that women are, or should strive to become, beings whose existence is *essentially* constituted by their relationships to others. It is all right, of course— indeed necessary—for a man to have "relationships" with others, provided that he is not passive and dependent in these relationships and that they do not distract him from his primary goal, the pursuit of individuality. And it is all right (in some quarters at least) for a woman to "have interests outside the home," even to have a "career"—provided that even in her "outside" work she puts relationships to others ahead of all other goals and that she does not allow such activities to interfere with her essential task of creating and perfecting her relatedness to husband and children. The differential assignment of relatedness and individuality to women and men assumes that no single person can be both fully an individual and fully related to others. Yet most of us who have been caught up in the women's movement have experienced moments when we *knew* that to be essentially related to other persons and, at the same time, to be essentially self-directing, unique individuals whose actions and concerns are valuable in themselves, are not two conflicting ways of being, but mutually supportive and mutually necessary aspects of every experience. But when we try to act on that conviction in our everyday lives—at work, at home, even with our friends—we find ourselves blocked again and again, not only by the expectations of others, but by *something in ourselves* which insists that if we wish to be individuals, we must sacrifice our relatedness to others, and that to preserve our relatedness we must suppress our individuality. And when we try to explain, even to ourselves, how all of us might become more androgynous in this sense, we find it very difficult to say how it is possible.

To understand why this is so, let us look more closely at the inherited assumptions which underlie our conceptions of individuality and relatedness.

To be an individual means, in traditional thought, to exist in a kind of psychic solitude—at least, a one-way solitude, like a pane of glass which is transparent from one side but opaque from the other. An individual is isolated from the influence of others, while exercising control over them; he is completely independent, self-sufficient, self-validating. To paraphrase Descartes' definition of "substance," an individual is someone who requires nothing but *himself* in order to exist. Obviously, no human being can meet these criteria, but the ideal is there, nonetheless, guiding and shaping our actions, our expectations of others, and our estimates of ourselves. To the extent that a man cannot meet such standards, he is apt to feel, and be perceived as, less than "masculine," hence a failure as a human being.

To be a fully related person, on the other hand, means in traditional thought to be wholly shaped by and oriented to others; it means to be entirely and uninterruptedly open to and supportive of *their* needs, desires, and achievements. Such a person is defined solely by her relationships; she has no identity of her own, no enjoyment in her own accomplishments, and no creative effect on the future. To paraphrase Descartes again, a fully related person requires nothing but *others* in order to exist. Obviously, no one can consistently meet these criteria either, but the ideal affects us profoundly. To the extent that a woman is dissatisfied with or incapable of living up to such standards, she will probably feel, and be perceived as, "unfeminine" and therefore a failure.

The metaphysical assumptions underlying this understanding of individuality and relatedness are inherently anti-androgynous. Not only are the two principles irreconcilable in any single instance of actuality; individuality (embodied in men) is inherently superior to and dominant over relatedness (embodied in women). Individuality (man) has intrinsic worth, whereas relatedness (woman) has value only as support for others. And the content of individuality itself is determined by these assumptions. Since to be an individual is to be superior and thus dominant, individuality (masculinity) both requires and *consists in* the expression and enforcement of superiority and domination. That is, "uniqueness" turns out to be comprised of the denigration, manipulation, and destruction of whatever lacks individuality. The results of a single-minded application of this view are plain to see in our economic, political and social life and in the ecological disasters we have created. *This* metaphysics surely cannot provide a model for androgynous life.

I now want to turn to Whitehead's concepts of individuality and relatedness, for he challenges those presuppositions of traditional thought which make any ideal of androgyny based upon them self-contradictory and dangerous.

I spoke earlier of Whitehead's philosophy as an androgynous vision. By this I do not mean that the term "androgyny" appears in his writings, nor even that he was a feminist in any explicit sense. Indeed, Whitehead appears to have been oblivious to certain issues of which feminists today are acutely aware, such as the extent of the sexist character of our language, social institutions and practice. Nor do I wish to claim that a detailed vision of an androgynous society can be immediately deduced from his metaphysics. Any such claim would be inconsistent with Whitehead's own view that the nature of particular forms of existence can never be deduced from the general principles which characterize all forms of existence. My aim is more limited: namely, to show that Whitehead's conception of the fundamental nature of things provides a general *model* for envisaging androgynous life.

As stated, the task of metaphysics, in Whitehead's view, is to describe, as accurately and adequately as possible, the *generic* character of those fully actual things which together constitute the world. And for Whitehead metaphysical analysis reveals that these fully actual entities or facts are not sticks and stones, nor physical particles, nor even human beings understood as entities which endure through time. All these are organized *groups* or aggregates (Whitehead calls them societies) of these more fundamental actual entities. According to Whitehead, these primary actual things which make up the world are "drops" or "buds" (William James' term) or "pulsations" of experience. Each pulsation is, in this schema, an individual process, with its own spatio-temporal boundaries, its own perspective on the past, its own aim and enjoyment of itself in the present, and its own influence on the future. And, as such, every actual entity is both a unique and individual occurrence, and an entity which is essentially related to the whole world.

Whitehead's paradigm for conceiving the world as made up of such pulsations of process is a human occasion of experience . . . such as the experience you are enjoying at this very moment. An occasion of human experience is not a static thing, but an activity—the activity of becoming what it is. Whitehead speaks of this activity of becoming as "concrescence," that is, the act of "growing together." This concrescence is the process by which many diverse experiences (or in Whitehead's terminology feelings) which make up the past completed world, are integrated into the unity of a new and unique present occasion of experience, into one, complete, fully definite feeling. For instance, at this moment, the components of your experience consist of many different feelings, some conscious, some unconscious. There are the feelings of the sound of my voice, of the specific odor and temperature of the air in the room, of the surface of the seats on which you are sitting, of being surrounded by other people, and so on. And there are other feelings which are part of your experience now that come from the more remote past—such as your feeling about sitting and listening to someone lecture—and others which refer to the future. So your experience at this moment consists of many diverse feelings, and what you are doing is bringing these feelings together in some way to form a unified pattern.

These occasions which you feel in your present process of becoming are occasions which have already completed their own acts of becoming. Past, completed occasions were once themselves activities of self-creation, once subjects synthesizing their own diverse feeling of *their* past world of experience into a unity. Having attained such unity, they now constitute the past world out of which your present experience arises. They are no longer creative processes of becoming but the completed "objects" there to be appropriated by you. They are, so to speak, the multiplicity of data which are given to you for creative synthesis; they are the elements out of which you are to create your own unique experience. Thus each present moment of concrescence is *essentially related to all past occasions* for they are its primary constituents.

Yet while these past occasions are fixed and given and hence determining, and you *must* feel them, synthesize them in some way, *how* you feel them and *how* you integrate them is not predetermined. Every completed occasion is felt in some way and with some degree of relevance by you (and by every other new concrescence) and every new moment of becoming is constituted by its relations, that is its feelings of, the occasions belonging to the past world out of which it arises. Yet you, in your present moment of experience, feel these past occasions in your *own* way, from your *own* perspective, for your *own* purpose, and you thereby synthesize them into a pattern unique to yourself. You, and all other activities of becoming, though constituted by relations to the past, are self-creative and free in those relations. This active, unique creation of the self comes about in accordance with what Whitehead calls your "subjective aim." A subjective aim is an occasion's urge to synthesize its inherited feelings in accordance with some new, novel possibility. In its initial form, your subjective aim is provided by God, who is among the components of your actual world. But even an occasion's initial aim is not fully determinate; that is, it is up to the occasion to decide in which of many different ways it will actualize its general aim. Thus the achievement of an occasion, while made possible jointly by God and antecedent occasion, is, in the final analysis, its own achievement, and this achievement has intrinsic value for the occasion itself. That is why Whitehead calls the final phase of concrescence the occasion's "satisfaction." Thus each concrescent occasion is *essentially* an *individual*—self-creative, unique, a being whose "existence is its own justification."[14]

When this act of concrescence has attained its unique, fully determinate synthesis, its life as a subject—that is, as the active creator of itself—is over. It perishes. But in perishing as a subject, the occasion passes over to a new kind of existence. It is now an object, a member of the actual worlds of new processes of concrescence. As such, it requires them in turn to take account of it—to make it part of themselves—in some way. Thus the value that the completed occasion achieved for itself becomes an element of value in the acts of concrescence which supersede it. In this way every occasion is *essentially related* to *all future occasions:* to make a difference in the world, for it is part of that world.

Obviously, occasions are not all on the same level with respect to the degree of novelty they can achieve, nor in the extent to which they can transmit their novel achievements to the future. The specific character of an occasion's environment may enhance or severely limit its chances for effective novelty. But despite these differences, all actual occasions exhibit the same three-fold structure: each arises out of and is constituted by its feelings of the past; each is the self-directing subject of its own becoming, attaining its unique satisfaction and enjoying its own self-worth; each contributes its achievements to the future. No occasion exists in "self-sufficient isolation."[15] Yet each is an individual, for there are no "vacuous actualities"[16] no occasions which are merely "vehicles for receiving, for storing in a napkin, and for restoring without loss or gain."[17] Every concrescence is a "moment of sheer individuality, bounded on either side by essential relativity."[18]

Up to now I have been speaking of individuality and relatedness as features of single actual occasions. But a human being is more than a single occasion of experience; more, even, than a linear succession of such occasions. A human being according to Whitehead, is a complex society of concrescent activities, both bodily and mental, so organized as to yield great

14. Whitehead, *Modes of Thought*, 109.
15. Ibid., 140.
16. Whitehead, *Process and Reality*, 43.
17. Ibid., 269.
18. Whitehead, *Adventures of Ideas*, 227.

depth of relatedness and intense individuality. Moreover, the society which is a human being is set within a larger society of societies (its natural environment, including other human beings) which contribute significantly to its individual uniqueness. I must stress that what I have said is a very inadequate account of Whitehead's theory of relatedness and individuality, especially as it applies to human beings. But since a human being is a society of actual occasions, each of which is both fully individual and fully related to the world, it is obvious that the life of every human being, male or female, is both unique and constituted by its relationships to others. In this limited but important sense, Whitehead's analysis of the relatedness and individuality of concrescent occasions offers a model for envisaging androgynous life.

It is clear that Whitehead's model differs radically from the traditional model which I outlined earlier. Not only are individuality and relatedness *compatible aspects of every actuality,* these two principles *require each other.* And since they require each other, *neither is more "real," important,* or *valuable than the other.* On the contrary, individuality and relatedness *support and enhance one another.* The more profound and complex an occasion's relationships to the world from which it arises, the greater its opportunity to achieve unique value for itself; and the more unique its individual satisfaction, the more valuable its potential contribution to the world which supersedes it. What Whitehead calls the "rhythm of process"[19] at the heart of actuality is a rhythmic alternation between giving and receiving, between the appropriation of others for the enrichment of oneself and the yielding up of oneself for the enrichment of others. Whitehead's description of the rhythm of process is a metaphysical rendering of what Nietzsche calls "the gift-giving virtue,"[20] in which the self eagerly pours out the treasures it has plundered the universe to obtain.

I mentioned earlier a series of dualisms which have pervaded Western culture, all exhibiting a pattern of domination and subservience and all associated with a dichotomous conception of male and female. I have tried to show that Whitehead's metaphysics involves a different understanding of one of these pairs—an understanding which denies the pattern of dichotomy and domination. In exploring Whitehead's view of individuality and relatedness, we have also glimpsed the dissolution of this same pattern with respect to certain other traditional dualisms: activity and passivity, self and other, subject and object. If time permitted, it could be shown that Whitehead dissolves all the destructive dichotomies associated with the distinction between the sexes, including the dualisms of creator and creature, humanity and nature, mind and body, reason and emotion—even the dualism of life and death.

This last dualism, the dualism of life and death, is in my opinion the most important issue awaiting feminist exploration, both because our dichotomous view of the relation between life and death is the wellspring from which all the other

---

19. Whitehead, *Modes of Thought,* 88.

20. Friedrich Nietzsche, *Thus Spoke Zarathustra* in Walter Kaufmann, trans., *The Portable Nietzsche,* The Viking Portable Library (New York: Viking, 1954) 187.

dualisms have arisen,[21] and because this is an issue about which feminists have not yet begun to think seriously enough. Although no adequate discussion of the relevance of Whitehead's metaphysics to overcoming the dualism of life and death is possible here, certain clues have already been mentioned. We know that, for Whitehead, the fundamental actualities which make up the world are living occasions of experience, brief in duration yet each with intrinsic worth and self-enjoyment. We know also that each occasion, when it has completed its process of self-creation, perishes. But in perishing as a living subject, it does not simply cease to be, as though it had never lived; the value it has achieved for itself is appropriated by occasions beyond it, contributing to their lives something unique and irreplaceable. So the rhythm of process is the rhythm of living and dying, in which living occasions are nourished by the dead and occasions which have perished live on in their successors. No particular occasion is indispensable to the rhythm of process, but each is a unique individual which *makes a difference*, for better or for worse. Each is alone in its self-creation; yet in its aloneness all that has lived is part of itself. Each is appropriated by others; but in being appropriated it remains its unique self. Just as relatedness and individuality are not in conflict within us but require and support one another, so living and dying are mutually enhancing.

It is true that complex societies of occasions which I call myself will someday cease to exist as that society; this is what we ordinarily mean by "death." Most of us find it easier to affirm the perishing of our particular occasions of experience than the death of our enduring selves. Yet the slightest shift in perspective is all that is needed to enable us to affirm the death of the enduring self also. "Perspective," Whitehead points out, is another word for "importance."[22] The question is: what importance do we attach to our enduring selves, in comparison with the vividness of our lives in the present moment—that present moment which, as Whitehead says, holds the sum of existence, backwards and forwards within itself?[23] The most basic assumption that we have inherited from patriarchal culture, and the one which feminists may find most difficult to overcome, is that the enduring self is the true locus of value, and that the death of that self is our greatest adversary. Until we have faced this fact honestly and probed the innermost recesses of our feelings about life and death, we shall not truly have arrived at the possibility of envisaging androgynous life.

The shift in perspective which would enable us to affirm death will not occur as a direct result of metaphysical inquiry, any more than will the shift involved in affirming the unity of relatedness and individuality. Feminists are well aware that when a new idea strikes us as valuable and right, we are not able immediately to act upon it; that old habits are not easily discarded; and, most important, that none of the personal effects of sexism can be overcome on the purely personal level, since these effects are continually reproduced

21. See, for example, Norman O. Brown *Life against Death: The Psychoanalytic Meaning of History* (New York: Random House, 1959); and Dorothy Dinnerstein, *The Mermaid and the Minotaur: Sexual Arrangements and Human Malaise* (New York: Harper & Row, 1976).

22. Whitehead, *Modes of Thought*, 9–11.

23. Whitehead, *The Aims of Education* (New York: New American Library, 1949) 14.

in us by our social institutions. The political is, indeed, personal; and the personal, political.

So androgynous life will not miraculously appear among us just because *we* find an adequate *way* of conceptualizing it. For that to happen, we need not only a vision of what we want, but practical plans for creating it. How to bring androgynous life into being is a question I have not addressed not because I think the question is unimportant, but simply because no one can talk about everything at once. Although there are clues in Whitehead's metaphysics which can be helpful in formulating such plans, no metaphysics can give us the concrete methods for effecting social change.

Still, what we think it is possible to achieve by social change is an essential ingredient in bringing it about. If the dichotomies which have been indissolubly linked with sexism in our culture cannot be overcome, then the prospect of overcoming sexism itself seems very dim. On the positive side, while the availability of a model of androgynous life will not create androgyny, it may help us to see more clearly what we are after.

Traditional theology has defined sin as humanity's attempt to transgress the limits of [its] creatureliness. Feminists might rephrase this in language once used by Charles Hartshorne: "man alone among the animals is able . . . to imagine that he can quarrel with the essential character of the universe while still living in it."[24] The task feminists have set themselves could then be said to be, finally to bring the quarrel to an end. In carrying out this task, Whitehead's metaphysics can be an invaluable ally. Since processes of concrescence are the fundamental actualities of our existence, Whitehead's thought not only provides a way of envisaging an as-yet-unachieved androgynous form of life, it also shows that even now, against the strivings inculcated in us by patriarchal culture, and in spite of the social structures which stand in its way, we are already aware, at some deep level of our existence, that to be is to be androgynous.

If process thought has correctly conceived the basic character of our existence, then what feminists are engaged in is, in an important sense, the attempt to create something new; but, in another and equally important sense, we are trying to make explicit and provide the conditions needed for a long-delayed flowering of what is already there: the ever-present androgynous structure of life itself.

---

24. [*Sic.* There is no citation in the original article.]

Commentary

Helene Tallon Russell

Valerie Saiving is famous for her groundbreaking essay, "The Human Situation: A Feminine View"[1] (1960), which shattered the misconception that the male situation and experience is the whole of the human situation and experience. Rather, she suggests women's situation and experience yield qualitatively different theological questions and insights. Both types of situations and reflections ought to be included in the writing of theology and its doctrines.

In this lecture, she continues her brilliant constructive work by exploring the interface between process thought and feminism. Using the common themes of the important role that experience as a source of knowledge plays for both schools of thought and a shared aversion to the dualistic and substance based rationalism of modern discourse, she argues that Alfred North Whitehead's thought offers a philosophical framework appropriate to feminist experience, consciousness and philosophical intuitions.

In addition to highlighting experience as a primary epistemological source, Saiving unpacks feminist criticism of dichotomous polarities and their pattern of dominance and submission as well as its desires to eliminate these dualisms and the gender roles associated with them. She names this goal as an androgynous ideal in which all persons are free to inculcate human qualities without regard to the stereotypical masculinity or femininity associated with it in our patriarchal culture, seeking to enable human flourishing beyond dominant and submissive gender roles.

Her analysis provides a clear foundation for ways that women's philosophical and theological endeavors can benefit from process metaphysics. In addition to Whitehead's organic empiricism being built upon experience, process thought provides a way of thinking about actuality that is consistent with many other feminist sensibilities. In a process worldview polarities are neither hierarchical nor dichotomous. They represent characteristics or realities that are mutually dependent upon each other, not mutually exclusive. As an example, Saiving examines a polarity between relationality and individuality. In modern metaphysical presuppositions, these two modes are understood as a dichotomy in which women are defined relationally while men are defined in terms of their independent individuality. Feminists have insisted that relationality and individuality are both important values in both men and women. Process philosophy offers a remedy by postulating a conceptual framework in

---

1. Valerie Saiving, "The Human Situation: A Feminine View," *Journal of Religion* 40 (1960) 100–112.

which all entities function both relationally and with individual freedom. Each entity is both formed out of relations with others and makes its own individual decision in becoming. Both modes are part of the process of concrescence or becoming concrete.

This theme will be picked up and developed theologically in other process feminist thinkers, most notably Catherine Keller's work in *From a Broken Web*.[2] As can be seen below, she analyzes the problematic nature of what she calls *separative* and *soluable* selves.

Although the androgynous ideal is not a common term for current feminist and womanist theology, the work of enabling persons of both genders to embrace various characteristics and modes is still a goal for most. Recently, the focus has shifted to an acceptance and appreciation of individual differences without resorting to the pattern of opposites or polarities.

This lecture paints a lucid picture of the beginnings of the process relational feminist movement and makes a compelling argument for the importance of an interface between them. Saiving focuses on the ways that process thought can benefit feminism by providing metaphysical grounding for the movement and its claims. Such a foundation has proven very fruitful and continues to influence and benefit new generations of process feminist thinkers. It started feminists thinking about other ways that process thought and feminism could engage each other fruitfully. One way in which this has progressed is that the beneficial influence happens in the other direction as well—process thought can benefit from feminist and women's theology as well. One thinker who explicitly develops the mutually enriching interactivity between process thought and feminist theology is Marjorie Suchocki in a paper entitled "Openness and Mutuality in Process Thought and Feminist Action."[3] Not only does the integration of these two schools of thought serve feminism and feminist theology, but also process theology gains by its interaction with feminism.

In this lecture, Saiving sets a process feminist movement afoot by engaging women's focus on experience in the reason-filled way given in process philosophy. This metaphysics provides a constructive world view in which all experience is constitutive of reality and thus enables the ethical claim that women's experience matters, the experience of the poor matters, the experience of persons marginalized for what ever reason are all to be taken into account. In a process worldview, this claim is not limited to a proscription, it is also a description of the way things are.

Saiving points out and develops a connection between Whitehead's developed metaphysics with feminist sensibilities. This is particularly evocative and noteworthy because women often come to process theology already feminists and in encountering the worldview imagined, articulated, and described in process philosophy and theology, we know that we have found a way of thinking that

---

2. Catherine Keller, *From a Broken Web: Separation, Sexism, and Self* (Boston: Beacon, 1986).

3. Marjorie Suchocki, "Openness and Mutuality in Process Thought and Feminist Action," in *Feminism and Process Thought: The Harvard Divinity School/Claremont Center for Process Studies Symposium Papers*, ed. Sheila Greeve Davaney, Symposium Series 6 (Lewiston, NY: Mellen, 1981), 62–82.

resonates with our own sensibilities. Saiving explicitly articulates this experience. It is as if Whitehead writes what we wanted to say. Many process feminist and womanist thinkers describe the experience of first encountering process philosophy as one similar to the sentiment in Etta James' blues song, *At Last*: finally a worldview that speaks to my experience and intuition of how the world is and works. This is another way in which process philosophy affirms women's experience.

Saiving's work here is significant for process feminist thought because she articulates an insightful and productive vision for the possibilities of an alternative worldview in which women, feminists, and process thinkers can say in one accord, *At Last*, we have found "a dream that we could speak through, a worldview that we can call our own."

STUDY QUESTIONS

1. What is meant by experience in this essay? How do you understand experience? Is experience a prominent part of your understanding of knowledge? What role does it play for your theology?

2. Saiving makes special reference to the traditional dichotomy of life/death and its pertinence to the future of feminist criticism. What does Saiving find particularly important about this dichotomy? What significance might the question of locating ultimate value in particular individuals and "enduring societies" have?

3. Note how this dyad of relationality and individuality plays itself out in other authors in this text, especially for Catherine Keller's concepts of separative and soluable selves.

4. Pull out what Saiving means by the "androgynous life." While this terminology has fallen out of use, which of the values and goals that Saiving describes are still desirable ideals in feminist endeavors? Why do you think this terminology is no longer used?

5 Methodology/God's Presence

Marjorie Hewitt Suchocki

Marjorie Hewitt Suchocki is a professor emeritus at Claremont School of Theology and Claremont Graduate University, where she taught theology and philosophy of religion from 1990 to 2002. She earned a PhD from Claremont Graduate School in 1974. She served as Dean at Claremont from 1992 to 1999, and at Wesley Theological Seminary from 1983 to 1990. She has served as the Director of the Whitehead International Film Festival since 2001 as well as the Director of Process & Faith Program of the Center for Process Studies. Perusing the bibliography will reveal that she has written many books addressing process thought and feminist theology. She has also published countless articles and is highly demanded as a speaker. She has served as mentor and inspiration for many feminist process theologians. This excerpt is taken from chapter one and chapter 5 of her first book, originally published in 1982.

Excerpt from *God, Christ, Church: A Practical Guide to Process Theology*

A RELATIONAL THEOLOGY

EACH GENERATION EXPRESSES ANEW the Christian conviction that God is for us. The immediate catalyst for these expressions may well be the profound conviction that God is a force for love, trust, and hope in a communal world. The conviction carries with it a drive for expression and the expression itself contributes to the creation *of* communities *of* love, trust, and hope. God is for us: therefore we speak, create a tradition, and live as a community called the church.

Expressions of faith, however, must partake of more than traditional categories if they are to be creative of community in the world. Communication is necessary to community, and communication depends upon using thought patterns that constitute the "common sense" of a time. If ordinary perceptions of the world deal in categories of subject/object, then expressions of faith will also use that language. Otherwise, the "God for us" message will not address the reality of the subject/object world of one's interpreted experience, and how then will the message even be heard? Likewise, if the world is understood in terms of substance and accidents, faith must also incorporate those categories or find itself addressing a story world unrelated to the "real" world of everydayness. And if the dominant understanding of the world is through categories of interrelationship, process, and relativity, then this sensitivity must be picked up by the language of faith. Theology, as the way in which we interpret existence in a world where God is for us, will be expressed in relational language.

The importance of expressing theology through the thought patterns of an age is hardly new. Augustine, for instance, gave an enduring formulation of faith by drawing heavily upon the understanding of the world which had been fashioned by the third century philosopher Plotinus. Plotinus, working from his own unique study of Plato, had powerfully defined the structure of existence. His thought provided a popular framework within which people could understand themselves in relation to the whole of reality. Augustine used Plotinian thought as a vehicle through which to express the faith which was his both through his personal redemptive experience and through his study of the Christian scriptures and tradition.

Centuries later Thomas Aquinas utilized the newly discovered teachings of Aristotle to provide a background within which to express the dynamics of faith. Christian experience, scriptures, and tradition spilled into the philosophy. "Philosophy is the handmaiden of theology," was the watchword of the day. By this it was indicated that philosophy did not dictate the content of faith, it was simply the tool through which faith was explicated systematically. A strong advantage of the method was the sense in which it allowed a unified vision of reality. The understanding of the natural world and the understanding of faith were compatible. The paralysis of a compartmentalized religion was avoided, and there was a vigor to Christian thought and life.

Augustine and Aquinas might be considered watershed figures in terms of shifting philosophical worldviews which became intermingled with Christian faith. But they are only two of the most outstanding examples of this dynamic. Implicitly or explicitly, positively or negatively, Christians tend to express faith in ways which are generally compatible with dominant understandings of the world.

Our own age is one which has seen profound changes. Darwin, Marx, Freud, and Einstein are familiar names to us. Each one has contributed to a shift in the way we see things. It is not simply a matter of understanding the details of what each man said, nor is it even necessary to speak of a general familiarity with the school of thought each man represents. Nor is agreement with the theories propounded by them the issue. Rather, the intellectual climate within which we all think has been changed. Even when we strive to repeat the thought patterns of a previous age, we must do so against the counterforce presented by the contemporary milieu. It is as if we view the world as a kaleidoscope, filled with shapes and colors which can be described in terms of a particular pattern. A period of time is like one particular viewing of the pattern. But then someone turns the kaleidoscope, and not only do all of the pieces shift, but it seems that some new ones have been added. There is familiarity and some continuity, for the colors are still there—but their tones seem somehow different in the altered positions, and while at first we try to see them still in their familiar form, we nevertheless find ourselves struggling to express the difference in the way of seeing. Finally we must recognize the newness of the pattern, and we reach toward a familiarity with the new which can be as assuring as that which we remember—or project—as belonging to the old. But the kaleidoscope will never repeat exactly the same pattern. Darwin, Marx, Freud, and Einstein have all turned the kaleidoscope of our world, changing the configurations of what we call reality.

Christians remaining true to their tradition will take the kaleidoscopic shift of our time seriously, and engage in the task of expressing again the redemptive realities of Christian faith with a critical openness to the critical openness to the changes entailed. They will inquire into a biblical understanding of the nature of God, of Christ, of the church, and of the reign of God, and seek to give these faithful expression in thought forms appropriate to our own day. The proclamation of faith in terms that speak to the whole of reality depends upon the church's self-critical and creative responsiveness to this task.

The most pervasive factor of the contemporary configuration is the heightened importance of relationality and therefore change, and indeed, most theology written in the mid- to late twentieth century gives far more positive importance to relational categories than was so in previous centuries. But the most explicitly relational theology is that known as process theology. The philosophical vehicle through which this mode of thought is expressed is that of Alfred North Whitehead, who formulated his particular understanding of reality as a result of his work in physics and mathematics in the early part of the twentieth century. Not content to confine his data to these fields, he drew as well from areas such as history, sociology, and philosophy. He gave particular priority to the data of religious experience. Therefore, even though his model of reality reflects his highly technical background, it ultimately rests upon a broad understanding of experience in a relativity-conscious age. By using this model to express Christian faith, we push toward the rewards of communicating Christian faith in thought forms that reflect a contemporary understanding of reality.

When one strives to express Christianity in new thought patterns, however, many critical issues emerge. What is the substratum with which one works? We speak of "Christian faith" as if it were indeed one thing, enduring throughout the ages, albeit expressed in different thought forms! Many scholars have devoted much effort to uncovering an "essence" of Christianity that pervades whatever thought form might be utilized. The difficulty, of course, is that the thought forms are inextricably woven into Christian faith. There is no abstract "Christian faith" apart from the living reality of people who are Christians, and who give expression to their faith. The thought forms they use not only define their faith, but their very lives. Thought forms are not so easily abstracted from living faith, leaving some "essence" to be discovered! Even the biblical witness, in its own time, is a contemporary expression of the living faith that God acts for us through Jesus Christ. Each new generation inherits the expressed witness of the previous generations, with a double transformation occurring. On the one hand, the new generation is shaped by the faith it inherits, but on the other hand, it transforms that faith through its own living witness. The "essence" of the Christian faith may well be that it is a malleable witness, depending upon transformations again and yet again of an inherited word that God is for us.

...

GOD AS PRESENCE

We exist in creative response to relationships; this means that existence is through and through relational. Despite this immersion in a world of relation, we sometimes experience a sense of isolation, of watching the crowd, of feeling that there is no real mattering of ourselves in relation to others: loneliness. Who can touch us in our loneliness?

The problem is intensified when we consider the importance of relationships in establishing our own individual sense of meaning. In the illustration of Catherine, it was obvious that her daily purpose and fulfillment were associated with the relationships of her life, whether family, studies, church, or profession. Meaning is found in the concrete relationships of our existence, or it is not found at all. Loneliness, then, carries as its bitter corollary a fear that there is no longer any meaning. In its most intense form, this fear extends beyond daily meaninglessness to an ultimate meaninglessness that reduces one's life to triviality and absurdity.

Inevitably, however, we judge loneliness to be out of kilter with the way things should be. We measure the hollow places of loneliness by the value of the relationships we wish we had, so that there is a restlessness and discontent with the condition of loneliness measured against the "might be" of our yearning. This loneliness is seldom the total absence of perceived relation; it is rather the experience that known relationships are insufficient to meet our deepest needs. In loneliness, we judge the concrete relationships of our lives as wanting, as transient, and without any ultimacy of meaning. It is as if the condition of loneliness takes us beneath the surface of those relationships, so that whether momentarily or longer, we are dissatisfied with those relations. But we are also dissatisfied with loneliness. Why?

We could almost speak of our experience as if it occurred in layers: the outermost layer of daily existence, and a deeper layer—the place of loneliness—where it seems that relationships cannot follow, so that the relationships are deemed insufficient for us. This deeper layer of loneliness does not seem to have ultimacy, for it itself is deemed insufficient. It is as if there were yet another depth beyond the place of loneliness, providing a place of judgment upon loneliness, just as loneliness has provided a place of judgment upon daily relationships.

The experience of loneliness thus indicates at least three dimensions to our experience. There is the surface dimension of eyerydayness, often experienced as sufficient for the requirement of meaning. Lurking beneath such daily relations is the recurring sense of emptiness, futility, loneliness despite relation. This dimension takes us inside ourselves, forcing us away from the surface of our living. In loneliness the insufficiency of daily relationships is that they do not follow us here, to the inwardness of ourselves; the relationships are therefore found wanting. But neither is there sufficiency in this inwardness: the lonely self exists in an echo chamber, crying against the prison of its own solitariness for a relation that can set it free. Since the surface relationships cannot participate in this inwardness, and are judged as "surface" precisely through the inwardness, those relations cannot suffice for release from loneliness. Nor, in their insufficiency, can those relations provide the source of the judgment that the loneliness is itself a negative state. There is, in the very sense of loneliness as negative, an intimation of yet a deeper dimension to reality that has the power of judgment over loneliness. Loneliness is then like a space between two forms of relation: the daily relationality above, and a depth relationality beneath. The dilemma of the lonely self is its alienation from both forms of relation. The former seems insufficient, and the latter seems inaccessible, or even illusory. Both forms become like the walls of the echo-chamber prison, intensifying the sense of alienation and loneliness.

If only one could rest content with loneliness! Then loneliness might seem more like a great hall than a narrow prison; one could stay the intensifying power; one could hold back the insufficiencies of daily relation and the judgment of ultimate relation, like a Samson braced between the pillars of the Philistine hall. "Loneliness," one could say, "is but part of our human condition, to be accepted in unquestioning endurance." In such a way, one might balance the pillars that hold up the roof of futility and despair, and find protection in the hall of emptiness. But too often we push against the pillars of denied relation, and the chaos of futility, alienation, and meaninglessness falls upon us, and we are lonelier still. The great hall is no less a prison than the narrow echo chamber.

What if the imagery be used in a different way: if loneliness is like a space or a room between two forms of relation—the one superficial, the other inaccessible depth—may we not consider the condition of loneliness not as a room but as a passageway? That is, if in loneliness we have longings for a form of relation that penetrates more deeply into our being than those relations of everydayness, and if this sense of a deeper relation becomes both the judge against superficial relationships and against loneliness itself, may not loneliness—which gives rise to the sense of such a form of relationality in the first place—become a mode of access to such a reality? If we intuit such a form of relation through loneliness, might we not go still further, and reach such a form of relation precisely through the prior condition of loneliness? Perhaps the human experience of loneliness becomes an entry point for an awareness of relation to a God who is usually hidden in the dailiness of life; perhaps we can move through loneliness to its further side, and begin to speak of the nature of the God who is for us as an ultimate presence.

How can this be? And what is the import of a God who is an ultimate relation, an ultimate presence? The process conceptuality comes to our aid in laying bare the dynamics by which loneliness becomes a component of our experience, and the sense in which loneliness can suggest the nature of God.

Every moment of existence begins in relationality through the transition of energy from the past to the present. The past *is* present to the becoming occasion. These physical feelings of the past are supplemented by a mental conception of what might be. This conception is the grasp of possibility, of the occasion's response to the moment-by-moment touch of God. God proposes an optimum way of being and the becoming occasion disposes of this as it wills.

The occasion is responsible for what it does with what it has received. In its becoming, it is alone with itself, determining the value of its universe. This activity can be portrayed as a spiral, wherein the occasion moves from its feelings of the past (including God) into its own integrative activity, intent upon becoming one reality in the midst of its manifold relations. Upon its completion, it bursts into transitional relation again, now hurling its effects upon the future, joining with God and the whole universe in calling that future into being, even as it itself was called into being. In the flashing movement of existence, every momentary act of becoming is followed by transitional relation, and every transitional relation is followed by a new act of becoming, called concrescence. Each concrescence is like the breathing space in the sea of relationality, the aloneness through which one becomes a self through integration of the many relations.

Thus far the model is more descriptive of aloneness in the midst of relation than loneliness in the midst of relation. The difference is crucial, for aloneness can be full of meaning, while loneliness involves loss of meaning. One can be alone, and yet intensely aware of relationships which are integral to the self, both constitutively and valuationally. To be lonely, however, is to experience the devaluation of relations, and an isolation despite relation. The fact that each moment of concrescence is an aloneness with itself is the basis for the further experience of loneliness, but it is not identical with loneliness. To push toward an understanding of loneliness, we need to expand the discussion of consciousness begun in our last chapter.

Each occasion of existence is both mental and physical, with the physical pole being defined as feelings of the past, and the mental being that capacity to generalize the past and to grasp a new possibility in relation to that past. Very few actual occasions appear to have consciousness, which is the awareness of the contrasts between data in light of some particular possibility for becoming. Consciousness is a possibility of the mental pole; it is a particular development of the mental pole, but it is not itself reducible to the mental pole. Consciousness comes to actuality through the strength of contrast between what is and what might be. Thus consciousness is a function of the contrasting integration of the mental and physical poles. It is, therefore, produced through concrescence, and is necessarily a late phase of concrescence. Consciousness cannot be produced in the initial stages of concrescence, for the physical pole, is the sheer feeling of energy from the past. Only as the many feelings are integrated can consciousness arise, for the activity of integration is the activity of contrasting.

What provides the contrast? There are two sources, with the first and foremost being a grasp of the "might be" in contrast to the "what is." In order for this type of contrast to obtain, however, the second source must also be present. There must be a wide range of positive feelings (or prehensions) of the past. If most of the past is felt negatively, so that only a narrow sphere of reality is admitted into positive influence during concrescence, then the contrasting activity will be minimal. Consequently, the mental pole will integrate the past with a minimum amount of novelty; and a relative repetition of the past will be assured. The vast proportions of occasions in our world are of this variety, with the result that there is a basic stability to the natural world. Its rate of change is slow relative to us.

When an occasion is open to a wide range of influences received positively into the concrescent process, then the manyness of influences itself presents a ground for contrast, plus a problem for integration. The more influences allowed, the more novelty is called for. The "might be" comes into play as ways of integrating the many into unity come to the fore. The contrast between the many and the "might be" produces consciousness as itself being a means of integration. Consciousness, then, relies upon an openness to novelty and thus a prominence to the mental pole, a prominence that increases through the intensity of contrasts which the occasion can sustain.

In loneliness, as contrasted with aloneness, the relations that are constitutive of the self are valued negatively. Ordinarily, relations are valued in varying degrees: they range from intense to minimal importance. Further, there is a fluctuation within each relationship, depending upon the immediate purposes of the individual. For instance, a son may be intensely important to a mother, but if the mother is involved in writing, the relationship to the son may well slip to the background of consciousness. When the mother and son are engaged in conversation, however, the values in the immediate experience may reverse. The writing may become background, and the relationship between mother and son becomes foreground. Thus daily existence admits a multitude of relationships, each with its own value, contrasted with the fluctuating purposes of existence. The contrasts of relation are varied. Not so, however, in loneliness. There is a leveling of relation through negativity. There is a painful sameness to all relations in loneliness, wherein the contrasting variability and interest is silenced.

Yet there is consciousness. What is the contrast that produces the consciousness of loneliness? It can only come from the "might be," but the "might be" in the process vision of reality is located precisely in the initial aim from God.

Earlier, we spoke of loneliness as a prison between two modes of relation, the devalued everyday relationships, and the sense of ultimate relation through which loneliness is judged as being askew. We are now in a position to correlate the existential sense with the philosophical model, wherein we can move into the implications for God. Loneliness follows from the devaluation of finite relations. Relationality cannot be negated, for existence is thoroughly relational. But the relationality can be devalued, and in the devaluation all finite relations are leveled to a sameness. One can, in this process of devaluation, live a robot-like existence, moving in a contrastless world with minimal consciousness. Yet given the propensity of human existence for consciousness, the contrast of the "might be" forces itself upon us, demanding that we visualize a relation that could follow us into our inward processes of existence, meeting us with presence and providing us with meaning.

The "might be" that comes from God is always for an optimum possibility for concrescence, given our situation. God not only begins our existence through the touch that mediates possibility to us. but God also feels us at the conclusion of each momentary existence integrating that which we have chosen to become into the divine awareness. We are surrounded by God as our source and destiny in every moment This indicates that the "might be" that comes to us in our devaluation of finite relations is in and of itself rooted in a unique presence, for there is no other reality in our experience that is both our source and our destiny, There is a uniqueness to the aim received from God that goes beyond its content to the uniqueness of its source in relation to ourselves.

This unique source is something that is experienced again and again by each successive moment in our existence. If God is always present, then there is no contrasting absence whereby God's presence could rise to conscious notice. This would mean that the very constancy of God's presence would paradoxically function to hide God's presence from consciousness. This hiddenness is further emphasized by the fact that the content of God's touch upon each concrescence occasion is toward an optimum mode of existence in the world. Thus God's aim directs us toward the world, not necessarily toward God, and again, God is present in a mode of hiddenness.

When, however, the contrasts of the world are leveled as in loneliness, might it not be the case that a new contrast emerges, touching the edges of consciousness with a sense of the divine presence? Whitehead speaks of a peculiar category known as "transmutation," by which he means the identifying of many occasions by a single characteristic that they all hold in common. As the contrasts of relationality are leveled, they are deemed insufficient, and their very variability becomes a part of that insufficiency. We might speculate that in loneliness, we tend to categorize all relations alike, negatively valuing the variability that ordinarily is the source of richness and contrasts. Transmutation occurs, and many relations are devalued for variability. Is there not then a natural contrast provided between the variable finite relations and the one invariable divine relation? And might not this contrast suffice to begin to lift this divine relation out of hiddenness into awareness?

We have mentioned the invariability of God's presence as one factor that contrasts with finite relationality. There is yet another factor of that follows from strict usage of this process model. Every finite occasion is felt by another as past, since no occasion is effective for another until it is determinate and therefore complete. Upon its completion of becoming, its concrescent energy becomes transitional energy, and the past becomes an object to be felt by the present. Whitehead calls this "objective immortality." Since God concresces conversely from every finite occasion, God's concrescence never ends: God is the only entity whose subjectivity continues even as it is being felt. This is not a violation of the metaphysics; it simply follows from the reversal of the polar dynamics as discussed in chapter three, and elaborated in the appendix.

Determinateness, established by all finite occasions *after* the unification process is established by God through the primordial quality of the mental pole. Finite occasions end in determinateness, thus allowing the transmission of energy. God begins in the determinateness of the primordial vision, so that God's transitional creativity is copresent with God's concrescent creativity. For finite occasions, determinateness is the result of subjectivity; for

God, determinateness is the presupposition of subjectivity. Hence God, unlike any other actuality, is felt by the finite occasion during the divine subjectivity, not after-for there is no "after."

If in loneliness the subject's feeling of God shifts from the world-oriented content of the initial aim to the God-derived nature of the aim, would not this peculiar feature, which surely differentiates this aim from all others, play a part in the resulting contrast? And would it not indicate a divine mode of presence to the subject that would differ markedly from finite modes of presence? Two points of discussion might clarify this: the nature of "objective immortality" in the process model and the account of mystical experience, which could be seen to illustrate the difference the continuing concrescence of God might make in the sense of the divine presence.

"Objective immortality" is the way the past functions in the internal constitution of the present, and therefore continues to "live on" in the present. However, the subjectivity that belonged to each element of the past in its own time of becoming is lost. The easiest way to illustrate this is through some great example from history: Martin Luther King, Jr., created a significant difference in American life that certainly continues in these decades since his tragic death. In that sense, he lives on. But his own subjective reality was cut down in 1968; King himself does not participate in the events that succeed him, even though he critically influenced what those events could be. He is "objectively immortal" in history. The subjectivity belongs to those in the present time who are influenced by him.

Process philosophy says that this illustration typifies what happens not simply with the great figures of history, but in every moment of existence, at every level of existence. Every instant of becoming *is* a becoming through the dynamic convergence of past and future: the past, through many divergent influences demanding an accounting; the future, through a transforming decision concerning how these many influences of the past might be unified. The present is the becoming of a new subject through this process of unifying the past and the future. "Objective immortality" is a critical and technical analysis of the transition that occurs when the becoming subject selectively incorporates aspects of the past into itself: This incorporation is first of all the subject's feeling (or "prehension") of the past, and then a comparison and evaluation of that past relative to the subject's own possibilities for becoming.

It belongs to the process that the present, by definition, signals the objectivity of the past. An occasion of experience feels the past, integrates it evaluatively into its own subjective becoming, and then itself becomes past for some new present. There is a rhythmic movement from subject, to object, to subject yet again—but the movement is of successive units of becoming; it is a process of "perpetual perishing," as Whitehead said, quoting Plato before him.

This process might also be described by the different modes of creativity it suggests. To feel the past and deal with it evaluatively is a subjective mode of creativity, or, in the language of the philosophy, "concrescent creativity." But once this act is completed, it has an effect upon a future, evoking that future into a new mode of becoming. This effect is the transition from subjectivity to objectivity, or the movement from concrescent creativity to transitional creativity. Transitional creativity, or effectiveness for a future, signals the completion of the subjective aspect of existence for that particular unit.

In personal existence, this moment by moment passage of subjectivity is quick and hardly noticeable, like the many distinct frames of a movie that nonetheless yield a sense of singular continuity. The illusion is of an overall subjectivity, but the reality is a series of discrete units of subjectivity, each of which feels and to some extent recreates the subjectivity of the past in each new present. The continuity of the self depends upon the subjective incorporation of one's own immediate and distant past into the present. To put it in more common terms, the sense of self-continuity depends enormously upon that which we call memory. Our yesterdays are objective to our todays; even the self of a moment ago is objectively past to the self of the presently becoming moment. Perpetual perishing characterizes even personal existence.

But there is one momentous exception to this rule. God is the only reality whose subjectivity continues even while God is effective for others. The reasons for this exception are not arbitrary; we have given them in chapter three and in the appendix dealing more technically with the process model. Every finite unit of existence begins by feeling the influences of the past. and concludes by unifying those feelings into one determinate reality, called "satisfaction" by Whitehead. God, as the source of possibility, must be a reversal of this process of becoming, "beginning" in the satisfaction of a unified vision of all possibilities, and concrescing by incorporating feelings of the world into the divine subjectivity. There is thus an essential openness to the divine reality, an everlastingness that is copresent with every finite reality whatsoever. God is before all time, with all time, and beyond an time.

Thus when a new finite occasion comes into existence, it does so through the feelings of a finite past that is now objective, and through the feelings of a God who continues in subjectivity. Every finite element in the occasion's past is completed, finished, devoid of subjectivity; it is present to the new subject only in the mode of objectivity. But God, who is also present to the new subject, is present precisely as subject. In this sense, the occasion's feeling of God is unique. Might not this uniqueness be conveyed to the occasion?

Mysticism offers a number of parallels to our usage of the phenomenon of loneliness, for the mystic tends to move into areas of inwardness in search of the divine presence. If loneliness is a leveling of finite relationality, constituting all finite relations as superficial, there is a parallel sense whereby the mystic at least initially, tends to categorize finite relations as insufficient for the soul's needs. The mystic frequently experiences a place of loneliness, a "dark night of the soul," in the inwardness of experience; the mystic, too, speaks of alienation and isolation. The parallel breaks down insofar as the person experiencing loneliness tends to do so not purposefully but meaninglessly. The individual does not seek loneliness, but is rather engulfed by loneliness. The mystic, however, usually intends the mystic journey. There is a purposiveness to the mystical experience of loneliness. The mystic seeks the divine presence on the other side of loneliness and indeed expects it, or at least hopes for it. The lonely individual is more apt to stumble upon the divine presence, or to sense it as an unnamed and haunting possibility at the boundary of loneliness.

The purposiveness of the mystic is an openness to the presence of God. In account after account, mystics speak of God breaking into the soul in a fullness of presence, so that the consciousness of the mystic becomes entwined with consciousness of God as the copresent one. For the mystic, God's presence is not simply *to* the soul, but *in* the soul. Why not, if God's subjectivity is everlasting, and thus everlastingly copresent to every prehending occasion?

When the continuing presence of God can be conveyed to and in the soul through the influence of God upon the soul (the "initial aim" in process terminology), then we indeed can account for the sense of ultimacy in the divine presence. The depth dimension to the relation to God is based in the tremendous contrasts provided between God and the world—contrasts that are ordinarily hidden in the invariable presence of God, and in the world—directive content of the influence from God. When these contrasts begin to emerge through the peculiar condition of loneliness—or indeed, mysticism—then God as the supremely present one begins to be revealed.

What is the result of the sense of God's presence? Is the world devalued in contrast to the ultimacy provided by God? Following the process model, it is necessary to say that the sense of God's presence must push one back into the relationality of the everyday world The understanding of God is of one who feels the world order to offer redemptive possibilities to the world. To have a sense of God is to have a sense of God's purposes toward the well-being of the world. The more surely one is attuned to the reality of God, the more surely one is conformed to the divine purposes. But if the divine purposes are toward the good of the world, then to be aware of the divine presence is to be directed again toward the good of the world. If one laboriously crosses the empty places of loneliness in order to reach God, then one is flung back across those places into the everyday world of finite relationships. Conforming to God's purposes involves being plunged headlong again into a world wherein meaning is constantly being created through relationships. The presence of God releases us from loneliness to presence in the world, and in that finite world, we find ourselves again involved in the creation of meaning.

What, then, can we say theologically about God, based on this understanding of God as presence? If we push the experience and the model further in conjunction with Christian faith, God as presence leads also to an understanding of the faithfulness and love of God. The process model portrays God as giving us birth in every moment through the touch of the divine will for us. The model further portrays God as our destiny since God feels our reality upon the completion of every concrescing moment of our lives. God surrounds our moments, embracing our lives with the ever living divine presence. There is in this an intense faithfulness to God, for the import is that God continually provides presence, and that even in our deepest loneliness we might become aware of that presence.

Long ago the Psalmist cried out in awareness of God's surrounding presence, and the patriarchs and prophets voiced the revelation of God as a guiding presence. As Christians we name Jesus as an ultimate presence of God in human history, calling him Immanuel, "God with us." The process model, working with the dynamics of the experience of loneliness, simply explicates for our own relativity-conscious times what faith has long proclaimed: the nature of God is expressed through presence, and that presence is one of divine faithfulness and guidance.

God's presence is faithfulness because it is unfailing. Existence is impossible apart from the presence of God to us in our beginning and in our ending. God's presence is guiding, because the content of God's touch is directive, making present to us a way of being in the world. In the process model this is necessarily so, for God is the source of possibility for us precisely through God's interweaving of the feelings of the consequent nature with the vision of harmony in the primordial nature. That which God offers us is the best that can be for us, given the circumstances with which we have to work. God's presence to us is therefore also God's love for us, since unfailingly to will the good of the other is assuredly a component of that which we call love. Given this, we can also say that God's presence to us contains judgment, for the initial aim is surely an evaluation of our own past in terms of its possible good, and in terms of the wider good of the world to which we contribute our existence.

To say such things of God goes far beyond the initial experience of loneliness that presses us to say that God is an ultimate presence. However, the sense in which loneliness is judged to be out of kilter with reality lends an existential basis to the statements. The restlessness in loneliness may give us the means to feel the aim of God. but to feel God as the source of the aim will lead to a renewed valuation of the content of the aim. And always, the aim of God will push us toward relation, creating value in the finite relations that are given to us, working for an optimum good. When in our loneliness we touch God we know ourselves as also touched by God, and in the knowing, we are open to the pervasiveness of the divine presence. But it is the nature of the divine presence to nudge us back to the world, pushing us toward renewed attention to the content of that touching, guiding, creating aim for our good. The aim inexorably directs us toward our best way of constituting ourselves through and for the world.

As the world again becomes for us a place of importance, the contrasting sense of God as presence may dim to memory: The memory, however, finds its echoes in the world of finite relation—not in hollowness in the prison of an empty self, but in the fullness of finite forms of presence. The inward presence of God turns to the outward presence of God, for the God who is present to us is present to others as well. The God who guides us guides others also the God who cares for us cares also for others. The whole world is touched by God, and therefore the world can mediate God's presence to us. Divine presence pervades finite presence, launching us into the world again, for its good and for ours. Meaninglessness fades, crowded out by presence, and presence—human and divine—insists upon and achieves the meaning of love.

Commentary

JEANYNE B. SLETTOM

First published by in 1982, Marjorie Hewitt Suchocki's *God—Christ—Church* was an explicit effort of mutual transformation aimed at: 1) providing an accessible introduction to the process philosophy of Alfred North Whitehead; 2) showing its applicability and compatibility with the Christian tradition; and 3) opening up new areas of exploration in both as a result of this mutually enhancing encounter. Revised in 1988 and 1995, it remains the "go to" book, not only for those who want a better understanding of Whitehead's philosophy, but also for those who want to see how it can be applied to such specific Christian theological categories as God, soteriology, ecclesiology, and eschatology.

Theology, Suchocki writes, must be expressed in the "thought patterns" of our time.[1] In the Christian tradition, critical moments have occurred "when shifting philosophical worldviews became intermingled with Christian faith" (2) exemplified by Augustine's appropriation of the Neoplatonist philosopher Plotinus, and Aquinas's appropriation of Aristotle. Suchocki writes that the world-changing ideas of relativity theory and quantum physics resulted in a new cosmological worldview, which in turn provoked Whitehead to propose a matching philosophical worldview. She claims, as did a handful before her, that the intermingling of process theology with Christian faith is presenting us with another critical moment in Christian history. But perhaps her most distinctive contribution is her contention that feminist philosophy is also a constituent part of the "shifting philosophical worldview" of our time. The "critical moment" thus requires us to express theology in both process and feminist thought patterns.

This critical intermingling—theology, feminism, and process philosophy—is a consistent theme in Suchocki's writing. Sometimes she emphasizes one element more than another, but the reader should recognize that all three are presupposed in her work. What binds together all three of these elements is the notion of relationality—that relationships are integral to who we are, to our identities and our existence. For Suchocki, process-relational theology provides the metaphysical ground for the relationality claimed by feminist experience, feminism leads process thought from abstraction to action, and both rescue theology, especially the doctrine of God, from patriarchal language and power constructs.

In the excerpted chapter on God's presence, Suchocki starts with this presupposition of relationality ("existence is through and through relational") but moves quickly to the contrasting state

---

1. See above, 46.

of loneliness, which she locates in the middle space between the surface level of our daily relationships and a deeper layer that we sense but cannot fully grasp. Caught in this middle space, we discern the difference between what is and what might be—and it is in this distinction that we become aware of our relation to God.

In process terms, the "might be" is called the initial aim of God, and it is present in every moment of experience. At this point, Suchocki goes to some lengths to unfold more of the process model, especially as it relates to the process by which an occasion receives the past, subjectively determines itself, and becomes an objective datum for the next occasion. She also explains how this process is the reverse for God. The crucial point, however, is that Suchocki appropriates the philosophical model of Whitehead to make ontological claims about the subjective presence of God in every moment of experience. The subjectivity of both the self-determining occasion and God constitute a co-presence, a "God-with-us" reality that informs every aspect of our lives (and, not incidentally, construes power very differently from patriarchal claims).

But Suchocki is not finished yet, and astute readers will learn to look for this in her work: the "so what" moment. As a Whiteheadian, Suchocki does brilliant speculative work, but as a feminist, these speculative flights must always land in some field of practical endeavor. In this context, her point is that loneliness may lead us to awareness of our relationship with God, but the God encounter will always lead us back into relationship with the world: "Divine presence pervades finite presence, launching us into the world again, for its good and for ours" (61).

STUDY QUESTIONS

1. Suchocki writes that theology must be expressed in the "thought patterns" of our time. How would you identify the "thought patterns" of our time? How do these thought forms shape your theology?

2. It is typical to contrast "presence" with "absence," but Suchocki chooses to contrast God's presence with the affective state of loneliness. Why does she do this? What is at stake here for both process and feminist theologies?

3. What are some ethical implications of God's subjective presence in human and nonhuman life?

6 Rejection of Dualism

Rosemary Radford Ruether

Rosemary Radford Ruether is the Georgia Harkness Emerita Professor of Applied Theology from Garrett-Evangelical Theological Seminary and the Carpenter Emerita Professor of Religion from Pacific School of Religion and the Graduate Theological Union. Ruether received degrees from Scripps College and Claremont Graduate School. An important formative thinker for feminist theology, she completed graduate work in historical theology that shapes her writing about gender in the Christian tradition and construction of feminist doctrine. Ruether writes as a feminist liberation theologian, but also as an ecofeminist theologian. The excerpts are taken from Sexism and God-Talk *(1983), where Ruether deconstructs dualism, and from* Gaia and God *(1992) where she analyzes types of ecological theology, including process theology, and proposes an ecofeminist theocosmology.*

Excerpt from *Sexism and God-Talk: Toward a Feminist Theology*

TOWARD A FEMINIST UNDERSTANDING OF GOD/ESS

THE FOUR PRECEDING BIBLICAL traditions may not be adequate for a feminist reconstruction of God/ess, but they are suggestive. If all language for God/ess is analogy, if taking a particular human image literally is idolatry, then male language for the divine must lose its privileged place. If God/ess is not the creator and validator of the existing hierarchical social order, but rather the one who liberates us from it, who opens up a new community of equals, then language about God/ess drawn from kingship and hierarchical power must lose its privileged place. Images of God/ess must include female roles and experience. Images of God/ess must be drawn from the activities of peasants and working people, people at the bottom of society. Most of all, images of God/ess must be transformative, pointing us back to our authentic potential and forward to new redeemed possibilities. God/ess-language cannot validate roles of men or women in stereotypic ways that justify male dominance and female subordination. Adding an image of God/ess as loving, nurturing mother, mediating the power of the strong, sovereign father, is insufficient.

Feminists must question the overreliance of Christianity, especially modern bourgeois Christianity, on the model of God/ess as parent. Obviously any symbol of God/ess as parent should include mother as well as father. Mary Baker Eddy's inclusive term, *Mother-Father God*, already did this one hundred years ago. Mother-Father God has the virtue of concreteness, evoking both parental images rather than moving to an abstraction (Parent), which loses effective resonance. Mother and father image God/ess as creator, as the source of our being. They point back from our own historical existence to those upon whom our existence depends. Parents are a symbol of roots, the sense of being grounded in the universe in those who have gone before, who underlie our own existence.

But the parent model for the divine has negative resonance as well. It suggests a kind of permanent parent-child relationship to God. God becomes a neurotic parent who does not want us to grow up. To become autonomous and responsible for our own lives is the gravest sin against God. Patriarchal theology uses the parent image for God to prolong spiritual infantilism as virtue and to make autonomy and assertion of free will a sin. Parenting in patriarchal society also becomes the way of enculturating us to the stereotypic male and female roles. The family becomes the nucleus and model of patriarchal relations in society. To that extent parenting language for God reinforces patriarchal power rather than liberating us from it. We need to start with language for the Divine as redeemer, as liberator, as one who fosters full personhood and, in that context, speak of God/ess as creator, as source of being.

Patriarchal theologies of "hope" or liberation affirm the God of Exodus, the God who uproots us from present historical systems and puts us on the road to new possibilities. But they typically do this in negation of God/ess as Matrix, as source and ground of our being. They make the fundamental mistake of identifying the ground of creation with the foundations of existing social systems. Being, matter, and nature become the ontocratic base for the evil system of what is. Liberation is liberation out of or against nature into spirit. The identification of matter, nature, and being with mother makes such patriarchal theology hostile to women as symbols of all that "drags us down" from freedom. The hostility of males to any symbol of God/ess as female is rooted in this identification of mother with the negation of liberated spirit. God/ess as Matrix is thought of as "static" immanence. A static, devouring, death-dealing matter is imaged, with horror, as extinguishing the free flight of transcendent consciousness. The dualism of nature and transcendence, matter and spirit as female against male is basic to male theology.

Feminist theology must fundamentally reject this dualism of nature and spirit. It must reject both sides of the dualism: both the image of mother-matter-matrix as "static immanence" and as the ontological foundation of existing, oppressive social systems and also the concept of spirit and transcendence as rootless, antinatural, originating in an "other world" beyond the cosmos, ever repudiating and fleeing from nature, body, and the visible world. Feminist theology needs to affirm the God of Exodus, of liberation and new being, but as rooted in the foundations of being rather than as its antithesis. The God/ess who is the foundation (at one and the same time) of our being and our new being embraces both the roots of the material substratum of our existence (matter) and also the endlessly new creative potential (spirit). The God/ess who is the foundation of our being-new being does not lead us back to a stifled, dependent self or uproot us in a spirit-trip outside the earth. Rather it leads us to the converted center, the harmonization of self and body, self and other, self and world. It is the *Shalom* of our being.

God/ess as once and future *Shalom* of being, however, is *not* the creator, founder, or sanctioner of patriarchal-hierarchical society. This world arises in revolt against God/ess and in alienation from nature. It erects a false system of alienated dualisms modeled on its distorted and oppressive social relationships. God/ess liberates us from this false and alienated world, not by an endless continuation of the same trajectory of alienation but as a constant breakthrough that points us to new possibilities that are, at the same time, the re-grounding of ourselves in the primordial matrix, the original harmony. The liberating encounter with God/ess is always an encounter with our authentic selves resurrected from underneath the alienated self. It is not experienced against, but in and through relationships, healing our broken relations with our bodies, with other people, with nature. We have no adequate name for the true God/ess, the "I am who I shall become." Intimations of Her/His name will appear as we emerge from false naming of God/ess modeled on patriarchal alienation.

Excerpt from *Gaia & God: An Ecofeminist Theology of Earth Healing*

TYPES OF CONTEMPORARY ECOLOGICAL THEOLOGY

Although the ecological crisis interjects a new urgency into this quest for a theology of nature, in many ways the tensions between Christian and anti-Christian proposals represent a restatement of this classic tension between Greek and Hebrew thought. For neo-pagan thealogians such as Carol Christ, the pagan gods and particularly the goddesses are being reborn to save us from antinatural Christianity. For Christian ecological thinkers, however, the biblical God and Gaia are not at odds; rightly understood, they are on terms of amity, if not commingling.

Three somewhat different versions of Christian cosmological theology circulate in the contemporary quest for ecological spirituality. One of these is Creation-centered spirituality, represented particularly by Matthew Fox (see chapter 6). Another has been developed by followers of the French paleontologist-philosopher Pierre Teilhard de Chardin (1881–1955), and a third is based on the process theology of Alfred North Whitehead (1861–1947). I will characterize each of these briefly, and then discuss the key elements in them for an ecofeminist theology of nature.

For Fox, original blessing is the intrinsic nature of things. True Christian spirituality remains rooted in this vivid sense of original goodness. Evil is present in history, but as distortion and alienation from original blessing, not as primary reality. Evil can be evaluated as evil only in its negation of primary goodness, which remains our true "nature." Goodness is fundamentally relational. It is the life-giving and celebratory interconnection of all things. Evil is the denial of that interconnection.[1]

In his *The Coming of the Cosmic Christ,* Fox reclaims the classical cosmological Christology we have discussed in this chapter. Christ is not simply confined to the historical Jesus, not-only related to human souls. Christ is the immanent

---

1. See Matthew Fox, *Original Blessing* (Santa Fe, NM: Bear and Co., 1983) 117, 157, 229.

Wisdom of God present in the whole cosmos as its principle of interconnected and abundant life. The cosmic Christ is not only the foundational basis of original blessing in creation, but is its *telos* or direction of fulfillment. Creation moves toward increasing fulfillment of this abundance of life. The cosmic Christ is thus another name for original and final blessing. It is both immanent divinity present in all things in their interconnection, and the fulfilled being of the cosmos, which it seeks to realize.[2]

For Christians, Jesus is the paradigmatic manifestation of cosmic wisdom and goodness. But he is only one such manifestation. The same wisdom and goodness underlies all other religious quests and has been manifest in many other symbolic expressions, such as the Tao, the Buddha, the Great Spirit, and the Goddess. Thus the truth manifest in Jesus is in no way exclusive, but links Christians in "deep ecumenism" with all other religions, not just the "Great Religions," but also native religions that have been despised as "paganism."[3]

Fox also calls for dialogue with secular wisdom cultures, such as psychotherapy, whose antireligious views have often been based on critique of the distortions of religion. The recovery of an ecological spirituality also means that we have to redevelop the "right brain" or intuitive part of our experience and culture atrophied by masculine dominance. This means attention to the arts and liturgy, dance and bodywork, to reawaken our deadened capacities for holistic experience.

I think that Fox is basically on target in these affirmations and values. His chief defect is a certain superficiality. He has, as it were, mapped the territory that needs exploring, but others have to follow up in greater depth.[4] Particularly problematic is his tendency to distort the Christian past by dividing it into two traditions, creation-based and fall/redemption. Although there is some element of truth in this distinction, he appropriates it in too simplistic a manner, exaggerating the similarities to his own views among medieval mystics, such as Meister Eckhardt or Hildegard of Bingen, with whom he identifies himself.[5]

In Fox's account the ambiguities of all these Christian thinkers, and the elements of social hierarchy and spirit-matter dualism in them, are erased. Fox tends to brush off the significant differences between these expressions of past Christian tradition and his view of creation spirituality, rather than grappling with the meaning of these differences. The deep questions of sin and death, which were central to Christian theology, need new answers for today, and not simply a denial that these are real questions.

The second and third types of ecological theology to be summarized here represent important efforts to incorporate new scientific understanding, the new earth story of evolution and the new subatomic physics or quantum mechanics.

2. Matthew Fox, *The Coming of the Cosmic Christ* (San Francisco: Harper & Row, 1988) 129–55.

3. Ibid., 235–39.

4. See Rosemary Radford Ruether, "Matthew Fox and Creation Spirituality," in *The Catholic World* (July/August 1990) 168–72.

5. Barbara Newman, author of *Sister of Wisdom: St. Hildegard's Theology of the Feminine* (Berkeley: University of California Press, 1987), has conveyed to me her critique of Fox's mistranslations and misinterpretations of the writings of Hildegard of Bingen. See her review in *Mystics Quarterly* 15.4 (December 1989) 190–94.

Teilhard de Chardin, whose writings only became available in the late 1950s due to church censorship, used the new insights from evolution to restate the sweeping cosmic vision of salvation history found 1,700 years earlier in Irenaeus. Not just humans, but all of nature is part of this salvation drama.

For Teilhard, the universe is a total system that ascends in successive systems of organization, from the atomic to the planetary level. This ascent to increasing organizational complexity is also a moral and spiritual ascent, moving toward the unification of consciousness in what Teilhard calls "the Omega Point." The different stages of the evolution of matter, from atomic energy to molecular organization to cellular life to plants and animals and finally humans, are not merely changes of quantitative complexity, but are qualitative leaps to new levels of existence.[6]

The universe evolves along the axis of the complexification of matter. Increasingly complex organization of matter increases the internal "radial energy." It is this interior aspect of the complexification of matter that Teilhard sees as responsible for "boiling points" that bring breakthroughs to new levels of existence. There arises from molecular organization the living cell, then increasingly complex organic beings that become more and more aware, and then human self-consciousness. Everything that appears in the process of cosmogenesis is latent from its beginning, but this does not change the reality of its historical birth, which can appear only when a critical level of evolution is reached.

Teilhard's thought would mesh well with the Gaia hypothesis, for he sees the planet earth as a living organism.[7] Earth is one living organism, not only spatially, but across time. The planet earth grows through stages of development that are not repeatable, any more than the stages of organic growth from fetus to adult are repeatable. Like an organism, it will also eventually die. The link between geosphere and biosphere is the organic cell, the highest unit of the molecular structure and the simplest unit in the organic structure. The breakthrough to life expresses a new level of centerness and unification, in which the whole structure becomes an organism participating in a common center and a common life. Unlike nonorganic structures that can be split up and each part survive, when the vital center of an organism is cut, the whole structure disintegrates.

Once organic life appears, its profusion ramifies into ordered types. The phyla become self-perpetuating along the lines laid out by specific types, and they cease to be able to cross-fertilize each other. There is a pattern of experimentation in evolution. First there appears the rudimentary type, then a series of modifications and experimentations with that type, until the most efficient form of that species is reached and its reproduction is stabilized around that form. Less successful experiments die out, and evolutionary changes within that species cease. The suppression of penults gives the impression of greater differences between phyla than originally existed when evolution of that group of related species was in progress.

---

6. Pierre Teilhard de Chardin, *The Phenomenon of Man* (New York: Harper & Brothers, 1959).

7. See James Lovelock, *Gaia: A New Look at Life on Earth* (New York: Oxford University Press, 1979); also Lovelock, *The Ages of Gaia: Biography of our Living Earth* (New York: Norton, 1988).

For Teilhard, the evolutionary tree has a privileged axis or *telos*. This *telos* is toward increasing interiorization and centricity, increasing coordination around the directing center of the organism. With vertebrates we arrive at an animal, not held together by an external shell, but from within by a central nervous system. From vertebrates to reptiles to mammals, the nervous system develops a unifying center in the brain. The increasing size and convolutions of the brain correspond to increasingly intelligent species of mammals, until we arrive at *Homo sapiens,* in which conscious thought appears.

For the last 100,000 years, humans have been the privileged axis of evolution, while the animal and plant kingdoms, from which humans arose, diminish. Now the age of animals is over, and the earth is more and more a human earth. Once the level of thought is reached, evolution takes place socially rather than organically. Humans are more adaptable than animals because they add new evolutionary developments, not as adaptations of their bodies, but as culture and technology. Human evolution through culture and technology is through the complementarity of increasing individuality and increasing collectivity.

Teilhard unabashedly sees Christian Western history as the privileged axis of cultural evolution. From the Neolithic revolution, there arose a limited number of classical civilizations, of which the Greco-Roman world was one. From the Renaissance to the twentieth century, a new stage of modernity began, which is now reaching around the globe, transforming all surviving Neolithic and classical cultures. Teilhard sees this new global stage of consciousness and technology as making possible a "noosphere" or world mind that is increasingly unified and centralized. Human minds together increasingly become one unitary Mind.

Teilhard sees this evolution toward unitary Mind as, in some sense, the evolution of immanent deity or the cosmic Christ. As increasingly collective consciousness develops, finally the organic substratum of the planet will die away, and Unitary Mind will be born from the finite earth into eternal life. The universe will fall away and die after having given birth to God, the ultimate communal consciousness, in which all that has gone before is gathered up and made immortal.[8]

This world picture contains some disturbing elements that need to be rejected. One is the way in which traditional hierarchical order has been "laid on its side," in an evolutionary concept of "progress," together with the confident faith in Western civilization and modernity as the privileged axis of this progress. The anticolonial movements and the ecological crisis have put this confidence in Eurocentric progress in grave question. Second, there is the sanguine acceptance of extinction of species as the acceptable price of progress. Does this not imply an acceptance of ethnocidal destruction of other peoples and cultures as also to be tossed aside by the triumphal march of Eurocentric progress?

Finally we must question the vision of the material underpinnings of consciousness as being tossed aside in the eschatological, culminating stage of evolution, a conclusion that contradicts the foundational insight of life and consciousness

---

8. See Teilhard de Chardin, *Phenomenon of Man,* 285–90; also his *The Divine Milieu* (New York: Harper & Row, 1960) 133–39.

as the inferiority of complexified matter. Surely this means that mind and body, the inside and the outside, cannot finally be separated. What is compelling about Teilhard's thought for today is precisely this insight that mind is the inferiority of matter, and it is continuous from the simplest molecule to the most complex organism.

Process theology, as developed by Christian theologians such as John Cobb and Marjorie Suchocki,[9] from A. N. Whitehead's work,[10] has many affinities with the thought of Teilhard de Chardin. Like Teilhard, process theology sees an element of "mentality" present even in the random movements of subatomic particles. "Mentality" is a capacity for interaction, which becomes increasingly self-determining and conscious as matter organizes itself at successive layers of organizational complexity. Process theology postulates, as underlying this process, a dipolar God. The Primordial Nature of God contains the whole of potentiality of all existing entities at every moment of actualization. This Primordial Nature of God provides the "initial aim" or best potential option for each entity at each occasion of existence. This "initial aim" relates to the total context of the past of that entity at that moment, and thus is interrelated with all that has been, ultimately, in the whole universe.

Each entity has, however, its own subjectivity. It adapts or actualizes this aim of God through actualizing one possibility that can only partially fulfill that aim, and can even thwart that aim in negative choices that are destructive. Thus the God of Process theology "lures," but does not coerce. It offers continual new possibilities, but the choice belongs to existent entities that can negate their own best options. There is freedom and risk in divine creativity, and with this risk, the possibility of evil. This possibility of evil increases as consciousness and power increase on the part of existent entities.

As entities opt for particular choices, these actualizations are taken into the being of God as God's Consequent Nature. The reality of God is thus shaped through interrelation with self-actualizing entities. God not only lures and offers new life, but also suffers, experiencing the pain of destructive choices as well as the pleasure of good choices.

Process theologians also postulate that this Consequent Nature of God, reflecting the memory of all that has been, is taken up in some way into the Primordial Nature of God, not only preserving immortally all that has been, but also incorporating it into the total vision of what could and should have been, to reconcile the evils and missed opportunities of history. In this way all that has been is not only remembered in the eternal being of God, but is redeemed as well.[11]

TOWARD AN ECOFEMINIST THEOCOSMOLOGY

Ecofeminist theology and spirituality has tended to assume that the "Goddess" we need for ecological well-being is the

---

9. See John B. Cobb Jr. and David Ray Griffin, *Process Theology: An Introductory Exposition* (Philadelphia: Westminster, 1976); also Marjorie Suchocki, *God, Christ, Church: A Practical Guide to Process Theology* (New York: Crossroads, 1989).

10. Alfred North Whitehead, *Process and Reality: An Essay in Cosmology* (New York: Macmillan, 1929) 519–33.

11. See particularly Marjorie Suchocki, *The End of Evil: Process Eschatology in Historical Context* (Albany: State University of New York Press, 1988) 97–114; also her *God, Christ, Church*, 183–216.

reverse of the God we have had in the Semitic monotheistic traditions; immanent rather than transcendent, female rather than male identified, relational and interactive rather than dominating, pluriform and multicentered rather than uniform and monocentered. But perhaps we need a more imaginative solution to these traditional oppositions than simply their reversal, something more like Nicholas of Cusa's paradoxical "coincidence of opposites," in which the "absolute maximum" and the "absolute minimum" are the same.[12]

As I suggested in chapter 2, something like this coincidence of opposites has appeared, surprisingly, in subatomic physics. Newtonian physics had seen reality as composed of indestructible atoms, like hard billiard balls, moved by external force in a fixed space. God was seen as constructing this world from outside it, like a clock-maker, and setting it to run by its own internal mechanism, but in no way participating in it as an immanent life-force. Eventually this external God was banished altogether as an unnecessary hypothesis. The universe came to be seen as a mechanistic system arising from random accidents.

But, as physicists continued to probe matter, seeking its ultimate "building blocks" or smallest "simple units," out of which everything else was composed by mechanistic combinations, they discovered smaller and smaller units. The atom was made up of vast space in which tiny particles or electrons moved around an extremely concentrated core or nucleus that contained most of the mass of the atom. The relation of the two can be envisioned if we imagine blowing up an atom to the size of the dome of St. Peter's Basilica in Rome. The nucleus would then be the size of a grain of salt.[13]

The nucleus itself was recognized to be held together by a distinct energy, nuclear energy, the same energy that fires the sun, but found rarely in earth in "loose" form. As the physicists penetrated the nucleus, they discovered that this too was composed of various particles, protons and neutrons. As techniques for detection of yet smaller particles increased, more and more particles were counted, until finally it became apparent that the whole concept of "particles," or elementary "building blocks" of matter, needed to be abandoned. What the physicists were discovering were energy fields in which energy "events" appeared and disappeared. Particles appeared out of energy and dissolved back into energy.

At the subatomic level, the classical distinction between matter and energy disappears. Matter is energy moving in defined patterns of relationality. At the level of the "absolute minimum," the appearance of physical "stuff" disappears into a voidlike web of relationships, relationships in which the whole universe is finally interconnected and in which the observer also stands as part of the process. We cannot observe anything "objectively," for the very act of observation affects what we observe.

As we move below the "absolute minimum" of the tiniest particles into the dancing void of energy patterns that build up the "appearance" of solid objects on the macroscopic level, we also

---

12. See Jasper Hopkins, *A Concise Introduction to the Philosophy of Nicholas of Cusa* (Minneapolis: University of Minnesota Press, 1978) 7–43; also Pauline M. Watts, *Nicolaus Cusanus: A Fifteenth-Century Vision of Man* (Leiden: Brill, 1982) 33–74.

13. The analogy comes from Fritjof Capia, *The Tao of Physics* (New York: Bantam, 1976) 54.

recognize that this is also the "absolute maximum," the matrix of all interconnections of the whole universe. This matrix of dancing energy operates with a "rationality," predictable patterns that result in a fixed number of possibilities. Thus what we have traditionally called "God," the "mind," or rational pattern holding all things together, and what we have called "matter," the "ground" of physical objects, come together. The disintegration of the many into infinitely small "bits," and the One, or unifying whole that connects all things together, coincide.

How do we connect ourselves and the meaning of our lives to these worlds of the very small and the very big, standing in between the dancing void of energy that underlies the atomic structure of our bodies and the universe, whose galaxies, stretching over vast space and time, dwarf our histories? Even our bodies, despite the appearance of continuity over time, are continually dying and being reborn in every second. Over a period of seven years, every molecule of our body has been replaced.

In this universe of the very small and the very big, can the human only appear lost, crying out with Pascal, "The eternal silence of those infinite spaces terrifies me!"?[14] Or is it a universe in which it makes sense to speak of values, of life and death, good and evil, as meaningful distinctions within which we can hope for a "better world"? Is it a universe with which we can commune, as heart to heart, thought to thought, as I and Thou?

As humans stand peering down through their instruments into the subatomic realm and outward into the galaxies, it cannot but be evident that, for us, the human remains the "mean" or mediator between the worlds. This is so because what we perceive can only be known and evaluated from the context of our own standpoints. But also because we are faced with the recognition that humans alone, amid all the earth creatures and on all the planets of these vast galaxies, are capable of reflective consciousness. We are, in that sense, the "mind" of the universe, the place where the universe becomes conscious of itself.

Reflective consciousness is both our privilege and our danger. At least for the last several thousand years of cultural history, male ruling-class humans have used this privilege of mind to set themselves apart from nature and over dominated women and men. Thereby they denied the web of relationships that bind us all together, and within which these males themselves are an utterly dependent part. The urgent task of ecological culture is to convert human consciousness to the earth, so that we can use our minds to understand the web of life and to live in that web of life as sustainers, rather than destroyers, of it.

But also, as Teilhardian and Process thought have argued, reflective consciousness, while it distinguishes the human from animals, plants, cellular bacteria and nonbiotic aggregates of molecules, it does so only relatively, not absolutely. The capacity to be conscious is itself the experience of the inferiority of our organism, made possible by the highly organized living cells of our brains and nervous systems that constitute the material "base" of our experience of awareness.

Consciousness is one type of highly intense experience of life, but there

---

14. Blaise Pascal, *The Pensées*, ed. J. M. Cohen (Baltimore: Penguin, 1961) 57.

are other forms present in other species, sometimes with capacities that humans lack, as in fish that can hear ranges of sound or animals that can see ranges of light not possible to our ears and eyes. Nor can we simply draw a line between us, together with large-brained mammals, and other beings, as a distinction of "living persons" and "dead bodies." For plants too are living organic beings that respond to heat, light, water, and sound as organisms, and even chemical aggregates are dancing centers of energy.

Human consciousness, then, should not be what utterly separates us from the rest of "nature." Rather, consciousness is where this dance of energy organizes itself in increasingly unified ways, until it reflects back on itself in self-awareness. Consciousness is and must be where we recognize our kinship with all other beings. The dancing void from which the tiniest energy events of atomic structures flicker in and out of existence and self-aware thought are kin along a continuum of organized life-energy.

Our capacity for consciousness, which allows us to roam through space and time, remembering past ages, exploring the inner workings of all other existing beings on earth or on distant planets, also makes us aware of the ephemeral nature of our "self." Our capacity for consciousness is sustained by a complex but fragile organism. Cut that organism at its vital centers, in the brain or in the heart, and the light of consciousness goes out, and with it our "self."

It is this juxtaposition of the capacity of consciousness to roam through space and time, and its utter transience in its dependence on our mortal organisms, that has generated much of the energy of what has been called "religion" in the past. Much of this religious quest has sought to resolve this contradiction by denying it, imagining that consciousness was not really dependent on the mortal organism. The mental self could survive, and even be "purified" and strengthened, by the demise of the body. This concept of the "immortal self," survivable apart from our particular transient organism, must be recognized, not only as untenable, but as the source of much destructive behavior toward the earth and other humans.

An ecological spirituality needs to be built on three premises: the transience of selves, the living interdependency of all things, and the value of the personal in communion. Many spiritual traditions have emphasized the need to "let go of the ego," but in ways that diminished the value of the person, undercutting particularly those, like women, who scarcely have been allowed individuated personhood at all. We need to "let go of the ego" in a different sense. We are called to affirm the integrity of our personal center of being, in mutuality with the personal centers of all other beings across species and, at the same time, accept the transience of these personal selves.

As we accept both the value and the transience of the self, we can also be awakened to a new sense of kinship with all other organisms. Like humans, the animals and the plants are living centers of organic life who exist for a season. Then each of our roots shrivels, the organic structures that sustain our life fail, and we die. The cutting of the life center also means that our bodies disintegrate into organic matter, to enter the cycle of decomposition and recomposition as other entities.

The material substances of our bodies live on in plants and animals, just as our own bodies are composed from minute to minute of substances that once were parts of other animals and plants, stretching back through time to prehistoric ferns and reptiles, to ancient biota that floated in the primal seas of earth. Our kinship with all earth creatures is global, linking us to the whole living Gaia today. It also spans the ages, linking our material substance with all the beings that have gone before us on earth and even to the dust of exploding stars. We need new psalms and meditations to make this kinship vivid in our communal and personal devotions.

But, even as we take into our spirituality and ethical practice the transience of selves, relinquishing the illusion of permanence, and accepting the dissolution of our physical substance into primal energy, to become matter for new organisms, we also come to value again the personal center of each being. My eye catches the eye of a bird as it turns its head toward me on the side of the tree, and then continues its tasks. Brendan spies me coming up the path, and with flashing red fur is at the door, leaping in circles with unfeigned delight. My body, stretching in the sun, notices a tiny flower pushing up through the soil to greet the same sun. And we know our kinship as I and Thou, saluting one another as fellow persons.

Compassion for all living things fills our spirits, breaking down the illusion of otherness. At this moment we can encounter the matrix of energy of the universe that sustains the dissolution and recomposition of matter as also a heart that knows us even as we are known. Is there also a consciousness that remembers and envisions and reconciles all things, as the Process theologians believe? Surely, if we are kin to all things and offspring of the universe, then what has flowered in us as consciousness must also be reflected in that universe as well, in the ongoing creative Matrix of the whole.

As we gaze into the void of our future extinguished self and dissolving substance, we encounter there the wellspring of life and creativity from which all things have sprung and into which they return, only to well up again in new forms. But we also know this as the great Thou, the personal center of the universal process, with which all the small centers of personal being dialogue in the conversation that continually creates and recreates the world. The small selves and the Great Self are finally one, for as She bodies forth in us, all the beings respond in the bodying forth of their diverse creative work that makes the world.

The dialogue can become truncated. We can seek to grasp our ego centers of being in negation of others, proliferating our existence by diminishing that of others, and finally poisoning the wellspring of the life process itself. Or we can dance gracefully with our fellow beings, spinning out our creative work in such a way as to affirm theirs and they ours as well.

Then, like bread tossed on the water, we can be confident that our creative work will be nourishing to the community of life, even as we relinquish our small self back into the great Self. Our final gesture, as we surrender ourself into the Matrix of life, then can become a prayer of ultimate trust: "Mother, into your hands I commend my spirit. Use me as you will in your infinite creativity."

Commentary

Kathlyn A. Breazeale

We can seek to grasp our ego centers of being in negation of others, ... finally poisoning the wellspring of the life process itself. Or we can dance gracefully with our fellow beings, spinning out our creative work in such a way as to affirm theirs and ours as well.

In this excerpt, Ruether presents her argument for why and how we should "dance gracefully with our fellow beings." Her instructions for this dance are the conclusion of her larger argument for the Christian sacramental tradition as a resource for healing the earth in chapter 9 of *Gaia & God: An Ecofeminist Theology of Earth Healing*. Ruether defines the Christian sacramental tradition as one of the "modes of relating to nature" and as the "cosmological tradition in Christianity" in which everything in the cosmos is interrelated, including God, humans, and nonhumans.

However, the Christian sacramental tradition must be freed "from patriarchal constructs" and brought "into dialogue with contemporary scientific knowledge and global realities" to be reclaimed for an ecofeminist theology. How Ruether accomplishes this reclamation is the significance of her work in this excerpt for the field of process-feminist theologies. First, her ecofeminist analysis of subatomic physics affirms a process understanding of the dipolar nature of God, yet she expands God's relationship to the world to include nonhuman as well as human creation. Second, she elaborates on Whitehead's concepts of mentality and subjectivity to define humans' relationship to nature as "mediators."

In the context of the critique of Christianity as "antinatural" and the current ecological crisis, Ruether argues that "the biblical God and Gaia are not at odds." Following her analysis of the Christian cosmological theologies of Matthew Fox and Teilhard de Chardin, she discusses process theology's contributions to an ecological spirituality, including how God is interrelated with the universe through God's Primordial and Consequent Natures. Ruether then explains how God and matter come together at the subatomic level as the distinction between energy and matter disappears in subatomic physics.

Humans play a key role as mediators between the subatomic realm and the vast galaxies because only humans "are capable of reflective consciousness." However, because ruling class males have used this consciousness to dominate nature, women and men, Ruether asserts: "The urgent task of ecological culture is to convert human consciousness to the earth, so that we can use our minds to understand the web of life and to live in that web of life as sustainers, rather than destroyers, of it."[1] Furthermore, because reflective consciousness distinguishes humans from other creatures "only relatively, not absolutely," Ruether holds that consciousness "is and must be where we recognize our kinship with all other beings." Consciousness also gives humans the capacity to recognize the finitude of our minds and bodies. Ruether offers a bold critique of our effort to deny human finitude with our religious imagining of immortality: "This concept of the 'immortal self,' survivable apart from our particular transient organism, must be recognized, not only as untenable, but as the source of much destructive behavior toward the earth and other humans."

In summary, the key points of Ruether's ecofeminist theocosmology are her doctrine of God and her theological anthropology. The Whiteheadian God who is the "great companion—the fellow sufferer who understands"[2] is also the "wellspring of life and creativity from which all things have sprung and into which they return . . ." This God is intimately interrelated to all creation. Similarly, Ruether's theological anthropology defines and underscores humans' close relationship to the earth. The crux of her position is her analysis of human consciousness and her criticism of the religious attempt to imagine a part of the human as immortal.

Since *Gaia & God*, Ruether's more recent thinking on ecofeminist theological issues includes her chapter in *Ecospirit: Religions and Philosophies for the Earth*.[3] Here she reviews the work of Vandana Shiva (India) and Ivone Gebara (Brazil) as well as elaborating her own position. Ruether's discussion of Shiva and Gebara underscores her commitment to promoting the work of theologians and women of faith from a diversity of cultures as previously demonstrated in *Women Healing Earth: Third World Women on Ecology, Feminism, and Religion* (Maryknoll, NY: Orbis, 1996) and *Integrating Ecofeminism, Globalization, and World Religions* (Lanham, MD: Rowman & Littlefield, 2005). Thus, possible directions for Ruether's sensibilities could include collaboration between process feminist theologians with women and men from other countries as well as further development of Ruether's doctrine of God and theological anthropology from process-feminist theological perspectives.

Although Ruether studied theology with John Cobb at Claremont, her training as an historian is evident in how her constructive theology is usually presented after an in-depth discussion of the broad historical context that preceded her ideas. Thus a suggestion for students seeking to understand Ruether's position is to read her theological construction at the end of the chapter first. Ruether is one of the "foremothers" whose early work established a foundation for the development of feminist theology. She

---

1. The conversion of human intelligence to the earth was previously discussed by Ruether as a conversion that overcomes the dualisms of dominant male linear thinking. See Ruether, *Sexism and God-Talk: Toward a Feminist Theology* (Boston: Beacon, 1983) 88–92.

2. Alfred North Whitehead, *Process and Reality*, ed. David Ray Griffin and Donald W. Sherburne, corrected ed. (New York: Free Press, 1978) 351.

3. Rosemary Radford Ruether, "Ecofeminist Philosophy, Theology, and Ethics: A Comparative View," in *Ecospirit: Religions and Philosophies for the Earth*, eds. Laurel Kearns and Catherine Keller, Transdisciplinary Theological Colloquia (New York: Fordham University Press, 2007) 77–93.

continues to be a prominent leader, urging us forward with her vision for healing the earth.

STUDY QUESTIONS

1. Briefly describe how Ruether supports her argument for the interrelatedness of God, humans, and nonhuman nature with one example from contemporary ecological theologies or subatomic physics.

2. Humans play a central role as mediators in Ruether's ecofeminist theocosmology. Do you think this focus on the importance of humans undermines Ruether's argument for dismantling the traditional hierarchy of humans over nature?

3. Ruether argues that only humans are capable of "reflective consciousness." Do you think other animals might also have this capacity? How would we know if they did?

4. Ruether states that our denial of human finitude with our religious imagining of immortality is "the source of much destructive behavior toward the earth and other humans" (69). Do you agree? Why or why not?

7 Sin

"The Sin of Hiding"

SUSAN L. NELSON

Susan L. Nelson served as Vice President for Academic Affairs and Dean and Professor of Theology and Culture at Claremont School of Theology and Professor of Religion at Claremont Graduate University from 2006–2010. She received degrees from The University of Rochester, Pittsburgh Theological Seminary, and Claremont Graduate School. Her teaching and research included constructive theology, women's studies and culture, and more recently in suffering in Christian theology. She lost her battle with a brain tumor in November 2010. The excerpt is taken from the journal *Soundings* (1982). The content reflects Nelson's interest in exploring how process feminist theology interprets the doctrine of sin using Reinhold Niebuhr's work, and she names the sin of hiding as the primary form of sin in women's lives.

Excerpt from "The Sin of Hiding: A Feminist Critique of Reinhold Niebuhr's Account of the Sin of Pride"

A WOMAN KNOWS GUILT for most of her life. She is guilty if she is too assertive; she is guilty if she is too feminine and therefore seductive. She is guilty if she is too brilliant, too articulate, too successful. If she becomes pregnant, she is at fault. If she chooses not to have children, she is guilty at best of denying her true femininity; at worst, of murder. If her children are maladjusted, if they fail at school, get involved with drugs, or exhibit inappropriate behavior, it is her fault. And, if her marriage fails, if her husband loses interest and chooses the attentions of another, it is because she has fallen short.

And, guilt is taking its toll. If violence against women has been recorded in footbinding, gynecological mutilation, rape, and pornography, it is also being etched into the secret lives of women who turn against themselves in self-hatred; who lose themselves in alcohol, drugs, starvation diets—or in the frenetic activity of trying to please everyone else.

Our sense of guilt is fundamentally rooted in our concept of sin, and is the result of the perception of our sinfulness in relationship to God. Guilt, then, is directly related to the way in which a religion focuses on the nature of sin and to the way it then names and proclaims the forms of sin. In Christianity, one knows one's sin and one's guilt, but one also is promised the forgiveness and love of God. Guilt does not stand alone, for sin is recognized within the context of the forgiveness and mercy of God which lead to regeneration and new life.

But the guilt of woman does not seem to have known this same redemptive promise. Rather than guilt leading to confession of sin, the knowledge of pardon, and the transformation into a new life, guilt has led woman into the very cycle of bondage to guilt and patterns of destruction that the Christian faith is supposed to shatter. What has gone wrong? Why has woman not experienced the reality of redemption? Why has she been locked into cycles of guilt, self-hatred, and violence against herself?

The key to solving this dilemma is, I believe, within the Christian tradition itself; for, in its development of sin as the sin of pride, and in its failure to develop fully what I shall call the sin of hiding—a sin which I believe to be the primary form of sin for woman—Christianity has perpetuated patterns of bondage and repression rather than breaking them. Thus, by encouraging woman to confess the wrong sin, and by failing to judge her in her actual sin, Christianity has both added to woman's guilt and failed to call her into her full humanity.

In order to illustrate this point, I shall refer to the work of twentieth-century Christian theologian Reinhold Niebuhr, and most particularly to his writings on the doctrine of sin. Although one cannot claim that Niebuhr is exemplary for all the strands of Christian tradition, he is an appropriate example both because he sees himself as standing within the mainstream of Christian theology, and because his work has been a major influence upon Christian thinkers in this century. Moreover, in his development of the sin of pride, Niebuhr, although allowing that pride has not been regarded as the primary sin for absolutely all of Christian thought, traces the emphasis on the sin of pride back to Augustine (who defined pride as ". . . the beginning of all sin . . ."[1]), Luther, Thomas Aquinas, and John Calvin.

What, then, is the fundamental, the primary sin? It is, Niebuhr says, "lack of trust in God."[2] It is a lack of faith in God, a turning away from the One in relation to whom one can know one's full humanity. Without this faith, one's world, so to speak, falls apart. One knows fragmentation and alienation from one's self and from others. It is a state of anxiety in which one seeks to find a center— a god other than God—around which to focus one's life.

This anxiety over holding one's life together is innate to the human situation, for Niebuhr understands human nature to be by definition dipolar—as holding in tension the two poles of finitude and freedom. In anxiety over maintaining this tension between the two poles, humanity turns from God and seeks to resolve its anxiety in other ways. Because of the dipolar nature of humanity, Niebuhr argues that human sinfulness is dipolar in its forms as well. Hence, when humanity "seeks to overcome [its] insecurity by a will-to-power which over-reaches the limits of human creatureliness," when it "pretends that [it] is not limited," its "intellectual and cultural pursuits . . . become infected with the sin of pride."[3] On the other hand, when humanity seeks to "solve the problem of the contradiction of finiteness and freedom . . . by seeking to hide [its] freedom and by losing [itself] in some aspect of the world's vitalities," its "sin may be defined as sensuality rather

---

1. Reinhold Niebuhr, *The Nature and Destiny of Man*, vol. 1 (New York: Scribner, 1941) 186 n. 1.
2. Ibid., 252.
3. Ibid., 178–79.

than pride."[4] Niebuhr here uses the term sensuality to describe this sin because he focuses on the loss of oneself in some bodily form of finitude. However, because the naming of this sin as sensuality reveals the lack of development of its full meaning as a state of escapism, I shall use the expression "the sin of hiding," which focuses more on the act, or nonact, of escaping rather than on the locus to which one escapes.

Although Niebuhr initiates the doctrine of sin in this broad fashion, he fails to develop it as fully. The very naming of the sin of hiding as sensuality betrays a certain narrowness of focus which eventually serves to lead him from his initial insight. Hence, although Nieburh describes the sin of hiding as an escape "from [one's] unlimited possibilities of freedom, from the perils and responsibilities of self-determination, by immersing [one's self] into a 'mutable good,' by losing [one's self] in some natural vitality,"[5] he later refers to the sins of sensuality "as expressed for instance in sexual license, gluttony, extravagance, drunkenness and abandonment to various forms of physical desire . . ."[6] Hence, from his broader understanding of the sin of hiding as the escape *from* one's freedom, he narrows his focus to the "forms of physical desire," thus turning his emphasis from hiding to sensuality. Moreover, his use of the term "sensuality" betrays as well his narrow focus on the aspect of finitude into which one can escape. Thus, he fails to realize that the forms of finitude into which one can escape need not be only aspects of one's own physical cravings, but may also be loss of one's self in other finite persons, institutions, or causes. Hence the sin of hiding can take the form of devotion to another—the expending of one's vital energies not in the acceptance of one's own freedom, but in the running away from that freedom by pouring those energies into the life of another. Had Niebuhr enlarged his understanding of the possible loci for such an escape, he would have realized the very insidious hiddenness of the sin of hiding and could no longer have termed it the sin of sensuality. Furthermore, Niebuhr loses his insight into the escapist nature of the sin of hiding as he develops his understanding of the overlapping of the two primary forms of sin. Because Niebuhr posits human nature as a tension between the two poles of freedom and finitude, humanity can never totally deny either of the poles. One can never become other than a finite creature; nor can one ultimately hide from one's freedom. In seeking to overcome finitude, one eventually succumbs to the self-conscious idolatry of some form of finitude, which is reflected in the knowledge that the idol one worships is truly finite and not transcendent at all—the sin of hiding. On the other hand, in seeking to escape from one's freedom, one betrays in the very intention to escape a desire to control one's own existence, which reflects the sin of pride. Hence, neither form of sin is totally without the taint of the other, and there is a certain ambiguity in the positing of two forms of sin, for the two overlap and each form becomes a secondary form of the opposite primary sin. Because of this overlapping of the forms of sin, Niebuhr develops the sin of pride in its primary form while also positing pride in

---

4. Ibid., 179.
5. Ibid., 186.
6. Ibid., 228.

its secondary form under the sin of hiding as the "bottom line" of the sin of hiding. Hence, he tends to equate the sin of hiding with the sin of pride, and hiding becomes one form of the sin of pride. Moreover because he calls the sin of hiding sensuality, he confuses the sin of hiding in its primary form with its secondary form under the sin of pride. This secondary form he also calls sensuality, but under the sin of pride, sensuality has the connotation of a self-centered devotion to sensuality, with the emphasis on the self-centeredness. Hence, whereas he first refers to the sin of hiding (called sensuality) as the "flight not to a false god but to nothingness,"[7] he ends up identifying it with the sensuality that is "an extension of self-love to the point where it defeats its own ends."[8] Niebuhr thus loses his initial, broader insight into the sin of hiding as the escape from freedom— not *in* freedom—into nothingness. And, this state of nothingness carries the connotation of dissipation rather than the notion of the fear of becoming someone.

Furthermore, Niebuhr, though affirming the polarity of finitude and freedom in human nature, tends to collapse finitude under freedom. That is, just as the sin of sensuality becomes subsumed under the sin of pride, so finitude is subsumed under freedom. Humanity, he feels, "cannot merely live."[9] That is, humanity can never be only finite; it is true human nature to ascend the rungs of freedom—to be continually more transcendent. Hence, not only does the sin of hiding, of totally denying one's freedom, never become a possibility, but the true law of human nature—humanity's true fulfillment—is in the law of self-transcendence, the transcendence of self that becomes the giving of self and ultimately the total giving of the self in self-sacrifice, for "he that findeth his life shall lose it; and he that loseth his life for my sake, shall find it."[10] That is, not only is the total denial of freedom just not possible, but the ultimate goal of human existence is expressed in one's total self-giving. The sin of hiding has become a nonpossibility, and the sin of pride has become *the* sin; and true humanity, as seen in the one true man Jesus Christ, is known through total self-sacrifice. Self-sacrificial love, then, becomes the goal, the supreme human virtue, for all of humanity.

Now Niebuhr's development of the doctrine of sin, as it tends eventually to negate the sin of hiding under the sin of pride, and his positing of the virtue of self-sacrificial love as the highest human goal, pose several problems. First of all, one must question whether self-sacrifice, as the total self-transcendence of that self which gives itself for another, is the highest form of humanity in its dipolar state of being finite and free, or whether it is in actuality an expression of the very desire to deny one's finitude totally, and thereby transcend one's finitude—which is the sin of pride.

Furthermore, in subsuming the sin of hiding under the sin of pride, Niebuhr fails to develop fully his insights into the sin of hiding, and the sin of hiding becomes for him not a real possibility. Hence, his doctrine of sin becomes a one-sided development of the sin of pride. Moreover, had he developed the sin of hiding

---

7. Ibid., 237.
8. Ibid., 240.
9. Reinhold Niebuhr, *The Children of Light and the Children of Darkness* (New York: Scribner, 1944) 20.
10. Ibid., 19.

more fully, Niebuhr would have realized that it stands in direct contradiction to his positing of self-sacrificial love as the goal of human life. He describes self-sacrificial love as the total giving of one's self for the sake of another. But the sin of hiding is the escape! from one's "freedom into other finite forms of existence—forms which Niebuhr narrowly identified with forms of sensuality," but which I have suggested could be the loss of self into some "other." Had he developed the possible forms of the sin of hiding more fully, Niebuhr would have realized that what he posits as humanity's highest virtue, the loss of self, is identical with the sin of hiding, the escape from one's self. The virtue and the sin are synonymous, and one must begin to wonder what the implications of such a contradiction are. Most obviously, by making self-sacrificial love the ultimate Christian virtue, one makes the sin of hiding into a virtue as well, and thereby encourages those already committing the sin of hiding to stay in that state. One then becomes glorified for never truly seeking to become fully human. Furthermore, by uplifting hiding to a virtue, and by denying the sin of hiding as a possibility, Niebuhr's theology has no understanding of how the one guilty of the sin of hiding can be judged in his/her sin and called to actualize his/her freedom. There is no judgment upon the one who escapes; there is no call to emerge from the state of hiddenness.

Now, what does all of this have to do with the guilt of woman? If Niebuhr does stand in the mainline of Christian tradition, what does this critique of his development of the sin of pride as *the* sin, and the virtue of self-sacrificial love as *the* human virtue, have to do with the relation of woman to Christian tradition? First of all, the failure to develop the sin of hiding bears directly on woman's situation. In stressing the fact that humanity can never totally escape from its freedom into finitude, Niebuhr seems not to realize how much of one's freedom it is possible for one to deny. And yet, inasmuch as woman has accepted the name of "Other" within a patriarchal culture, inasmuch as she has accepted a role, a place, a name without realizing her human freedom to name herself, she has been guilty of the sin of hiding; inasmuch as she has poured herself into vicarious living, inasmuch as she has denied her sense of self in total submission to husband/father/boss or in total self-giving to children, job, or family, she has been guilty of the sin of hiding. As she has been afraid to dream a dream for herself as well as for others, and as she has trained herself to live a submerged existence, she has hidden from her full humanity.

Moreover, not only has the Christian tradition consigned woman to her state of nonbeing by failing to emphasize that hiding is a sin, it has also perpetuated her state by lifting up for her to emulate the virtue of self-sacrificial love, which is synonymous with her sin. As long as the highest human virtue is self-sacrifice, and as long as the long-suffering, totally self-giving wife/mother is the symbol our tradition uplifts as true woman, then woman cannot answer the call to accept her human freedom without knowing the guilt of being named by the tradition, as well as by herself, as assertive, self-centered, unfeminine—and, finally, as sinner. A theology that recognizes pride as the primary form of sin, that fails to understand that the sin of hiding is in actuality a hiding under the guise of self-sacrifice, and that fails to teach that the call of God to full humanity is the call into the freedom to name oneself, to assert one's selfhood, and to know pride in one's self—such a theology seeks to perpetuate woman's bondage to her hiddenness. Furthermore, because self-assertion is equated with the sin of pride, the knowledge of her desire to be a self is often experienced by a woman with guilt and anxiety. Hence, the need to be a self is placed in opposition to being the good woman—the good wife and mother—whose total devotion to others is her virtue. Not only, then, does woman know the guilt of submerged desire that puts her into hidden conflict with the virtues she is called upon to emulate, but that desire itself creates a state of guilt and anxiety within her. As long as the sin of pride remains *the* sin and as long as the sin of hiding remains an unnamed sin, woman is caught in a double bondage to her guilt.

And finally, by associating the sin of hiding with sensuality, Niebuhr, while not overtly misogynist, stands within a tradition that has associated the sin of sensuality—or of carnality, as it is often called—with woman. Just as Niebuhr ends up subsuming finitude and bodiliness under the higher pole of freedom in human existence, so Christian tradition has tended to uplift the soul or spirit over the body. And, inasmuch as woman has been to that tradition Eve, the seductress, the carnal one, she has been culpable for luring man—the spiritual one—into the sin of carnality. As the early church father, Tertullian, for example, said: "You (woman) are the Devil's gateway. You are the unsealer of that forbidden tree. You are the first deserter of the divine Law. You are she who persuaded him whom the Devil was not valiant enough to attack. You destroyed so easily God's image of man. On account of your desert, that is death, even the Son of God had to die."[11] It is woman as Eve who is responsible for the fall of man, and who continually lures man away from the higher pursuits of the spirit. Hence, by narrowing the sin of hiding to the sin of sensuality, a theology not only denies a fuller understanding of sin that can judge woman in her escapism and beckon her on to a fuller humanity, it also sets the stage for a patriarchal culture to name her the source of all carnality. And so, she is caught in her bondage to guilt: the guilt of desiring to be more fully human than the patriarchal culture tells her she should be; the guilt of being Eve, the seductress, the carnal one; and the deepest guilt of all, the guilt of not becoming a self. And the guilt lives within her, reaping acts of violence against her and against any woman who dares to defy such a judgment.

Cut off from herself, alienated from others, hidden woman lives a submerged existence. She is the woman who accepts the wisdom of the world and bears the name of evil, fallen woman when she seeks to have a career, to fulfill herself in ways other than the role of mother. She is the woman who spends thousands of dollars and several years of her life to get a college education, only to stop driving a car when she becomes pregnant. She is the woman who discovers that one baby and one husband will not fill all the empty hours of a day no matter how hard she may try to make her housework more difficult. She is the woman who waits seven years for her

---

11. Quoted in *Religion and Sexism*, ed. Rosemary Radford Reuther (New York: Simon & Schuster, 1970) 157.

husband to decide who *he* is going to be so that she can know who she is. She is the woman who feels guilty for every dollar spent on babysitting or continuing education and every moment spent away from her home, and who agonizes over every slip that reveals a submerged motive. She is the woman who constantly apologizes for having her own thoughts and who in guilt hides her creativity because it seems too much like self-assertion. She is the woman who is consumed by a guilt she can never assuage through total self-sacrifice because deep down it is a guilt goaded on by an even deeper sense of guilt, the guilt of not being a self, the guilt of denying her full humanity and hiding in a deformed existence. Until women repent of their real sin, the sin of having no self to sacrifice, they will know no end to the cycle of guilt and violence turned inward. For as long as a theology focuses on the sin of pride, as long as it uplifts the one virtue of self-sacrificial love, as long as it worships a judgmental Father in the sky who demands self-sacrifice and is not known to sound the call that beckons one on to full humanity through the acceptance of one's freedom, the full humanity of women will continue to be sacrificed on the cross of self-sacrifice.

The emergence of woman's full consciousness and her repentance for her primary sin of hiding marks a challenge to any theology that persists in a one-sided development. For to challenge one doctrine of a theological system is to know that the other doctrines will have to be challenged as well. Woman needs to lay claim to the more perceptive and inclusive insights of the Christian tradition—insights such as those we have seen initially in the thought of Reinhold Niebuhr—that have persisted on its fringes only to be lost and negated by patriarchal one-sidedness. Woman needs to affirm the basic insight that humanity is body *and* spirit, finite *and* free, and to challenge any theology that seeks to negate the one or to lose the tension of the both/and-ness of the polarity, And woman needs to assert that human sinfulness is not just the sin of pride, but is also the sin of hiding; that the God who judges human pride must also judge human hiding and passivity, not by demanding a sacrifice of the self, but by beckoning the forgiven self to affirm her full humanity through grasping and claiming her call to freedom.

To confess her sin of hiding is a deeply threatening thing for any woman to do. We have believed for so long that femininity and assertiveness cannot be held together, that we persist in hiding behind husbands/fathers/children/bosses, and in the busyness of being somebody's "something" rather than in the demanding task of becoming who we are. Rather than show our hands, our "manus," and reveal ourselves, we manipulate from the shadows. And in our manipulation, we accept the name that has been thrust upon woman throughout tradition: Eve, the feminine, the dark side of humanity. By confessing the sin of hiding, woman stands revealed to the world and to herself. She stands exposed in her insecurities and self-doubts, revealed in her true vulnerability, for, while escaping from herself, she has not learned how to cope either with her own shortcomings, or with her talents and desires. She has been cut off from her human calling to dare to hope. But in her new exposure she is *on* the record; she is given a forum, an arena, a *life* to be lived.

Asserting her selfhood need not threaten a woman's femininity. Woman in search of herself, woman who seeks to know herself as something more than wife/mother/daughter, is caricatured as bad mother, evil woman, who cares only for herself and who, in her evil desire to be human, bears the burden for the malfunctioning of the world. But this is caricature. It is *not* the picture of the true femininity/humanity to which woman aspires when she emerges from hiding. To assert one's selfhood is to accept responsibility for oneself. It is to be the person one *is*, whoever and whatever that may be, with the talents and weaknesses she has, with the network of relations that she has built. It is to become a responsible, committed person who enters *into* relationships, who seeks not to live only for herself, but who seeks both to care for and *to be cared for* by others. Motherhood, then, which has often been denied to or by women who have sought to emerge from the shadows of their hiding, can be affirmed and not denied. For as a woman emerges from her hiding, true motherhood, the true caring for and nurturing of *another*, becomes a real possibility.

Because of the onus of being the carnal one, a woman who emerges from the shadows may wish to deny the myth that "anatomy is destiny." But the emerging woman, seeking full humanity, also must affirm that anatomy *is part of her* destiny. To fail to do so is not only to be guilty of the sin of pride, of the denial of one's bodily finitude, but is also to leave the understanding of motherhood and femininity as it has persisted for too long: as a state of truncated, one-sided human existence, cut off from its true and full humanity. Rather, emerging woman should reclaim her motherhood and femininity. For woman, as she emerges from the womb of escapism, truly gives birth to herself, and she knows that she can be known and loved by another, not because she is a passive reflection of patriarchy's archetype, but because she is the fully human, fully vulnerable person she has become. And she knows that, with the birth of children, she is mother not by losing herself in that infant "other," but by nurturing that child into its own full human existence, an existence that is *not* her own. Perhaps then as well, with the emergence of woman from the womb of her hiding, a new concept of family can be born, a concept that does not depend upon one person in the middle who has no separate personhood of her own but seeks only to serve the others; a concept of family that recognizes mutuality, independence, responsibility and commitment in its members; a concept that reflects the realization that when mother is freed from her submerged existence, her children are freed as well from submerged and manipulative motives, are freed to realize themselves as separate individuals.

Women have been hiding long enough. The patriarchal culture that has robbed them of their selfhood, that has sapped their vital energies, has deprived the world of the creativity they could and should bring to it. It is time that we confessed our real sin, the sin of hiding, and reclaimed our full humanity. It is time for us to challenge a theology that has kept us in bondage to guilt rather than setting us free for a new life. It is time for us to give birth to ourselves, and to be midwives to one another, as we emerge from the womb of our escapism. And, it is time for us to wean ourselves from the cultural conditioning that has stunted our growth, and to learn not to hate ourselves any longer.

For as woman refuses to hide herself behind the walls that patriarchy has built to protect itself from her; as she dares to name the reality that has lived unnamed within her for countless generations; as she knows the fear and vulnerability that accompany the affirmation of life; and as she finds in herself a faith in a deity who judges her passivity and escapism and who beckons her onward; then she knows the courage to demand that the world be transformed, that oppression and bondage be named and fought wherever they exist, and that a vision of a reality beyond fragmentation, beyond violence, and beyond guilt, be born.

Commentary

Nichole Torbitzky

In "The Sin of Hiding," Susan Nelson tackles the very personal area of sin and powerfully points out that even sin is not free of gender inequality. With this article, Nelson asks us to think again about the nature of sin. She challenges the traditional definition of sin as primarily sins of pride. At the same time, she asks us to consider who is included as human when we address questions of the "human condition." In line with the works of feminist theologians like Valerie Saiving and Judith Plaskow, Nelson continues the feminist (and also process relational) reconstruction of primary Christian doctrines, including the doctrine of sin. Situated in what has been commonly (if not popularly) called the Second Wave of feminism, Nelson's critique of Niebuhr picks up the revolutionary themes of the day: that official and legal inequalities were inextricably linked to unofficial and social inequalities. The personal is inextricable from the political as even the most deeply personal parts of women's lives are affected by and reflective of the misogynistic power structures.

Her analysis of Niebuhr reveals that for most of mainstream Protestant theology, sin has been cast in almost exclusively male terms as the sin of pride. Women's sins tend not to fall into this category. Nelson develops what Niebuhr only hinted at, that women have been inclined to sin by shirking their freedom. This insight brought feminist theology to a pivotal point. No longer can women hide from the responsibility of freedom. She names and proclaims women's sin. Naming and proclaiming is powerful in that it affords access to the structures of God's promised forgiveness. Guilt proclaimed is guilt that can be, and is, forgiven, which, in Nelson's words, "lead[s] to regeneration and new life." Her work allows women access to forgiveness of sin that the blindness of generations of male theologians has never been able to offer.

The significance of Nelson's article encompasses more than the lasting impact it had on the feminist canon. She wrote from a process relational point of view that became more noticeable in her later works. Her work with the sin of hiding develops a natural theology of sin based on experience and relation to the world, as opposed to a supernatural theology of sin. For Nelson, the sin of hiding is not sinful simply because God said so. In her later work, *Healing the Broken Heart*, Nelson describes the sin of hiding as not one single sin, but a complex web. She explains that hiding is sinful because it short-circuits healthy relationship through destructive self-sacrifice. The sin of hiding is sin because it avoids the risk of possibility. Hiding is sinful because it is a refusal of the creativity necessary for one to fulfill her self and her rightful place in relationship to the rest of the world. This relational view of sin develops the process theological themes of God as love and Christ as creative transformation. Her endeavor to enlarge our definitions of sin brought process-relational theology to a new place. Most process theologians were working from a view of sin that was still relatively supernatural. As God is integrally related to each of our becoming moments, to deny the beauty and creativity that God has in store for us is to sin and turn away from God and the transformation we are offered in each moment. Nelson prompted process relational theologians to look at sin in terms of its relational and experiential dimensions.

The influence of Susan Nelson's work on sin prompted those working in the field of theology and philosophy to think carefully not just about sin, but also about sin from the perspective of women. Using a natural theology and process metaphysic, she set the stage to further develop notions of "women's experience" and "women's sin." Her work provided room for other process thinkers to explore womanist, mujerista, and countless other views of sin. She led the way in reconstructing Christian doctrine in order to challenge old standards and limited thinking so that each of us is empowered to follow the lure of God toward creativity and fullness of life.

STUDY QUESTIONS

1. If Niebuhr had considered the "sin of hiding," he might have categorized it as injustice perpetrated upon women and not sin at all. Some have seen Nelson's article not as an attempt to liberate women from sin, but as an instance of blaming the victim and heaping more guilt upon guilt. Is Nelson blaming the victim?

2. If we can accept the idea of complicity in sin as sin, what role does justice play in addressing women's sin? What is the place for seeking justice in the confession of the sin of hiding?

3. Both process and feminist writers have undertaken the monumental task of rewriting Christian doctrine and re-interpreting Scripture in order to address the needs of women and an ever-developing world. How could Nelson's theological insights open new understandings of grace in interpreting Christian Scripture, and what influence could Scripture have on the assertions Nelson makes in her article?

4. Self-sacrifice is named as sin in this article. Is there a time or place where self-sacrifice is not sinful for women? Is there a time or place for self-sacrifice at all?

5. Nelson writes from the perspective of a white, middle class, educated, American woman. How helpful can her insights be to African-American women or Hispanic-American women? Can her insight be applied to women in developing nations who are more concerned with the daily struggles of life, or to other women who haven't enjoyed such privileges of race, class, and country of origin? How do these privileges or lack thereof affect our view of the sin of hiding?

6. Does the sin of hiding apply to men?

8 Self and God

Catherine E. Keller

Catherine Keller is a professor of constructive theology at the Graduate and Theological School of Drew University. She earned a PhD from Claremont Graduate School. She has published many article and books on process and feminist theologies as well as ecological and poststructuralist theory and is currently examining the confluence of the apocalyptic turn in theology, Christian mysticism, and recent physics. As director of the Drew Transdisciplinary Theological Colloquium, she gathers various scholars into a polydoxy of thinkers for re-creating theology. She continues to inspire many blossoming constructive theologians and scholars. The following excerpt is taken from chapter one and chapter five of *From a Broken Web: Separation, Sexism, and Self*.

Excerpt from *From a Broken Web: Separation, Sexism, and Self*

> For to weave is not merely to predestine (anthropologically), and to join together differing realities (cosmologically) but also to *create*, to make something of one's own substance as the spider does in spinning its web.
>
> —Mircea Eliade, *Patterns in Comparative Religions*

> But I waste my heart away in longing for Odysseus; so they speed on my marriage and I weave a web of wiles . . . In the daytime I would weave the mighty web, and in the night unravel the same.
>
> —Penelope in *The Odyssey*, trans. S. H. Butcher.

IN THE CLASSIC WESTERN novel, Penelope waits while Odysseus wanders. As he intrudes, escapes, and seduces his way through time and space, he creates an ego of epic independence, positing it over and against a world of dangerous opponents. Enemies and elements, monsters and magical ladies exist only to strengthen his self-identity and to test the powers of his autonomy. After his separation from home, he completes the archetypal hero's journey by returning to faithful Penelope. Having created nothing, she merely remains: intact, yet "wasting away." Daily weaving and unweaving her tapestry, she has preserved herself—but is it a self?—for him, in a fixed space, in a cyclical time. He is loosed; she is bound. To be "loosed away from" is the etymology of the Absolute: that which is complete in itself, independent of and separate from everything else. Thus Simone de Beauvoir's now-classic thesis: "He is the Subject, he is the Absolute—she is the Other."[1] But

[1]. Simone de Beauvoir, *The Second Sex*, trans.

would Penelope, as she binds and looses the threads of daily survival, want to be the Absolute—even were her fate, like her shuttle, in her own hands?

The classical pair personifies a familiar pattern. We encounter it in endless tales of errant knights and wandering cowboys, adventuring against an emotional background of waiting women: "In song and story the young man is seen departing adventurously . . . she is locked in a tower, a palace, a garden, a cave, she is chained to a rock, a captive, sound asleep: she waits."[2] Most of us know this complementary dyad through the less heroic familiarity of familial history. Even more intimately, we know it because we have not altogether escaped *being* it. The pattern congeals into two different sorts of self, completely dependent upon each other; but the task of one is to assert its apparent independence, the task of the other to support that appearance. If now the Other is asserting her independence, she will want to avoid setting herself loose only to find herself bound up in the subjectivity of the (apparently) separate and supreme ego. And if he begins to extricate himself from the politics of the "male ego," one hopes he does not resort to passive dependency. Moreover, if we wed both sets of gender roles to produce what is sometimes called androgyny, we may simply redouble the force of the stereotypes by internalizing their complementarity.[3]

H. M. Parshley (New York: Vintage, 1952) xix.

2. Ibid., 84.

3. However problematic the notion has become, androgyny has proved a valuable ideal for many feminists, pointing beyond the restrictions of gender stereotype to the cultivation of the full range of human capacities by both sexes. However, the very metaphor presupposes the recapitulation of stereotypical sex distinctions.

NO-ONE'S SEPARATION

An occasional antihero notwithstanding, the myth of the warrior-hero has dominated Western imagining of what it is to be a "man," that is, a full human being. Within the most sublimated contexts, far from any battlefield, the Homeric heroes continued in the mind of every schoolboy to savage their opponents, while Christian soldiers marched onward against each other and other enemies of the Lord. The archetypal hero fashions human personality in his own image, projecting an ego armored against the outer world and the inner depths. His philosophical descendant is the separate, self-enclosed subject, remaining self-identical throughout its exploits in time. Its relations do not affect its essence. Indeed, to sustain its sense of independence, such a subject is always liberating itself from its bonds as though from bondage. Intimacy, emotion and the influence of the Other arouse its worst anxieties, for somehow it must keep relation external to its own being, its "self." It proves its excellence through the tests of separation, establishing a mobile autonomy as its virtue (where *vir* means "man"). Virility lies above all in impermeability.

A contemporary male here recalls his education in the integrity of separateness: "I was raised to be authentic, to be my own man. I was told that the way to success was to be self-possessed, to love difficulty and isolation, independence and self-sufficiency, as the strength of not needing others. I discovered the philosophy of authenticity as if I had lived it all along."[4] A philosophical economist, Wikse here brings into play the economics

4. John R. Wikse, *About Possession: The Self as Private Property* (University Park: Pennsylvania University Press, 1977) 10.

of the separate self: it is its own property, possessing itself. We may add that its Other, its complementary opposite, must also be possessed; for this independent ego is in fact dependent upon its array of waiting and attendant Others, largely women. Thus the Greek word *ousia*, from the verb *to be*, traditionally translated as "substance," denoted at once "reality" and "realty": Odysseus reclaimed his own substance upon his return to Ithaca, where wife and real estate awaited him.

Man's self-possession seems to have required woman as his property. So the theft of woman warrants war. Helen's beauty launched a thousand ships—in defense of the system of masculine self-possession. If Menelaus loses her, the heroic integrity of all Greeks fails. Wikse reports how in childhood an American myth formed his sense of authenticity. His father regularly narrated to him the Saga of Cowboy Jack, a wandering good guy who saves the town but steers clear of all attachments—so that he can go on wandering and saving. Certainly the self-identity of the heroic ego involves impressive disciplines of self-denial in the pursuit of its successful career. (The static self-sacrifice of the waiting woman pales by contrast.)

But is the self-denial of the heroic ego simultaneously other-denial: a repression of its own deep interrelatedness with everything else, and a suppression of the legitimate claims of any others? However much the ego feels single and apart, this feeling may represent not truth but denial. It is less precise to call this ego separate than *separative*, implying an activity or an intention rather than any fundamental state of being. The separative self is identifiable historically, but neither essentially nor necessarily, with males and the masculine. Its sense of itself as separate, as over against the world, the Other, and even its own body, endows it with its identity. It is *this,* not *that.*

Virginia Woolf's character Louis (an exceptional male) bemoans the prevalence of separateness:

> These attempts to say, 'I am this, I am that,' which we make coming together, like separated parts of one body and soul, are false. Something has been left out from fear. Something has been altered, from vanity. We have tried to accentuate differences. From the desire to be separate we have laid stress upon our faults, and what is particular to us.[5]

Fear and vanity motivate both males and females, but within the culture of sexist complementarity it motivates them differently. As a self-shaping, primary force, this accent on differentness is part of the cultivation of the heroic ego. Continuous, self-imposed exposure to fear and a defiant vanity seem fundamental to the character of the hero. But his woman's fear is of *him,* and her vanity reflects her image in his eyes. Thus her difference from him is often little more than a reaction to him, a secondary role formation.

Fortunately, even the *Odyssey* contains—however subtextually—certain ironies that belie the defiant self-identity of the male ego on its journey and the sheer passivity of the female at her immobile loom. Irony, as the incongruous juxtaposition of what is said with what is true, provides a possible methodological perspective for approaching

---

5. Virginia Woolf, *The Waves,* in *Jacob's Room/The Waves* (New York: Harcourt, Brace and World, 1959) 270.

androcentric traditions and texts. According to Kierkegaard "irony is the incitement to subjectivity."[6] An ironic perspective is inspired, if not intended, by the *Odyssey's* most classic pun: The monstrous Cyclop (son of Earth and rebel against the order of Zeus) asks Odysseus his name. Odysseus knows the Cyclop will then call for help from his one-eyed friends and so tells him: "No-one is my name." No One, *oudeis*, puns upon the word *Odysseus*. After escaping, Odysseus hurls his real name at the Cyclop expressly to contribute to the fame of that name and so to his own immortality. On the surface of the text, these are ironies enough.

But a deeper incongruity suggests itself. The last laugh may be on our hero and on the kind of ego he so splendidly embodies. Perhaps Odysseus told the truth when he meant to dissemble. For if such a subjectivity ultimately loses itself in its own bid for fame, name and immortality, then here it inadvertently names its repressed anxiety: "No-one is my name." I am not important. Not real. Not one. Not *one*. Not a self-possessed monad. By this account, the hero illustrates what Kierkegaard calls the "despair of defiance," which he equates with "the despair of manliness."[7] "That self which he despairingly wills to be is a self which he is not (for to will to be that self which one truly is, is indeed the opposite of despair)." An authentic self wills to be what it is. And so if Odysseus calls out that he is No-one, does he in his very defiance voice the despair of a yet unacknowledged self-contradiction? What if the controlling ethos of heroic egoism, foisted upon millennia of males (and lately upon white middle-class professional females) smacks of an unrecognized self-doubt? After all, it received its ultimate modern rationalization as the Cartesian ego, a concept that was forged in the depths of self-doubt. Descartes divided human reality into two independent substances, cogitating ego and lifeless matter, while meditating in solitude about whether he existed at all.

Incitement to a fresh notion of the self and its subjectivity may prove the only solution—though not as just one more argument against dualism or substantialism. But the stubbornly entrenched presupposition of the separateness of selves militates even below consciousness against any alternative. For as we will see, it is fortified by the even more massive self-defenses of patriarchy itself.

WOMEN IN WAITING

What of Penelope's self? Of late she has been disrupting the static fidelity of her ancient persona; she has been exploring the apparently endless psychic and social ripples of her peculiar ontological status in history: woman's self as no self of her own, and thus a false, an owned, self, somehow not quite a self at all. She seems dispersed, diffused, defused, meant to glory in her being-for-him, named even by his name. In her devoted anonymity,

---

6. S. A. Kierkegaard, *The Concept of Irony*, trans. L. M. Capel (New York: Harper & Row, 1965) 234.

7. S. A. Kierkegaard, *The Sickness unto Death*, in *Fear and Trembling/The Sickness unto Death*, trans. Walter Lowrie (Princeton: Princeton University Press, 1968) 200–203. The heroic energy of defiance emerges vividly in the account: "So the despairing self is constantly building nothing but castles in the air, it fights only in the air. All these experimental virtues make a brilliant showing . . . such self-control, such firmness, such ataxiasia, etc. . . . and also at the bottom of it all there is nothing. The self wants to enjoy the entire satisfaction of making itself into itself," 203.

she has collaborated in his self-deception, fostering in him that covert dependency upon her by which he sustains his sense of independence. In our epoch the incongruities mount as she encounters old "feminine" inauthenticities in tandem with her new temptation to a "masculine" defiance. Inasmuch as economic self-sufficiency has become an option for women (though the prospect remains bleak for all but middle-class white career women), the separative urge to claim "I am this," "I am that," becomes harder to resist.

Kierkegaard defines sin as despair, the despair summoned by the failure to be who we are, by the desperate attempt of the self to escape being itself. He goes on to distinguish between specifically "masculine" and "feminine" forms of despair. If the masculine sin is "potentiated defiance"—a refusal to accept the ultimate terms of selfhood—the feminine analogue is "potentiated weakness." Kierkegaard perceptively links woman's weakened sense of self to her self-loss in service to others, that is, to her devotion. He recognizes that the traditional feminine devotion is a sin, not a virtue, because it is a form of despair and self-abnegation: "by devotion (the word literally means giving away) she has lost herself."[8]

Kierkegaard might seem to be anticipating the contemporary reevaluation of sin by feminist theology. Theologians Valerie Saiving, Judith Plaskow and Sue Dunfee demonstrate how the traditional notions of sin as pride and self-assertion serve to reinforce the subordination of women, whose temptations *as* women lie in the realm of "underdevelopment or negation of the self."[9] But unfortunately Kierkegaard, who like most thinkers cannot distinguish between the effects of patriarchal culture and woman's nature, only turns the screws tighter, as the above passage in its fuller context reveals:

> But the fact that devotion is woman's nature comes again to evidence in despair. By devotion she has lost herself, and only thus is she happy, only thus is she herself; a woman who is happy without devotion, that is, without giving herself away (to whatever it may be she gives herself) is unwomanly.[10]

While he correctly exposes the despair concealed in women's devotion, he at the same time sentences us to self-loss as the very condition of our happiness! This typically androcentric pronouncement on women's "nature," mistaking a femininity required by masculine arrogance for some feminine essence, renders the intolerable inevitable. Such a relapse into essentialism eclipses Kierkegaard's own existentialism, injecting it with a certain bad faith. Moreover for the masculine sin there is no comparable double-bind. One does not read that a man must commit the despair of defiance in order to be manly.

If in Danish, *devotion* means "to be given away," we find that the archaic definition of the English word is "doom." Women know the doom of devotion all too intimately: a mother who has sacrificed

8. Ibid., 183.

9. Valerie Saiving, "The Human Situation: A Feminine View," in *Womanspirit Rising: A Feminist Reader in Religion,* ed. Carol Christ and Judith Plaskow (San Francisco: Harper & Row, 1979) 37. Also see Sue Dunfee, "The Sin of Hiding: A Feminist Critique of Reinhold Niebuhr's Account of the Sin of Pride," *Soundings* (Fall 1982) 316–27.

10. Kierkegaard, *The Sickness unto Death*, 183.

untold possibilities of self-development to see to her children's opportunities observes them retreating emotionally when she most needs support because they resent her history of selflessness for its implicit demand; or a woman who devoted herself to the support of her husband's ego and career now finds herself cast off as he discovers the excitement of self-assertive women (not depleted by his own need); or a daughter who feels her success subtly poisoned by sorrow at her mother's unrealized potential. In these stereotypical but still typical situations, women trapped between stages of a culture that is only begrudgingly changing sometimes feel scorned by feminism as well—as though their despair is indeed sinful. The generations of devoted and desperate women haunt us like a chorus of furies.

Psychologist Maggie Scarf offers the case of a wife and mother who, within an externally ideal family situation, is a near victim of suicide in her late forties. This woman expresses the feminine despair with precision: "I've got no identity in particular . . . I'm not *anybody,* you know, not really a person. I've surrendered that part to Bob."[11] Her self was his to receive but not to return. Thus, while Odysseus calls himself No-one only by virtue of being a public someone, the woman is someone only by virtue of being no one; that is, of belonging to him. If this is Penelope's irony, it has incited only the subjectivity of the possessed: just by being owned can she gain her own public identity. She encounters herself always already as someone else's. If even at sea his image retains its separate solidity, hers, even in its grounded fixity, suggests the deliquescence and dispersion of any selfhood.

Let us designate this sort of self, neither necessarily nor essentially but historically embodied by women, the *soluble self*. In the classical dyad, it complements the separative self, which works upon it as a solvent. Women's tendency to dissolve emotionally and devotionally into the other is a subjective structure internalized by individual women, but imposed by the superstructure of men. Woman is to wait: for her very self, her self-definition, and the advent of the hero who will bring her joy. Simone de Beauvoir captures the self-contradicting state of women's passivity:

> Now, what peculiarly signalizes the situation of woman is that she—a free and autonomous being like all human creatures—nevertheless finds herself living in a world where men compel her to assume the status of the Other. They propose to stabilize her as object and to doom her to immanence since her transcendence is to be overshadowed and forever transcended by another ego *(conscience)* which is essential and sovereign.[12]

In de Beauvoir's thought, "immanence" means to exist within an already established reality, to remain within any *status quo ante*. For her, immanence designates the ultimate in human doom, the stagnant acquiescence in given conditions resulting thus in the failure of freedom; one has given oneself over to the given, the past, "nature," the path of least resistance. Authentic subjectivity, by contrast, arises "through exploits or projects that serve as a mode of transcendence."[13]

---

11. Maggie Scarf, *Unfinished Business* (New York: Ballantine, 1980) 417.

12. De Beauvoir, *The Second Sex*, xxxiv.
13. Ibid., xxxiii.

For de Beauvoir as for Sartre, this secularized sense of transcendence implies no religious movement upward toward a God or a Heaven, but keeps its feet—moving—on the ground. Existential authenticity occurs as we step beyond static patterns into the pursuit of creative projects. But Penelope at her loom, weaving, unweaving, reweaving the same fabric every day, creates nothing. Woman's subjectivity becomes objectified in such a futile cycle, characteristic of our assigned activity throughout history: "The domestic labors that fell to her lot because they were reconcilable with the cares of maternity imprisoned her in repetition and immanence; they were repeated from day to day in an identical form, which was perpetuated almost without change from century to century; they produced nothing new."[14] Mere repetition produces only the objectification of the one who repeats. Subjectivity is ground down in the routines of survival, where nothing new takes place. To take part in history, in the creation of our worlds, is to transcend ourselves and so to realize novel possibilities. The voice of transcendence—"Behold, I am doing a new thing" (Isaiah 43:19)—articulates the heroic history of men, not the domestic heritage of women.

For de Beauvoir, as for the Hegelian-Sartrian tradition as a whole, all class, race or mass oppression stems from the reduction of the Other to immanence, that is, to the status of object. Women's oppression is the most universal instance of such objectification. Though we will shortly challenge a certain presupposition at work in her particular opposition of immanence and transcendence, de Beauvoir's rich analysis and documentation of women's objectification stands as irrefutable.

As women we know well the cast of Sleeping Beauties, Snow Whites and servile Cinderellas sustaining a mythos of feminine passivity intact through the ages. The imagining of our futures has been channeled into a soporific hope for the redeeming prince. In his embrace, adolescent passivity melts into maternal devotion: this womanhood grows from waiting for its self to giving its self away. Its ontology is—at least partly—that of the object, the object of the hero's adventure. His the agency, hers the patience.

. . .

THE SELF-ABSOLVING ABSOLUTE

The hero-warrior lives a transcendence without immanence, a separative oneness based on opposition to the Other. With de Beauvoir we acknowledge that the very structure of subjective freedom must be *achieved,* for by definition it cannot be something already given. But then why should we receive the subject-object opposition itself as though *it* is a given? We may with her appreciate a dynamic account of the genesis of subjectivity; but nonetheless we must doubt the desirability or possibility of the subject's achievement of absolute independence from nature or from others. For we begin to suspect that the ideal of autonomous self-assertion is implicated in a sort of ontological belligerence, and we see that the hostility, glorified by the image of the warrior, discloses after all a specific historical beginning and so no universality.

In contrast to the soluble self, which dissolves into relation, the separative self makes itself the absolute in that it absolves

14. Ibid., 71.

itself from relation. It brooks no other subjects and so it turns them into the nonsubjective other, the object, whenever it can. But does it not in fact require these objects, as though to complete something missing in itself? What would it be that it misses? What lack in itself could motivate its violence of conquest and dominance?

Perhaps we can gain a clue to the motives of objectification if we reexamine the notion of immanence. If the other enters my experience, then it enters as an influence upon me: it makes a difference, and so I am no longer quite the same. But influence, to be more precise, is not working *upon* me so much as *into* me; in-fluence is, that which flows in. If the other flows into the self, then the other is immanent to the self, to the inside being of that self. This is the philosophical meaning of internal rather than external relations: relations between different subjects that are internal to what those subjects *are*—part of their very essence, for good or for ill. But then a self has no shield to protect it from others, no hard bronze off of which influences bounce like intercepted arrows. The in-flowing other must feel to a defensive ego like an aggressive intrusion, a threat to its self-containment. So it will redouble its fortifications and can justify its own aggression as defense. Indeed it will declare itself an absolute in the original sense of the word: to be "cut loose" from-the-other, we presume, who faced with the self-absolutizing I soon appears as the alien Other. Relation to others, once ousted from the self's inside and so experienced as external, must be *kept* outside by a policy of psychic isolationism. Thus the ego denies the streams of influence entering into it and tries to control—and so to possess—their sources. Only by subduing and possessing the Other can it feel truly in possession of itself. Externalizing relation, it in fact projects both the threats and comforts of relationship onto the Other. Then woman, as man's most intimately threatening yet most comfortingly controlled Other, is there to fill his lack: the lack of immanent relations—of the sense of an intimate interconnection with the world. But the lack is in a way as illusory as his absoluteness-because willy-nilly each subject exists in interdependence with its world. And so in a bizarre sense, by objectifying the Other the subject compensates for a lack that it does not really have—for it is only the feeling, not the reality, of isolation that cuts it off from the in-flowing other.

Where does the cycle begin? Later chapters may shed light on causes, both mythic and psychological. For now let us claim that any fundamental opposition of self and other serves the double purpose of establishing the self's sense of its inner independence from influence and compensating for the haunting fear that the independence is illusory. As it cannot embrace interdependence, it ironically comes to depend upon the dependent Other, in reality or fantasy.

. . .

BEING HERE/BEING NOW

. . . No wonder this ego despises maternity, mother-goddesses, childhood and everything that reminds it of "first times." It does not *want* first times, it wants the endurance of the same. The more repetitive it can remain, the more it can exclude influx of the different, the new, the world; the more it can deny its ontological feelings, and the more its sheer redundancy creates the narcissistic illusion of an immutable essence. It tries to stop time by sheer rigidity. The subject turns itself into its own object (or tries to) in emulation of a stone—the petrified hero hiding in marble monuments to his immortal glory. The Medusa-mother, who with her writhing snake hair resembles the spider and all things radiating out of bounds, mocks in her monstrosity not time but the timeless ego.

What is the self-timing of connective selves? They participate in the spirals of becoming and perishing, of micromoments and of monthly periods, of moon cycles and solar rounds, of daily and seasonal metamorphosis. The complex continuum—not the simple line—of a flow of events finally excludes no moment of human history nor any wriggle of worm or burst of star in its timing; through this continuum the groundswell of the past empowers the present. The present self may adjust the tempo to its own desire, but first I meet these complex rhythms as an immanent choreography. They cannot be evaded. If, however, I move consciously with the wider dance of nature and history, I may find the knots of my personal compulsions, my patterns of mistiming, easing into an ampler grace.

The future? It is already there, *as* future, that is, not as predetermined, but as probability or possibility. The present pregnant with the future does not know that future as any fait accompli; it does not foreclose, does not control, does not subscribe to the ontology of insurance policies. Yet this future is neither a gaping abyss, God (as the contemporary German theologians Pannenberg and Moltmann would have it), or The End. We can feel the future forming in ourselves now, for this my present self will be endlessly taken up and reiterated. The future will—if only to the most trivial degree—feel this present. My soul, my body, my world: ongoing, they will have to take me in. So if I learn to feel the subtle movement from past to present, I may begin to discern the transformation of vast relational patterns, personal and social, as they roll through my present. But we cannot—and neither can any God or Goddess-foreknow or control the future. It is by definition not yet. However well we read the portents and the promises, neither divinity nor humanity can extinguish the spontaneities with which future presents will self-create. The heroic ego feels thwarted by the uncontrollability of the future. Instead of his time-paranoia, we may learn a new time-trust. Time is the dynamism of relation.

This seems all rather vast. Let us recall the particularity of timing—that timing is ever of the essence, that a friendship, a desire, an interest, a decision that is not possible right now may become possible at another time. The content may remain quite identical: the timing literally makes the difference. For with every moment, the self becomes another. It comes to be a *different* self. And if I can live with the light, butterfly continuity of soul, and the amassed, changing commune of body, forfeiting the rigid self-identities of the ego, I become not less but more responsible. Rhythmically entraining with *my* world, I can *respond* to its desires. I become ever more skillful in the space-time dance of self with other, of same with different, of here with there. Freed really to *feel* the others in their claims upon my future, I will need neither to tense up in defensive rebellion against their influence nor to comply in self-aborting imitation of their impulses. Moving in synchronism with others, community is created and communication not only relays information but effects transformation.

The emergence of community out of the implicit sociality of selves is a matter of timing. Consider examples of shared life rhythms, where empathy and freedom must intertwine to generate intimacy. The skills of intimacy and communication, as well as politics and confrontation, are matters of timing. But we see that self-timing and self-spacing are inseparable processes: as I create space, I am also creating time. To say "I need some space," seems hardly distinguishable from "I need some time:" Whether I have time (in the midst of the busiest of schedules) is a function of whether I create it. And this creativity is a matter of taking in the world—and expanding it from the inside out. Such elaboration is my contribution to worldspace. As I flow into my next moment of self, I *take place:* I am a space-time event. These "drops of experience" (James) have nothing to do with clocks or maps: they are the organic timespaces that come to be as the essence of our self-composition.

"A wild patience has taken me this far"—a distance as much of time as of space, and measurable only in selves. The organic interactions *of* timing and spacing—sometimes feeling mistimed and misplaced, sometimes feeling right on time and right in place—are what I am. How far I have come cannot be counted in years and miles. What counts is only the incalculable integrity of what I am becoming. As the many become one, and many again, as the public becomes private, and public again, as the physical becomes the mental, and physical again, space becomes time, and space again. Space and time have everything to do with the relational self—for space and time are nothing in themselves. They are nothing but metaphors with which we describe the relations between beings. We connect, all of us, spaciously, timefully.

DIVINING THE WEB

"Be what you are becoming, without clinging to what you might have been, what you might yet be," says Irigaray, thus reversing Nietzsche's "Become what you are." We can no more return to the past than we can control the future. Only a self forged in the image of an impenetrable inner hardness, mistaken for integrity, could separate itself from the matrix *of* all life. Without clinging to the others or to our own past and future selves, we can connect and reconnect in freedom: there is so much to remember, to reread, to revision, to redeem. There is always the world, coming in: its immanence. We make something *of* it, flowing out: our transcendence. Remembering in its work of immanence, of taking in and reconnecting, breaks into imagining, in its work of transcendence, of envisioning the possible.

We arise from the matrix; we redesign its elements; we are woven back into the matrix. This is the religious action of reconnecting. As the word itself tells us, matrix is always *mater,* mother. No inert matter here; there is no such thing. All beings come tied to the matrix of interconnection by what poet Judy Grahn calls "the one true cord, / the umbilical line / unwinding into meaning, / transformation, / web of thought and caring and connection."[15] In a matricidal civilization such as we have known for the extent of our textual history, the umbilical line is denied, ignored, violated, feared, and almost—catastrophically—severed. But even selves who declare their heroic freedom *from* the matrix, in place of freedom *within* the matrix, cannot kill it. The Spider Mother spins on. Tehom still undulates within and among us.

What do such disparate metaphors as the oceanic mother Tehom/Tiamat and the airy spider share, we might wonder? One goes deep, the other reaches wide. One is heavy, the other light. One takes in, the other creates. One embodies the tidal currents, belying opacity and separation. The other filigrees her body's substance into complex patterns of differentiation. Neither knows any hardness, any rigidity, in herself. Both express themselves with the fluency of interconnection. In their different dimensions and domains, both horrify the self-forgetting fixity of other—opposed egos. The sea monster is the dread, suppressed face of the liquescent, the influent; the spider, in order to spin, extrudes viscous fluid from her body.

These are metaphors, demanding their own multiplicity of images: no single metaphor can be privileged as the truth, without forfeiting its own relational life. Many have pronounced the very metaphor "God" dead. Nelle Morton suggested above that identifying "God" with male rulership and control drained the life out of the image. I would only add that its competitive exclusivism, which resulted in the simple One, stifles imagination and so kills image at the source. For the unimagining, Deep and Spider seem ungodly.

Tapping the source freshly, Morton relates a late-life experience of metaphor which came to her as a vision:

> Immediately on the right side of the window appeared an enormous spider with a gray body and orange legs. She lifted one leg high above the other as she walked toward me on the darkness. I was not afraid, somehow. As the spider reached me she held out her two front legs on which hung some woven material. All she said was, "Your mother spun this for you." As I took the material the spider dissolved into me, as did the Goddess and then my mother. I opened my eyes.[16]

Eye-opening in more ways than one, this arachnean epiphany offers an alternative vision, a complex discernment of the sacred and personal forces at work in us. The spider has a gift to offer: the mother's material, the transformation of matter into art, the "ancient skill." Nelle Morton experiences quite literally an infusion of grace, almost in the old Catholic sense—the wisdom, the energy and the images of the revelation now into her, become her. Interestingly, the spider vision is multiple, indeed triune—a gynomorphic community of Goddess, Mother, and Spider, three distinct persons revealing different facets of one reality. The reality of woman's Self? Certainly the triune Goddess symbolizes the Self of all women and, indeed, may lend men an indispensable link to their own deeper personality.[17] But if Goddess

---

15. Judy Grahn, "Helen you always were the factory," *The Queen of Wands* (Trumansburg, NY: Crossing, 1982) 92.

16. Nelle Morton, *The Journey Is Home* (Boston: Beacon, 1985) 163.

17. For the clearest statement of the role of the Goddess today as symbol of woman's self-empowerment, see Carol P. Christ, "Why Women Need

symbolizes Self, it is just as true that the Self incarnates Goddess.

The divine is always becoming flesh—what else does the Eros desire? Of course, stories of God becoming Man have eclipsed the revelation of Her becoming Woman. But now, in our becoming, vision begins slowly to clear.

A multiplicity of self-occasions "in flowing movement" naturally gives rise to a pluralism of vision itself. Thus Morgan, speaking for the archetypal spider-self: "Let me sit at the center of myself / and see with all my eyes."[18] The radical remembering of postpatriarchal religion disallows any monofocal vision. Reconnection requires polyscopic discernment. We can no more immobilize the divine element in the universe in the form of a single name, a single sex, a single code, creed or cult, than we can freeze the fluid transformations of the universe. A postpatriarchal perspective, expressing a self that is many in one, learns a limpid, diversifying discernment of all things dancing as many in one.[19] But all things together do not add up to a deity. Any simple pantheism, deifying the universe, might squelch profound possibilities of relation. For in community, in the matrix of interconnections private and public, we encounter a holiness of Self and Other that is irreducible to any one self or any one other. It has life-lives-of its own. Yet we cannot know this holiness—this elusive wholeness—directly. It calls us from the depth of ourselves, from where we are not ever yet conscious. Any being in the universe can be its metaphor. Such wholeness attunes us to a deep frequency of relation itself; yet in all our relations we also relate to this frequency. It is not simply the principle of relationship, for it is always becoming flesh, specific, unique. We relate *to* it when we relate to the metaphors that move us. From dreams and imaginings, myths and poems, straggling intuitions and clear perceptions, from all the stories we tell each other, the images emerge, resonating with the deep frequency. The divine Eros, the luring Love, frequents the world: its incarnations and revelations are never delivered once and for all. And as Spider, Goddess and Mother dissolved back into the one envisioning them, the images dissolve back into our selves. They are there to get embodied and ensouled, not literalized and idolized.

For now we will sidestep any theological conclusion, any final fix on the Wisdom that weaves the Web. Let us not tie up or tie down the ontological status of a deity: the arachnean religion requires us only to keep on tying *together*. The immanent Desire provokes our own transcendence, and no doubt transcends us in turn. Metaphors of self arise from, give rise to, the Self of all metaphors. All this, every moment. But let us at present try thinking not of some substantialized divinity, but of our own process of *divining*.

---

the Goddess: Phenomenological, Psychological, and Political Reflections," in *Womanspirit Rising: A Feminist Reader in Religion*, ed. Judith Plaskow and Carol P. Christ (San Francisco: Harper & Row, 1979) 228–45. And for the classic connection between psychological-archetypal pluralism and the image of the Goddess as woman's self, see Naomi R. Goldenberg, *Changing of the Gods: Feminism and the End of Traditional Religions* (Boston: Beacon, 1979).

18. Morgan, "The Network of the Imaginary Mother," 84.

19. Fanchon Shur's choreographic work *Taalit: Prayer Shawl* (based in Cincinnati) is a ceremonial dance which de-patriarchalizes an ancient Jewish symbol, enacting in motion the holy inclusiveness of community and cosmos.

The Greek word for "divining" is *mantikē*, the oracular discernment over which the serpentine pythia once presided. This word, *mantic*, stems from the same root (*mens*, "mind") as does *mania*, the divine madness (by which the profane insanity of separation is overcome); *mens* is also the origin of *minna*, old German for love (the singing Eros) and of "memory" as the Mother of the Muses, Mnemosyne (whose inspiration holds it all together). And of course from this root springs the radical *monstrum* herself, the admonishing-remonstrating-demonstrating monster-mother who has been carrying us in her belly and spewing us out all along.

What patterns reveal themselves in the tensions, contradictions, and contrasts of the many becoming one in me? What in my public warp of relations, in my private woof of introspections, do I *divine*? Divining my own desire I make connection with yours; divining each others', we sense our own; and often only your divination of my truth divulges it to me. Feeling my feelings, and feeling among my feelings the feelings of all those to whom and to which I relate, I may tune in to the deeper frequency.

Such divining, we sense, is infinitely difficult. Some part of us would still like a parental God or god-person just to give us the answers. And because nothing stays quite the same, the metaphors and methods of our best discernment never work quite the same way a second time. But when we stop divining, even for a few moments, we seem to forget ourselves, to drift toward solubility or separation, to lose connection. The recurrent patterns, the rhythmic continuities that constitute selves, allow only the loosest predictions. So this difficult process of divining requires genius: the spider's genius.

Such genius does not reside in a swollen IQ, but in heedful awareness, drawing on all of our innumerable senses. *Religio*, though etymologically stemming from the Latin "tying back together," has as its first dictionary meaning "careful observation." To divine is certainly a religious act, and its "genius" is our self to whatever extent we can claim our connections: our con-geniality. The word "genius," which translates the Greek *daemon*, a tutelary spirit or indwelling deity, dwells in everyone. Thus Daly calls women to reclaim our "tidal genius," the oceanic daemon (*demon* to the patriarchy) that will trespass all fixed shorelines. Oceanic depth and arachnean breadth: when we are what we are becoming, interfusing spaciously and intertwining timefully, feeding each other and exceeding ourselves, we will divine new signs and portents. The new *monstrum* demonstrates what is possible in and between our Selves.

Commentary

KRISTA E. HUGHES

IN THIS SELECTION WE hear from Keller two inter-related proposals: the self be understood as relationally constituted and such insight shifts not only our understanding of the human person but also our conception of God at work in the world—in and with us.

Keller offers the concept of the relational self, at once feminist and process in its sensibilities, as an alternative to the classically gendered separative and soluble selves. That is, she questions both the classically masculine tendency to eschew relational connection and the classically feminine tendency to be overly determined by one's relations. The answer to woman's solubility is not, Keller makes clear, to pursue the separative tactics of man. Rather, the self ought to be reconsidered altogether: as that which is internally constituted by its relations with others. Significantly, Keller extends her critique beyond Western philosophy's dualistic anthropology and addresses how the separative self has also been projected onto God, who becomes the Separative Self par excellence. Is it not, instead, that God too is constituted by relations—actively, intimately becoming with/in the world, with/in us?

Since weaving her early Web, Keller has gone on to spin yet larger and more intricate theological tapestries—moving from anthropology to cosmology, from apocalypse (back) to the depths of genesis, from ecology to empire. Yet strikingly, if unsurprisingly, many of the thematic threads of Keller's evolving corpus are discernable in *From a Broken Web*. It seems that those first radials she established to weave her vision of the relational self continue to support her ever-expanding theological web. Now, as then, Keller combines fearlessness in challenging certain sacred orthodoxies with the tenderest regard for the heart of the Christian tradition and its people.

While addressing a wide range of concerns, Keller has been consistent in her diagnosis of the fears that seem to underpin the hierarchical power relations funded by Western philosophy and Christian theology. In particular she has exposed the patriarchal and imperial fears of (gendered, sexual, cultural, racial) otherness and multiplicity—and of the epistemological ambiguity to which these give rise. In doing so, she continually questions the reification of an absolute, self-enclosed One—be that God or "Truth." Instead, she celebrates the dynamic, diverse multiplicity at the heart of all becoming. "[M]ultiple integrity, while always unfinished, is no less whole or coherent than that of a closed substance," the early Keller of *From a Broken Web* insists. Indeed, it is precisely this integrity that "unbreaks the brokenness by weaving the fragments into a new—if provisional—whole. "Not multiplicity," she continues, "but the refusal of multiplicity, fragments."[1] One wonders whether Keller today, in exploring the possibilities of polydoxy and theologies of the manifold, recalls her own earlier words.

In challenging theological-philosophical tradition, Keller is ever careful to seek what is good in that tradition while also resisting any simplistic feminist reversals. Like Whitehead, she mines the tradition for all that she finds promising. Yet her appreciation for deconstruction allows her to find the fissures in tradition, which she pries open to release new possibilities. From these she suggests a "third way" beyond the thorny dualisms that plague theological discourse and in turn material lives. In addition to a relational conception of the self, Keller gives us a counter-apocalypse to challenge the good-evil dualisms that fund apocalyptic thought and a creation *ex profundis* ("from the deep") as an alternative to a creation from nothing that would seek to deny the bubbling potentiality of the primordial deep. These and the other "third ways" she proposes are never static or singular but always invite multiplicity and becoming.

Keller has likewise modeled in her robustly transdisciplinary methodology that feminist-process thought need not always name itself in order to ground and inspire transformative theologies. "My own thought [has] not concentrated on gender for some time," says Keller in a 2008 essay, "though no doubt I have always been writing through it."[2] Regarding the project of "feminist theology" more broadly, Keller speculates that its name "will lose its caché." Yet, she insists, it is "neither losing its influence nor passing away...We will find its traces written on the edge, *ta eschata*, of any future theology worthy yet to unfold."[3] In sum, process feminism may do some of its most profound theological work when it is so fundamental as to be unseen.

In the last chapter of *From a Broken Web* Keller commends the "spider's genius" of web-making as a fresh image for religion—one constituted by "the very process of reconnection" rather than the worship of a separative, untouchable deity. Such "arachnean spirituality is," she says, "a way of becoming not prescribed from the outside but sprung from the whorl of internalized relations." As such, it is "a way of radical integrity."[4] Keller herself might be said to possess, and express, the spider's genius: weaving intricate transdisciplinary webs of thought that sparkle with both incisive truth-telling and theopoetic lyricism—despite beginning "from a broken web" of theological constructs that inhibit creaturely flourishing. That is, Keller mimics Arachne's own web-spinning by shying away from neither the ugly truths of our world nor the power of beauty in our interpretations of and responses to those truths[5]—in an echo of Whitehead himself, who tells us that "truth matters because of beauty."[6] In this she exemplifies one of her most key

---

1. Catherine Keller, *From a Broken Web: Separation, Sexism, Self* (Boston: Beacon, 1986) 228.

2. Catherine Keller, "The Apophasis of Gender: A Fourfold Unsaying of Feminist Theology," *Journal of the American Academy of Religion* 76 (2008) 906–7.

3. Ibid., 930.

4. Keller, *From a Broken Web*, 225.

5. Ibid., 216–17.

6. Alfred North Whitehead, *Adventures of Ideas* (New York: Free Press, 1933) 267.

contributions to process feminism—eschewing any notion of static, unitary "perfection" in favor of a dynamic, multiple, creative poiesis. If God is poet of the world, then in our own "divinings," Keller seems to suggest, we too are poets of ourselves and of one another.

STUDY QUESTIONS

1. Describe the separative self and the soluble self. What problems does Keller identify in each?

2. In the process notion that the self is internally constituted by her relations, Keller finds a "third way" of understanding the self. Why is this not simply a reinscription of solubility?

3. In what ways do traditional images of the Christian God resemble, and even reify, the separative self?

4. What does Keller mean when she says that metaphors for the divine "are there to get embodied and ensouled, not literalized and idolized"? Why is a multiplicity of metaphors for God important?

5. Keller suggests that we participate in "our own process of divining"—and that we ought to. Some might say she is promoting human idolatry. How might Keller respond from a feminist-process perspective?

9 Christology and Eros

RITA NAKASHIMA BROCK

Rita Nakashima Brock is the founding codirector of Faith Voices for the Common Good, an organization dedicated to educating the public about the values and concerns of religious leaders and organizations. She received her PhD from Claremont Graduate School in Theology and Philosophy of Religion. She has written many texts including the following excerpt, which is from her award-winning Journeys By Heart: A Christology of Erotic Power, *which earned the Crossroads/Continuum Publishing Company award for the most outstanding manuscript in women's studies in 1988.*

Excerpt from *Journeys by Heart: A Christology of Erotic Power*

ALL POWERS, INCLUDING THE most destructive, depend on relationships. But once this insight begins to sink in, how we interact with each other becomes a far more crucial question. For if we choose some element of domination, no matter how benevolent, we reduce the presence of the other in the relationship, and thereby diminish the creativity of connection and the wonder and mystery of erotic power.

Alfred North Whitehead and Charles Hartshorne have argued that the key to human awareness and action is *experience*, experience understood in its integrating complexity. Hence how we perceive, understand, and organize the events of our lives has a great deal to do with our behavior. As Hartshorne states in *The Logic of Perfection*:

While experience is certainly influenced by its data (which are its only conditions), it seems evident that it can never be wholly determined by them. A "creative synthesis" is required, without which the experience would be merely the given data over again.[1]

Erotic power is the energy that produces creative synthesis, and is enhanced by the relationships that emerge from creative synthesis. It produces not fusion and control, but connectedness. While various forms of dominance exist in society, if we can begin to experience them differently, we will begin to break down the damaging power hierarchies that destroy heart. We can then begin to see power as the fluid product of a highly interactive process that begins with birth and buoys us throughout life. Erotic power emerges in and maintains the play space allowing

---

1. Charles Hartshorne, *The Logic of Perfection* (LaSalle, IL: Open Court, 1962) 230.

the engagement of our whole being and world of experience. Such a view of power may seem new, but it, in fact, is a more primal awareness of life that taps the energy sources of our earliest beginnings when, as children, we were most vulnerable and needed to connect to others. The childhood birth of play and the rebirth of heart lead us into the many realms of erotic power.

Erotic power integrates all aspects of the self, making us whole. Erotic power grounds the concreteness of our experiences of empathy, passion, creativity, sensuality, and beauty. Erotic power resides in the matrices of our connectedness to self, to the body, to others, and to the world. Through it we experience in the richness of our lives—in our bodies, psyches, and spirits—the flowering of ourselves and our worlds. Erotic power in human life has been richly articulated by several feminist theorists, including those whose works are briefly discussed below.

Unlike agape, which is often defined as a disinterested, or objective form of love, most exemplified in the dispassionate divine love, Eros connotes intimacy through the subjective engagement of the whole self in a relationship. It is sometimes confused with lust, or sexuality. Trask's analysis in *Eros and Power* of Freud and Marcuse suggests that patriarchy under capitalism turns Eros into sexual domination by the repression of sex instincts through childhood and puberty, "during which time the body is progressively desexualized by parents and other authorities."[2]

This process submits women to male dominance as the object of projections of Eros. Hence women are the core of the repression of sexuality.

This repression of sexuality brings people into line with the demands of an acquisitive, aggressive society prescribing heterosexual possession and prohibiting spontaneous liaisons and nongenital sex as *"immoral* or *unnatural."* The end result of this repression is an alteration of sexuality from an expressive aspect of the entire person into a specialized function,

> a means to an end, . . . a desexualization of the body for the fulfillment of the performance principle, that is, alienated labor . . . the "toneless" pleasure principle is subjugated to the performance principle [which] decrees an acquisitive, aggressive ego.[3]

Trask sees the feminist articulation of Eros as moving well beyond the identification of passion and love with genital sexuality to a sense of the body and a power that cherishes life in its multiplicities of feelings and forms.

In "Uses of the Erotic: The Erotic as Power," Audre Lorde, describes the erotic as the ability to feel our deepest passions in all aspects of our lives as the root of our lives' deepest meanings.[4] The life force behind the creative, empowering energy of our lives is the erotic. The erotic bridges the passions of our lives by a sensual span of physical, emotional, psychic, mental, and spiritual elements.

The erotic cannot be felt secondhand; it can only be felt through our own unique presence and the presence

---

2. Haunani-Kay Trask, *Eros and Power: The Promise of Feminist Theory* (Philadelphia: University of Pennsylvania Press, 1986) 9.

3. Ibid., 9–10.

4. In Audre Lorde, *Sister Outsider* (Berkeley: Crossing, 1984) 53–59.

of others to us. The erotic underlines all levels of experience, openly and fearlessly, with intense joy. As we feel deeply the complex, many dimensions of ourselves, we begin to want the joy that we know emerges through the erotic. We begin to examine our lives for the excellence and fulfillment we glimpse in erotic power. We are empowered to refuse the convenient, shoddy, conventional, and safe. The erotic compels us to be hungry for justice at our very depths because we are response-able. We are able to reject what makes us numb to the suffering and self-hate of others. Acts against oppression become essential to ourselves, empowered from our energized centers. Through the erotic as power we become less willing to accept powerlessness, despair, depression, and self-denial. The erotic is what binds and gives life and hope. It is the energy of all relationship and it connects us to our embodied selves. The empathetic sharing of any pursuit with another person helps us understand what is not shared. Hence differences become less threatening as we are empowered to affirm all persons in our lives, and to see through the faint, fearful, broken heart of patriarchy.

In *Pornography and Silence* Susan Griffin describes Eros as the basic yearning for others and for self-discovery. Our deepest selves—our hearts—seek the intimate relationships toward which Eros lures us. To be in relationship with a changing world is to recognize, according to Griffin, that we are constantly changing. To choose domination and isolation is to deny Eros. However, Griffin acknowledges that the surrender to such a process is not an easy one. For she is aware of the damage we all carry. Surrender means recognizing that we are fragile and interdependent, subject to forces outside ourselves. To be such open selves is to be easily damaged, yet to be so is essential to healthy psychic survival. The reunion inside us of nature, of desire, of sensuality, of change, of darkness, of death, of vulnerability, of receptivity, and of the child in us are, for Griffin, the only way to become whole.

All power emerges from erotic power either, in life-giving form, from our acknowledgment of it and our ability to live in that understanding or, in destructive form, from the brokenheartedness that refuses to understand it. The erotic is the basis of being itself as the power of relationship, and all existence comes to be by virtue of connectedness, from atoms to the cosmos. Erotic power is the fundamental power of existence—as-a-relational-process. Metaphysically, nothing can exist without the connections that make it what it continues to become through space and time. Connection is the basic power of all existence, the root of life. The power of being/becoming is erotic power. Erotic power leads us, through the human heart, toward life-giving cocreating.

Erotic power, unlike control, domination, or authority (which we believe, self-deceptively, we can possess), cannot be fixed or clung to because it cannot be controlled, won, possessed, or created. We are born in it as we are born in the physical structures of the universe. Erotic power is the very foundation of life and the source of energy for human selves that compels us to search for the whole of life. This power affirms, creates, and is recreated in human existence by heart. As the foundation of heart, erotic power compels us toward compassion, collective action, integration, self-acceptance, and self-reflective memory in our critical recollection of the past.

But as brokenheartedness poignantly reveals, our patriarchal society can cut us off from the life-giving power of the erotic. Patriarchal ideologies require that we split off parts of ourselves so that we may be self-righteously "correct" and good, no matter what the cause—feminism, Christianity, civil rights, liberation, and so on. Such a self-righteous split divides self and world so that psychological self-examination and personal responsibility are set against the political realities of institutionalized oppression. The personal and political—the therapeutic and ethical—are sharply divided. Such polarization tends to set distinctions and differences as oppositions, heightening conflict while making it difficult for us to recognize or integrate conflict.

In "The Way of All Ideology" Susan Griffin calls for us to relearn thinking.[5] Our reflection must explore self and world with a desire to integrate. Without the integration of sensation, feeling, and thinking, our dialogues with each other and the shape of our efforts toward liberation will be imprisoned behind ideologies that erase our sometimes contradictory and paradoxical experiences. She suggests that in both the psychological and political quests for understanding are hope for changing the world for the better and a profound acknowledgement of our own woundedness and the damaged state of the world. Griffin sees in both perspectives a passionate desire to heal suffering and a forgiving vision of the world. In the desire to understand and to rejoin what is broken, they seek for the whole.

And this desire to know is perhaps finally a way to loving. For the desire to know deeply all that is, as part of our outrage over injustice and suffering, accepts the truth, the whole and compassionate being.[6]

THE HEART OF THE UNIVERSE

Out of our acceptance of the whole and compassionate being, new awarenesses emerge that lead us to a knowing from the heart that transforms worlds. Elizabeth Janeway speaks of messages from the self's interior, of dream, fantasy, and myth—messages of feeling in which the realm of play becomes magic in its transformative capacity. In this realm, images well up from experience and emotional need and communicate what is puzzling, frightening, or challenging and what has not been satisfied by events in the outer world.

> Dreams give us happy endings to desires when the world won't; and sometimes they also hint slyly why it is that the world refuses to grant our wishes. Thus they provide practice for ordering and reordering the inner images of reality.[7]

In so-called primitive societies, trances are important as a source of healing and wisdom. In trances spirits which dwell in the concrete world of reality—ancestral spirits, the recently dead, nature deities, tricksters, and other cosmic powers that touch life—can be called upon for messages of wisdom, healing, and foresight. The messages of shamanistic trances

---

5. In *Signs* 7.3 (1982) 641–60.

6. Ibid., 660.

7. Elizabeth Janeway, *Powers of the Weak* (New York: Knopf, 1980) 66.

are often playfully symbolic, vague, and allusive, requiring both intense focused concentration by the medium and wise interpretation. The shift from trance to dream, from a more conscious awareness of the magic of the play space and memory, to a more unconscious state may represent a shift from egalitarian societies with horizontal cosmologies to male-dominant societies with vertical cosmologies and more distant, alienated gods. In "Patriarchal Revolution in Ancient Japan," Robert Ellwood argues that the ancient shamaness trance spirituality of prepatriarchal Japan was replaced with a male priest-centered religion in which gods sent messages in dreams.[8] Marjorie Shostak in *Nisa* and Richard Katz in *Boiling Energy: Community Healing Among the Kalahari Kung* describe the egalitarian healing trances of the !Kung, trances that bind and heal the entire community. But our society has lost its capacity to listen to trances or dreams.[9]

Our technocratic, rationally oriented society has great difficulty dealing with dreams and the shamanistic magic of mythic images, except to relegate them to fiercely rational psychological analysis, or to images as art. In rejecting anything that might smack of supernaturalism, we draw our truth concepts predominantly from cognitive awareness. The literalism and reductionism of scientific thinking and its reliance on objective truth results in a one-to-one fusion of self and world, cause and effect, predictability and control. The self disappears into its objective observation of objects and pretends it has removed itself. This outmoded but still common concept of objectivity in Western thought assumes that a neutral place exists from which an observer, whose presence does not interfere with the event taking place, can tell what "really" occurred. This assumption of objectivity grounds the scientific method and is used to subordinate ideas that overtly take an advocacy position. This myth of objectivity has been challenged in Marxist, feminist, and process thought and by relativity physics.

Many cultures, especially those that the intellectual West has called "primitive," and that are more relationally oriented, delve far deeper into the subjective realms of dream and magic and give these realms external reality. Awake, we ignore the richness of subjective connections to others and the play space provided by multivalent images because we tend toward logical linearity. Hence we lose connections to our own creative insights. Yet, as Janeway reminds us, "each of us civilized human beings has to expect to spend some hours of every day in a world where emotional linkage operates with vivid actuality."[10]

The distinction between the imaginative, interactive play space of myths, feelings, and dreams and the linear, cognitive orientation of our technocratic culture can also be seen in the difference in orientation to reality between oral and literate cultures, a difference that can be discerned in the development from foraging societies to advanced agrarian empires. Gerda Lerner notes the political implications of the development of writing in

---

8. In *Journal of Feminist Studies in Religion* 2 (Fall 1986) 23–38.

9. Marjorie Shostak, *Nisa: The Life and Words of a !Kung Woman*; and Richard Katz, *Boiling Energy: Community Healing among the Kalahari Kung* (Cambridge: Harvard University Press, 1984).

10. Janeway, *Powers of the Weak*, 80.

agrarian societies as it allowed greater control for an elite class and a different orientation to time and space. Writing strengthened the leadership of elite classes by giving them greater control over governance and sacred knowledge. The gradual cultural shifts involved in writing moved people toward a worship of the power of abstraction, which can become a means of controlling illiterate masses, and of a more linear orientation to time and a visual orientation to space. Through abstraction the observable facts of female reproduction can be transmuted into a symbolic creativity of the word to the concept of the "creative spirit of the universe." Without such a move, exclusive monotheism is impossible. With such a move, large numbers of people can be persuaded to imagine and follow an abstract, more unilateral orientation to reality, as a writer can be detached from social context and exercise a great deal of control over composition and idea.

In *The Oral and Written Gospel*, a discussion of oral culture and written canon, Werner Kelber claims that in oral cultures people have access to the same memory capacities as their leaders and story tellers.[11] The people's participation in and cocreation of political and sacred knowledge is well developed. Oral language is personal, holistic in its involvement of persons, and resonant interactively among participants. Sacred knowledge is not made true through its historical reliability, "but on the authority of the speaker and by the reception of the hearer."[12]

While we cannot escape belonging to a literate society, I believe we must pay closer attention to the differences between an oral and a literate orientation to reality. For oral culture allows a multifaceted, flexible orientation to language and reality that is highly interactive, contextual, and transformative. Language carries complex feeling; time is cyclical, constantly doubling back on itself; space is multisensory. We cannot return to oral culture, for we are too thoroughly literate and historical. A more accurate sense of history is an important element in understanding our own patriarchal past. History is the primary way our society has chosen to understand its past. However, the oral roots of human society may be an important dimension of ourselves, our society, and the sacred.

This attention to the oral is especially crucial if we want to understand human memory and spirituality. Attention must be paid to oral roots both in a historical sense and in a psychological sense. The play space of human selves is developed in an early oral environment. Literacy develops out of our earlier oral experiences and the linguistic skills we learn there. Its roots are interpersonal, interactive, cyclical, multisensory, and contextual. Play space becomes attenuated when external control enters the picture. When imagination is too literal, when its creations are understood to correspond one to one with reality, it shrinks. Hence a too cognitive, too literal, and too alienated orientation to reality reduces its spiritual power, its erotic power. The flexibility of

---

11. Werner H. Kelber, *The Oral and Written Gospel: The Hermeneutics of Speaking and Writing in the Synoptic Tradition, Mark, Paul and Q* (Philadelphia: Fortress, 1983).

12. Ibid., 71.

oral cultures parallels the capacity to play. This fluid world of play, where the self interacts with its world and creates itself and reality anew, is, I believe, a crucial aspect of the mysterious whirling realm of erotic power.

As the dancing mystery of the sacred, the magic of connection is the confirmation of divine presence in human life. This power affirms, creates, and is recreated by heart. It is the very foundation of our lives and the center of an energy that compels us to search for the whole of life, which is its fullest ongoing incarnation.

Erotic power is incarnate in heart. It binds the life-giving, healing heart of ourselves with each other, if we possess the courage to claim it. For courage itself wells from the heart. And heart enhances erotic power through our connections to others. Searching for connections is the heart's search, the search to heal suffering and brokenness.

Heart lives in erotic power, the power of our loving each other at the depths of our being. In expanding the feminist concept of erotic power to include its sacred dimensions, I am developing its theological implications as the incarnation of divine love. The presence and revelation of erotic power is the divine dimension of human existence. It grows and moves with us as the resilient, flexible vulnerability that reveals our existence in relationship and our cocreation of each other. Erotic power is with us at the origins of our own concrete lives and sustains us lifelong.

In the beginning is the divine Eros, embodied in all being. As the incarnate, life-giving power of the universe, divine erotic power is the Heart of the Universe. In *Omnipotence and Other Theological Mistakes* Charles Hartshorne suggests we move beyond theological analogies of parent-child relationships to the more intimate and accurate analogy of mind and body as descriptive of the divine relationship to the world.[13] But the connection of mind to rationality and logos and its history of dualistic separation from the body limits the usefulness of the mind/body analogy, even when it is explained in the nondualistic, relational terms of process thought. Imagining the divine presence in the world as Heart leads us to a greater sense of the whole of life as sacred.

Seeking for Eros, according to Griffin, leads us to the sacred. We become part of an ineffable ecstasy that binds us to the whirling mystery within ourselves, to the deepest unspeakable mystery of the sacred. But to be open to the creative insights of erotic power, we must be open to connection, to feeling, to sensuality, and to the play spaces of the fullness of experience, to images, dreams, myths, and magic. Janeway recognizes such openness as powerful in its political implications for transforming society.

> To change ourselves, to change relationships, to change the world–all these work together and can't be separated, and all of them will supply us with new data, as we update our chart . . . I like to imagine . . . a few features dating back to a time when play and poetry and metaphor were not excluded from serious business . . . let us . . . work toward a map of uncertain prediction connecting to memory, a map of promise, a map of possibility, of an unbounded future that will not be limited by an end.[14]

13. Charles Hartshorne, *Omnipotence and Other Theological Mistakes* (Albany: State University of New York Press, 1984).

14. Janeway, *Powers of the Weak*, 321.

This unbounded future begins with Eros.

Eros is what Alfred North Whitehead in *Adventures of Ideas* calls the divine incarnation that moves us into the future.[15] He describes Eros as that which urges the human soul to a synthesis of a "new fact which is the Appearance woven out of the old and the new—a compound of reception and anticipation, which in turn passes into the future."[16] In such a process, Whitehead urges that all human experience, not simply rational, cognitive thinking, be explored for truth. Without Eros—the divine yearning for playful becoming-new unities within the individual cannot emerge for the future.

The spiritual quest is an attunement to the graceful moments of life, according to Bernard Meland in *Fallible Forms and Symbols*.[17] He insists on culture and actual experience as resources for understanding. He criticizes the quest for rational certainty in our culture as that which cuts us away from an attunement to the depth of human experience, an attunement he calls "appreciative awareness." Meland insists *"we live more profoundly than we can think . . . even when we address ourselves in the profoundest way possible to the issues of our existence."*[18]

Meland believes the task of theology is to dwell on the margins of our structures of existence, margins with "an unmanageable depth of grace and freedom that opens into a relational ground" and exceeds the reach of concepts, concepts which become false gods. To create life anew and to relate to a larger world requires receptivity toward the depth of lived experience, which is far more than the technical, critical, and intellectual. Under the guise of knowing, rational thinking can project limited and fallible symbols upon the "more than we can think." For Meland, a sole reliance on reason is divisive and alienating because it demands allegiance to one strain of thought or an ideology. He calls for a more sensitive

> encounter with realities at the edge of our being . . . In a world of contextual meaning, dissonance takes on the import of qualitative distinctions which, in themselves, carry values to be cherished and sustained . . . Such dissonance can mean a readiness to live together with differences in the interest of retaining, cherishing, and hopefully participating to some degree in the complexity of meaning and value which these . . . differences offer.[19]

Meland, like Janeway and Griffin, is calling for religious life to be lived in the play space, in the realm of imaginative open interaction with the world.

Another process thinker, Henry Nelson Wieman develops an extensive argument for the primacy of connection in *The Source of Human Good*.[20] Wieman believes the only reliable basis for absolute good in human existence is relationship. Good is grounded in our deep awareness of others, our willingness to participate in mutual transformation, the expansion of quality, the increase of meaning that comes from increasing connectedness,

---

15. Alfred North Whitehead, *Adventures of Ideas* (New York: Free Press, 1967).

16. Ibid., 275.

17. Bernard Meland, *Fallible Forms and Symbols* (Philadelphia: Fortress, 1976).

18. Ibid., 82.

19. Ibid., 130, 198.

20. Henry Nelson Wieman, *The Source of Human Good* (Carbondale: Southern Illinois University Press, 1967).

and the deepening communion among all who participate in relationship. Because no single person can achieve such good alone, the good that emerges is suprahuman. The good that includes but moves beyond our own individual existence to become sacred emerges from the risks each of us takes to be vulnerable to relationships. Mutual support, intercommunication, and sensitive openness, the only avenues of divine power that create good, require enormous risks.

Wieman argues vehemently that no appeal to eternity or transcendent power can save us. If we cannot develop a faith that makes sense of our most concrete, puzzling, and problematic experiences, we have no redemptive faith. Wieman calls for a radical redirection of human devotion to the deepest sources of our connectedness that generate and recreate ongoing relationships. Hence, like the feminists cited above, Wieman is calling for a demystification of faith. Through it, we can come to understand what leads us to spiritual life.

We are led, according to Wieman, by signs, the shorthand codes that communicate experience and expand our capacity for connection to all that is. Wieman's notion of signs is similar to the idea of play images and to Janeway's map into the future. Signs connect us through our imagination to worlds beyond our immediate apprehension. Signs reveal "the secrets of many hearts."[21] In doing so, signs participate in the life of conscious awareness and take on richer qualitative meanings.

> As these meanings form a rich network of interconnective events comprehending all that is happening in the world, this universe becomes spiritual . . . It becomes more deeply and pervasively meaningful. It becomes the house of the human spirit . . . Events cease to be material things merely and become a language, a prophecy, a song.[22]

Wieman claims as long as signs remain flexible and move in relationships (they remain playful) and not fixed in final form, they perform their spiritual function. These signs point us to the deepest sources of our connectedness, to heart.

But an open play space can only happen if some element of grace is maintained in a life. We are vulnerable, fragile. The self at times may not be able to open such a space if its world will not help create it. Inner conflicts that paralyze the self indicate brokenheartedness. The conflicts of a broken heart have the potential of ultimate self-destruction, but, as the heart struggles to surface, the destruction can be seen as a sign of the heart's presence. Similarly, the revolutions and battles of groups of oppressed people to free themselves from tyranny, even when they hurt the oppressed themselves, are clear signs of the presence of the fundamental human need for love and dignity, for right relationships. If we turn deaf ears to such outcries of pain and numb ourselves to such destruction, we will miss important clues to how we can heal such brokenness and reclaim heart.

Reproducing patriarchal family structures and seeing power as the possession of a self or group over and against others raise serious questions about sanctifying, in a written canon, such oppressive divine images and theological

---

21. Ibid., 22.

22. Ibid., 23.

doctrines. Christian theology has done so, both through almost exclusively masculine symbols such as father, king, lord, and savior through theological doctrines of omnipotence and divine *apatheia*, judgment, and reason. At times, unconventional use of male-dominant images has shattered the hierarchal hold by a transmutation of the image into its opposite, for example, when the messianic king becomes a servant. However, the doctrine of omnipotence, by connection to such images, has tended to reinforce their hierarchical, controlling aspects. While each of these images conveys something of our understanding of authority, unilateral power, and selfless giving, they are a patriarchal legacy, symbol systems of hierarchical and oppressive societies. And the images have, I believe, reinforced the dynamics of mutuality sustained by paternalism. They have not often brought us to transforming insights that lead to erotic power because they tend to reinforce patriarchal structures of power as dominance and authority and love as obedience.

Christianity is afflicted with a hierarchical view of power that undercuts its understanding of love in its fullest incarnation—that we are all part of one another and cocreate each other at the depths of our being. In recognizing how we have been afflicted with the broken heart of patriarchy, we can begin to see the territories of connection beyond patriarchal powers. Heart is the guide into those new territories; erotic power is the energy of incarnate love.

Commentary

Marit A. Trelstad

In *Journeys by Heart: A Christology of Erotic Power* (1988), Rita Nakashima Brock writes: "As the dancing mystery of the sacred, the magic of connection is the confirmation of divine presence in human life ... It is the very foundation of our lives and the center of an energy that compels us to search for the whole of life, which is its fullest ongoing incarnation. ...Searching for connections is the heart's search, the search to heal suffering and brokenness."[1] This quotation illustrates three main themes which are present in Brock's written work to date: creative collaboration and relationship, an emphasis on healing and a lived experience of salvation, and a persistent concern that theological reflection never be disconnected from embodied experience.

Throughout *Journeys by Heart*, she emphasizes erotic embodied love, divine and human; it is a sacred love that pays attention to the particulars of a person's experience and builds healing relationships and connections. This incarnational emphasis is a hallmark of her past two

1. Rita Nakashima Brock, *Journeys by Heart: A Christology of Erotic Power* (New York: Crossroad, 1988) 45.

decades wherein several of her books have contributed to the theological categories of Christology and soteriology. These include *Journeys by Heart*; *Proverbs of Ashes: Violence, Redemptive Suffering and the Search for What Saves Us* (2001); and *Saving Paradise: How Christianity Traded Love of the World for Crucifixion and Empire* (2008).

Before delving into her work in detail, it is important to note that Brock does not self-identify as a process theologian even though she here uses the work of Whitehead and Hartshorne in conversation with feminist theorists to explain heart and Eros. Her non-dualistic and relational theology is, of course, compatible with the commitments of process theology. For process theologians, Brock's interpretation of Christic power in *Journeys by Heart* certainly advances the development of a process Christology.

Across her publications, Brock maintains broad understandings of incarnation and salvation, which include but do not begin or end with the person of Jesus Christ. An example of this comes from *Journeys by Heart* where Brock emphasizes the interrelationship between Jesus of Nazareth and the community. The power of healing and salvation are ultimately centered in the Christa/Community in which Jesus participates. Instead of being the lone hero, Jesus's power is interlaced and interdependent with the power of those around him, particularly in the Gospel of Mark. Using Brock's imagery, Jesus is like the visible whitecap on the ocean swell of incarnational, erotic power present in the community, and it is collaborative Eros rather than singular, individual action which saves.

In keeping with this commitment to creative mutuality, all of Brock's books after *Journeys by Heart* have been fully coauthored texts. While process theologian John B. Cobb Jr. has also co-written books, Brock's career is unique in its embodiment of feminist commitments to collaborative relationship. This novel approach to scholarship in theology also challenges patriarchal conceptions of hierarchical authority and power. Indeed, beyond the possible exception of Brock's co-authors, there is no other feminist theologian to date whose work has been so thoroughly and intentionally collaborative. She has worked alongside Susan Brooks Thistlethwaite in *Casting Stones: Prostitution and Liberation in Asia and the United States* (1996). And has co-authored two volumes with Rebecca Ann Parker: *Proverbs of Ashes* and *Saving Paradise*. In addition to this, she has coedited at least two volumes: *Setting the Table: Women in Theological Conversation* (1995) and *Off the Menu: Asian and Asian North American Women's Religion and Theology* (2007).

From *Journeys by Heart* to *Saving Paradise*, Brock has focused on healing and a lived experience of salvation. On the way to this goal, she has worked to expose the theological and social ideas that foster and justify disconnection, domination, brokenness and violence. She has challenged several traditional Christian doctrines by examining their actual impact on human life. In particular, she is concerned when beloved doctrines justify, reinforce and produce pain rather than connectedness and healing. She insightfully points out places of collision between feminist insights and Christian theology. At the same time, she works constructively to transform foundational Christian doctrines from a feminist perspective and a lived commitment to countering multiple forms of oppression.

Journeys by Heart deconstructs notions of Jesus' singular authority and power in favor of a non-hierarchical understanding of cooperative power. Where patriarchal power demeans and destroys, relational power heals and saves. In *Saving Paradise*, her theological work comes full circle. She and Parker argue that the Western Christian tradition has come to affirm that salvation comes through violence and death, both Jesus' and others. In response, they claim that early Christians emphasized paradise, baptismal waters and healing as the central images of salvation. They uncover a healing orthodoxy running deeper than the patriarchal theological tradition that too often conflated redemption with the violence of domination.

Lastly, from the inception of her work, Brock displays a passionate commitment to grounding all theological work in the concerns of real, embodied people and communities. She has steadily drawn our attention to the impact of patriarchy and patriarchal theology on the bodies, hearts and minds of all women and Asian/Asian American women in particular. Throughout her publications, she has addressed patriarchal and feminist understandings of the self in relation, family patterns of brokenness and domestic abuse, the Global Sex Market, and the connections between Christianity and violent empire.

STUDY QUESTIONS

1. Define erotic power, according to Brock. What limits erotic power? What fosters or nurtures it? What roles do play and imagination have in the erotic?

2. How is erotic power connected to our experience of the divine or sacred? Through what avenues does one experience erotic power or the divine, according to Brock?

3. Can you think of examples from everyday life that illustrate the power of hierarchical domination versus the erotic power of connection, relationship, and creativity that Brock mentions?

4. How would this understanding of power affect one's overall theological claims about God's power or Jesus' power in relation to humans?

10 Ecofeminism and Nature

SALLIE MCFAGUE

Sallie McFague is Distinguished Theologian-in-Residence at Vancouver School of Theology and Carpenter Professor of Theology Emerita from Vanderbilt University Divinity School. McFague earned degrees from Smith College, Yale Divinity School, and Yale University. Her contributions to feminist theology range from metaphorical theology to ecological theology, which constitute the methodological and substantive focus of her work toward ecojustice in theology. The excerpt is taken from *The Body of God* (1993). In the selection, McFague constructs an alternative to both the classical organic model and the mechanistic model of God and the God-world relationship, and she proposes that the world as God's body is a promising model for centering nature and transforming how humans relate to nature. Her model of God and the God-world relationship is a process-agential model.

Excerpt from *The Body of God: An Ecological Theology*

EMBODIED KNOWING, EMBODIED DOING

ATTENTION EPISTEMOLOGY, THE KIND of knowing that focuses on *embodied differences,* is illustrated by feminist epistemology. Probably the most widespread criticism that feminists of many different persuasions have made against Western thought is that, while masquerading as universal human thought, it is really from the perspective of and for the benefit of men. This perspective is seldom acknowledged; in fact, innocence and ignorance join hands to strengthen the case of "objectivity." The sincere belief by the dominant voice (in the West, the voice of white, affluent, educated, straight males) that it speaks for everyone, makes it all the more convincing. The cloaked or masked character of essentialist thinking (thinking that merges all differences into one essence) must be, feminists claim, revealed for what it is: concrete, situated, particular, and limited. In other words, it is *embodied* thinking, as is all thought, including, of course, the criticisms by the feminists themselves.[1] Since time immemorial

---

1. For a general treatment of the relationship of knowledge and embodiment, one that insists that concepts have a bodily basis, as seen, for instance, in our tendency to structure the world in cycles (hours, days, weeks, years) and from cycles in our bodies (heartbeat, breathing, digestion, menstruation, waking and sleeping, circulation), see Mark Johnson, *The Body in the Mind: The Bodily Basis of Meaning, Imagination, and Reason* (Chicago: University of Chicago Press, 1987). Feminists would claim, however, that such a treatment deals with the body in a universalist, essentialist way, since no gender, class, racial, or other context of embodiment is considered in the analysis.

women have been identified with the body and, by extension, with nature, and while there are some feminists who focus on the female body as the primary context for thought and action, this focus can result in a new essentialism.[2] The feminists who have become increasingly conscious of the ways in which, within feminism itself, essentialism has cloaked the real embodied *differences* among women will be more important for our project, since we are developing ways of thinking and doing that underscore differences among bodies (as well as the special ways they are united). A case study will be instructive.

The contemporary women's movement began in the 1960s principally as a white, Western, middle-class phenomenon concerned with liberation from the particular forms of oppression these women experienced. But the movement was slow to realize the depths of its own universalist thinking, even as it increasingly criticized the social constructions of gender by the dominant male institutions of Western culture. Initially, feminists spoke from a position "as women," which assumes a monolithic voice. (Often still one hears the weary question. What is the women's point of view on this issue? as if there were *one*. The comparable question, What is the men's point of view? is never asked, for we assume that men have many, varied, different perspectives on issues—in other words, that they are the full human beings.) Increasingly, however, feminists have come to realize the radical differences that separate women, one of the most painful in this country being the history of relationships between white and African-American women during slavery when, among other things, white women were often mistresses over African-American women, who were in turn mothers by the husbands of their mistresses.[3] As recent feminists have become aware, *embodiment* is a complex notion, and it is no longer sufficient to speak of the "oppression of women." The way that a poor, Hispanic, lesbian woman experiences each of these forms of devalued embodiment in our culture is not simply additive; she is not poor *and* Hispanic *and* lesbian, but is herself all three at the same time and each qualifies and changes the others (if, for instance, she were poor but white and straight, her experience would be different).[4]

These feminists say that we need to overcome both "somatophobia" and "pletherophobia," disdain for the body and fear of different kinds of bodies.[5] These are issues about bodies that refer to devalued tasks done by those with particular kinds of bodies, as well as devalued differences associated with particular bodies. In our culture, for instance, men's work is associated with the mind and women's with the body; hence, we favor jobs requiring mental activity over those requiring bodily activity, especially those directly concerned with the body, such as cleaning up after it, feeding it, washing its clothes (the

2. This criticism has been leveled against some of the French feminist deconstructionists as well as against Mary Daly. For one such treatment, see Chris Weeden, *Feminist Practice and Poststructuralist Theory* (Oxford: Blackwell, 1987).

3. For a discussion of this phenomenon, see Barbara Hilkert Andolsen, *"Daughters of Jefferson, Daughters of Bootblacks": Racism and American Feminism* (Macon, GA: Mercer University Press, 1986).

4. Elizabeth V. Spelman, *Inessential Woman: Problems of Exclusion in Feminist Thought* (Boston: Beacon, 1988) 129–30.

5. Spelman, *Inessential Woman*, 126–27.

so-called dirty work). Moreover, body work is disdained because it is associated with women and certain races and classes; white, upper-class males seldom do it (except at the most elite level of clothes designer and chef). Our culture not only disdains the body but also fears the differences associated with certain kinds of bodies (such as those with wombs, frizzy hair, or dark skin). Our culture devalues these bodies as not simply different but inferior (in contrast to bodies without wombs or with straight hair and light skin). Another strategy of pletherophobia is to elide or pass over the differences in a well-intentioned search for equality; if bodies, in all their differences, are seen as the cause of discrimination, then the best strategy is to eliminate them, become sex-blind and color-blind.[6] But of course what emerges once again is "woman," the generic, nonhistorical, nonexisting essential woman, who is no particular woman.

While there are problems with radical particularity and difference without some forms of interconnectedness, recent feminist analysis and critique of essentialist thinking makes a substantial contribution to our organic model. It helps to remind us that the particular, concrete, situated *differences* among human beings, who at the same time exist together within the body of the planet, must be starting points for knowing and doing, for embodiment is radically particular.

We have been highlighting attention epistemology (and feminist epistemology as an example of it) as a kind of knowing and doing intrinsic to the organic model that emerges from the common creation story. Embodied knowing and doing rest not upon the one ideal body (the white, fit and able, male, human body) that would absorb all its parts and all differences into itself for its own well-being. Rather, embodied knowing and doing should rest, for all intents and purposes, upon the infinite number of bodies in all their differences that constitute the universe. That backdrop serves as the relativizing context for the more operable notion of the forms of embodiment on our planet: *all* bodies are included, but we can conceive of only a finite number and, in our daily lives, interact with many fewer still. But to be able to learn from and guide one's behavior through attention to others—to have an attention sensibility—one needs only a few others, perhaps only one other, for each one, in its own unique, different embodiment, is the *other*. If we were to see *one* other with full attention, that is, loving it, acknowledging that this something other than oneself is really real, then it might follow that we would have to acknowledge the reality of many, perhaps all, others. On such a basis we might build an ecological ethic—a way of being in the world that respects the intrinsic value of the many different beings that comprise our planet—and begin to see as well where we human beings, as particular kinds of beings with special gifts and limitations, fit into the scheme of things.

. . .

SPIRIT AND BODY

My essay undertakes such a task, although with a profound debt to the organic and agential models of Teilhard and process theology. The agential model preserves transcendence, while the organic model underscores immanence. Alone, the

---

6. Spelman, *Inessential Woman*, 128.

agential model overemphasizes the transcendent power and freedom of God at the expense of the world. Alone, the organic model tends to collapse God and the world, denying the freedom and individuality of both. But if the model were that God is related to the world as spirit is to body, perhaps the values of both the agential and organic models could be preserved.

Two related issues, however, face us immediately. The first is the suitability of *any* personal language for God as being compatible with contemporary science. The second, assuming that we can provide reasons for retaining agential language, is the *kind* of personal imagery that is most appropriate. The dilemma set by these issues is an acute one: the Hebrew and Christian traditions are profoundly and, I would argue, indelibly agential; yet postmodern science, as we have seen, does not appear to permit any purpose or agency apart from local causation. This dilemma has caused some theologians to retreat from personal language for God except in worship.[7] The implication is that personal language does not really refer to God but is necessary for liturgical purposes, while the proper way to speak of God in the context of postmodern science is impersonally. One unfortunate result of this position is a willingness to continue to use traditional metaphors for God such as God as lord and father (since they are "only" liturgical images), without working toward more appropriate ones.

This approach permits, I believe, too strong a control of science over theology. If it can be shown that *all* personal metaphors are incompatible with postmodern science, the case becomes stronger. But since little reconstructive work on such models has been attempted, the images in question are traditional ones, not necessarily all personal ones. I agree that the monarchical, triumphalistic, patriarchal imagery for God is impossible to square with an evolutionary, ecological, cosmological framework. Even some of the more intimate models—God as mother (and father), lover, and friend—need to be balanced by other, less anthropocentric ones.[8] But are all personal models worthless, discordant, incongruous from the perspective of contemporary science? Moreover, if we do discard them all and speak of God only or principally in impersonal terms, can we any longer pretend that we still belong within the Western religious paradigm? Finally, is not the refusal to imagine God in personal terms a gesture in the direction of disembodiment: *we* are embodied agents, and is it not therefore natural and appropriate, as the outermost contemporary

---

7. See James M. Gustafson, *Ethics from a Theocentric Perspective*, vol. 1, *Theology and Ethics* (Chicago: University of Chicago Press, 1981) 179–89. See also Gordon Kaufman's critique of Gustafson's position ("How Is *God* to Be Understood in a Theocentric Ethics?" in *James M. Gustafson's Theocentric Ethics: Interpretation and Assessments*, ed. Harlan K. Beckley and Charles M. Swezey [Macon, GA: Mercer University Press, 1988] 13–35), as well as Kaufman's own highly nuanced discussion of nonreified uses of personal metaphors for God (see especially chaps. 22 and 23, *In Face of Mystery: A Constructive Theology* [Cambridge: Harvard University Press, 1993]). Although the positions of Gustafson and Kaufman are substantially different, both are wary of agential personalism and neither suggests new personal metaphors in place of the traditional ones.

8. This present work is meant, in part, to balance the limitations of my use of these metaphors in *Models of God*. However, there is a basic compatibility and complementarity between the model of spirit and those of mother, lover, and friend.

evolutionary phylum, to imagine our creator "in our image"?

The major model we are investigating in depth is the combined agential-organic one of the universe (world) as God's body, a body enlivened and empowered by the divine spirit. We have dealt in some detail with the organic aspect of the model, the universe as God's body, but what of the agential or personal aspect, the spirit? To begin framing an answer to this question, we need to start with ourselves as the concrete, embodied beings we are. We are embodied personal agents, and if we are not to be surds or outcasts in the world, we need to imagine God's relationship to the world in a way that includes us, that makes us feel at home. Mechanistic, impersonal models exclude us; personal, organic ones include us. If the history of the universe and especially the evolutionary history of our planet makes it clear that we do, in fact, belong here and that evolution has resulted in self-conscious beings, then does it not make sense to imagine the relationship between God and the world in a manner that is continuous with that evolutionary history, especially if, as we shall suggest, there is a way of modeling personal agency that also touches one of the deepest traditions of Christian thought?

That tradition is of God as spirit—not Holy Ghost, which suggests the unearthly and the disembodied, nor initially the Holy Spirit, which has been focused largely on human beings and especially the followers of Christ, but the spirit of God, the divine wind that "swept over the face of the waters" prior to creation, the life-giving breath given to all creatures, and the dynamic movement that creates, recreates, and transcreates throughout the universe.[9] Spirit, as wind, breath, life is the most basic and most inclusive way to express centered embodiment. All living creatures, not just human ones, depend upon breath. Breath also knits together the life of animals and plants, for they are linked by the exchange of oxygen and carbon dioxide in each breath inhaled and exhaled. Breath is a more immediate and radically dependent way to speak of life than even food or water, for we literally live from breath to breath and can survive only a few minutes without breathing. Our lives are enclosed by two breaths—our first when we emerge from our mother's womb and our last when we "give up the ghost" (spirit).

Spirit is a wide-ranging, multidimensional term with many meanings

9. Even a very brief survey from an encyclopedia makes this point. In the Hebrew Scriptures, the Spirit of God is active in history, prophecy, and many other ways, but especially as the source of life: "As the divine power is evident in a special way in the bringing forth and the maintenance of life, the Spirit of God is considered as the source of life (Gen. 1:2, 2:7, 6:3; Ps. 33:6, 104:29f, 146:4; Job 12:10, 27:3, 34:14f; Ezek. 37:7-10)" (article on the Holy Spirit, in *Encyclopedia of Theology: The Concise "Sacramentu Mundi,"* ed. Karl Rahner [New York: Seabury, 1975] 643). In the New Testament, the redeemed community is constituted by the Holy Spirit. Christ is conceived through the Spirit, equipped with the Spirit at baptism, and driven into the desert by the Spirit: "The Spirit is the moving power behind every activity of Jesus. The opposition of men [sic] to the Spirit is called by Christ the unpardonable sin." Christ promised the Spirit in his absence and it was given at Pentecost: "The pentecostal outpouring of the Spirit is the beginning of the communication of the Spirit which continues through all time." In Paul one finds a wide field of Spirit theology too complex to define. The Spirit is active in everyday life, is the animating principle of the church, and is especially connected with baptism and the life of the baptized as well as the pledge of eschatological fulfillment (*Encyclopedia of Theology*, 643).

built upon its physical base as the breath of life. We speak of a person's spirit, their vigor, courage, or strength; of team spirit, the collective energy of people at play; of the spirit of '76 or the spirit of Tiananmen Square, the vitality, grit, and resolution of a people banding together in a common cause to oppose oppression; of a spirited horse or the spirit of a sacred grove—animals, trees, and mountains can also have spirit.[10] All these connotations are possible because of the primary meaning of spirit as the breath of life: "Then the LORD God formed man [sic] from the dust of the ground and breathed into his nostrils the breath of life" (Gen 2:7). Bracketing the sexism of the Genesis 2 creation story, it nonetheless suggests the prime analogy of this essay: the dust of the universe enlivened by the breath of God. Each of us, and each and every other part of the body as well, owes our existence, breath by breath as we inhale and exhale, to God. We "live and move and have our being" in God (Acts 17:28). Indeed we do. That is, perhaps, the most basic confession that can be made: I owe my existence at its most fundamental level—the gift of my next breath—to God. God is my creator and recreator, the One who gives and renews my life, moment by moment, at its most basic, physical level. And so does everything else in creation also live, moment by moment, by the breath of God, says our model.

We are suggesting, then, that we think of God metaphorically as the spirit that is the breath, the life, of the universe, a universe that comes from God and could be seen as the body of God. Both of these terms, *spirit* and *body,* are metaphors: both refer properly to ourselves and other creatures and entities in our experience of the world. Neither describes God, for both are *back,* not *face,* terms. Nonetheless, even with these qualifications, questions abound. Let us look at a few of them. Why choose *spirit* rather than other personal, agential terms such as *self, mind, heart, will, soul,* and the like? Does spirit language for God make sense in terms of postmodern science and the Christian tradition? Does contemporary science substantiate such language, or does it accommodate or allow it? Can Christians use the model of God as embodied spirit, and, more pointedly, in a transcendent sky-God tradition, is it pantheistic? Does it collapse God and the world?

One reason for suggesting spirit as the way to speak of divine agency is that it undercuts anthropocentrism and promotes cosmocentrism. Only a human being has a mind or self, whereas spirit, while able to include mind and self, has a much broader range. Most attempts to use the body metaphor in regard to God rely on the analogy of mind/body: God relates to the world as the mind (self) relates to

---

10. Steven G. Smith, in his study of the concept of spirit, notes that there are two central traditions: one, connected with Hegel, which posits spirit in history and mind; the other, from Martin Buber, which sees spirit in nature and especially in relationships. The first tradition focuses on spirit as mind, the second on spirit as breath or life. See *The Concept of the Spiritual: An Essay in First Philosophy* (Philadelphia: Temple University Press, 1988). It is obviously the second tradition that an ecological theology relies upon, as it allows not only for continuity across all forms of life, but also for relationship among the diverse forms. Jürgen Moltmann makes a related point when he notes that definitions of human death either unite or dissociate us from other forms: if death is defined as "brain death," the focus is on the head, but if breath is the criterion of life, then life is located in the whole living body (*God in Creation: A New Theology of Creation and the Spirit of God* [San Francisco: Harper & Row, 1985] 255).

the body. Not only does this form of the analogy involve difficult, often dualistic, arguments concerning the mind/body correlation, but, just as important for our considerations, it implies that divine activity in relation to the world is primarily intellectual and controlling: God is Mind or Will.[11] This is an old, deep tradition in the Hebrew and Christian traditions as manifest in Wisdom and Logos theologies: God creates the universe as its orderer, as the One who gives it direction, limits, and purpose. The emphasis is on the work of the mind, the work of intelligence and control. It is precisely this concern that surfaces in the ancient

---

11. The literature on this analogy for God's action in the world is large and complex. A classic essay on embodiment within a nondualistic mind/body framework is P. E. Strawson's "Persons," in *Individuals: An Essay in Descriptive Metaphysics* (Garden City, NY: Doubleday-Anchor, 1963) 83–113. Theological positions range widely from Grace Jantzen's view of God's more or less total embodiment as a solution to both divine immanence and transcendence (*God's World, God's Body* [Philadelphia: Westminster, 1984]) to John Polkinghorne's rejection of divine embodiment as resulting in either God's tyranny over the world or capitulation to it (*Science and Providence: God's Interaction with the World* [Boston: New Science Library, 1989]). The tradition is full of examples of God's tyranny over the world, due to its refusal to consider any kind of embodiment, but God's absorption into the world is also a genuine problem if the classic organic model is operative. Thus, Thomas Tracy says that if we "construe our world as a single, functionally unified individual," then "to say that the world is God's body is to say that the processes unfolding in the universe are the processes of God's life, that God does not exist except in and through these processes" (*God's Action and Embodiment* [Grand Rapids: Eerdmans, 1984], 112). Our embodiment model attempts to avoid that collapse, while it also tries to avoid tyranny. Some other recent treatments of God's action in the world that radicalize both divine immanence and transcendence are the following: 1) Jay McDaniel's process relational panentheism, in which the world has some degree of independence, even as our bodies have some independence from our psyches, a view that sees both God and the world as agents and patients (*Of God and Pelicans: A Theology of Reverence for Life* [Louisville: Westminster John Knox, 1989]); 2) Arthur R. Peacocke's unitive mind/brain/body view with top-down (transcendent) as well as bottom-up (immanent) action: "Just as our human personal subjectivity (the sense of being an "I") is a unitive, unifying, centered influence on the conscious, willed activity of our bodies, and this is what characterizes personal agency, so God is here conceived as the unifying, unitive source and centred influence of the world's activity" (*Theology for a Scientific Age: Being and Becoming—Natural and Divine* [Oxford: Blackwell, 1990] 161); 3) Catherine Keller's claim that the "politics of individualism" and a "theology of sheer transcendence" are connected—that a view of the self as separated from others and the world underlies a view of God as "pure structure of reflexive selfhood," curved in upon the divine self and essentially unrelated to the world (*From a Broken Web: Separatism, Sexism and Self* [Boston: Beacon, 1986], 37–43); 4) Gordon Kaufman's reconstruction of divine immanence and transcendence in terms of biological and cultural historical evolution, a view that, while not using the embodiment model, speaks of God as "the serendipitous cosmic process" in a way that at the same time preserves the mystery and transcendence of God, since God is beyond all our constructions as their "ultimate point of reference" (*In Face of Mystery*, chap. 19). What all of these attempts (including my own) to speak of divine action in the world have in common is the desire to avoid occasional or interventionist divine action while stressing the continuity and thoroughness—but non-controlling and non-deterministic—character of the action. The sensibility behind this perspective was well expressed in 1889 by Aubrey Moore: 'Those who oppose the notion of evolution in defence of a 'continued intervention' of God seem to have failed to notice that *a theory of occasional intervention implies as its correlative a theory of ordinary absence*" (as quoted by Arthur R. Peacocke in *Religion and Public Policy*, ed. Frank T. Birtel [New York: Crossroad, 1987] 32). See also Owen Thomas's helpful anthology of a variety of theological positions on divine action (*God's Activity in the World*, AAR Studies in Religion 31 [Atlanta: Scholars, 1983], and Barbour's critique of various contemporary positions (*Religion in an Age of Science*, chap. 9, "God and Nature").

enterprise of natural theology: the need to answer the questions of why and how. But a spirit theology suggests another possibility: that God is not primarily the orderer and controller of the universe but its source and empowerment, the breath that enlivens and energizes it. The spirit perspective takes seriously the fecundity, diversity, range, and complexity of life and of life-supporting systems. It does not claim that the divine mind is the cause of what evolutionary theory tells us can have only local causes; rather, it suggests that we think of these local causes as enlivened and empowered by the breath of God. A spirit theology focuses attention not on how and why creation occurred either in the beginning or over the evolutionary aeons of time, but on the rich variety of living forms that have been and are *now* present on our planet. The breath of God enlivening each and every entity in the body of the universe turns our attention to a theology of nature, a theology concerned with the relationship of God and our living, breathing planet. The principal reason, then, for preferring spirit to alternative possibilities is that it underscores the connection between God and the world as not primarily the Mind that orders, controls, and directs the universe, but as the Breath that is the source of its life and vitality. The connection is one of *relationship* at the deepest possible level, the level of life, rather than *control* at the level of ordering and directing nature. And since, as we recall, our tendency is not only to model God in our image but to model ourselves on the models with which we imagine God, the metaphor of breath rather than mind might help us to support, rather than control, life in all its forms. Thus, in a spirit theology, we might see ourselves as united with all other living creatures through the breath that moves through all parts of the body, rather than as the demilords who order and control nature.

But is this model commensurate with twentieth-century science? If one understands the spirit of God as the source *of* the dynamic vitality of the universe and especially as the breath of all life-forms, then our focus is not on the purpose or direction of divine activity but on our dependence on God as the present and continuing creator. Our concern is not primarily intellectual but aesthetic and ethical: wonder and awe at the immensity, richness, and diversity of creation as well as gratitude and care for all its forms of life. Our response to this model is as grateful recipients of life rather than puzzlers over its mysteries. Contemporary science does not mandate or even imply such a model, but it is commensurate with an organic interpretation of its story. Since we and all other creatures and entities are in some sense inspirited bodies (even trees and oceans move with the winds), then if we were to think of God as in some sense continuous with this evolutionary history, one way to do so would be as the spirit of the entire body of the universe. This is not, of course, a scientific description nor is it a theological one; rather, it is a way of thinking about God and the world that makes sense in terms of postmodern science. It allows us to understand ourselves who have evolved into spiritual, embodied creatures as neither freaks nor surds in our world. It also allows us to think of God as the source of our being, the source of all being, not as the one who intervenes from the outside to initiate creation, patch it up, or direct it, but as the one who supplies us with the breath for all the incredible rich, teeming fecundity and variety of life.

It is a model of God and the world that focuses on "the wonderful life" that has emerged from evolutionary history, rather than on the divine ordering of the process. It does not attempt to enter into scientific discussions on the how and why of that history, but suggests that if one is *already* a person of faith (which cannot be arrived at or substantiated by postmodern science), then the picture of reality as an organic whole, a body, dependent on and sustained by the spirit of God, is one that fits with, is appropriate to, evolutionary history. This theology of nature is not a natural theology: it does not say that the scientific story gives evidence (even the tiniest bit) for belief in this or any other model of God and the world. All it says is that this way of conceiving of God and the world makes more sense in terms of the scientific picture than alternatives such as the deistic, dialogic, and monarchical models. But this is enough. A theology of nature does not ask for scientific proof, only for a picture to help us think and act holistically about God, ourselves, and our world.

Where does this model stand in regard to the Christian tradition? We can answer that question on one level simply and forthrightly by recalling the theme of the 1991 World Council of Churches assembly in Canberra, Australia: "Come, Holy Spirit—Renew the Whole Creation," or the affirmation from the Nicene[12] Creed: "I believe in the Holy Spirit, the Lord and Giver of Life." While the spirit of God, now the Holy Spirit, has often played a lackluster role in relation to the Father and the Son in Christian trinitarian thought, its credentials in both the Hebrew Scriptures and in the New Testament are more than solid.[13] The motif that runs throughout is the spirit as the source of life and the renewer of life: a theology of the spirit focuses on God as the creator and redeemer of life. The trajectory begins with the spirit of God hovering over the waters of chaos and breathing life into living beings; the spirit renews creation in the gift of baptism, the second birth; and fulfills it in the eschatological vision of all creation in harmonious union. One

---

12. One of the richest and most moving treatments of the Holy Spirit is Korean theologian Chung Hyun-Kyung's address at the Canberra assembly. Here she invokes the Spirit through the spirits of all the oppressed, from the murdered "spirit of the Amazon rainforest" to the spirits of exploited women and indigenous peoples, victims of the Holocaust and of Hiroshima, as well as Hagar, Jephthah's daughter, Malcolm X, Oscar Romero and all other life forms, human and non-human, that like "the Liberator, our brother Jesus," have been tortured and killed for greed and through hate. The closing words sum up this stunning hymn to the Spirit that moves through and empowers all life. "Dear sisters and brothers, with the energy of the Holy Spirit let us tear apart all walls of division and the culture of death which separate us. And let us participate in the Holy Spirit's political economy of life, fighting for our life on this earth in solidarity with all living beings and building communities for justice, peace, and the integrity of creation. Wild wind of the Holy Spirit, blow to us. Let us welcome her, letting ourselves go in her wild rhythm of life. Come Holy Spirit, renew the whole creation. Amen!" ("Welcome the Spirit; Hear Her Cries: The Holy Spirit, Creation, and the Culture of Life" [*Christianity and Crisis* 51 (15 July 1991) 223]).

13. For an introductory overview of the Spirit tradition, especially as oriented in an ecological direction, see Krister Stendahl, *Energy for Life: Reflections on the Theme "Come, Holy Spirit—Renew the Whole Creation"* (Geneva: World Council of Churches, 1990). For an extensive, ecologically oriented theology of the Spirit, see Jürgen Moltmann's *The Spirit of Life: A Universal Affirmation* (London: SCM, 1992).

of the great assets of the model is precisely its amorphous character in contrast to the highly human, personal, and androcentric nature of Father and Son: spirit is not necessarily human, personal (though it is relational), or male. In fact, it often has been designated female; but it may be best that, for once in Christian reflection, we let God be "it."[14] "It" (the divine spirit) roams where it will, not focused on the like-minded (the fathers and the sons—or even the mothers and daughters), but permeating, suffusing, and energizing the innermost being of each and every entity in creation in ways unknown and unknowable in our human, personal categories.[15]

The joining of the spirit that gives life to every creature with the Holy Spirit that renews all creation suggests a connection between Christian theology and the two forms of evolution—biological and biocultural. Creation, the gift of the spirit, could be seen as the action of God in the aeons of evolutionary development, which has resulted in the wonderful life we see about us as well as in ourselves. (This is a retrospective reading of creation in evolutionary terms.) In the model of the universe as God's body, divine incarnation is not limited to redemption but is everywhere evident in the bodies that live through the breath of the spirit. Within this model of the universe as God's body, God's presence and action are evident as the breath of life that gives all bodies, all forms of matter, the energy or power to become themselves. This understanding of divine action in light of evolutionary development focuses on *empowerment*, not direction. It does not claim that God is guiding the process in general or in particular; rather, it suggests that *all* life, regardless of which individuals or species prosper, is dependent upon God. God's creative action is not intermittent or occasional; on the contrary, it is continuous and universal, for without the sustaining breath of God, all the wonderful life, including our own, would fade and die. The "purpose" of creation from this perspective, however, is not human beings (or any other species), but the fecundity, richness, and diversity of *all* that is bodied forth from God and sustained in life by the breath of God. Needless to say, creation in this picture involves enormous waste, suffering, and death for all kinds of bodies—to suggest anything less or different is sentimental and false to the contemporary scientific picture of reality.

In Christian theology, however, the spirit of God is also the Holy Spirit, the spirit shaped and made known in the Hebrew Scriptures as well as in the life, teachings, and death of Jesus of Nazareth and the community that formed around him. Moreover, evolution is not only biological; with self-conscious creatures it enters a historical, cultural phase. At this point divine purpose can be spoken of within the evolutionary process in a new and special way. It is not only empowerment of but also a *direction* for all that teeming

---

14. Stendahl supports this usage, as it frees us from the overpersonalism of the tradition: "The Spirit is the indispensable vehicle to take us towards an all-inclusive theology" (*Energy for Life*, 5).

15. Alice Walker makes this point in the following excerpt between Celie and Shug: "It? I ast. Yeah, It. God ain't a he or a she, but a It . . . It ain't something you can look at apart from anything else, including yourself. I believe God is everything, say Shug. Everything that is or ever was or ever will be" (from *The Color Purple*, in *Weaving the Visions: New Patterns in Feminist Spirituality*, ed. Carol P. Christ and Judith Plaskow [New York: Harper, 1989] 103).

life, a direction expressed by Christians in the stories, images, and ideas of the Hebrew people, its paradigmatic founder Jesus, and all the lives and understandings of disciples over the centuries. The guide for interpreting that direction is called the Holy Spirit, and it works *through* human beings: we become the mind and heart as well as the hands and feet of the body of God on our planet. Christians claim that God has been in the natural process as its creator and sustainer (the spirit of the body) since the beginning, but now that process has been given a particular direction (a "new creation") characterized by inclusive love, especially for the vulnerable and oppressed. For Christians, the spirit has been qualified or given shape and scope by the Holy Spirit and is a direction or purpose for life that depends on our cooperation as God's partners.

Hence, we can say that God's action as the spirit of the body is twofold. The spirit is the source of life, the breath of creation; at the same time, the Holy Spirit is the source of the renewal of life, the direction or purpose for all the bodies of the world—a goal characterized by inclusive love.

One central issue remains in regard to our model of God as the spirit of life bodied forth in the universe: Is it pantheistic? This is a complex issue in Christian theology with intricate historical dimensions we cannot settle here. Nonetheless, the criteria for models of God and the world operative in this essay—commensurability with postmodern science as well as our own embodied experience and the well-being of our planet—cause us to lean toward an interpretation of Christian faith that accommodates this model. Since the model is commensurate with contemporary science, mirrors our own experience as embodied spirits, and connects us at the basic level of life-giving breath with all other life-forms on our planet, we are encouraged to look to those traditions within Christianity that emphasize the spirit in similar ways. These traditions can be characterized as neither theist nor pantheist, but pan*en*theist: "God is not exhausted by finite beings, not even all finite beings, yet God is *in* all finite creatures and apart from God there is nothing; nor is God 'apart' from anything."[16] This description of a panentheistic view of the relation of God and the world is compatible with our model of God as the spirit that is the source, the life, the breath of all reality. Everything that is is *in* God and God is *in* all things and yet God is not identical with the universe, for the universe is dependent on God in a way that God is not dependent on the universe. We joined the agential and organic models in order to express the asymmetrical and yet profoundly interrelational character of the panentheistic model of God and the world: while we, as members of the body, are radically dependent upon the life-giving breath from the spirit, God, as the spirit, is not so dependent upon the universe. Pantheism says that God is embodied, necessarily and totally; traditional theism claims that God is disembodied, necessarily and totally; panentheism suggests that God is embodied but not necessarily or totally. Rather, God is sacramentally embodied: God is mediated, expressed, in and through embodiment, but not necessarily or totally. It

---

16. Raymond Keith Williamson, *Introduction to Hegel's Philosophy of Religion* (Albany: SUNY Press, 1984) 254.

is, as we recall, the back and not the face of God that we are allowed to see.

Panentheism is, I would suggest, a strong motif in both Hebrew and Christian traditions that take seriously the mediation of God to the world.[17] These traditions deny, on the one hand, a picture of God as an external superperson (or Unmoved Mover) distant from and alien to the world and, on the other hand, a view of God as immediately available to the mind of human beings or as identified with natural processes. Rather, the panentheistic tradition is found in all those passages in the Hebrew Scriptures that mediate the divine presence through human words and acts as well as natural phenomena and in the New Testament in its central declaration that "the Word was made flesh" in Jesus of Nazareth. In all these instances, mediation and incarnation are central and, therefore, are open to, or ought to be open to, the embodiment of God, especially in its panentheistic form of the world (universe) as God's body and God as its spirit.

To sum up: we have suggested that God as the embodied spirit of the universe is a personal/organic model that is compatible with interpretations of both Christian faith and contemporary science, although not demanded by either. It is a way of speaking of God's relation to all matter, all creation, that "makes sense" in terms of an incarnational understanding of Christianity and an organic interpretation of postmodern science. It helps us to be *whole* people within our faith and within our contemporary world. Moreover, the model does not reduce God to the world nor relegate God to another world; on the contrary, it radicalizes both divine immanence (God is the breath of each and every creature) and divine transcendence (God is the energy empowering the entire universe). Finally, it underscores our bodiliness, our concrete physical existence and experience that we share with all other creatures: it is a model on the side of the well-being of the planet, for it raises the issue of ethical regard toward *all* bodies as all are interrelated and interdependent.

---

17. Apart from process theology, two other notable panentheistic traditions are the Hegelian and the Tillichian. In spite of Hegel's focus on history to the detriment of nature, he insisted on both intimacy between God and the world and the mediation of God in the world: God "is not the world, nor is the world God, but the world is God's appearing, God's activity of self-manifestation, appearing which is completed in man. The world, and man in it, are real only to the extent that God is in them, and their true being is in God, which is another way of saying that the finite is the appearing of the infinite and has its being in the infinite" (quoted in Williamson, *Hegel's Philosophy of Religion*, 270). One of Tillich's central contributions was his insistence that Spirit is the most adequate term for God as it unites power (the depths of the divine) with meaning (the Logos) and together they account for "life" or the spirit: "The statement that God is Spirit means that life as spirit is the inclusive symbol for the divine life" (*Systematic Theology*, vol. 1 [Chicago: University of Chicago Press, 1951] 250). One of the values of Tillich's position is that life rather than mind is the primary designation of the divine spirit; hence, a foundation is laid for an inclusive theology. A contemporary follower of the Hegelian/Tillichian panentheistic tradition, Peter Hodgson, moves it yet further in that direction: "When I say 'world,' I mean the whole world—the cosmos as we know it, the stars and planets, biological life, human consciousness, culture and history. This whole world is the figure, shape, or gestalt of God in the moment of *difference*; It is 'God's body.' 'God's got the whole world in his hands'" (*God in History: Shapes of Freedom* [Nashville: Abingdon, 1989] 106).

Commentary

Kirsten A. S. Mebust

When I invited my colleagues into conversation about Sallie McFague's influence on theology in the twenty-first century, the first things they named were not the importance of the universal creation story or the emphatic clarity of her prose. Instead, McFague reveals to us a potent new starting place for theology: taking a root metaphor and passing theological reflection through it like a gem, allowing the crystal structure to aim light into new places and bring new experiences into focus. Metaphorical theology integrates the theological tradition with contemporary experience and individual reflection with the context of community and culture, so that the word of God rings fresh and relevant in response to our daily dilemmas and decisions. "I didn't know theology could be done like this," said one. Beginning with fresh metaphors allows us to evaluate and re-engage with the ancient doctrines of the church. "Whatever you do," McFague once said in the classroom, "find the place in the tradition where your metaphor has been used before, and claim the connection." McFague's *Body of God* connects with the ancient patristic work of Irenaeus of Lyons, and the philosophical theology of Charles Hartshorne and Alfred North Whitehead, clarifying and reinvigorating this tradition for feminist and ecological theologians in our generation.

McFague critiques the patriarchal and abstract language that has dominated the Christian theological tradition as dangerous and idolatrous. By refusing to recognize traditional God-language as metaphorical, thereby excluding the experiences of women, non-Westerners, and people of color from the reigning metaphors of Christian worship and theology, Western theologians commit what Alfred North Whitehead referred to as the fallacy of misplaced concreteness. Idolizing a metaphor leads ultimately to the loss of its capacity to recognize and point to the plenitude and present reality of a living God. McFague has helped theologians the world over recognize the necessary metaphorical grounding of human religious language and acknowledge the finite perspective that all religious efforts to speak of God entail.

The method of metaphorical theology insists on integrating theology and ethics. When we imagine the world as the body of God, we realize that what we do in, with, and for the world enters into the experience of God. What happens in the world is filled with divine importance, intensifying the meaning of the particular everyday events of which the world is created. McFague affirms the concrete, situated, particular and limited perspective we bring to the feminist epistemology of attention, not only as very good, but as sacred spiritual engagement that reveals God's very life to us through our own and nature's radical embodiment. To be divine is to be radically incarnate, embodied in the very finite and wondrously alive things of this earth. What we believe matters; and thanks to McFague, we can see that what we believe and do about our backyards and our beaches, our food and our clothing, our social and cultural relationships, our travel and our political processes matters in the life of God. If we understand the world as the body of God, worship is a matter of our responsibility to each other and to the ecological and human systems and bodies in which we are embedded; the *telos* of our prayer and our actions is in the very matter that supports and sustains our lives. No twentieth-century theologian has more clearly redirected the aims of Christian spiritual life and work.

Reading McFague sometimes feels like taking a cold shower. The clarity and vigor of her language bring her critical points home to the heart. Her love of the particular and the concrete illuminate her arguments with vivid examples and awaken sleepy imaginations to the implications of our words and deeds. Her gift for linear argument coexists in a rare, happy harmony with her delight in poetic image. Readers are not often in doubt about what she means when they finish one of her books. The greater challenge in an encounter with McFague's prolific theological imagination is the claim it makes on the whole life of the reader. Like Martin Luther's *Small Catechism*, in one way or another, all of Sallie McFague's works contain the question, "What does this mean for us?"

STUDY QUESTIONS

1. What is the difference between the arrogant eye and the loving eye? Where do you see them at work in your own embodied experience?

2. McFague sees much of our culture and the Christian tradition as functioning out of "somatophobia" and "pletherophobia." What does she mean by these terms? Make a list of ways in which you can see these two fears at work in your life and in the life of your religious communities. How does a feminist epistemology of attention help us overcome these phobias?

3. McFague proposes that "spirit theology" enables us to use the metaphor of the world as the body of God to overcome anthropocentrism in the theological tradition. What has been the problem with past interpretations of the relationship of spirit and body? How can McFague's version of spirit theology overcome somatophobia?

11 Holy Spirit and Womanism

Karen Baker-Fletcher

Karen Baker-Fletcher is Professor of Systematic Theology at the Perkins School of Theology at Southern Methodist University. She received degrees from Wellesley College, Harvard Divinity School, and Harvard University. Her research interests include systematic theology, process theism, ecology, relational theologies, women and theology, contemporary and historical African American religious thought, nineteenth-century holiness women, global theologies, Wesleyan theology, intercultural constructive theology, religion and literature, religion and culture. This excerpt is from chapter seven of Dancing with God: The Trinity from a Womanist Perspective *(2006) where Baker-Fletcher articulates a doctrine of the Holy Spirit based on the ways in which historical black women have responded to the lynching of their sons.*

Excerpt from *Dancing with God: The Trinity from a Womanist Perspective*

THE HOLY SPIRIT AND DANCING WITH GOD

IN HER WORK AS a producer and performance artist, Vanessa Baker feels led by the Holy Spirit to create Christian art. In the artistic representation of Mamie Till-Mobley in the Baker-Swann choreo-poem, as well as in images captured by photo-journalists, one finds parallels between Mamie Till-Mobley before the coffin of Emmett Till and the Pieta, the image of Mary holding her son at the cross. Mamie Till-Mobley had an open-casket funeral. She had her son photographed in his casket to be viewed in magazines. She was like Mary, mother of Jesus, asking the world to look and to repent. She was like many other black women who had seen the horror, and couldn't bear another look. But Mother Till-Mobley found courage to say, "I'M NOT TAKING THIS! LOOK!" "Look, world, don't you see?" "Look at my son's face! Look at his body!" "World, get delivered of your demons and Look!" The viewing and funeral lasted four days. Thousands came to look. The world began to change until it forgot. Then the families of Medgar Evers, Martin Luther King Jr., and James Byrd Jr. followed, issuing calls to stop the hate that produces unnecessary violence. The struggle continues.

So, over the years the story of Emmett Till and his mother has been retold in scholarly publications, through Internet publications, community events, and educational programs to keep the story within the collective consciousness. The story is significant not only because of its tragic dimensions and moral challenge to cease hate crimes, but because of the faith of Till's mother.[1] She found courage to shout, "NOOO!" to hatred of another's life and unnecessary violence through her faith in a resurrecting God. She refused to merely bear the cross Money, Mississippi, gave her when they lynched her son, and instead sought justice to overcome it, bravely appearing at the trial of her son's accused killers at the risk of her own life. If we can ever speak positively about what it means to "bear one's cross," then she demonstrated it in her Christlike willingness to risk her own life by making every effort to bring her son's lynchers to justice. If there is any positive meaning in what it means to "take up your cross and follow me," it is what we learn through Mamie Till-Mobley.

To overcome the cross with Christ, then, includes being willing to risk your own life in the process in the call for justice. Yet, this is not a path that glorifies suffering and rationalizes that suffering is redemptive. Suffering is deepest and most severe when it is the spiritual suffering called despair that leads to cynicism. That is the worst kind of suffering. It is part of the problem that perpetuates hatred, injustice, and unnecessary violence. To overcome the cross by taking up one's cross is to claim divine and personal power over all crosses. It is the power that turns the cross into two pieces of wood instead of a tool of destruction. It is to choose the path of the old spiritual, "I shall not be moved."[2] It is the path of resistance against evil. It is the path of confronting evil and staring it in the face. This path is not death-loving. This path is life-loving. Where there is courage and truth, there is life. Where there is a call for justice, there is life. Where there is a call for love instead of hatred, there is life. This life resurrects itself again and again. Mamie Till-Mobley lived in the knowledge of resurrection faith.

Resurrection faith is the source of power and courage to say "No" to evil and destruction. Mamie Till-Mobley, who became a church mother in the Church of God in Christ, chose to carry the message of overcoming racial violence and hatred, in effect a message that crosses, hanging people from trees, are to be overcome. She was clear that such acts should not be repeated. In memory of her and of all women from the time of Christ who have mourned loved ones hung from trees, the teenage girls of St. Luke's (United Methodist Church in Dallas, Texas) performed a sacred dance. It gave everyone a new vision of human community, of God, and of trees. Protestant Christians need to remember Mary, because we continue to hear her story through the stories of Myrlie Evers, civil rights widow of activist Medgar Evers. We continue to hear

---

1. See Cheryl Townsend Gilkes, *If It Wasn't for the Women* (Maryknoll, NY: Orbis, 2001) for a discussion of Mamie Till-Mobley's influence as a Christian activist as a church mother in the Church of God in Christ. Comparing Mother Till-Mobley with the late Mrs. Lillian P. Benbow, also of the Church of God in Christ and a former president of Delta Sigma Theta sorority, Gilkes finds, "Mrs. Mobley is not the only "saint" to have an effect on the ethical and political culture of the black experience. Mrs. Benbow urged black sororities and fraternities to abstain from their annual dance and give the money they usually spent on "The Dance" to benefit the larger black community instead.

2. This spiritual is influenced by several scriptural sources, including Psalm 16:8 and New Testament literature, particularly the synoptic gospels, regarding Jesus' crucifixion on the cross. One line, for example, proclaims steadfastness and unmoveability even when one's cross is heavy. The spiritual emphasizes that in the face of injustice one must stand strong, "like a tree planted by the water."

her story in the biography of Mamie Till-Mobley and the story of Stella Byrd. We continue to hear her story in the story of every woman who has survived the unjust killing of a loved one.

If Mary were not the mother of God, then Christ's humanity would come into question. Was Christ fully human and fully divine or not? If Christ was not human and Christ does not continue to live in the hearts of believers like Mamie Till-Mobley today, then Christianity is a dead religion. However, it is not inevitable that we come to that conclusion. Mary *was* the mother of Jesus the Christ. As Hayes reminds us, she bore the humanity of God into the world in the flesh. In a process-relational understanding, energy produces matter, and matter produces energy. Likewise, spirit produces matter, and matter produces spirit. So of course Jesus is matter and spirit, divine and human, creature and creating, beloved and loving. Moreover, Mary is an integration of matter and spirit, who experiences the full possibilities of bearing and raising a child who is the full embodiment of God, who is the all-inclusive power of life, abounding in love, and continuously creating and renewing. She is therefore an appropriate bearer of God who is Spirit and who is embodied in Jesus the Christ, because God is omnipresent in creation. Mary at the cross witnesses the life and death of her own flesh and blood, because Jesus is flesh of her flesh and heart of her heart.

The blood shed on the cross takes on new meaning. It is Jesus' blood, it is Mary's blood, and it is the blood of Immanuel, God with us. The heart pumps blood to give life. Life flows from God's heart, to Mary's heart, in Jesus' heart, to all humanity. This God on the cross suffers with us in persecution and oppression. This resurrected God rejoices with us in victory over evil and suffering. Jesus' blood is a symbol of abundant life and unsurpassable love. I spent some time as a young girl in a Roman Catholic school. I was taught by nuns for three years. They always linked Jesus' love with Mary's love as mother of God in Christ. From them I learned about the sacred heart of Jesus. Paintings of the sacred heart of Jesus as well as paintings of Mary have influenced my Christian consciousness, although I am Protestant. To preach Christ and him crucified, it is necessary to focus on the heart of Jesus the Christ and on the heart of Mary. This is a new idea for Protestant womanists, but I believe it is essential. Otherwise, we literally lose the heart of the Christian message, and the relational understanding of womanist theology becomes compromised.

Vanessa Baker's production of sacred dance, music, and poetry moves beyond the moaning of past generations to a prophetic lament and shout. This lament and shout functions as a call to resistance against evil and to action for a world in which crucifixion is no more, a world in which we are no longer forced to bear crosses. Emmett Till is mirrored in Baker's sacred dance by the Christ figure that carries him lifted up in the cruciform of Christ-like arms. Even so Mamie Till-Mobley evokes memories of the story of Mary, mother of Jesus, who kneels at the cross and, who, in Christian artwork, holds his body as could only one who loved him from conception. Similarly, women, including Christian women, have fought to change rape laws and domestic violence laws, seeking justice in rigorous love. These are people who do not simply bear the crosses placed in their paths.

They pick up these crosses to overcome them and to overcome the production of crosses. They actively seek to bring an end to unnecessary suffering and violence. They refuse to acquiesce to evil.

...

THE HEALING, RESURRECTING POWER OF THE SPIRIT ON EARTH

Resurrection is not just an event of the past, but of the present and the future. Evil, suffering, and death have not, cannot, and will not overcome the world. Sin is a handicap that God in Christ, through the power of the Holy Spirit, overcame and continues to overcome. God, through Christ, in the power of the Holy Spirit, has overcome the evil that is in the world. We know this because love and creativity still exist in the world. We know this because Word/Wisdom is omnipresent in the world. We know this because comfort, healing, and encouragement to heal others are omnipresent in the world. The goodness of God in the land of the living is omnipresent and permeates creation, ever renewing and recreating. There is resurrection promise and resurrection hope in the world. Resurrection begins with the Spirit and ends with the creation of a new thing that is integratively physical and spiritual, a new, spiritual body, visibly incarnating past and present loving ways of being and becoming, visibly embodying future possibilities of becoming, creating faith, hope, and love in others.

The earliest Christian theologian, Paul, responded to questions about resurrection. New and prospective Christians in Paul's day were as perplexed as many today about resurrection. It made no more scientific sense in Paul's time than for many today. Paul, as pastor and theologian, said, "But someone will ask, 'How are the dead raised? With what kind of body do they come?'" Like many pastors today, he must have heard this question more times than he could count. Like some pastors and evangelical theologians today, he responded impatiently: "Fool! What you sow does not come to life unless it dies. And as for what you sow, you do not sow the body that is to be, but a bare seed, perhaps of wheat or of some other grain." Paul goes on to explain that God gives it a body as God has determined, "and to each kind of seed," God gives "its own body." Moreover, "Not all flesh is alike, but there is one flesh for human beings, another for animals, another for birds, and another for fish. There are both heavenly bodies and earthly bodies, but the glory of the heavenly is one thing, and that of the earthly is another" (1 Corinthians 15:35–40). In other words, the resurrected body is a spiritual body. It has its own splendor or beauty. It integrates body and spirit in a new way, a way that many find difficult to imagine. "So it is with the resurrection of the dead," Paul continues (1 Corinthians 15:42a). This spiritual body is everlasting and will not perish. The resurrected body is a spiritual, imperishable body that is not subject to decay.[3]

3. Katie Cannon, *Katie's Canon: Womanism and the Soul of the Black Community* (New York: Continuum, 1996) 113–21. Also, see Marjorie Suchocki, *God, Christ, Church: A Practical Guide to Process Theology* (New York: Crossroad, 1992) 205–6, 244. For Suchocki, "God, and only God, can feel the entirety of the other. Thus the flow of feeling that takes place as God prehends the other is a flow of the full subjectivity of the other into the full subjectivity of God. This is subjective immortality for the world within the life of God... There will be a new heaven and a new earth, but the locus

Similarly, Monica Coleman observes that Whitehead in *Process and Reality* defines evil as the fact of perpetual perishing, the element of loss in every process of becoming. We are saved from "the fact of perpetual perishing, the element of loss in every process of becoming, by immortality." Specifically, "salvation is effected by assuring everlasting life for the actual entities that are lost and by God's lure of the temporal world towards specific goals."[4] In other words, God's grace is saving in that there is promise of everlasting life in God, which overcomes temporal perishing and death. [Marjorie] Suchocki puts it another way in her discussion of resurrection and redemption, writing, "Applied to God, God receives the world so fully that God resurrects the world, and then integrates the resurrected world into the depths of the divine being according to the divine character." In other words, God judges the resurrected world according to God's own loving, just, creative nature. God does this within God's consequent nature, which, like the economic nature of the Trinity, is the divine response to the world. The world is continuously resurrected. Moreover, God continues to feel the positive and negative effects of the actions of the entities that make up the world, discerning which are consistent with divine love, creativity, and justice. Specifically from Suchocki's Whiteheadian perspective, "Applied to God, God evaluates, contrasts, judges the world according to God's own character till the world is conformed to God."[5] For Suchocki, this means that God, who feels the feelings of the world, feels the agony and joy of the world. Resurrected subjects, knowing themselves as God knows them, feel the effects of their actions, agony or joy, on others.

Suchocki paraphrases 1 Corinthians 13:12, observing that in resurrected, everlasting life with God, "We shall know as we are known." We shall experience ourselves as God experiences us. This indeed, Suchocki concludes, would be judgment. Her theology suggests that God is both heaven and hell."[6] At this point, problems emerge in Suchocki's understanding. The strength of her understanding is that everlasting life is relational and that we know ourselves as God knows us. The weakness of her understanding is the notion that God is both heaven and hell. Psalm 139 simply says that God is even in the depths of hell, with emphasis on the fact there is no place where one can flee or hide from God. Psalm 8:1 describes God's name as "majestic . . . in all the earth," and says that God has set God's glory "above the heavens." The writer of Psalm 108:4–5

---

of both is God's own being through God's power of resurrection. This resurrection is spiritual, not material." Suchocki derives this understanding from Whitehead's understanding of God as "feeling of feeling," in which God alone feels, experiences, or prehends all others in their entirety. For Whitehead, the temporal, finite world experiences only "objective immortality." Suchocki argues that given divine feeling of the feelings or the world, in the everlastingness of subjective resurrection in God there is also *subjective immortality*. This is not only logical, but satisfying in contrast to Hartshorne's nearly exclusive turn to *objective immortality*. See Alfred North Whitehead, *Process and Reality* (New York: Free Press, 1978) 211–12, 240.

4. Monica A. Coleman, "Walking in the Whirlwind: A Whiteheadian Womanist Soteriology," PhD dissertation, Claremont Graduate University, 2004, 36.

5. Marjorie Suchocki, "The Last Word?" in *Strike Terror No More: Theology, Ethics, and the New War*, ed. Jon Berquist (St. Louis: Chalice, 2002) 219; and Suchocki, *God, Christ, Church*, 208–10, 211–16. God, in God's justice and judgment, is for Suchocki the "overcomer of evil."

6. Ibid.

describes God's love as "higher than the heavens," and says "let your glory be over all the earth." First Kings 8:27 describes Solomon's prayer dedicating the temple he built for God as asking, "But will God indeed dwell on the earth? Even heaven and the highest heaven cannot contain you, much less the house that I have built!" Moreover, Isaiah 66:1 describes Isaiah prophetically speaking as God's mouthpiece,

> Thus says the LORD:
> "Heaven is my throne
>   and the earth is my footstool;
> what is the house that you would
>   build for me,
>   and what is my resting place?"

The point is that, scripturally, God who dwells in heaven and earth also transcends heaven and earth. According to Genesis, God created heaven and earth. This theme is carried forward throughout Hebrew Scriptures, particularly in the Psalms and in the book of Job. Neither heaven nor earth can contain God. Therefore, God is not heaven as Suchocki states. Nor is God hell. God, the Creator of all things—who continuously, everlastingly, dynamically creates—is not heaven, earth, hell, nature, or the universe. The latter are God's creations, not God.

God is in all places, but God is not a place. Suchocki fails to attend to the fact that "heaven" and "hell" are metaphors that describe the joy or agony of God's experiencing the feelings of others in resurrected experience. These are not metaphors for describing God. They are metaphors for describing the experiencing of joy and agony, the effects of every entity of the world on other entities. They are metaphors for divine judgment and selectivity regarding these experiences of freely and consciously participating in divine creativity or rejecting it to participate in the evil of harming others. Suchocki's understanding of the redemption of evil is also unclear and problematic. She claims, "Evil, even terrible evil, is felt by God in order to be redeemed by God—partially in history, but fully within the divine nature."[7] It depends on what she means. If she means that God uses what some intended for evil and transforms it into good, this works biblically as well as metaphysically. If she means that unrepentant sinners who have rejected participating in divine love, creativity, and justice are redeemed, then this contradicts her earlier understanding of judgment and New Testament understandings of heaven and hell. Suchocki argues that her understanding of judgment is true because in history we have a choice to go with or against God, whereas in God we do not have that power. "We must be conformed to the divine image, transformed into the insistent depths of a God whose 'nature and whose name is love.'"[8]

What happened to the persuasive God? Apparently, being in the direct presence of divine love is irresistible. Evil is transformed into good. "Redeemed" may not be the right word here. Coleman's understanding of "creative transformation" makes greater sense. God creatively transforms even evil into good to effect God's creation with blessing, in spite of tendencies among entities in the world to violate others. Still, Suchocki's understanding leaves doubts in the minds of many Christians. Divine everlastingness sounds

7. Ibid.
8. Ibid.

strongly deterministic rather than persuasive. Second Peter 3:13 indicates that God creates "new heavens and a new earth." Biblically, however, there is no reference to redeeming those who experience everlasting life as hell or agony. Theoretically, some Christians have argued, it could be possible. Metaphysically, from a Whiteheadian perspective, it makes some sense, but not enough if suddenly God is strongly deterministic rather than persuasive. Biblically, there is insufficient warrant for this claim. Metaphysics takes us only so far. It is enough to leave this a mystery known only to God and in God's everlasting realm.

Finally, Suchocki does not have a strong doctrine of the Holy Spirit. Understanding of resurrection healing and life is incomplete without attention to the power of the Holy Spirit. The Holy Spirit is the power of healing and resurrection in life everlasting and in temporal existence. The Holy Spirit is not like a genie in a bottle, which is what it has become for some: "Call on the Holy Spirit and all your ills, weaknesses, and money problems will disappear. A true believer, a true Christian, is wealthy, healthy, and fully lives out the American dream of prosperity." This notion of "healing" always means that there is no visible illness or disability remaining. Healing must evidence itself in the utter disappearance of an affliction. Those who suffer are weak in faith or have some hidden sin that keeps them in poverty, illness, or disability. If God does not heal the people in the visible, dramatic way expected, then those people have not prayed hard enough. Their faith is weak. They need to repent more and pray harder. They have not "allowed" the Holy Spirit to work through them. Among those who think in this way the claim to "know" what God *can* do becomes a tyrannical dictation of what God *must* do. This view, like the perspective that God only comforts during the "age of the church," looks for control. Unconsciously, however, this perspective reveals a desire to control God and knowledge of the nature of God. "God must heal *only and always* in the way I understand," the believer seems to be saying. Moreover, little attention is given to Paul's experience of asking for healing three times only to accept his difficulty as a gift with the understanding that God's grace is sufficient (2 Corinthians 12:1–10). Whether intentional or not, it seems that from this perspective God's grace *is not* sufficient. There is little or no awareness that an individual can rejoice in being alive and performing God's work in spite of disability or lack of wealth.

An opposite perspective goes to a different extreme that ends with the same result of revealing an unconscious desire to control God and knowledge of God. In this view, miracles are mythic accounts of what the ancients could not scientifically explain or, in the case of dispensationalists, they have ceased because God no longer needs to perform them. In this perspective, Christians claim to know what God *cannot do* or, at best, claim to know exactly in which historical period God chooses to do it. This closes off the meaning of the testimonies of persons for whom prayer works according to personal, family, communal, medical, and scientific accounts. Although doctors and scientists generally note they hope for a scientific explanation one day, the studies that demonstrate the effectiveness of prayer in such healing suggests that those who believe in the healing and miracle working power of the Holy Spirit have experienced *something*. They frequently call this something *God*. William James, in his study of varieties of religious experience, called it "the More," not limiting it to Christian experience but always focusing on the transformative effects of a belief in the life of a person of faith. For Christians who believe in the power of prayer to heal, "the More" would be understood as God, Christ, and/or the Holy Spirit, with particular attention to "the movement of the Holy Spirit."

. . .

The Holy Spirit, by whose power the Jesus of the four gospels heals and performs miracles, is not a genie we can manipulate to make all wishes come true. There is a difference between answer to prayer and the granting of wishes. Prayer may be answered in unexpected ways. Children want to receive their wishes exactly, sometimes to the wisher's disappointment if the wish has been ill-conceived. The answer to a prayer may be, "No," or, "Wait," as well as, "Yes." Prayers are answered according to the greater wisdom and power of a transcendent God through the power of the Holy Spirit who searches the mind of God. It is in the power of the Holy Spirit that God meets the *needs* of believers, not their wishes.

Healing and resurrection power are the particular characteristics of the divine action or revelation of the Holy Spirit. Healing and resurrection power are also the work of the entire Trinity. Healing and resurrection power are revelations of divine love in the world. The Holy Spirit is the power of love, but all three actions or relations of the Trinity are loving. All three relational actions create, recreate, and renew. Scholars know less about the Holy Spirit than the other two persons of the Trinity, because New Testament writers say more about "God the Father" and "Jesus, the Son, the Word, and Christ" than about the "Holy Spirit." Bruce Marshall has written that Jesus witnesses to God the Father and to the Holy Spirit. The Holy Spirit witnesses to the first two persons of the Trinity, but the Holy Spirit does not witness to the Holy Spirit. This makes the Holy Spirit more mysterious than the other two persons of the Trinity.[9] There are clues, however, to the nature of the Holy Spirit in the four gospels and in the Pauline letters. Secondarily, there are clues to the nature of the Holy Spirit in the written and oral accounts of Christian experience throughout the ages. The latter, secondary resources are accountable to descriptions found in scripture and when they fail to give adequate attention to the primary resource of scriptural accounts they tend to distort the nature of the Holy Spirit as noted above. In Genesis 1, many Christians interpret "the Spirit" to be the "Holy Spirit" of New Testament literature. The Holy Spirit, in New Testament literature, is also called "the Spirit" in several texts. Beginning with Genesis, one might offer a contemporary poetic rendering as follows:

In the beginning, there was dance. The Spirit of God hovered over the water. The author of all creation danced with the Spirit and the Word, which sang let there be light, let there be . . . let there be . . . Divine, everlasting community said let us create *adam*-earth creature-male and

---

9. Bruce Marshall, lecture notes, "Interpretation of the Christian Message I," Fall 2002; and Marshall, *Trinity and Truth* (Cambridge: Cambridge University Press, 2000) 180–81, 254–56.

female, in our image, reflecting our creative, communal dance with one another and it was so. An entire interrelational universe freely became through the power of persuasive, divine, creative, loving community, integrating spirit and matter, and it was good. Earth creatures, male and female, became greedy, wanting more than their share of power. Taking the freedom they were created in by persuasive, loving, divine community, they greedily grasped at more than their share of power. This created an imbalance, leaving divine community, which was already eternally creating, creating anew what had been whole and now was broken. The creation that took millennia to become whole spiritually strives to find wholeness again. Some desperately seek wholeness through false, destructive means—the idolatry of grasping at more than one's share of power in the universe. Some find authentic wholeness through the preventing grace of the Author and Parent of the universe, through the redeeming, restoring grace of Word and Wisdom, and the through healing power of the Holy Spirit. Resurrection hope is in the latter.

Divine preventing grace in the providence/nurture of God keeps evil from overcoming the freedom to consciously experience and participate in divine love. Without preventing grace, evil and hatred would overcome the creaturely freedom to participate in divine love. Preventing grace makes it possible for human beings to literally *feel* convicted by omnipresent, divine love. Divine, justifying grace in the Word/Wisdom of God receives the persuaded, convicted hearts of the world to free them from hatred and unnecessary violence. The Word/Wisdom of God frees, justifies, and redeems those who desire to participate in divine love so that they may love others. The sanctifying grace of God, in the power of the Holy Spirit, heals the wounds inflicted by evil actions and perfects the love of followers of the Word/Wisdom of God to make them whole. The entire community of God restores followers of Word/Wisdom to God, freeing them from broken relationship with God and the world. Then heaven and earth rejoice, because God's initial aim is realized on earth as in heaven. This happens day by day and is also a future event as creation moans, groans, and strives towards full redemption, the creation of a new heaven and a new earth in the fully realized reign of God.

The grace of God moves through the entire Trinity. It is present in God who is like a Parent, which reflects God's dynamic, providing, nurturing love. It is present in God's dynamic, creative relation of incarnate, passionate, and redeeming love. This is the power of God in Christ who is the Word and Wisdom of God. It is present in God's compassionate, comforting, and resurrecting love, which is the power of the Holy Spirit. It is the power of the Holy Spirit who unites the first two. This understanding is similar, in one respect, to Augustine's understanding of the Trinity. All three relational actions of the divine community create and love. The Holy Spirit is the power of divine creativity and love, empowering and encouraging divine community into creativity and love.

Referring to 1 John 4:16, Augustine said, "God is love." He understood the Trinity as the one who loves, the one who is loved, and love. In other words, one might describe God as Lover, Beloved, and Love. For Augustine, "the Father and Son and Holy Spirit are one God, creator and ruler of the entire creature." Yet the specific work of each person is not alien to the other in love. The Father is not the Son, nor the Holy Spirit the Father or the Son, he writes, "but . . . there is a trinity of mutually related persons and a unity of equal substance."[10] He associated the dynamic power of Love itself with the third person of the Trinity. This power of Love, found in the Holy Spirit, he wrote, unites Lover and Beloved. All three persons participate in divine love.

The source of love, for Augustine, always is God, because God in every aspect of God's nature inspires love. This was Augustine's description of the immanent Trinity and how the three persons of the Trinity relate to one another within God's one nature. There are moments such as these, when Augustine moves toward a relational concept of God, that comes close to understandings in process metaphysics. For Augustine, God is Trinity and functions as a type of relational community. Overall, however, most process metaphysicians find that Augustine viewed the hypostases, or "persons," as substances rather than nonstatic, dynamic relations.

There is something powerful, something more than mere flesh and blood. It is the very energy that creates flesh and blood, that makes love in the midst of hate crimes possible. In the experience of existential evil, the temptation to hate in kind, along with the temptations to give in to bitterness, passivity, or nihilism is ever-present. A power greater than flesh alone makes it possible to choose love instead. There is something greater and more persuasive than the impulse to seek revenge that is present in this world. God in all three relational actions or *hypostases* is persuasive. The distinctive action of the Holy Spirit in God's persuasive activity is multiple. Not only is it comforting, guiding, instructing, healing, discerning, and empowering; but it is also encouraging. According to Romans 12:8, encouragement, leadership, generosity, and mercy are all gifts of the Spirit.

Theologians in recent years, particularly Jürgen Moltmann,[11] have given much attention to empowerment through the Holy Spirit. The fullness of the Holy Spirit's grace in the body of Christ is understood only when the gifts are understood in relation to one another. In a world in which many have become apathetic, failing in faith and hope regarding creative transformation, the regenerating gift of the Holy Spirit, encouragement—the strengthening of the heart—helps clarify how the Holy Spirit empowers. The Holy Spirit lifts up the faint of heart, giving them courage to receive other gifts. This encouragement is contagious. It spreads through the body of Christ so that it is able to receive the other gifts to become a fuller realization of the church or *ecclesia*, so that all the gifts—wisdom, understanding, knowledge, mercy, leadership, prophecy, encouragement, discernment, healing, miracles, helps, teaching, apostleship, and, yes, the least of these gifts, which is speaking in tongues (*glossolalia*)—are present in the body of Christ. The Holy Spirit gives different gifts

---

10. Augustine, "Augustine of Hippo's On the Trinity, Book 9," in *The Trinitarian Controversy*, ed. William G. Rusch (Philadelphia: Fortress, 1980) 164–77.

11. See, for example, Jürgen Moltmann, *The Church in the Power of the Spirit: A Contribution to Messianic Ecclesiology* (San Francisco: Harper & Row, 1977).

to members of the body of Christ. When one looks at the traditions and denominations within the church universal, there are some traditions and denominations that exercise some of these gifts more than others. Together, they form the holy catholic church in its original meaning, which is simply holy *universal* church.

According to the teachings of John Wesley, we can do nothing without the Holy Spirit. The specific work of the Holy Spirit is sanctifying grace, but the Holy Spirit as grace is present in the prevenient and justifying activities of the first and second persons of the Trinity. For Wesley the sanctifying presence and power of the Holy Spirit is evident in works of mercy. The entire Trinity gives gifts of prevenient, justifying, and sanctifying grace to the world. The Holy Spirit, however, is the specific hypostasis in which we find God's work of sanctifying grace-gifts. The entire Trinity loves because God loves the world enough to send God's only Son that we might have abundant life. Yet, it is in the sanctifying activity of the Holy Spirit that we learn what it means to love. The Holy Spirit is (1) our comforter, who nurtures us like a mother; (2) our teacher and guide who leads us into all truth, which is the Wisdom/Word of God who justifies us in divine grace; (3) our advocate, who with Word/Wisdom advocates for us before God the Parent and in response to the world of profound injustices; (4) the power of life, who, like a mother, bears and births us (John 3:3–8), and in perfect Love; (5) a divine witness to the Word and Wisdom of God; (6) one who intercedes for us with sighs, groans, and moans when words are inadequate for expressing what is in the depths of our hearts; (7) the *hypostasis* of the One God who makes church a reality.

Those who are wise draw from the sagacious power of the Spirit to create beauty out of ugliness, celebrate life in the midst of suffering, and walk in love in the midst of hate. Womanists attribute the power of love to the Spirit. Womanists and other peoples tend to employ the term "Spirit" in two ways: (1) to refer to God who is a spirit; and (2) among Christian womanists and Christians in general, to refer to the Holy Spirit. The Holy Spirit is a distinctive, relational action or mode of being in the Trinity. Or, to emphasize the dynamic movement of the Holy Spirit, one might say that "she" is the dynamic agent of divine healing revealed by Jesus the Christ. Her constant unchanging nature is to comfort, heal, renew or recreate, and instruct. She is the power through which God "creates a new thing."

A healing comes to mind. A healing big enough to hold anger and turn it into justice seeking, rather than vengeance seeking. A healing big enough to hold bitterness, transforming it into peace. A healing big enough to hold hate and transform it into love. A healing big enough to overcome death and create new life. God is big enough to hold our anger. God is big enough to hold bitterness. God is big enough to hold hate. God is big enough to overcome death. God takes the hotness of anger, the ferment of bitterness, and the sourness of hatred to work with it, creatively transforming it into something sweeter. Existence alone ranges from bitter to bittersweet. Conscious, committed existence in God is more. The very presence of a moment of sweetness, comfort, or joy testifies to the presence of goodness in the land of the living. The Holy Spirit is the power of resurrecting healing. The distinctive work of the relation Christians call "the Holy Spirit" is healing, renewing, comforting, instructing, guiding, and encouraging the people of God; not only healing them, but also empowering them with gifts to go out and heal others.

CONCRETE SOCIAL MANIFESTATIONS OF THE HEALING MOVEMENT OF THE HOLY SPIRIT

The Holy Spirit inspires the dance of God, calling all to participate in the dance of divine love, creativity, healing, justice, and renewal. Healing is contagious. It is something that those who have experienced healing share with others. In the case of the Byrd Family, the Holy Spirit gave them gifts of finances, love, and teaching that empowered them to create a center for racial healing. In the case of James Byrd, he received gifts of finances, funds, love, teaching, writing, and speaking to create the Black Holocaust Museum in Milwaukee, Wisconsin. Many people such as these around the world find divine courage. They literally take heart and commit their lives to receiving and participating in the grace of divine healing.

. . .

The Holy Spirit and Social Activism

Mamie Till-Mobley was not simply concerned about the lynching of her own son when she held a nationally attended open-casket viewing and funeral in 1955. She was protesting the entire institution of lynching and racial hatred. As a Christian, she felt led by the Holy Spirit to make the horrific tragedy of Emmett's death an event for protest and a call to righteous, just love. She went on to speak out against racial violence nationally and as an educator.

For this reason the artist Vanessa Baker observes that, "There are many stories that circulate throughout history, then become pivotal in the mind's eye. One is the case of Emmett Till." Baker recalls, "I first heard of him as I listened in on one of the many discussions that went on between my mother and my paternal grandmother. They discussed everything—the past, the present, the future; they discussed religious views: who was in and who was out—politically; and the weather. They debated issues concerning what then typified the current status of society. These were *our* stories." Storytelling, historically, has been an important aspect of African American family life. The elders told stories not simply to entertain, but to educate. They shared, and many still do share, history. Even folk tales carry with them the same intent as the parables of Jesus, to tell truth in a way that anyone of any age in a community can understand. Baker's elders, like many, shared historical stories. Baker observes, "Some, such as Emmett's, were painful. But within that pain, even as a young child, I saw inspiration. Emmett's life stood as an ever-existing mirror angled before the face of humanity. It was placed before us through the agony, yet determination, of a courageous mother, Mamie Till [Mobley], who helped to teach me that all things—including one's afflictions—are woven into one's wholeness."[12] Baker found wisdom about wholeness in the story of the Till family.

Baker believes that by faith and in divine grace, she is called to provide more

---

12. Interview responses from Vanessa Baker, April 20, 2005.

opportunities for educational healing through artistic events in which young people and mature adults alike participate. While some experience God, "the Spirit," or, in the case of Christians, God in the power of the Holy Spirit calling them to create centers or museums for human tolerance and the healing of racial hatred, the Spirit gives many more gifts to the world. Vanessa Baker experiences her artistic talents as gifts of the Holy Spirit that she is to use in the work of education and healing."[13] As a Christian artist, Baker's faith in the Holy Spirit to empower and inspire her has led her to respond to a calling to create poetry and dance that tell healing stories of the past. As she puts it:

> My hope is that sincere concern and interest in regard to these stories continue to rekindle in each of us. Maybe we'll see less handcuffed youth, declaring the significance of a "color" while sporting jeans that cup the thigh instead of the waist. Maybe when we reunite as a community of pride-filled people, those who attack us to create an everlasting subservience will cease their tactics of intimidation. The rewards to us for clinging to our legacy are limitless.[14]

Theologians such as Joanne Terrell in the 1990s [in her book, *Power in the Blood?: The Cross in the African American Experience*] and myself in the twenty-first century have been moved by the Till story and stories like it to give theological attention to such events in relation to systematic theology, specifically christology. Like the story of Mary, mother of Jesus, the story of Mamie Till-Mobley teaches that the power of faith, drawn from an ever-present God revealed in Christ, inspired by the breath of God's own spirit, brings new life. What we learn from her story is that we need not be overcome by the second death that tries to take the soul. Mother Mobley was contemplating suicide when the phone rang, and from seemingly nowhere a place that could only be the quiet, nudging voice of God—she found courage to tell a reporter she planned to go back to school. The reporter helped her register for college. After only three and a half years, she became a teacher to what would become, in time, thousands of children. She did not give in to despair.[15] Held by the power of God, she was not overcome by bitterness that kills the soul. In her lowest moment, she found what Katie Cannon, a womanist ethicist from the South, calls "unshouted courage."[16]

"Unshouted courage" comes from that place where God "makes a way out of no way." It is what the old and the wise have in mind when they say God can "make something out of nothing." Feeling suicidal is to feel that you are nothing, that there is nothing to hope for, no reason to continue on. Life has lost its meaning. All looks and feels dark when one is in the depths of despair. Yet, in the depths of that abyss, there is a light that shines, a voice that calls, an energy that lures or draws the soul forward from the darkness and into a place of light, where gradually a sense of purpose is renewed. Mamie

13. Ibid.
14. Ibid.

15. Mamie Till-Mobley and Christopher Benson, *Death of Innocence: The Story of the Hate Crime That Changed America* (New York: Random House, 2003) 217–18.

16. Katie G. Cannon, *Black Womanist Ethics* (Atlanta: American Academy of Religion, 1988) 143–48.

Till-Mobley's legacy is her lived testimony to this light that shines in the darkness:

> All things came into being through him, and without him not one thing came into being. What has come into being in him was life, and the life was the light of all people. The light shines in the darkness, and the darkness did not overcome it. There was a man sent from God, whose name was John. He came as a witness to testify to the light, so that all might believe through him. He himself was not the light, but he came to testify to the light. The true light, which enlightens everyone, was coming into the world. (John 1:3–9)

Already a Christian woman, Mamie Till-Mobley experienced this light in her darkest moment. Through divine, preventive grace, the telephone rang; and it came into her mind that she would go back to school instead of jump out of a window.[17] She did not keep the light of God's presence to herself, but shared it with others. She taught the knowledge that in God each of us has a purpose. She shared this message in one way as a school teacher, encouraging children to live up to their full potential. She shared this in other ways as a community leader and church mother in the Church of God in Christ. Like John, she herself was not the light. Like Mary, she was simply a bereaved mother whose son died a brutal death.

Before she died, Mamie Till-Mobley said to her biographer, "I have come to realize that we are all here for a purpose and we have unique gifts to share with the rest of the world." She knew her time was near and said further,

> I have enjoyed a full, rich, meaningful life because I was able to discover my reason for being and to perfect my gifts in fulfilling my purpose, touching so many lives in the process. Hopefully, I have left each one just a little better than I found it. Hopefully, I have made a difference. That is, after all, how our lives are measured. By how many other lives we touch and inspire. By how much of life we embrace, not by what we reject. By what we accept, not by what we judge."[18]

Mother Mamie Till-Mobley acknowledged that even with all the goodness and joy she had come to experience in her life, especially through touching the lives of others, she still cried about Emmett sometimes.

> But I see much more clearly now through my tears, and that is a good thing. Rainy days always help us appreciate the sunny ones so much more, don't they? Besides, it is in crying that we are able to let go. In letting go, I have experienced what it is like to bring hope from despair, joy from anguish, forgiveness from anger, love from hate. And if I can do it, I know anyone can. And if everyone does it, just imagine how much better we all can be.[19]

Indeed the Holy Spirit graces followers of Jesus with many gifts to *edify* or *build up* the church, which is the *body of Christ*, to fulfill its call to participate in God's loving, healing activity with heart, head, and body (1 Corinthians 12). Mother Till-Mobley knew that by the grace of God and in the power of the Holy Spirit, she truly

---

17. Till-Mobley, *Death*.

18. Ibid., 283.

19. Ibid.

could do "all things through [Christ] who strengthens me" (Philippians 1:13). She did not sink into victimhood and wallow in suffering. She became an overcomer and a leader in the civil rights movement before Martin Luther King Jr. became the leader of the bus boycott in Montgomery, Alabama, in 1955, a boycott initiated by another great woman of God—Mother Rosa Parks. Mother Till-Mobley, like Rosa Parks, was a faithful witness to the light, the divine energy that calls us forward into realizing active hope in the full potential of humanity. She knew the wisdom so many African American women have taught their children and practiced; "You have to rise to the occasion!" As a follower of Jesus, she took heart, because she knew the living Christ had overcome the world. In courage she became a leader for righteousness, justice, and tough love. In Christ she became a leader in overcoming a world of crucifixion. She did not ask, "What should I do?" She listened to the Spirit, and she did it! The community knew she was a woman in the Spirit and did not cynically ask, "Well, what should we do?" and wait for a miracle. They listened to the Spirit, too, and in so doing *became the miracle*. An ordinary woman and bereaved mother, Mother Mobley became a prophet and mother to many in her commitment to helping an entire nation understand that it must be transformed . . . May we all learn not only from her life well-lived, but from her life's testimony to the gracious power of the Spirit to move even the most despairing of believers forward, one dynamic step at a time. Like Coretta Scott King, she walked and she did not faint. She carried the banner for peace, love, and healing of racial hatred. Already led by the Spirit to commit her life to racial healing, she shared the Christian and Gandhi-inspired values of the twentieth-century human rights movement led by Dr. Martin Luther King Jr., Coretta Scott King, Rosa Parks, Ella Baker,[20] and a host of others, female and male, of diverse racial-ethnic, religious groups and nationalities.

Women like Mother Mamie Till Mobley, Mother Rosa Parks, Mother Ella Baker, and First Lady Coretta Scott King could have hated, but walked in love. They could have sunk to violent rage, but instead they walked in holy indignation and holy dignity. They led others as they followed Christ in the comforting, encouraging, and healing power of the Holy Spirit. God in Christ bore them up on wings like eagles (Isa 40:31). They showed the world the meaning of resurrection, Holy Spirit power. One step at a time, may we all take heart. One step at a time and by the grace of God, may we all follow Christ's example, Mary's example, Mother Mobley's, Rosa Parks's, Ella Baker's, and Coretta Scott King's examples. One dynamic step at a time, may we all dance with the Trinity in the power of the Spirit! May we do so in love for an entire creation, following the example of Coretta Scott King who, as the first lady of the civil rights movement

---

20. Ella Baker is known as the "Mother" of the Student Non-Violent Coordinating Committee (SNCC) and was a leader of the Southern Christian Leadership Conference (SCLC), which helped young people found SNCC. Members of SNCC initiated the "sit-ins" in restaurants and diners that discriminated against people of color and Jews. As far as I know, she is not related to myself and my family. Still, however, given the disruption of name family relationships during slavery and all she stood for, I feel kinship with her as a Baker in name and simply as an ancestor that should be admitted by all of us as one of our spiritual mothers in the communion of saints.

throughout her adult life, met with freedom and human rights activists of all religions and from around the world as a follower of Jesus. May we who are Christian, like these women of the Spirit, realize that when we truly follow Jesus—with all our hearts, minds, strength, and souls, loving our neighbors as ourselves—we are the miracle. We are the miracle when we live in the wholeness of divine grace toward all creation. This is the good news of Jesus, the Christ! This is the dance with God! Amen.

Commentary

MONICA A. COLEMAN

Dancing with God: The Trinity from a Womanist Perspective is most explicitly about how the metaphorical understanding of dance (both performative and instinctual) is well suited to describing how black women manage to live in the midst of tremendous unnecessary violence. *Dancing with God* revolves around the two most famous lynching stories in the last century of African American history—the murders of Emmett Till in 1955 and James Byrd Jr. in 1998. Separated by over forty years, these murders reflect not only the precarious reality for many African Americans in a racist society, but also the courage that their respective mothers took in responding to these incidents. Amazed at how these women could go on after the lynching of their sons, Karen Baker-Fletcher establishes courage as a theological category that, infused with Spirit, allows black women to creatively transform the world around them. The excerpt from the last chapter that is presented here is where readers see Baker-Fletcher connect most succinctly the historical narratives, Protestant and Catholic Christianity, contemporary issues in theology and social activism.

In this work, Baker-Fletcher is doing what she terms "integrative theology," a theology that draws from various theological sources to make its conclusions. Baker-Fletcher's theology uniquely draws together process theology, Christian evangelical theology, and womanist theologies. Readers can see *Dancing with God* reflect both Baker-Fletcher's own personal commitments as a "Christian relational womanist," and larger trends within process theological reflection.

Although readers can see Baker-Fletcher's flirtations with process-relational theology in *Sisters of Dust, Sisters of Spirit* (1998),[1] she is most explicit in *Dancing with God*. She acknowledges the ways in which former colleagues at the Claremont School of Theology influence her: notably, John B. Cobb Jr. and Marjorie Hewitt Suchocki. At Perkins School of Theology at Southern Methodist University, she has increased interaction with

---

1. Karen Baker-Fletcher, *Sisters of Dust, Sisters of Spirit: Womanist Wordings of God and Creation* (Minneapolis: Fortress, 1998).

Theodore Walker Jr., an African American ethicist in the Hartshornean tradition of neoclassical metaphysics. Influenced by both Whiteheadians and Hartshorneans, Baker-Fletcher seeks common ground between both schools of process thought. She remains relatively unconcerned with the details of the metaphysics because she wants to highlight the broad themes of process thought that contribute to her understanding of God and world. For this reason, she will refer to her work as "relational." Indeed, an increasing number of feminists and womanists prefer the term "relational" when invoking many of the tenets of process thought.

Baker-Fletcher is also part of the long-standing conversations between process thought and Wesleyan thinkers. It is no mere coincidence, some have asserted, that many Christian process theologians are also Methodists. Schubert Ogden, John B. Cobb, Jr., and Marjorie Hewitt Suchocki have been forerunners in noting the resonances between process thought and Wesleyan theology. More recently, Bryan P. Stone and Thomas Jay Oord compiled various writers to discuss explicitly these connections in *Thy Nature and Thy Name Is Love: Wesleyan and Process Theologies in Dialogue* (2001).[2] These conversations continue in the American Academy of Religion's Open and Relational Theologies Consultation. Historically posited against one another, evangelical and process theologians with shared commitments to open theism and relational thinking discuss the ways in which they contribute to the contemporary theological enterprise.[3] Baker-Fletcher is grounded in the holiness tradition that reflects both experiences in Wesleyan/Methodist heritage and black church religiosity. She invokes the Wesleyan/Methodist quadrilateral in her method (Scripture, tradition, experience, and reason), while also discussing the importance of Spirit for how many people of faith actually experience God. And, unlike many other process theologies, her integrative theology will affirm the following: the Bible is authoritative for matters of salvation; conversion from sin is possible through Jesus Christ and necessary for salvation; and Christians should evangelize and transform the world around them.

The last significant ingredient in Baker-Fletcher's theological cauldron is the one for which she is most known: womanist theological reflection. Baker-Fletcher's work is womanist in that she makes the lived experiences of black women the center of her theological reflection. As she does in *A Singing Something: Womanist Reflections on Anna Julia Cooper* (1994),[4] Baker-Fletcher grounds *Dancing with God* in the historical experiences of black women. We also see her kinship to womanist theologian Delores S. Williams, who asserts that while liberation is important, survival and quality of life may also be a goal of womanist theology. Baker-Fletcher's most well-known contribution to womanist theology is in *Sisters of Dust, Sisters of Spirit*, her

---

2. Bryan P. Stone and Thomas Jay Oord, eds. *Thy Nature and Thy Name Is Love: Wesleyan and Process Theologies in Dialogue* (Nashville: Kingswood, 2001).

3. See Thomas Jay Oord, "Evangelical Theologies," in *Handbook of Process Theology*, eds. Jay McDaniel and Donna Bowman (St. Louis: Chalice, 2006) 251–61.

4. Karen Baker-Fletcher, *A Singing Something: Womanist Reflections on Anna Julia Cooper* (New York: Crossroad, 1994).

book-length engagement with ecological justice and the ways that environmental racism impinge upon the lives of ordinary black women. Her assertion that everyone is both dust and spirit, human and divine, echoes throughout *Dancing with God*.

Like Alice Walker (who coined the term "womanist"), Baker-Fletcher is interested in the well-being of the whole community. Baker-Fletcher also shares Walker's habit of making alliances with other people seeking liberation. Thus Baker-Fletcher's integrative theology incorporates feminist and *mujerista* theologies, and more centrally Andrew Sung Park's Korean theological understanding of *han*. Unlike Walker, a self-described pagan-Buddhist, Baker-Fletcher is committed to reflection within the realm of Christianity.

Although many process theologians reflect on the categories of systematic theology, Baker-Fletcher's work is a prime example of ways to utilize women's theologies and process theology within a more evangelical Christian framework. Her work opens the door for evangelical Christian women theologians, who may have eschewed the natural-theology leanings of process theology, to participate in process-relational theology. Baker-Fletcher also offers a way forward for Christian theologians of color, who historically have resisted the metaphysics of process thought and/or its more liberal theological assertions. Baker-Fletcher convincingly shows how process thought can undergird a theology grounded in history and liberation.

STUDY QUESTIONS

1. Baker-Fletcher suggests that women's activism against violence is a way of "taking up the cross." How do women "take up the cross" in your own community? How might you?

2. Baker-Fletcher draws upon women process theologians when discussing heaven, hell, and redemption. She critiques Suchocki for locating "heaven" in what Whiteheadian process thinkers refer to as "the consequent nature of God." Is this one of the places where Baker-Fletcher departs from process thought? Or does she offer a helpful revision to process metaphysics? If so, how?

3. How does Baker-Fletcher use Wesleyan concepts of justifying, preventing, and sanctifying grace to discuss the Trinity and resurrection?

4. What is the role of commemoration and education in Baker-Fletcher's understanding of the work of the Holy Spirit?

12 Theological Anthropology

NANCY R. HOWELL

Nancy R. Howell is Professor of Theology and Philosophy of Religion at Saint Paul School of Theology and Adjunct Professor of Bioethics at Kansas City University of Medicine and Biosciences in Kansas City, Missouri. Howell received degrees from The College of William and Mary, Southeastern Baptist Theological Seminary, and Claremont Graduate School. Her research interests include science and religion, theological primatology, feminist theology, and process theology. The excerpt is taken from the journal Theology and Science, where the article titled "The Importance of Being Chimpanzee" was first published in 2003. The article reflects on recent primate studies that name chimpanzee behavioral traits that challenge theological claims about human uniqueness. Process-feminist theology informs Howell's ecofeminist reconstruction of theology in response to primate studies.

Excerpt from "The Importance of Being Chimpanzee"

WHAT COUNTS AS HUMAN uniqueness becomes more difficult to defend as science becomes more skilled in observing and interpreting animals. Primate studies fascinate us because we continue to be surprised that animals we presuppose to be rather distinct from humans gradually display characteristics that humans have guarded as our own. Chimpanzees (and other animals) amaze humans with language-related skills, culturally transmitted knowledge, and behavioral precursors of morality In light of the closing gap between our definitions of human uniqueness and our understanding of primates, what is left of human uniqueness? How have science, philosophy, and religion established presuppositions about human uniqueness, which may need to be revised in response to primate research? As the characteristics defining human uniqueness are identified in other primates, humans are caught in the tension between protecting a sense of human nature and identity and recognizing that humans, too, are animals. While scientific research clearly makes the case that humans are very closely related to chimpanzees, truly claiming kinship with primates is difficult. Perhaps one factor that makes humans reluctant to recognize our place in nature is a history of associating some humans with animals and nature in order to justify subordination, inferiority, or oppression.

The habits of thought, language, and experience that preserve human uniqueness in relation to animal inferiority are challenged by primate studies, and how humans draw boundaries between themselves and animals seriously shapes how we understand justice among humans and animals. To make a case for this justice claim, this article will review what primate studies teach us about chimpanzees, name what questions about human uniqueness emerge from reflection on science, and recall how the history of science, philosophy, and theology demonstrates some conformity in presuppositions about human uniqueness and animal inferiority.

PRIMATE STUDIES: CLOSING THE GAP BETWEEN HUMANS AND CHIMPANZEES

Genetics is the first basis for demonstrating the kinship of humans with chimpanzees. A 1967 study of blood proteins led Vincent Sarich and Allan Wilson to conclude that human and chimpanzee protein molecules are very similar.[1] In a 1975 study comparing human and chimpanzee proteins, Mary-Claire King and A. C. Wilson discovered that the genetic differences between humans and chimpanzees are relatively small in light of significant morphological and behavioral differences in the two species.[2] In the early 1980s, more sophisticated genetic comparisons reported by Charles Sibley and Jon Ahlquist concluded that humans and chimpanzees share a 98.4% similarity in DNA. The genetic similarity of humans and chimpanzees is greater than the similarity of gorillas and orangutans with chimpanzees.[3] Because of genetic data, primate taxonomy now groups chimpanzees, gorillas, and orangutans as *hominids*, a term once reserved for humans and human ancestors.[4] Genetic and evolutionary continuity between apes and humans suggests that an understanding of human nature depends on understanding apes. Craig Stanford makes this claim in *Significant Others: The Ape-Human Continuum and the Quest for Human Nature,* but he cautions that extrapolation between ape and human species must keep in mind that apes are not primitive humans.[5] Stanford examines feeding, mating, hunting, and other behaviors that give insight into human nature. For example, the contrasting behaviors of chimpanzees and bonobos suggest interesting alternatives in evolutionary ancestry. Chimpanzees demonstrate highly aggressive and violent behavior, which includes the struggle to maintain rigid dominance hierarchy, sexual coercion and beating of females, and patrol of perimeters and attacking or murdering neighbors.[6] Bonobos, however, maintain social organization through social cooperation, sexual social communication, and alliance formation.[7] Chimpanzees are known to be especially brutal and violent hunters who capture monkeys

---

1. Vincent Sarich and Allan Wilson, "Immunological Timescale for Human Evolution," *Science* 158 (1967) 1200–203; cited in Roger Fouts, *Next of Kin: My Conversations with Chimpanzees* (New York: Avon, 1997) 54.

2. Mary-Claire King and A. C. Wilson, "Evolution at Two Levels in Humans and Chimpanzees," *Science* 188 (1975) 107–16; cited in Stephen Jay Gould, *Ever Since Darwin: Reflections in Natural History* (New York: Norton, 1977) 50–51.

3. Charles G. Sibley and Jon E. Ahlquist, "The Phylogeny of the Hominoid Primates, as Indicated by DNA-DNA Hybridization," *Journal of Molecular Evolution* 20 (1984) 2–15; cited in Fouts, *Next of Kin,* 55.

4. Ibid., 57.

5. Craig Stanford, *Significant Others: The Ape-Human Continuum and the Quest for Human Nature* (New York: Basic Books, 2001) xviii, xv.

6. Ibid., 23.

7. Ibid., 24.

and kill them "either by a bite to the neck (for small-bodied juveniles) or by thrashing them against the ground or a tree limb (for adult colobus)."[8] The chimpanzee high-ranking males share the meat with kin *and* allies, but withhold meat from rival chimpanzees. Alternatively, bonobos capture monkeys but tend to use them as dolls or playthings rather than food. The monkeys are released without harm.[9] What do these two behavioral patterns teach us about human nature? Craig Stanford writes:

> These recent findings about bonobos have led anthropologists to place humans squarely at an evolutionary crossroads. One path leads to a chimpanzee world of male brutality and violence, where might makes right and the low guy on the totem pole must grovel to avoid taking a beating from his higher ups. The other path leads to a vision of humanity in which violence is not strength and compassionate bonding is not a weakness. It's not Camelot, it's bonobo society.[10]

Stanford cautions that the studies of bonobos and chimpanzees have compared captive bonobos with wild chimpanzees and may reflect political biases of researchers, yet social bonds among females may be a real difference between bonobos and chimpanzees.[11]

CHIMPANZEE CULTURE

Recently, culture and learning among chimpanzees is reported in scientific literature. Claims about culture in chimpanzees are controversial because they depend upon a rather inclusive definition of *culture*, more comfortable for biologists than anthropologists. Frans de Waal defines *culture* as follows:

> Culture is a way of life shared by the members of one group but not necessarily with the members of other groups of the same species. It covers knowledge, habits, and skills, including underlying tendencies and preferences, derived from exposure to and learning from others. Whenever systematic variation in knowledge, habits, and skills between groups cannot be attributed to genetic or ecological factors, it is probably cultural. The way individuals learn from each other is secondary, but that they learn from each other is a requirement. Thus, the "culture" label does not apply to knowledge, habits, or skills that individuals readily acquire on their own.[12]

De Waal's theory is that primate social learning is rooted in the "urge to belong to or fit the social organization."[13] De Waal's acronym for the process of learning motivated by conformism is BIOL, Bonding-and-Identification-based Observational Learning. Observations suggest that this learning process is present in both wild and human-reared chimpanzees.

Imitation appears to be one mode of learning associated with tool use, grooming behavior, vocalization (pant-hoots), and self-medication. The case of self-medication is particularly interesting.

---

8. Ibid., 23–24.
9. Ibid., 27.
10. Ibid.
11. Ibid., 29.

12. Frans de Waal, *The Ape and the Sushi Master: Cultural Reflections of a Primatologist* (New York, NY: Basic Books, 2001) 31.
13. Ibid., 231.

For example, the juice of *Vernonia amygdalina* is extremely bitter, and the plant's bark and leaves contain toxins. However, chimpanzees remove the outer bark and the leaves of young shoots of *Vernonia* and chew the pith to extract the juice. Chimpanzees who do this show symptoms including diarrhea, listlessness, and worm infections. Fecal analysis showed a drop in nematode infection in one chimpanzee following chewing the bitter pith, but no corresponding drop in infection was observed in chimpanzees that did not use the medicine. African human groups use *Vernonia* to treat malaria, dysentery, and intestinal parasites.[14] In another example, from Gombe and Mahale, chimpanzees use their tongues to fold hairy, rough *Aspilla* leaves so that the leaves may be swallowed whole. Because the leaves are not chewed, *Aspilla* seems to act as a mechanical device to remove intestinal parasites. Chimpanzees are observed to swallow the leaves in the morning before foraging for food. More than thirty different plant species' are used similarly across Africa, which suggests that cultural transmission plays a role in learning self-medication. Chimpanzee self-medication is a risky and difficult practice. De Waal indicates that because "self-medication seems hard to acquire without the example of others and is assumed to assist survival, it remains high on the agenda of research into chimpanzee culture."[15]

Active teaching, which stops just short of symbolic communication, is another form of social transmission. Active teaching requires the ability to adopt a perspective outside oneself in order to assess another's knowledge and its deficiencies and. then to address the deficiencies through instruction.[16] De Waal provides a clear example of active teaching in chimpanzees. In the Taï Forest, mother chimpanzees may actively teach infants the skill of nut cracking. When adults finish eating nuts, they usually take their nut-cracking tools with them. However, mother chimpanzees sometimes leave nuts, rock hammers, and anvils ready for use and in the presence of infants. As they attend to the direction of the infant gaze, mothers, sometimes show the normally rapid nut-cracking motion in slow motion. Sometimes mothers correct unsuccessful infants by removing the nut from the anvil, cleaning the anvil, repositioning the nut, or reorienting the hammer held by their infant. Mothers and infants appear to be involved in active learning, but too few observations currently support this claim and more research is needed.[17]

Tool use among chimpanzees is diverse across Africa, and the most reasonable explanation is cultural variation and learned traditions.[18] Even familiar chimpanzee tool use, such as fishing for termites, shows variation in different chimpanzee traditions. While tool use is now commonly accepted in chimpanzees symbolic meaning in tool usage has been reserved for humans. However, Craig Stanford provides examples that may show symbolic meaning in chimpanzee tool usage. Male chimpanzees may use tools to signal females that they would like to mate. At Gombe, male chimpanzees rapidly shake a small bush or branch

14. Ibid., 254.
15. Ibid., 255.
16. Ibid., 262.
17. Ibid., 262–63.
18. Stanford, *Significant Others*, 112–14.

several times to signal readiness to mate. After the signal, the female approaches the male and presents herself to him. In Mahale, male chimpanzees use leaves to initiate courtship. The courtship gesture involves plucking a leafy branch and noisily tearing off the leaves with teeth and fingers. The gesture, called leaf clipping, is only used when signaling to a particular female that the male is ready to mate. In addition to using tools in courtship gestures, chimpanzees may symbolically groom leaves to signal desire for grooming from a social partner.[19]

CHIMPANZEES AND LANGUAGE

Four decades of primate language studies with chimpanzees started with the work of Allen and Beatrix Gardner in the 1960s and continues in the work of Roger and Deborah Fouts at the Central Washington University Chimpanzee and Human Communication Institute. Washoe is the female chimpanzee that without reward or punishment learned American Sign Language as a very young chimpanzee. Washoe not only learned hundreds of signs, but also was able to improvise signs and signed to herself (when looking at magazine photographs).[20] Later, Washoe successfully taught her adopted son Loulis to sign as human researchers limited sign language in his presence.[21] The cultural transmission of language to offspring and the demonstration that chimpanzees used American Sign Language in the absence of human researchers were important accomplishments in primate language studies.[22] While chimpanzees do not have the same vocal anatomy as humans, their facility and neural apparatus are similar to humans.[23] As chimpanzees gesture naturally, American Sign Language was a more successful approach to primate language study than spoken English. Social interaction is important for learning language. Chimpanzee calls have both a genetic and a learned component, and in the wild, chimpanzees imitate the subtleties of their companions' calls. Chimpanzee calls have different dialects in East Africa, and chimpanzees may adapt their calls to sound more like their companions. Craig Stanford indicates that the ability to imitate calls is characteristic of socially complex animals.[24]

CHIMPANZEES AS MEAT EATERS

Meat eating and hunting are part of complex social interactions among chimpanzees. Stanford notes three differences in human and chimpanzee predation. First, humans in traditional societies search for prey, while chimpanzees are opportunistic meat-eaters who capture prey when they happen upon them. Second, while humans use weapons, chimpanzees do not. Third, humans are capable of killing and eating large prey because they use weapons and carving tools, while chimpanzee prey is limited to animals of 20 pounds or less.[25] Stanford also notes similarities between human and chimpanzee meat-eating. First, both prefer to eat meat even though meat makes up a small percentage of their diets. Second, both probably eat

---

19. Ibid., 114.
20. Fouts, *Next of Kin*, 71.
21. Ibid., 240–41.
22. Ibid., 302–3.
23. Stanford, *Significant Others*, 158.
24. Ibid., 159.
25. Ibid., 54–55.

meat for the fat content since protein and calories are more plentiful in other components of their diets. Third, chimpanzees and humans are omnivores who decide when they will hunt.[26] Stanford's theory is that meat eating is part of a market economy in apes and early humans. The social market economy of chimpanzees requires individuals to keep a tally of social debits and credits. Because chimpanzees keep a "balance sheet of relationships," meat (which contributes so little to the diet) may be a currency bartered to form alliances and to pay social debt.[27] Stanford argues,

> that since the energy and time that chimpanzees spend hunting is rarely paid back by calories, protein and fat gotten from a kill, we should consider hunting a social behavior done at least partly for its own sake. When chimpanzees barter a limited commodity such as meat for other services—alliances, sex, grooming—they are engaging in a very simple and primitive form of a currency exchange . . . It may be that two chimpanzee cultures two thousand kilometers apart have developed their distinct uses of meat as a social currency.[28]

Stanford suggests that similar systems evident in humans may share roots with the chimpanzee social economy.

CHIMPANZEE ART AND MORALITY

Among the intellectual abilities of chimpanzees may be art and aesthetics. Frans de Waal offers a number of examples of chimpanzees engaged in art. First, Desmond Morris worked with a young chimpanzee painter whose work was exhibited in 1957. Congo's painting is described as very controlled and beautiful with qualities such as energetic style, symmetrical coverage, rhythmical variations, and eye-catching color contrasts.[29] Second, a chimpanzee named Bella seemed to have a strong sense of completion in paintings. When her zookeeper at the Amsterdam Zoo interrupted her painting, Bella lost her temper. Similarly, Congo was disturbed when someone attempted to remove his painting before he was finished or when someone encouraged him to continue painting after he put down his brush. Once Desmond Morris succeeded in taking a fan-shaped painting away from Congo, but when he returned the painting, Congo completed the pattern started in the painting.[30] Third, a chimpanzee named Kunda painted with French artist Lucien Tessarolo. Kunda and Tessarolo collaborated on paintings and sometimes Kunda responded favorably to the figures that Tessarolo contributed. Other times, Kunda rubbed out Tessarolo's figures and waited for him to add something new before continuing to paint herself. Kunda apparently reacted to Tessarolo's figures based on a sense of how the completed painting should look.[31]

De Waal has also reported that chimpanzees (and other animals) may demonstrate behaviors that are clues to the evolution of morality. By looking for sympathy-related traits, norm-related characteristics, reciprocity, and getting along, de Waal investigates whether

---

26. Ibid., 55.
27. Ibid., 51.
28. Ibid., 116–17.
29. De Waal, *The Ape and the Sushi Master*, 169.
30. Ibid., 172.
31. Ibid., 173.

"some of the building blocks of morality are recognizable in other animals."[32] Sympathetic behavior is observed in wild and human-raised chimpanzees. In the wild, chimpanzees were observed to express a kind of sympathy upon finding the body of a male who broke his neck in a fall. The chimpanzees displayed, embraced, touched, and mounted, and an individual juvenile female stared at the body for more than an hour.[33] A human-reared chimpanzee, Lucy, responded to her human mother's illness by becoming disturbed, comforting the human, bringing her food, and grooming her.[34] Deception, another component of moral behavior, is evident in chimpanzees. In the wild some DNA studies show that female chimpanzees conceived offspring with enemy males outside their group. Because the females were absent from the resident group for a very short period of time, the "resident males were led to believe that one of them was surely the father of the ensuing offspring, when in fact none of them were."[35] The captive chimpanzee Washoe set up a deception of Roger Fouts (then a graduate student) when she was a young chimpanzee. Washoe pretended attention to something in the rock garden, and her intent interest drew Fouts into the garden. When Fouts remained in the garden to writes notes, Washoe climbed into a tree and waited until he became so absorbed in his writing that she could rush down the tree, into the house, and steal soda from an unlocked cabinet. Fouts writes, "Washoe must have noticed that the cupboard was unlocked during breakfast, suppressed her natural impulse to raid it when my back was turned, and instead devised this plan for distracting me long enough to drink the soda. This was a level of planning and deception beyond anything I thought her capable of."[36] While de Waal would not take anecdotal evidence of behaviors as proof that chimpanzees are moral beings, he does conclude that constituent behaviors of morality are present in animals.[37]

Jane Goodall suggests that chimpanzees may experience something similar to spirituality. She notes that awe is a feeling that humans articulated with language and that led to religious belief and worship. Chimpanzees express something like awe at a spectacular waterfall in the Kakombe valley. Goodall describes watching the chimpanzees at the waterfall:

> For me, it is a magical place, and a spiritual one. And sometimes, as they approach, the chimpanzees display in slow, rhythmic motion along the river bed. They pick up and throw great rocks and branches. They leap to seize the hanging vines, and swing out over the stream in the spray-drenched wind until it seems the slender stems must snap or be torn from their lofty moorings.
>
> For ten minutes or more they may perform this magnificent "dance." Why? Is it not possible that the chimpanzees are responding to some feeling like awe? A feeling generated by the mystery of the

---

32. Frans de Waal, *Good Natured: The Origins of Right and Wrong in Humans and Other Animals* (Cambridge: Harvard University Press, 1996) 3.

33. Ibid., 56.

34. M. K. Temerlin, *Lucy: Growing Up Human* (Palo Alto, CA: Science and Behavior Books, 1975); cited in de Waal, *Good Natured*, 60.

35. Stanford, *Significant Others*, 73.

36. Fouts, *Next of Kin*, 45–46.

37. De Waal, *Good Natured*, 210.

water; water that seems alive, always rushing past yet never going, always the same yet ever different. Was it perhaps similar feelings of awe that gave rise to the first animistic religions, the worship of elements and the mysteries of nature over which there was no control? Only when our prehistoric ancestors developed language would it have been possible to discuss such internal feelings and create a shared religion.[38]

While far from sufficient to demonstrate religion or even spirituality in chimpanzees, Goodall's observation of chimpanzees at the Kakombe waterfall indicates that some primatologists are alert to behaviors that relate to human spirituality.

Chimpanzees are rather remarkable and share a number of traits with humans. While further observations are necessary to confirm the existence of or discern the level of behavioral traits, chimpanzees show some evidence of culture, social complexity, learning, symbolic tool use, language, aesthetics, morality, and spirituality. These very traits are those used to defend human uniqueness.

PHILOSOPHICAL AND THEOLOGICAL REFLECTIONS ON THE CLOSING GAP BETWEEN HUMANS AND CHIMPANZEES

A number of philosophical and theology perspectives are challenged by the closing gap in behavioral traits common to chimpanzees and humans, and advances in primate studies offer an occasion to refine philosophical and theological reflection on a number of points.

One point for reflection is nature-culture dualism. While feminist theology and other holistic perspectives have challenged nature-culture dualism, de Waal offers a further challenge from the standpoint of primate studies. While he acknowledges the value of dichotomies for organizing ideas, he is concerned that dichotomies neglect complexities. For both humans and chimpanzees, genetics, learning, and environment affect behavioral traits.[39] De Waal points out that culture is a created environment and that natural selection has crafted species that possess cultural traits.[40] Humans and perhaps chimpanzees are nature-creating culture, which, means that nature and culture are closely intertwined rather than opposites. Ironically, cultural constructions prevent humans from seeing the world. De Waal writes,

> Culture is an extremely powerful modifier-affecting everything we do and are, penetrating the core of human existence—but it can work only in conjunction with human nature. Culture takes human nature and bends it this way or that way, careful not to break it. That we have trouble looking through the false dichotomy is due to a peculiar uncertainty principle: we are unable to take off our cultural lenses, and hence can only guess at how the world would look without them. That is why we cannot discuss animal culture without seriously reflecting on our own culture

---

38. Jane Goodall, with Phillip Berman, *Reason for Hope: A Spiritual Journey* (New York: Warner, 1999) 188.

39. De Waal, *The Ape and the Sushi Master*, 8.
40. Ibid.

and the possible blind spots it creates.⁴¹

Exactly because nature and culture are so intertwined, humans must be especially attentive to control beliefs or cultural lenses that block full awareness of animal nature and culture.

A second point for philosophical and theological reflection is the issue of continuity and discontinuity. Stephen Jay Gould, Frans de Waal, and Craig Stanford urge us to abandon thinking of the difference between humans and chimpanzees as a difference in kind. Instead, the differences between humans and chimpanzees might better be described as a difference in degree, which emphasizes continuity rather than discontinuity. Something nagging in my mind makes me uncomfortable even with difference in degree, not because I want to ignore the differences between humans and chimpanzees, but because difference in degree can still be used to establish value judgments or conclusions inappropriate to scientific or scholarly "objectivity." I am suspicious that difference in degree can take over the role that difference in kind played in establishing the arbitrary divisions between humans and chimpanzees. What shall we make of similarities and differences between chimpanzees and humans? In effect, the power of the similarities between the species rests in obvious morphological and functional differences. For example, even if cognition and hand morphology are very different, how much more marvelous and interesting it is that humans and chimpanzees are able to communicate with American Sign Language in spite of the differences! I suggest that the similarities require philosophy and theology to become much more articulate about human uniqueness, which means that we must be far more aware of advances in primate studies.

A third point for philosophical and theological reflection is appropriate comparability or analogy. Both difference in kind and difference in degree comparisons of chimpanzees and humans set human abilities as the benchmark for comparison. For example, when Craig Stanford assesses chimpanzee language skills, he uses comparisons with humans. His scorecard for chimpanzees and bonobos includes the following statements:

> Chimpanzees and bonobos understand human speech sounds, but maybe not as well as we do. They can use words, but word-like units in their natural communication (and in that of some monkeys) lack proper word properties. Chimpanzees lack the ability to make complex, abstract representations of word meanings; their ability to do this is at the level of a two-and-a-half-year-old child. They can comprehend and produce simple syntactical structures. In the realm of cognition, they can comprehend things about the state of mind of others, but not to the same degree as human children. They can imitate, but not well, or perhaps only emulate. And they have concepts of number sequences, sums, and fractions at the level of a three-year-old child.⁴²

My point is not to diminish how the comparison can assist us in understanding chimpanzee and bonobo language abilities, but my concern is how much

---

41. Ibid., 9.

42. Stanford, *Significant Others*, 161.

comparison with humans may mask our perceptions of chimpanzee communication. Communication, for example, is not limited to the grammar, syntax, or symbolism expressed in the best of human communication (and note that not all humans demonstrate competence with grammar, syntax, and symbolism). Perhaps we should look at a much larger and unexpected profile of social communication (verbal and nonverbal). Are there more neutral criteria for assessing abilities that set traits and behaviors in the ecological and adaptational contexts of each species? Perhaps we should look for incomparable traits and abilities, where among similarities we may discover incomparable values.

A fourth point for philosophical and theological reflection is the definition of *personhood*. I have suggested in another article that we should examine how we define *personhood* and expand the term to include chimpanzees.[43] The case for chimpanzee personhood is supported by three observations. First, chimpanzees have a sense of self-identity. Unlike monkeys or other animals, chimpanzees recognize and inspect themselves in mirror reflections.[44] Second, chimpanzees have awareness of their place in the social order. They carry the balance of social debits and credits, alliances, kinship, reconciliation, and deception in their memories and act on their sense of place in the social order. Chimpanzees also seem to have long-term memories of relationships. When Washoe was reunited with Allen and Beatrix Gardner after a long period of separation, she clearly recognized them, for example.[45] Third, chimpanzee self-formation occurs in the context of family and the larger social group. For example, Washoe's self-image was human rather than chimpanzee because of being reared within a human family.[46]

A fifth point for theological and philosophical reflection is morality and sin. Deception, lethal aggression, and infanticide are among behaviors shared by humans and chimpanzees. Some explanations for the brutal and aggressive behaviors of chimpanzees suggest that such behaviors are related to survival and adaptation. If humans and chimpanzees have both a common and parallel evolutionary history, what do naturalistic explanations of such behaviors mean for humans? At the practical level, naturalistic interpretations of aggressive behaviors create problems in imagining legal interpretations of and deterrents for such behavior. At the theological level, a natural interpretation of aggression and deception creates difficulties in interpreting immorality and sin. If sin is natural, is it a product of human adaptation and socialization rather than rebellion against God or harm to another person? Does a natural interpretation of sin mean that chimpanzees sin, too, or is sin a null category? As we learn more about our nearest primate relatives, interpretations of sin, salvation, *imago Dei,* and the soul may require a fresh look. Theology may need a transformation as remarkable as the decentering of humans as the focus of the God-world relationship.

---

43. Nancy R. Howell, "A God Adequate for Primate Culture," *Journal of Religion & Society* 3 (May 2, 2001) 1–11; online: http://moses.creighton.edu/JRS/toc/2001.html.

44. De Waal, *The Ape and the Sushi Master,* 59.

45. Fouts, *Next of Kin*, 169–71.

46. Ibid., 121–22, 160, 206, 210.

SOCIAL JUSTICE: CLOSING THE GAP BETWEEN THE HUMAN AND THE NOT-QUITE-HUMAN

What does it mean to be an animal? Unfortunately, the word *animal* has not been applied in value-neutral ways, but has often been used to signify that individuals are not human or not fully human. Nancy Tuana argues that science, philosophy and religion participated in associating women and Africans with animals. In *The Less Noble Sex*, Tuana surveys the three fields from the classical period through the end of the nineteenth century giving special attention to control beliefs that shaped attitudes toward gender and ethnicity.

Tuana, for example, surveys how philosophers and theologians understood distinctions in the soul. In a summative statement, Tuana writes.

> Western ethical and legal theories, strongly influenced by Christianity, refer most commonly to the soul or the mind to demonstrate human superiority over all other animals. Some theorists, claiming that *only* humans possess a soul, view this as proof that humans alone are "in the image of God."
>
> The idea of woman as a misbegotten or unevolved man typically incorporated the belief that these "higher" faculties of soul and mind would be less developed in woman. In other words, woman was a fainter image of God.[47]

The nature of the soul differentiated humans and animals and designated status as the image of God. Unfortunately, since woman was considered misbegotten or unevolved, her undeveloped mind and soul became justification for inferior status. Plato concluded that woman was inferior because of the nature of her soul which was bound to the appetites and limited in ability to grasp rational truths. Plato's philosophy also included a slave class, which possessed none of the elements of the soul and was considered barely human.[48] Aristotle based the inferiority of the woman's soul on her biological inferiority. Gratian believed that woman had no soul and was not in God's image because she was created second to Adam. Philo believed that woman must become man in order to be the image of God, and Augustine argued that woman has an inferior soul and is a fainter image of God.

Science too suggested distinctions between the minds of women and men, and between Europeans and Africans. Tuana's close reading of Darwin's theory natural selection discovers that Darwin considered the male more fit mentally than the female.

> Darwin rejected any attempt to argue that any differences in the intellectual abilities of the sexes might be caused even in part by socialization, and denied that such differences could be erased or even minimized through education. Darwin insisted that if every possible effort were made to increase woman's intellect, man's intellect would still outstrip woman's, for biology would dictate that men "maintain themselves and their families; and this will tend to keep up or even increase their mental powers, and, as a consequence, the present inequality between the sexes." Woman's natural role includes

---

47. Nancy Tuana, *The Less Noble Sex: Scientific, Religious, and Philosophical Conceptions of Woman's Nature* (Bloomington: Indiana University Press, 1993) 53.

48. Ibid., 54.

the bearing and care of children, while man's role is to support and protect the family. The latter, according to Darwin, requires more intelligence than the former. For Darwin, biology is destiny.[49]

In addition to evolutionary explanations for the mental inferiority of women, scientists used craniology studies to document differences in the size and structure of brains. Results of craniology studies were used to combat the women's movement of the nineteenth century and to justify slavery.[50] Skewed results in the Studies were apparently acceptable to scientists whose prejudices prevented them from questioning the testing conditions or contaminated results. In one diagram of brain size, a bushwoman's brain is depicted more like a gorilla's in comparison with a drawing of the brain of the mathematician Gauss.[51] In another diagram of the evolution of skulls, the angle of the skull was falsely extended to make a "Creole Negro" appear more like a young chimpanzee than a Greek male.[52] Control beliefs created the problem of falsely justifying the inferiority of women and Africans by making them appear closer to animals (including apes) than European males.

Where we draw the line separating humans and animals is important, and whom we place on the border between humans and animals is equally critical. Frans de Waal reminds us "if history has taught us anything, it is to be cautious about postulating difference. It is not too long ago that it was said that 'savages' were incapable of organizing themselves into societies."[53]

The effort to draw lines separating humans and apes and preserving human superiority is not just historical. Stephen Jay Gould claims that ties to our religious and philosophical heritage compel us to seek criteria by which to separate humans from chimpanzees, even though the chimpanzees continue to cross the lines.[54] Craig Stanford names contemporary keepers of the differences between humans and apes. Creationism maintains that biology teaches nothing about humanity. Evolutionary psychology ignores the relevance of primate studies for understanding human behavior and locates human uniqueness in the mind. Social sciences and humanities describe scientific theories as mere social constructions of reality.[55] De Waal avers that we suffer from *anthropodenial,* which is the "a priori rejection of shared characteristics between humans and animals when in fact they may exist."[56] De Waal sees religious heritage as part of the cause of anthropodenial. Western religion claims that humans are separate from nature, even as science understands humans as part of nature. Religion provides a control belief that influences science to reject anthropomorphism: "A clear desire to stay at a distance from animals is the reason for rejecting anthropomorphism."[57]

---

49. Ibid., 66. Within the quotation, Tuana quotes Charles Darwin, *The Descent of Man, and Selection in Relation to Sex* (New York: Collier, 1901) 728.

50. Tuana, *The Less Noble Sex*, 68.

51. Ibid., 69.

52. Ibid., 45.

53. De Waal, *The Ape and the Sushi Master*, 31.

54. Gould, *Ever Since Darwin*, 51.

55. Stanford, *Significant Others*, xiv.

56. De Waal, *The Ape and the Sushi Master*, 69.

57. Ibid., 82.

Accepting kinship with chimpanzees does not mean diminishing the differences between humans and chimpanzees or minimizing human cultural accomplishments. Accepting kinship with chimpanzees may mean that we can learn to de-center humans long enough to focus on the animal's perspective—an approach that de Waal calls *animalcentric anthropomorphism*.[58] In learning to take a chimpanzee perspective, we stand to learn more about human evolution and culture. De Waal writes,

> Where does all this leave us? I see little life left in the position that we humans fall outside of nature, and that it is culture that sets us apart. A retreat to "symbolic culture" as the hallmark of humanity may provide some relief, but in the long run I see a much more fruitful challenge for scholars in search of typically human accomplishments. The time has come to define the human species against the vast common ground we share with other life forms . . . We and other animals are both similar and different, and the former is the only sensible framework within which to flesh out the latter.[59]

A more refined understanding of chimpanzee uniqueness and human uniqueness depends upon knowing our commonalities, and justice depends upon high regard for both the similarities and differences among us.

Commentary

Ann M. Pederson

The nature of what it means to be human is at the heart of the theological work of Nancy R. Howell. From the article in this volume, "The Importance of Being Chimpanzee," to her other articles, chapters in books, and texts, Nancy R. Howell offers a theological anthropology that challenges traditional boundaries and categories. Nancy Howell's work is, in the best sense of the word, prophetic. Whether in her writings on process-feminist thought or her leadership in the religion and science discussion, Howell has raised questions, offered constructive arguments, and provided leadership that has expanded the horizons of traditional scholarship.

Howell's foundational work in process thought began as and continues to be expansive in its scope. What has often been relegated to the periphery of traditional theological and philosophical work Howell draws to the heart and center. An example of this is in her work, *A Feminist Cosmology: Ecology, Solidarity, and Metaphysics*, in which she utilizes feminist philosophy to build an all-encompassing framework for explaining the cosmological relationships between God, human,

---

58. Ibid., 77.

59. Ibid., 362.

and creation.[1] The diversity of all life finds its unity within the web of interdependent relationships. Like Whitehead, she links diversity and unity as part of the same metaphysical movement of the creative advance. Cosmology is the movement where the many become one and are increased by one.

If human beings are situated in the midst of a vast cosmos, what does that mean for their self-understanding? More specifically, what does it mean to interpret the Christian notion of *imago dei* in light of the dialogue between religion and science? I believe that the most important contribution that Howell has made and will continue to make is her constructive work on theological anthropology situated within the religion-and-science conversation. She aligns her work with others like Philip Hefner, who know that while we are created by God, humans are creating themselves—through advances and new technologies in the life sciences and biotechnology. We are in the process of becoming human, and the nature of that is always changing and fluid. The boundaries between human animals and non-human animals, nature and culture, machine and nature, male and female have imploded. Howell's work interprets the significance of this implosion for Christian theology and for the ethics of how we live together on this planet Earth.

In her article "The Importance of Being Chimpanzee," Nancy Howell sharpens the focus of this question of human uniqueness and her response through her use of primate studies. She asks two specific questions: "In light of the closing gap between our definitions of human uniqueness and our understanding of primates, what is left of human uniqueness? How have science, philosophy, and religion established presuppositions about human uniqueness, which may need to be revised in response to primate research?"[2] Her conclusions lead to helpful directions, not only for the science-and-religion dialogue, but also for the way human persons are interpreted and viewed within medical science and biotechnology. The rate at which humans are changing their environment and their own nature often exceeds the rate at which theologians and philosophers can keep pace. This has enormous implications for how society lives together, the way animals are treated, access to healthcare, and human self-understanding. The strength of Howell's response is that it acknowledges the complexity of the question and the nuances of the answers. She ends this article by saying that "a more refined understanding of chimpanzee uniqueness and human uniqueness depends upon knowing our commonalities, and just depends upon high regard for both the similarities and differences among us."[3]

This need for a more refined understanding extends not only to the human/nonhuman distinctions, but also to and within human similarities and differences. Howell is right to be worried about giving in to the notion that all understandings are "socially-constructed," but neither is she willing to accept forms of reductionism that mark some sciences or interpretations of science. Howell can

---

1. Nancy R. Howell, *A Feminist Cosmology: Ecology, Solidarity, and Metaphysics* (Amherst, NY: Humanity, 2000).

2. Above, 145.

3. Above, 157.

develop the work of de Waal and others like him more extensively to help those who want to work this path between a kind of relativism and absolutism. Here I see her work resonating with other feminist philosophers like Sandra Harding and Donna Haraway. Like Haraway, she calls for traversing a path of understanding that acknowledges ambiguity, finitude, and the messiness of how human animals and nonhuman animals live together. Howell is not a sentimentalist about animals. She understands and respects the distinctions between species.

The current trajectories of Howell's work provide promising directions for her ongoing contributions to Christian theology, the relationship between religion and science, and her work as a process feminist thinker. My hope is that her interpretive work on what it means to be human will be seen and used by others for the prophetic voice it is. And that she, herself, takes this prophetic challenge by pushing and expanding her own theological boundaries even further. Other scholars in the feminist process movement can use her work for challenging boundaries in the area of bioethics. Her work is provocative, imaginative, synthetic, and opens doors where fresh air is needed. These open windows and doors will illuminate the ways both the sciences and religious traditions have often appeared to turn off the lights on the validity and contribution by women about what it means to be human.

STUDY QUESTIONS

1. How might Howell's perspectives on human uniqueness be applied to other boundary issues like gender and sexuality?

2. Why do humans have an investment in claiming that their species is unique? Does uniqueness imply superiority?

3. What might those who make policy decisions regarding medicine and healthcare be challenged by and find helpful in Howell's arguments about the relationship between human animals and nonhuman animals?

13 Creativity, Christology, and Science

Ann Milliken Pederson

Ann Milliken Pederson is Professor of Religion at Augustana College in Sioux Falls, South Dakota. She is also Adjunct Associate Professor in the Section for Ethics and Humanities at the Sanford School of Medicine of the University of South Dakota. She received degrees from Montana State University–Bozeman and the Lutheran School of Theology at Chicago. Her research interests include Christian theology, with particular emphases in religion and medical sciences, feminist theologies, and Lutheran constructive theology. This excerpt is from chapter 2 of God, Creation and All That Jazz: A Process of Composition and Improvisation, *where Pederson uses the improvisational nature of jazz music as a metaphor for understanding how God and creation co-create.*

Excerpt from *God, Creation, and All That Jazz: A Process of Composition and Improvisation*

MARY CATHERINE BATESON— LEARNING ALONG THE WAY

Mary Catherine Bateson has been my guide on an absorbing journey, offering rich metaphors for navigating my way through a crazy, topsy-turvy, spinning world. In a world marked by rapid change, diverse cultures, and expanding technologies, Bateson's work provides strategies for negotiating this postmodern landscape. She claims that *how* we learn relates to *what we* learn. Instead of simply clinging to one tried-and-true way of being in the world, Bateson teaches her reader how to learn in new ways, how to see things in new ways. She leads her reader through stories in a myriad of places that link multiple perspectives. The reader learns to look for new patterns in the familiar, old patterns in the unfamiliar. Bateson offers learning strategies for making one's way through the kaleidoscope of an interdependent, multidimensional world:

> Ambiguity is the warp of life, not something to be eliminated. Learning to savor the vertigo of doing without answers or making shift and making do with fragmentary ones opens up the pleasures of recognizing and playing with pattern, finding coherence within complexity, sharing within multiplicity.[1]

---

1. Mary Catherine Bateson, *Peripheral Visions: Learning Along the Way* (New York: HarperCollins, 1994) 9.

Underneath her writing is a profound optimism that life is a place where we are always learning. She uses many different metaphors to explain this lifelong educational process. We learn through the metaphors and stories we construct to make sense of our world. When we retell each other's stories, we make connections between the familiar and unfamiliar.

Bateson explores the metaphor of improvisation in *Composing a Life*. "Life is an improvisatory art, about the ways we combine familiar and unfamiliar components in response to new situations, following an underlying grammar and an evolving aesthetic."[2] She examines the lives of five women who creatively worked through the possibilities and difficulties their lives presented. This study of improvisation is a study of creativity. Each woman discovers the patterns along the way instead of conforming to a predetermined essence. In a stable, homogeneous society, where everything fits neatly together, the typical artist creates something in a traditional, formed style. Bateson, however, is addressing a different world, one where "the materials and skills from which a life is composed are no longer clear."[3] Bateson uses an analogy from music, particularly that of jazz musicians. Jazz exemplifies a kind of creativity that holds together the individual and community, freedom and constraint, structure and chance. Improvisation helps us deal with the ambiguities life presents because it helps us confront the unfamiliar with the familiar, the chaotic with order.

In her book *Peripheral Visions*, Bateson reaches deeper into this model of improvisation and connects it to the theme of vision. How we look at the world will shape how we cope with the world. If we look at the world through a single-vision lens, we miss those things in our peripheral vision. We are blinded to the diversity, multiplicities, and ambiguity within our range of sight. Bateson develops this metaphor extensively in a chapter called "Improvisation in a Persian Garden." She explains how single models, that is, a sort of "visionary reductionism," don't fit the complexity of life's landscape. "Openness to peripheral vision depends on rejecting such reductionism and rejecting with it the belief that questions of meaning have unitary answers."[4] In our rapidly changing world, we can no longer see through just one lens, especially if we think that it is the only one through which everyone should look. Instead, we must learn to see multi-dimensionally, to live with competing visions, to explore new ideas. We live this way in concert with others.

Learning is the art of improvisation. Learning and improvisation share the same qualities for those who are open to the world around them:

> Improvisation and new learning are not private processes; they are shared with others at every age. The multiple layers of attention involved cannot safely be brushed aside or subordinated to the completion of tasks. We are called to join in a dance whose steps must be learned along the way, so it is important to attend and respond. Even in uncertainty, we are responsible for our steps.[5]

2. Bateson, *Composing a Life* (New York: Grove, 1989) 3.

3. Ibid., 2.

4. Bateson, *Peripheral Visions*, 11.

5. Ibid., 10.

We are held responsible as lifelong learners in a constant process of creative discovery. We are responsible for how we learn what we learn and what we do with what we know. Knowing and doing, epistemology and ethics, are connected.

Bateson's own background brought her to many cultures and different peoples. Her family, both when she was a child and later, after she married, lived all over the world. The temptation would be to think that her multicultured, well-traveled worldviews are a matter of privilege. To some degree this is true. Yet whether we live in rural South Dakota or London, England, we all face how we deal with the differences in our complex world. We are no longer exempt from the possibilities and problems that diversity brings. Many think there are only two options: We can deal with diversity by running from it, shoring up the defensive walls and hunkering down, or we can assume that truth is determined merely by one's personal taste, and relativism rules in its anarchic way. Those are our fears, yet we all live with commitments. How can we live in a committed manner and yet be open to the voices of those who are different from us? Is there a third option? Answering this question is part of Bateson's task. Improvisation is a creative solution to this dilemma. What we learn to do is to maximize diversity instead of minimizing it. Thinking we are all alike is a kind of homogeneous imperialism. As we live and work together, we realize that differences do matter. But they can matter for the good. The improvisational model moves us away from warlike metaphors that pit one against the other, an "us-them" attitude. "It is curious that the sins of disobedience against God have been emphasized so much more than the sins of hatred between brothers."[6] Bateson's genius is her emphasis on creativity. To learn is to create in partnership and through difference.

In a similar manner, Alfonso Montuori, an educator and musician, develops the theme of improvisation as a metaphor for the learning community. He is critical of the way academic communities stifle creativity and set up barriers to genuine collegial dialogue. The academic world has often modeled itself as a battleground where scholars compete to outdo one another's theories. Competition instead of collaboration is the means by which learning takes place. This battleground means that we are afraid to sound ignorant, afraid to show that our models might not be the final truth:

> In public, in journals, conferences, and presentations, we generally present our models, theories, and methods but do not account for the complexities, ambiguities, and uncertainties which preceded them. In public, we show what we know, and what we do not know becomes minimized, obscured, defended, feared, a source of embarrassment: We are afraid we may have missed something, that we will be caught with our pants down, unable to answer the pointed question, locate the vital reference.[7]

Many of us have made presentations at conferences where the whole agenda was to try to shoot holes in the presenter's paper. Academics are trained to shoot down their competitors, not to collaborate. Once we find teaching positions, we

---

6. Ibid., 194.

7. Alfonso Montuori, "Social Creativity, Academic Discourse, and the Improvisation of Inquiry," *Revision* 20.1 (1997) 34.

attend conferences and write grants about collaborative learning. However, our entire academic process has worked against the kind of creativity that leads to fertile collaboration with other colleagues. The lone scholar myth still pervades most graduate schools.

Montuori challenges this model of learning and offers an alternative metaphor. His own background in music leads him to the theme of improvisation. He finds rich resources in the works of African American theorists, who have been critical of European music. Jazz provides an alternative way to think about creativity in contrast to the tight, precise, and controlled music of many Euro-American composers and musicians. Jazz focuses on a community of conversation, in which the give-and-take creates ongoing fresh statements. "In jazz, spontaneity, improvisation, ambiguity, uncertainty, and even mistakes—particularly mistakes—are used as avenues for new explorations and also as a testament to the improviser's ability to think on his/her feet."[8]

Montuori applies the musical model to the academic community. For knowledge to be creative, one must be willing to take risks in a trusting community. The old "battleground" model wages war and reinforces distrust among colleagues. The jazz model encourages trust, community, and an enthusiasm for the process of creating music together. Montuori notes that he is not calling for abandoning high standards for intellectual rigor, but is calling for a different way of going about it. "Creative, collaborative inquiry is in some sense the delightful shadow side of the instrumental, technological, self-contained knowing."[9] Learning in this kind of system will feel risky; we will "expose" our weakness at first until we learn to trust those around us. But when we do, the spirit of collaboration will allow for a new kind of work, a different kind of creative spirit. Montuori and Bateson both encourage work that is not only creative but also and necessarily transformative. Creative work leads to the transformation of knowledge and the learning process.

FLOW: MIHALY CSIKSZENTMIHALYI

Mihaly Csikszentmihalyi, a professor of psychology and education at the University of Chicago, has spent his life studying the process of happiness and creativity. His studies define his conception of "flow": that experience of losing oneself to a creative process.[10] Flow is not an elitist concept reserved for the brilliant artist. Like the music of jazz, flow is the music from beginning to end, the reason one plays. Csikszentmihalyi's methods lead him to research in many cultures, in many different kinds of social and vocational settings. The emphasis of flow is on the process, not just on the end result, the product. He explains that many psychologists have studied the aberrant personalities, the psychotic, the despondent. But how are we to learn about that which gives life, that which perpetuates the good, if we only study its opposite? His research goal to study creativity is to study that which creates happiness, that which produces life and well-being.

8. Ibid., 4.

9. Ibid., 5.

10. Flow: "a state of consciousness in which concentration on activity is so intense that complete absorption is achieved," in "How to Find Flow," interview with Mihaly Csikszentmihalyi, *Free Inquiry* 18.3 (1998) 25.

To define creativity, Csikszentmihalyi doesn't ask what creativity is, but instead explores *where* creativity happens. He dispels the myth of creativity as the process of a lone, crazy, individual spirit. Creativity is a social phenomenon occurring within systems. He notes, "Creativity does not happen inside people's heads, but in the interaction between a person's thoughts and a sociocultural context. It is a systemic rather than an individual phenomenon."[11] Creativity is a social process that requires a social context. Likewise in jazz, creativity is a way of life, a preoccupation of the artists. Paul Berliner explains: "When performers speak of jazz as a way of life, they refer to the performer's constant preoccupation with musical ideas and notions of creativity . . . they refer to Barry Harris's students continually reviewing music history while riding on the subway . . . they refer to Lee Konitz whistling new melodies to the beat of his footsteps as he walks his dog in the evening."[12] Creativity occurs within the natural rhythms and happenings of everyday life.

Three major components are required for creativity: the domain, the field, and the individual.[13] The domain "consists of a set of symbolic rules and procedures."[14] Domains can be separate fields of knowledge, such as religion, math, legal systems, or physics. Each system has its own rules and symbols. Domains belong to the realm of cultural evolution. The field is necessary to determine whether or not the novelty produced will become part of the dominant culture. Csikszentmihalyi notes that a culture can only absorb so much new information, and, consequently, cultures are conservative by nature to assure their own survival. Thus, competition exists between memes (discrete units of cultural information).[15] A field is a way of passing judgment that determines whether or not the creative innovation will survive. He defines a field's makeup as a group of "experts in a given domain whose job involves passing judgment on performance in that domain. Members of the field choose from among the novelties those that deserve to be included in the canon."[16] Fields can use narrow or broad filters and encourage novelty when they are culturally appropriated. Finally, one must consider the contributions of the individual person. Yet, even in this discussion, creativity is still seen as a property of the overall system. The person making the creative contribution must internalize the domain within which he or she works, understand the criteria of judgment, and relate the work to the larger culture. The systems model of creativity has important implications: "The level of creativity in a given place at a given time does not depend only on the amount of individual creativity. It depends just as much on how well suited the respective domains and fields are to the recognition and diffusion of novel ideas."[17]

---

11. Csikszentmihalyi, *Creativity: Flow and the Psychology of Discovery and Invention* (New York: HarperCollins, 1996) 23.

12. Paul F. Berliner, *Thinking in Jazz: The Infinite Art of Improvisation* (Chicago: University of Chicago Press, 1994) 486.

13. Martin H. Levinson, "Mapping Creativity with a Capital 'C,'" *ETC: A Review of General Semantics* 54 (1997) 447.

14. Csikszentmihalyi, *Creativity*, 27.

15. Ibid., 41.

16. Ibid., 42.

17. Ibid., 31.

Csikszentmihalyi's description of the creative person is developed from many interviews and has much in common with the jazz musician, whom Red Rodney describes: "You keep playing, keep studying, keep listening, keep learning, and you keep developing. Jazz is not a nine to one [a.m.] job, once or twice a week. It's a way of life."[18] The creative process, as Rodney sets it out, resonates with what Bateson and Montuori said. "Creative individuals are remarkable for their ability to adapt to almost any situation and to make do with whatever is at hand to reach their goals. If nothing else, this distinguishes them from the rest of us."[19] The creative personality is *not* the lone, crazy individual working in splendid isolation. From many interviews of scientists, artists, and writers, we come to know the creative person as one who has access to the domain, to the field, and is open to the twists and turns of experience. The creative person is finally a complex person, one who exhibits the contradictory extremes in life and brings them together in fruitful possibilities. Csikszentmihalyi lists ten sets of opposites that embody the creative personality.[20] For example, creative individuals have a great deal of energy, and yet they also know when to take time to be alone and rest. Developing the creativity within oneself depends on practicing the art of careful attention to the environment. Creative acts do not come de novo, but often as the result of hard work, attention to detail, timing, and some element of luck.

Csikszentmihalyi's description of the creative person is much like Whitehead's notion of creativity, in which the many become one and are increased by one. Creativity is the creation of that which is new. Csikszentmihalyi notes,

> Creativity involves the production of novelty. The process of discovery involved in creating something new appears to be one of the most enjoyable activities any human can be involved in.[21]

In earlier works, Csikszentmihalyi described this experience as *flow*.[22] Whitehead is famous for his methodological airplane ride in which he explains the

---

18. Red Rodney, quoted in Berliner, *Thinking in Jazz*, 485.

19. Ibid., 51.

20. 1. Creative individuals have a great deal of physical energy, but they are also often quiet and at rest 2. Creative individuals tend to be smart, yet also naive at the same time. 3. A third paradoxical trait refers to the related combination of playfulness and discipline, or responsibility and irresponsibility. 4. Creative individuals alternate between imagination and fantasy at one end, and a rooted sense of reality at the other. 5. Creative people seem to harbor opposite tendencies on the continuum between extroversion and introversion. 6. Creative individuals are also remarkably humble and proud at the same time. 7. In all cultures, men are brought up to be 'masculine' and to disregard and repress those aspects of their temperament that the culture regards as 'feminine,' whereas women are expected to do the opposite. Creative individuals to a certain extent escape this rigid gender role stereotyping. 8. Generally creative people are thought to be rebellious and independent 9. Most creative persons are very *passionate* about their work, yet they can be extremely *objective* about it as well. 10. Finally, the openness and sensitivity of creative individuals often exposes them to *suffering and pain yet also a great deal of enjoyment*." Csikszentmihalyi, *Creativity*, 58–73.

21. Ibid., 111.

22. Flow has nine main elements: "1. There are clear goals every step of the way. 2. There is immediate feedback to one's actions. 3. There is balance between challenges and skills. 4. Action and awareness are merged. 5. Distractions are excluded from consciousness. 6. There is no worry of failure. 7. Self-consciousness disappears. 8. The sense of time becomes distorted. 9. The activity becomes autotelic." Ibid., 111–13.

creative action as a combination of particularity and generalization. The play of free imagination is grounded in the details of observation. Whitehead explains that "the true method of discovery is like the flight of an aeroplane. It starts from the ground of particular observation; it makes a flight in the thin air of imaginative generalization; and it again lands for renewed observation rendered acute by rational interpretation."[23] The imagination brings the familiar into new territory. We see the familiar in new ways. Creativity is an evolutionary process in which the past unfolds into the possibilities of the future through the reality of the present.

Csikszentmihalyi explains that creativity used to be the domain of the gods. Humans were weaklings subject to the whims and tantrums of the deities. But somewhere along the way the scenes changed, and the humans became the creators, the gods. Creativity is our evolutionary calling. "It is not surprising that as we ride the crest of evolution we have taken over the title of creator."[24] Whether our destiny will be our fall is yet to be seen. But we bear an ultimate responsibility for how we use this gift. "It's a random coupling of behavior type with a feeling, which over time achieved a greater survival or reproductive advantage. And now we are in a sense 'designed' to want to be in flow."[25] We are designed to be creative; we feel good when we discover something new. Novelty is necessary for the future of who we are as a species on this planet.

23. Alfred North Whitehead, *Process and Reality: An Essay in Cosmology* (New York: Free Press, 1978) 5.

24. Csikszentmihalyi, *Creativity*, 5.

25. Mihaly Csikszentmihalyi, *Omni* 17.4 (1995) 73.

Csikszentmihalyi claims that we construct our future through the creative process of flow. Our future is emergent, not predetermined in the past. We discover who we are along the way. "Individual enjoyment seems an evolutionary potential in humans, responsible in large part for technical and social advances, in future-oriented goals. It's intrinsic interest that keeps people going."[26]

PROCESS AS CREATIVITY: WHITEHEAD AND COBB

Bateson and Csikszentmihalyi confirm the notion that creativity is the means by which each of us lives out our evolutionary calling in life. Both authors agree that to understand the process of creativity is to understand how we develop worthwhile strategies for living in the world. Creativity is a social process in which novelty arises from that which is given. With some traditional theological perspectives, we have feared that by attributing creative power to humans, we diminish the creative power of God. However, my theological claim is that creativity is not solely the work of God. The rest of creation shares in the ongoing creative act. Process theology, along with other contemporary voices, such as feminist theology, challenges this notion that God's creation is a divine fiat that happened only once, only "in the beginning." In a way similar to process theology, Dorothee Soelle claims:

> We are mistaken if we assume that the life of the creator diminishes as the created live more fully. The power of life is not a flat sum that must be divided, unequally, between the creator and the created,

26. Ibid., 9.

although the mainstream theology often conveys this strange impression. On the contrary, the more a person develops her creativity, delves into the project of liberation, and transcends her own limitations, the more God is God. God does not cling to creational power, making it his possession, but shares it knowing that good power is shared power.[27]

Whitehead, whose work is foundational for process theology, emphasizes creativity as the means by which God and the world are related to each other. Whitehead's vision of the relationship between God and the world is similar to the vision of the jazz ensemble, in which power is mutually shared, creativity is intrinsically related to freedom, and the creative process is as important as the final product.[28] Creativity in Whitehead's system, like a performance in jazz, resists being held captive in a final form. God is continually creating life anew.

A brief explanation about Whitehead's life helps to explain the origins of his philosophical works. His life and work reflect the goal he envisioned for all of life: to live and to live well. In 1890, Whitehead's marriage changed his outlook on life. He remarked about his wife, "Her vivid life has taught me that beauty, moral and aesthetic, is the aim of existence; and that kindness and love, and artistic satisfaction are among its modes of attainment."[29] This love of the aesthetic informed his primal vision of God and the world. For Whitehead, Christianity was not assent to correct doctrine, but a way of life that evoked meaning and concern. Whitehead feared that Western theology had so aligned God's power with brute force that the persuasive power of beauty and grace had been eclipsed. For Whitehead, beauty is the creative expression of God's imaginative power to transform death into life, old into new. God does not fight force with force; "he does not create the world, he saves it: or, more accurately, he is the poet of the world, with tender patience leading it by his vision of truth, beauty, and goodness."[30] Although some have criticized this vision of God as sentimental, Whitehead's correction of divine power as coercive fiat deserves attention again in a world marked by ugliness and manipulative, coercive power.

Of the three traditional metaphysical values—goodness, truth, and beauty—Whitehead chooses beauty as the ultimate value for life. This choice of beauty, as Whitehead notes, somewhat shifts the ordinary philosophical emphasis upon the past. It directs attention to the period of great art and literature, as best expressing the essential values of life."[31] Creativity is that universal that applies to all of life. To create is to love beauty. Beauty lures us into the goodness and value of the creation. Dorothee Soelle calls Christians to participate in this aesthetic education:

> To love creation means to perceive its beauty in the most unexpected places. An aesthetic education that

---

27. Soelle, *To Work and To Love: A Theology of Creation* (Philadelphia: Fortress, 1984) 39.

28. "Whitehead, *Process and Reality*, 348. "God and the World are the contrasted opposites in terms of which Creativity achieves its supreme task of transforming disjoined multiplicity, with its diversities in opposition, into concrescent unity, with its diversities in contrast."

29. Whitehead, *Essays in Science and Philosophy* (New York: Philosophical Library, 1947) 15.

30. Whitehead, *Process and Reality*, 346.

31. Whitehead, *Science and Philosophy*, 15.

deepens our perception is not a luxury for the elite but a cultural necessity for everyone. To believe in creation is to perceive and to engage in the aesthetic model of perception . . . We become better lovers of the earth when we tell the earth how beautiful it is.[32]

When we see the creation as beautiful, we look at it in new ways, with new possibilities. To engage in that which is beautiful is to become part of the imagination of God. To create is to be in partnership with God to create that which is new. Jazz musicians sense this creative partnership when they enter into something that is "the big picture." The music carries them into another world, where "they feel a deep sense of reverence for 'all living things.' In spiritual communion, they merge together in the shrine of a universal life force—timeless, peaceful, yet energizing and euphoric."[33]

This principle of creativity and beauty is used in the contemporary theological writings of John B. Cobb Jr. Cobb uses the philosophy of Whitehead to develop his theological understanding of the relationship between God and the world. Cobb's work is particularly helpful because he explains creativity within an aesthetic framework as the means by which God acts in the world. Cobb's book *Christ in a Pluralistic Age* connects the metaphysical principle of creativity to his vision of Christ as creative transformation. Using the work of Andre Malraux, Cobb traces the visual representations of Christ throughout the history of art. "Here there is a striking movement from radical transcendence through incarnation to crucifixion and assimilation through suffering humanity."[34] This tour through the history of Western art demonstrates the inextricable relationship of the present meaning of Christ to the interpretative history. Cobb demonstrates that the Christian may discern Christ as creative transformation in the changing styles and forms comprising the forms of Western art. Like the author of Colossians, Cobb identifies Christ as the one in whom all things cohere, the one in whom "all things were created." Christ himself is the process of creative transformation and cannot be identified with one absolute image. Creative transformation is the living image of Christ's presence in the world.

Cobb's christology, in a way similar to Bateson's, addresses the postmodern concerns of relativism, pluralism, and secularism. The language of christology must include not only "theological" vocabulary but also the terms of the world in which it lives. Cobb's theological language makes contact with both God and the world because christology is the focal point around which the meaning of God and the world ultimately matter. A postmodern christology can have nothing to do with a doctrine that imperialistically ignores the world in which it was formed. God's grace is at work in all the world and not apart from the world.

Cobb's christology addresses a world that converses in multiple conversations rather than in homogeneous monologues. Cobb's efforts in interreligious dialogue support his christological formulations. The best way to approach interreligious dialogue is through a christological formulation that not only acknowledges multiple conversations but also affirms

---

32. Soelle, *To Work and To Love*, 48, 49.
33. Berliner, *Thinking in Jazz*, 498.
34. John B. Cobb Jr., *Christ in a Pluralistic Age* (1975. Reprinted, Eugene, OR: Wipf & Stock, 1999) 43.

transformation of those involved through the conversations. Like Bateson, Cobb opposes those who reduce Christianity to a single essence, to a single narrative. Many centers of meaning exist in the world. Cobb comments in *Christ in a Pluralistic Age* that "Christ, as the image of creative transformation, can provide a unity within which the many centers of meaning and existence can be appreciated and encouraged and through which openness to other great ways of mankind can lead to a deepening of Christian existence."[35] Christ, as the principle of creative transformation, excludes dogmatic finality and yet does not give in to a relativism lacking content or norms. Christ is the center around which other centers find a new and deeper meaning. In the language of jazz, unity is found amidst the diversity of styles. "Similarly, as music systems around the world provide jazz performances with additional sources of inspiration, improvisers may have the sense of participating in a global discourse among music thinkers, negotiating musical ideas that transcend cultural and historical boundaries."[36] Creative moments in jazz, according to Berliner, inspire a humility that "envelops the artists in the grip of such awe-inspiring aspects of creativity" that the musicians renew "their sensitivity to life's spiritual qualities and great mysteries."[37]

However, Cobb fears that many people in our world are facing a great spiritual and moral crisis; they are apathetic to the environmental, economic, political, and cultural forces that threaten to destroy the planet. Cobb describes this world as one that is constantly on the brink of facing its own self-destruction. How do we begin to address this crisis? In his essay "Christ Beyond Creative Transformation," Cobb notes that theological thinking can begin from several starting points. One could begin with the historical Jesus, with the preaching of the early church, with christological debates of the early centuries, the doctrine of God, or recent christologies. However, all these ignore the urgent context of the world, which the word must address. Cobb begins with salvation as the starting point for christology because the problems raised in the postmodern world are so urgent.[38] The word must be able not only to address the world in speech and deed but also to transform the world. The most comprehensive and responsible place to begin is with the nature of salvation for the entire creation. The questions of salvation are too pressing to ignore. Note Cobb's emphasis:

> We should not use the symbol *Christ* for anything less than the power that works savingly in this comprehensive way. *Christ* must be the life that struggles against the death-dealing powers that threaten us and the way that leads through the chaos of personal and global life to a just, participatory, and sustainable society in which personal wholeness is possible.[39]

The symbol of *Christ* is a "living" symbol.[40] We crucify this living symbol when we limit it to common or proper nouns that reduce its soteriological function beyond the redemption of the entire

---

35. Ibid., 21.
36. Berliner, *Thinking in Jazz*, 491.
37. Ibid., 492.
38. Cobb, "Christ Beyond Creative Transformation," in *Encountering Jesus*, ed. Stephen T. Davis (Atlanta: John Knox, 1988) 142–43.
39. Ibid., 143 (italics are in the original).
40. Ibid., 141.

world. As Gregory of Nazianzus, the Cappadocian, said, "What is not assumed, cannot be healed."

Christ is that symbol that works in a comprehensive way against all "death-dealing" powers; Christ brings life and hope for all creation. In an unpublished paper entitled "Postmodern Christianity in Quest of Eco-Justice," Cobb explains that the worth of all creation is the joy God experiences. He obscures the distinction between humans and other creatures to explain the benefits of salvation: "But God and the created order in their intimate connection constitute the context of all our thought and life."[41] Salvation is a participatory process including God and the world in which all work together for well-being, vitality, and enjoyment. Cobb's understanding of salvation results from his choice of beauty as the ultimate principle in life, for all of creation has intrinsic value. Creation has benefit and value not only as it relates to others but also in its relations to itself and before God. The intrinsic value of each created entity is "enjoyed" by God.

The purpose of Jesus as the Christ is not only to reveal how God works in the world but also to be the one through whom the new force of creativity works in all the world. Jesus Christ becomes the principle of creative transformation, the one through whom all things are made whole and well. Jesus Christ is God incarnate in the world, whether the world consciously recognizes it or not. In an article titled "The Presence of the Past and the Eucharist,"[42] Cobb shows how Jesus is specifically present in the eucharist and also present in all creation. He shows how the past is efficacious in the present. The sacramental presence of Christ affirms that God's transformative and gracious power is effective in all creation, in the finite stuff of the world. The sacraments are particular expressions of God's universal love and presence. The principle of creative transformation is at work in the world regardless of its being realized. This can be illustrated in Janna Tull Steed's comment about the music of Duke Ellington, whose music has been labeled "sacramental."

> Duke Ellington has been blithely called a cultural icon. The word "icon," in its original sense, refers to a prayerfully created and dedicated work of art, a picture or an image through which the divine nature or word can be mediated to the viewer. As such, the image is no longer a lifeless object, but one animated by a living spirit. In this sense, Ellington is an icon. And his music is sacramental, too; because it is also a mediator of life-giving spirit. His art unveils the glory of what is luminously holy, but hidden, in the material world and in human flesh.[43]

God's grace is manifest in all of creation. This theme of God's grace is improvised on as creatures develop the theme through their own freedom. Like the music of Ellington, the life of Jesus unveils the glory and grace of God. Christ is the sacramental presence that names that which is salvific to the community of believers. The purpose of Christ for the world is more than revelatory, that is, to show the world what God is accomplishing. In

---

41. Cobb, "Postmodern Christianity in Quest of Eco-Justice," 3, (public lecture in Chicago, February 1990).

42. Cobb, "The Presence of the Past and the Eucharist," *Process Studies* 13 (Fall 1983) 218.

43. Janna Tull Steed, *Duke Ellington: A Spiritual Biography* (New York: Crossroad, 1999) 164.

other words, Christ does more than demonstrate or illustrate to the world what it already knows about God. Christ transforms the world.

These christological images of hope and salvation, whether transcendent or immanent, move the world through ambiguity and death to meaning and life. For the vision of the kingdom brings present injustices to light and "supports the claims of the weak and the powerless."[44] The way that Christ works in the world is through the valley of the shadow of death, through those historical structures riddled with ambiguity. God in Christ accompanies the world through the valley of the shadow of death. However, Christ is more than just a friend on the way. Christ is the one through whom transformation and new life occur. But this transformation always occurs through the ambiguity, not by avoiding it. This is the risk of the creative advance in which God and the world participate. Thus, Christ is not only creative transformation but also the suffering one through whom all cohere and have their end. Christ offers the world hope.

Cobb equates faith in Christ with hope in the future. The past, present, and future are not separable from one another. Their relationship constitutes Cobb's understanding of the role of the future and hope. "Jesus opens us to the present working of the Logos by assuring us of our future."[45] Christ is not to be identified idolatrously with particular results or accomplishments of the past. Christ corrects this distorted view of the past in order to "remove the obstacles to faith as openness to creative transformation."[46]

The structures of hope are none other than the structures of creative transformation. Whitehead's theme of adventure is evident when Cobb explains that the problem of our contemporary culture is not that we "believe too much but that we do not believe enough."[47] The structures of hope are formed when eschatological images "break courageously into transcendence."[48] These structures of hope are not merely wishful thinking but are grounded in the possibilities of the present world. The ordering of the possibilities comes from the transcendent Logos. Thus, the structure of hope is "the incarnation of this Logos whereby it is the effective structuring of actual experience. Hence, the structure of hope is Christ."[49] Creative transformation is the reason for hope, because it is at work everywhere in the world, confronting the negative with possibility. It is that "whose nature it is to bring into being just that which cannot be predicted until it occurs."[50]

Christ is the central image of hope, incarnate in the world. Images of hope that guide humanity into the future must not only have the possibilities presented through creative transformation as the Logos, but they must be grounded in the actual existence of the present moment. These images are at once transcendent and immanent. They are incarnate; they work from the present into the future. The task of Christians is to conceptualize images that do not return idolatrously to past images or look hopefully to some supernatural forms that are not grounded in reality. The task of finding images of hope

44. Cobb, *Christ in a Pluralistic Age*, 228.
45. Ibid., 185.
46. Ibid., 186.
47. Ibid., 187.
48. Ibid., 182.
49. Ibid., 183.
50. Ibid.

is a large one for the Christian community, and Cobb gives criteria for naming these images of hope. These are the four criteria for calling an image one of Christian hope: (1) The image must be a recent product of creative transformation, not simply a resuscitation of old images; (2) the image must be reformable through a continuing process of creative transformation; (3) the image must be open to the process of creative transformation in the present; and (4) the image must have arisen through encounter with Jesus' words or as a result of immersion in his field of force.[51]

However, no new orders of liberation or images of hope ensure a utopian future. At the very heart of reality is "always the dream of youth and the harvest of tragedy."[52] The creative advance brings "decay, transition, loss, and displacement."[53] Tragedy is marked by what has been along with what was not and what could be. Ambiguity is inherent in the structures of reality. At the heart of nature is ambiguity. Hope lies in peace, in Christ as the truth, in the one in whom all things come together. Christ, as truth, is the imagination of God that inspires within us the hope that something lies beyond the bondage of our own vision. And yet hope is only possible as it is incarnate in the lives of individuals. Incarnate hope lives in the world, in the present moments of daily life. Hope lives from this world into the next world, where it receives its ultimate fulfillment. Thus, in Christ as the way, the truth, and the life, God is both the lure of possibility and order and the one in whom all comes to fulfillment.

Hope in God through Christ inspires the world as music inspires the performer. Jazz artists develop the growth of their creative potential over an entire lifetime. From this life of creativity comes a moral obligation to share their talent with others. The survival of music is grounded in the present spirit of the players. In a commitment to share with others, jazz musicians offer a vision of hope for the musical world:

> They hope to make their mark on a world plagued by social conflict and preoccupied with materialistic values. Improvisers view performance as a positive force that can redress this imbalance, if only in a small way, by replenishing the earth's soundscape with music possessed of beauty and vitality, integrity and soul to remind listeners of these finer universal expressions of human aspiration.[54]

To improvise on Whitehead's language: "God is the improviser of the world, with tender patience, composing it with her vision of truth, beauty, and goodness." Our role is to be part of God's imaginative soundscape of beautiful music.

CREATED CO-CREATOR: PHILIP HEFNER

Theologically, we take account of the two-natured human animal who is both conditioned and free by asserting, first of all, that *the human being is created by God to be a co-creator in the creation that*

---

51. Ibid.

52. Whitehead, *Adventures in Ideas* (New York: Free Press, 1961) 296.

53. Ibid., 286.

54. Berliner, *Thinking in Jazz*, 503.

God has brought into being and for which God has purposes.[55]

Philip Hefner develops an understanding of creativity that is rooted in the Christian doctrine of creation viewed from an evolutionary perspective. Hefner, setting forth his agenda in *The Human Factor*, tries to make sense of the contents of the Christian faith in light of contemporary sciences. The central questions for Hefner are, Who are human beings and what are their purposes? To answer these questions he draws on theologians like Irenaeus, John Hick, Ralph Burhoe, and Joseph Sittler. Using Imre Lakatos' philosophy of science, Hefner constructs a project that works around a core hypothesis with auxiliary hypotheses. His main task is to present theological proposals for discussion. "What is essential is that the proposal appear to be interesting and fruitful for exploration—fruitful above all."[56] Hefner's method is one of the great strengths of his theological proposal. The strengths of his theology are in the fruits that it produces. Hefner's theology is not confined within the walls of ecclesiastical domains but encompasses human identity situated within the vast cosmos of God's creation. Hefner takes the world seriously as the place for theological reflection.

The core of his proposal, the theory of the created co-creator, becomes grist for the theological mill. We are created by God as creatures and simultaneously endowed with the responsibility and gift of freedom to co-create the world with God. The primary shape of Hefner's proposal provides information for humans to work with as they struggle in life-and-death situations on this planet. Hefner provides a narrative of self-understanding from the Christian perspective that will help humans to live "wholesome" lives and be responsible for the creation around them. Hefner's non-dualistic framework joins what much of the Enlightenment has put asunder: nature from culture, humans from technology, religion from science. He says, "my view holds that both humans and technology are parts of nature."[57]

We understand who we are in relationship to the cosmos in which we live. Creation is both creation out of nothing (*creatio ex nihilo*) and continuing creation (*creatio continua*). Nature is the birthplace of human understanding. In a rather interesting reversal of metaphors, Hefner describes our "place" in the following way:

> Our lives are not so much a traveling through nature's space and time, as if we were making progress on a journey or conquering obstacles in our way towards a destination that is important to us, as they are stations on a journey whose traveler is something that transcends us, and for whom still more stations lie beyond us. We are not so much moving through and over nature, as we are natural creatures who represent a discrete station on nature's way. We are not sovereign over nature, but rather an occasion with nature's sovereignty.[58]

Our journey is not from this place to another, as if the goal of faith were to leave where we were created. Our calling in life is to be located in this place God put us, in the garden. To find our niche in nature

---

55. Philip Hefner, *The Human Factor: Evolution, Culture, and Religion*, Theology and the Sciences (Minneapolis: Fortress, 1993) 35.

56. Ibid., 17.

57. Ibid., 49.

58. Ibid., 55–56.

is to find our theological placement and self-understanding. We find ourselves already in relationship with the natural matrix that gave us birth. Nature is the place where we discover the sacred.

We are created co-creators rooted in our evolutionary history. "We are, first of all, thoroughly natural creatures. We have emerged from the natural evolutionary processes."[59] Hefner draws on a biocultural model that emphasizes our two-natured character as human beings. We are developed from our inherited genetic data. Also creatures of culture, we construct frameworks of meaning in order to understand who we are and to assess the world around us.[60] The evolutionary process is the means by which God created us as free creatures. We are dependent on God and the evolutionary past from which we came. Thus, we are "created." Yet we are not destined to be determined by our genes, and we are free creators with God. Freedom is both the condition of our existence and the means by which nature is "stretching itself" toward that which is new.

Christ is the one who embodies true humanity. Hefner, along with other theologians, shifts the primary focus of redemption to creation. In other words, the doctrine of redemption only makes sense if it is viewed in the large focus of the doctrine of creation. Nature and grace are not separate but are resolved in the understanding of the purpose of God in Jesus Christ for the benefit of all creation. In Christ, we know who we are and who God is for us. Hefner believes that we have the possibility to develop a new phase of evolution. In Christ, we find out what it is and who it is that God intends for us to be. "Jesus Christ becomes the central event for understanding what it means for humans to be God's proposal for the future of the evolutionary process."[61] In sacramental language, Hefner claims that it is precisely nature that is a fit vehicle (*finitum capax infiniti*) for God's grace. This is preeminently understood in the incarnation of God in Jesus the Christ.

If we understand that nature is the vehicle fit for God's grace, we must have a corresponding theological interpretation of humanity's relationship to nature, particularly in a scientific and technological age. As noted before, many theologies and Enlightenment philosophies bifurcated nature from technology and humanity from nature. Hefner's proposal offers a more helpful way of interpreting how humans are situated in the natural world. He develops a theology of *techno-nature* that corresponds to his anthropological notion of the created co-creator. Humans are placed firmly within the evolutionary process, and, consequently, technology is viewed as "natural." However, this is not to assume that Hefner is uncritical of humans' use of technology. On the contrary, he urges critical responsibility in our use of and discernment about technology. Concerns of social justice, war, and destruction are the ethical frameworks for comprehending this connection between techno-nature and the created co-creator. "Technology must be interpreted; it is a behavior to be guided; and it must interface in a wholesome or well-synchronized manner with the full range

---

59. Ibid., 19.
60. Ibid., 29.

61. Hefner, "The Evolution of the Created Co-Creator," in *Cosmos as Creation: Theology and Science in Consonance,* ed. Ted Peters (Nashville: Abingdon, 1989) 417.

of earth's physico-biogenetic information systems."[62] Like the other voices analyzed in this chapter, Hefner links our ability to survive in the future with our ability to further our creative endeavors in ways that are wholesome and life-giving for the planet.

We are drawn into the future of what we will be. God is not finished with the world yet. We participate in constructing a world that is more wholesome for the entire cosmos. "The essential *humanum* that is emerging is being continually called by its destiny, and our ability to participate as an ordained co-creator is the result of the creative thrust of God."[63] We are not yet who we will be. God is drawing all the creation into a new destiny. What this means for Hefner is that God's creative work is also God's redemptive work. Our work as co-creators is part of God's redemption and re-creation of all of life. Our vocation is linked to the future of all creation. Our identity was shaped by the evolutionary history of billions of years, and our destiny is tied to that very same process through which God works. God's future is our future; we are not on the journey, but God's journey is moving through us.

Commentary

Caryn D. Riswold

My teacher, Ann Pederson, preached Whitehead at our Lutheran church wedding. I begin this discussion of her work with that story because, as she says, "the stories we tell about ourselves reveal our self-understanding." The stories others tell about us similarly reveal the effects of our relationship with the world. A primary way in which Ann Pederson relates to the world is as a teacher-scholar, and the six ideas about creativity that she identifies in this chapter as emerging from four individuals can be effectively applied to describe her teaching: It is an aesthetic process to create and perceive beauty; it creates what is natural in students with their own idiomatic parts; it works within students and not as an additional force outside of them; it creates with the students; it carries an inherent risk; and it is about hope for the future. The body of Ann Pederson's work extends, therefore, beyond her books and chapters and articles, and into the lives of college graduates around the world who have learned from her theological practice in the classroom and on campus.

In this excerpt from the chapter "Creativity as Creaturely Vocation," Pederson models the theological vision that she describes: creative transformation that draws together images and ideas from disparate sources. This is how she

---

62. Hefner, *The Human Factor*, 154.

63. Hefner, "The Evolution of the Created Co-Creator," 418.

creates theological jazz in her 2001 book, *God, Creation, and All That Jazz: A Process of Composition and Improvisation*, with improvised connections, spontaneity, and a flow of ideas that provokes resonance. Whether it be articulating the sacramental heart of Christian theology with Whiteheadian language or using Montuori's metaphor of improvisation to describe the learning community, Pederson brings together meaningful pieces of philosophy, theology, experience, and music here and throughout her work. She mentions "Whitehead's notion of creativity, in which the many become one and are increased by one."[1] Likewise, Pederson's creativity brings us an entirely new product as a result of her connections among the many. She does what she quotes Bateson as describing: combining "familiar and unfamiliar components in response to new situations, following an underlying grammar and an evolving aesthetic."[2] She invokes Whitehead at the wedding.

Specifically in this section, the way in which Pederson draws in and builds on Philip Hefner's construct of the created co-creator encapsulates both method and substance in this work, as well as in her 1998 book, *Where in the World is God? Variations on a Theme*.[3] As created, owing our existence to something other than ourselves, human beings are dependent, contingent, and humbled. As co-creators, bearing a deep responsibility for the world that we inhabit and shape daily, human beings are independent, free, and empowered. As a theologian by vocation, Pederson is created, depending on the familiar treasures of her own teachers and tradition. As teacher and scholar, she is co-creating, drawing in new and sometimes unfamiliar resources, constructing theology and enabling learners to respond to the challenges of making justice in the twenty-first century. Her current work is writing and teaching in the area of medical ethics, in the state of South Dakota, a recent and ongoing battleground for women's health care. She continues to transform her theological vision with renewed relevance and application. She brings the often esoteric discussions about religion and science, process and feminist theologies, down to the ground, to the embodied location of our human and political lives.

Pederson's focus on the embodied reality of human life is threaded throughout the body of her work because of reasons that she describes in this excerpt: "It is precisely nature that is a fit vehicle (*finitum capax infiniti*) for God's grace. This is preeminently understood in the incarnation of God in Jesus the Christ." Taking familiar Christian themes like the incarnation and improvising on them with an eye specifically to women's experience, feminist theology, and a process vision, Pederson's work has served to bridge church, academy, tradition, and the future. In her article "Christmas and the Reality of the Incarnation: *Finitum capax infiniti*," in a 2007 issue of *Word & World*, Pederson further connects this ancient theological metaphor to "economic realities, political histories, religious struggles, and formidable social boundaries," thereby transforming its relevance for life in the world today.[4]

---

1. Above, 165.
2. Above, 161.
3. Ann Pederson, *Where in the World Is God? Variations on a Theme* (St. Louis: Chalice, 1998).
4. Pederson, "Christmas and the Reality of the Incarnation: *Finitum capax infiniti*," *Word & World* 27 (2007) 382.

In the book she coauthored with Arthur Peacocke in 2006, *The Music of Creation*, she claims in the prelude to have contributed "ideas about communal and ongoing creativity."[5] Her sections of that book are titled "Working at Creation" and "Ongoing Creation." Themes of Ann Pederson's work in print and in the classroom are aptly described with those titles: We have to work at creation, and that work is ongoing. In the chapter excerpted here, we have a sample of her creative transformation to consider.

STUDY QUESTIONS

1. What are the gifts and challenges of the metaphor of improvisation as a way of describing how humans live and create?

2. Does Csikszentmihalyi's idea of "flow" or "losing oneself to a creative process" apply effectively to God as well as to humans? What might the issues be in thinking of creativity this way?

3. What are the implications of Pederson's ideas about "creativity as creaturely vocation" and about divine power for discussions about theodicy and the problem of evil?

4. For whom is embracing ambiguity "at the heart of nature" good news? For whom might it be risky? How might these ideas connect to queer theories and theologies?

---

5. Arthur Peacocke and Ann Pederson, *The Music of Creation* (Minneapolis: Fortress, 2006) xii.

14 Jewish Feminism

SANDRA B. LUBARSKY

Sandra B. Lubarsky is director of the Master's of Arts Program in Sustainable Communities and Professor of Religious Studies at Northern Arizona University. She received degrees at Pomona College, the University of Chicago, and Claremont Graduate University. Her research interests include sustainable communities, philosophy of religion, interreligious dialogue, religion and the environment, aesthetics and Jewish feminism. This excerpt, "Reconstructing Divine Power: Post-Holocaust Jewish Theology, Feminism and Process Philosophy" is from Women and Gender in Jewish Philosophy *edited by Hava Tirosh-Samuelson, a ground-breaking collection of essays on Jewish and feminist philosophies.*

Excerpt from "Reconstructing Divine Power: Holocaust Jewish Theology, Feminism, and Process Philosophy"

INTRODUCTION

NO OTHER EVENT HAS crystallized the problem of evil and problematized power more than the Holocaust. In a midrash on Leviticus 21:1–3, 10–12, in which the priestly caste is forbidden from making contact with corpses for fear of a loss of their trust in God, Shlomo Carlebach wrote, "Ever since the Holocaust we are all like priests who have become contaminated by death."[1] Indeed, the faith of many modern Jews has been corrupted by contact with the corpses of the Holocaust. Though modern science and philosophy had spun their disenchantments on Jews as much as on anyone else, the Holocaust was an unequivocally Jewish tragedy that multiplied by immeasurable degree the crisis of meaning that gripped Europeans and Americans in the twentieth century. Where had the all-powerful, all-good God of the covenant been at Auschwitz?

What had been hoped for, even expected, had not happened. The classic Jewish hope is for a world that is in accord with God's will—a world made meaningful by standards of justice, the fulfillment of promises, and an increase in holiness and peace. Jewish covenantal expectations have revolved around the understanding that each partner in the divine-human relationship has specific responsibilities and duties and although the human partners may, indeed, will, fall short of their obligations, it is understood that God will hold true to the partnership despite humanity's

---

1. Cited in Rodger Kamenetz, *The Jew in the Lotus: A Poet's Rediscovery of Jewish Identity in Buddhist India* (Northvale, NJ: Aronson, 1995) 157.

failures. It goes without saying, then, that the relationship between divine justice, love, and power has been, for Jewish thinkers, the theological and philosophical challenge of the hour. In the struggle to make sense of either justice or love in the face of the Holocaust, divine power plays a pivotal role.

Post-Holocaust Jewish theologians have probed the meaning of divine and human power, seeking to understand how power could have become so deeply perverted in the mid-twentieth century. What is striking is that power continues to be understood by and large, in traditional terms: most thinkers assume divine omnipotence (even if they opt for divine self-limitation) and assume power's primary form to be coercive.

Important critiques and reconstructions of power have come from two quarters: feminist thought and process philosophy. Having assessed modernity as a particularly egregious advocate and sponsor of the use of dominating power, they have provided sophisticated analyses that have helped to unveil the complex dynamics of power. Feminist thinkers have been masterful in exposing the absences on which power thrives as well as in detailing the privileges and exclusivity of power that is bonded to patriarchy. Process thinkers have focused on modernity's marriage to mechanism and materialism and the subsequent uses and abuses of power. Both feminist and process thinkers have developed a thorough critique of dominating power, but this critique has had little impact on the construction of post-Holocaust theodicies by Jewish thinkers.

This essay brings feminist thought and process philosophy into conversation with Jewish theology on the topic of divine power and covenantal relations in a post-Holocaust era. It begins with an examination of "divine hiddenness" and "divine self-limitation" as responses to the Holocaust with specific attention given to the writings of Eliezer Berkovitz and Irving Greenberg.[2] For both thinkers, God is assumed to be omnipotent and to wield coercive power but to voluntarily become less powerful in order to accommodate human freedom.

The second part of the essay is a critique of the idea of "divine hiddenness" based on feminist re-evaluations of power and powerlessness. Feminist scholars have given considerable attention to documenting alternatives to dominating power—alternatives drawn from the life experiences of those who have survived generations of oppressive conditions. In so doing, they have illustrated, on the one hand, that "hiddenness" is not "powerlessness" when power is expanded to include such powers as come with affection and relational interdependence. On the other hand, it is also clear that although the status of being invisible is not without its power, it is nonetheless indicative of an oppressive imbalance of power. When the negative consequences of the "hiddenness" of women are acknowledged, "hiddenness" as a theological strategy becomes suspect.

The third section offers an analysis of power based on the principles of process philosophy. In ascribing the powers of

---

2. Editors' note: Cf. Irving Greenberg, "The Relationship of Judaism and Christianity: Toward a New Organic Model," in *Twenty Years of Jewish-Catholic Relations*, ed. Eugene J. Fisher et al. (New York: Paulist, 1986) 191–211; and Eliezer Berkovits, *Faith after the Holocaust* (New York: Ktav, 1973).

self-determination and causal efficacy to all experiencing beings, process philosophy insists on the metaphysical necessity of power at the same time that it favors persuasive power as the form of power most in line with freedom and relationality. A process understanding of power offers ways to name the power of "hiddenness" positively—as *persuasive* power—and, in fact, to assert that such power is not a compromise, but a fundamental characteristic of divine action.

Taken together, feminist critiques of dominating power and explications of the "hidden" power of the oppressed, and process philosophy's reconstruction of divine power based on a relational metaphysics, have important implications for the development of post-Holocaust theodicies and theologies.

. . .

FEMINIST CRITIQUE OF DOMINATING POWER

In asking for clarification of the difference between a God who restrains the use of power and a God who is actually limited in power, Steven Katz makes the sardonic observation that, "If the non-presence, non-power, non-involvement of God proves his Presence, then by a similar demonstration we could 'prove' all sorts of entities and attributes into existence."[3] Indeed, the strategy of hiddenness, insofar as it continues to assume divine omnipotence and limit the expression of power to physical force, is unable to fulfill its intentions.

Though absence theologians like Berkovitz and Greenberg hold on to traditional notions of divine power, they verge on proposing an alternative understanding of power, both human and divine. When they speak of the presence of the "hidden God" as guiding, nurturing, and caring, they are identifying alternative notions of power. Were these alternative forms of divine activity recognized as forms of power, it would be possible to develop a theodicy that does in fact fulfill the intention of upholding covenantal relationality.

Feminist thought has revolved around a critique, dissection, and reconstruction of power. An ongoing fugue, played and replayed through the voices of many women, power is the major theme composing feminist inquiry. Power is acknowledged to be both the instrument of oppression and the means of liberation. Feminists have evaluated the power of power as it appears in political and social institutions, cultural traditions, and by way of tacit knowledge, including the "anonymous," "unbound," disciplinary power that permeates cultures.[4] In the most general terms, feminist examinations of power can be divided into two broad categories: (1) various critiques of dominating power, and (2) illuminations of multiple forms of alternative power.

It is dominating power, power "over," that is the trademark of patriarchy and the hallmark of women's experience in patriarchal cultures. Undergirding dominating power is a dualistic and hierarchical

---

3. Cited in David Wolpe, "*Hester Panim* in Modern Jewish Thought," *Modern Judaism* 17 (1997) 26.

4. Sandra Bartky, "Foucault, Femininity and the Modernization of Patriarchal Power," reprinted in *Feminist Philosophies,* ed. Janet A. Kourany, James P. Sterba, and Rosemarie Tong (Englewood Cliffs, NJ: Prentice Hall, 1992) 112.

vision of reality: the world is divided along gender lines into two kinds of beings—men who are superior and women who are inferior—and operates hierarchically, with those who are superior having power over those who are inferior. In a patriarchal framework, it is assumed that power is a limited commodity so that power relations are understood as competitive, with a gain on one side yielding a loss on the other. Moreover, power is used to exact privilege from those who might not otherwise oblige; it is, to put it simply, coercive.

When feminists have turned to an examination of religion and power, they have focused attention on such issues as God-language, authority structures, and textual and ritual traditions. Feminist theologian Nancy Howell has pointed out that "Feminists do not seem particularly preoccupied with the topic of divine omnipotence."[5] And yet, the traditional doctrine of divine omnipotence is absolutely central to the reconstruction of a non-patriarchal theology. For divine omnipotence has been construed as congruent with patriarchal power and hence both mirrors and anchors the power relations that are found in social and political settings. Even in a largely secular culture, images of God, whether accepted as literal or literary, give support to deep-seated messianic hopes, nationalistic desires, and interpersonal relations. Thus, when God is conceived of as warrior, king, and supreme ruler, men have hoped to attain such status and both women and men have accepted the roles of soldiers and servants of God. When God is described as masculine, men have been given normative status and women perceived as "other." And when God is imaged as an all-powerful being whose power takes the form of overwhelming coercion (e.g., through "signs and wonders"), then those who desire to act in consonance with the divine image learn to hope for unlimited power and to mimic divine dominance.

To feminist thinkers we owe significant insights into the power of language to shape our expectations and experiences. As Carolyn Merchant has written about the cultural shift: that occurred in early modern attitudes toward nature, "Descriptive statements about the world can presuppose the normative; they are ethic-laden . . . The norms may be tacit assumptions hidden within the descriptions in such a way as to act as invisible restraints or moral ought-nots."[6] Language and images of God's power as dominance belie an ethic of brute power and a world in which relationality is contingent and autonomy is valued over interdependence. The tacit assumption behind a conception of God as an omnipotent being who wields aggressive, imperious, even tyrannical force, is a theology of domination. Judith Plaskow, the Jewish feminist theologian who has so cogently addressed gender relations, cites with approval the insight of Rosemary Radford Ruether that "Such images of God's dominance give rise to the terrible irony that the symbols Jews have used to talk about God as ultimate good have helped generate and justify the evils from which we hope God will save us."[7] Even when God is cast as

---

5. Nancy R. Howell, *A Feminist Cosmology: Ecology, Solidarity, and Metaphysics* (New York: Humanity Books, 2000) 107.

6. Carolyn Merchant, *The Death of Nature: Women, Ecology, and the Scientific Revolution* (San Francisco: Harper & Row, 1980) 4.

7. Judith Plaskow, *Standing Again at Sinai:*

a loving parent, Plaskow notes, it is as an authoritarian father who demands obedience, punishes independence, and shows little restraint in using power to achieve this.

Once the alignment between divine omnipotence and patriarchal power is acknowledged, the significance of feminist critiques of power for post-Holocaust Jewish theology becomes clear. For it is patriarchal power that continues (unnamed) to inform the thought of most post-Holocaust theologians. Omnipotent power is taken to be dominating power, and thus both violent and competitive. In the theologies of Berkovitz and Greenberg, we are given images of a God who fears that without self-restraint, not only evil but the very structure of human existence will be destroyed.

An oppositional dynamic is in place in which God must self-limit in order to allow for human freedom. Thus we are presented with a flawed emancipatory project, based on the idea of power as a zero-sum game, in which one party's gain in power entails the other party's diminishment.

In a patriarchal model, power connotes physical presence and effect and powerlessness connotes invisibility. When absence theologians couple divine hiddenness with powerlessness, God joins the ranks of many women who have suffered the same fate under the conditions of patriarchy. While humanity gains power, God takes up the classic female role of suffering both with those involved in power struggles and because of them. Berkovitz describes the hidden God as long-suffering and patient; Greenberg speaks of the self-limited God as "suffering, sharing, participating, calling." These are attributes that have been assigned to women and are associated with helplessness. Although it will be argued momentarily that such attributes are in fact bearers of non-dominating power, here it is important to note that in connecting hiddenness and helplessness, Greenberg and Berkovitz repeat the pernicious conditions for silencing that women have experienced.

Alternative Forms of Power

In contextualizing power so that it is understood as something that functions differently in different circumstances, feminist analyses have led to the realization that dominating power is neither the singular nor the superior species of power. Attention is given to more complex forms of power, identified as relational or empowering power. In contrast to "power over," alternative forms of power speak of influence, interdependent relationality, and mutual empowerment.

The contrast with oppositional power is striking. "Formal male power" has been described as "a form of compulsion" and as "direct pressure on a social actor to perform a specific action." Such power becomes a " 'thing in itself,' measurable like amps on an electricity meter."[8] Operating as an external force "on" another being or object, formal power takes place between independent, separate beings and results in an effect that is visible and measurable. Informal, female power, by contrast, functions as influence, which has been

---

Judaism from a Feminist Perspective (San Francisco: Harper & Row, 1990) 132.

8. Jean Bethke Elshtain, "The Power and Powerlessness of Women," in *Beyond Equality and Difference: Citizenship, Feminist Politics and Female Subjectivity,* ed. Gisela Bock and Susan James (London: Routledge 1992) 112.

described as "in-fluence," in which the effect of another "is not working *upon me* so much as *into* me; in-fluence is that which flows in."[9] Its effect is internal and thus may not be immediately or even ever discernible in the same way as dominating power. It is often the quiet, gentle power of sympathy, patience, care and support. Moreover, because it is cooperating power, it does not overwhelm, but rather increases capacity and competence.[10] And empowering power is abundant, contributing to the power of another without diminishing the power of those who enter a relationship. Relational power takes many forms. It can, for example, guide, encourage, cooperate, and respond. Its hallmark is sensitivity to the other and thus, in this sense, it is contingent power. In its most intimate form, it is the power of love, expressed by parents, friends, children, lovers—and by God. Such power *is* real power, but it is so different from the paradigm of dominating power that it is often not recognized to be an alternative power, let alone the most elemental, pervasive power at work in the world.

Because Berkovitz and Greenberg limit their interpretation of power to dominating power, they remove God from the world in order to make room for human freedom and responsibility. Though they wish to strengthen the covenantal relationship, they actually undercut it. God is bereft of power and humanity is bereft of a response-able relationship with God. The mutual participation and responsibility required by covenant is dissolved. Were Berkovitz and Greenberg, however, to attribute the power of influence and relationality to the "powerless presence" of the hidden God, they would actually gain expressed corroboration of their own insights. Invisibility does not necessarily mean powerlessness; nor does "powerlessness" require invisibility. Power has its hidden, quiet forms; and those deemed invisible because excluded from formal power structures, have always had informal power.[11] The naming of "invisible" power as real power also maintains a continuum of responsibility throughout all relationality, thus breaking the dualism between power and responsibility and powerlessness and irresponsibility. For when divine hiddenness is equated with powerlessness, God is excused from responsibility because God is helpless to act. Non-dominating power assumes the ability to act, albeit in non-coercive ways, and thus entails responsibility as well.

---

9. Catherine Keller, *From a Broken Web: Separation, Sexism, and Self* (Boston: Beacon) 27.

10. This point is nicely made by Rachel Adler in *Engendering Judaism: An Inclusive Theology and Ethics* (Philadelphia: Jewish Publication Society, 1998) 94. It is, however, important to note that not all non-coercive power is affirming or empowering power. For example, Miriam Peskowitz details the use of the feminine gaze and women's gossip/storytelling to control women in obedience to patriarchal standards. She writes, "In the absence of more formal modes for enforcing rabbinic visions of culture, law, and society, the informalities of public gazes and chatter are not to be underrated," in *Spinning Fantasies: Rabbis, Gender, and History* (Berkeley: University of California Press, 1997) 149.

11. See, for example, Leila Ahmed's now almost classic essay "Western Ethnocentrism and Perceptions of the Harem," *Feminist Studies* 8 (1982) 521–34, in which she describes some aspects of the power and control available to women in separatist structures. For example, she writes, "Although in its explicit formulations, Saudi society gives individual men control over individual women, nevertheless, the *shape* of that society allows men considerably less control over how women think, how they see and discuss themselves, and how they see and discuss men" (528).

Feminist proposals for understanding relational power offer important correctives to the theological strategy of divine hiddenness. Based on an examination of women's experiences as more or less hidden from the formal, public domain, and yet not dispossessed of power, not helpless, and not irresponsible, alternative forms of understanding divine activity in the world become available. God may indeed be in the world, actively guiding it and responding to it without overwhelming human freedom or undercutting human responsibility.

PROCESS PHILOSOPHY ON DIVINE POWER

Based on the thought of Alfred North Whitehead (1861–1947) and Charles Hartshorne (1897–2000), process philosophers have developed a detailed analysis of power as relational and a model of divine agency that affirms neither dominating nor omnipotent power. God's power is redefined in two ways: (1) God is understood as the most powerful existent being, but because other creatures have some power, power is not confined to the Godhead, and (2) God's power is the power of persuasion, not the power of brute force; were God to act with violence toward any creature, God would violate a vital aspect of what is implied in the image of God as a perfect being.

Process philosophy, unfortunately, has received only limited attention in contemporary Jewish thought, even though some leading Jewish thinkers in the twentieth century were indebted to it. Max Kadushin in his 1938 book, *Organic Thinking: A Study in Rabbinic Thought*, spoke of Whitehead's philosophy as "the most comprehensive philosophy of organism" and proposed that many of Whitehead's "metaphysical concepts can be taken as generalizations of the characteristics of rabbinic theology."[12] The scholar of Gnosticism and philosopher of science, Hans Jonas, expressed strong appreciation for and affinities with process thought, calling it a philosophy "whose intellectual force and philosophical importance are unequaled in our time."[13] Jonas embraced the process emphases on becoming over being, on freedom and value as characteristic of all of life, and on limits to divine power. In the 1950s, Milton Steinberg spoke of his indebtedness to Charles Hartshorne's "neo-classical" reconception of divinity in which God is neither immutable nor omnipotent. Rabbi Levi Olan, too, adopted Hartshorne's reinterpretation of divine perfection in which " 'be ye perfect' does not mean 'be ye immutable!' "[14] Most recently, Rabbi William E. Kaufman has contributed a book on *The Evolving God in Jewish Process Theology* and David Griffin and I have published a collection

---

12. Max Kadushin, *Organic Thinking: A Study in Rabbinic Thought* (1938; reprint, New York: Bloch, 1976) 247–50.

13. Hans Jonas, *The Phenomenon of Life: Toward a Philosophical Biology* (Chicago: University of Chicago Press, 1966) 96.

14. Charles Hartshorne, "Philosophical and Religious Uses of God," in *Process Theology: Basic Writings,* ed. Ewert H. Cousins (New York: Newman, 1971) 111–16. See Steinberg, quoted in Simon Noveck, *Milton Steinberg: Portrait of a Rabbi* (New York: Ktav, 1978) 87, 262. On Levi Olan's affinities with process thought, see his essay, "The Prophetic Faith in a Secular Age," reprinted in *Jewish Theology and Process Thought*, ed. Sandra B. Lubarsky and David Ray Griffin, SUNY Series in Constructive Postmodern Thought (New York: State University of New York Press, 1996) 25–34.

of essays entitled *Jewish Theology and Process Thought*.[15]

The starting point for process philosophy is an analysis of power as a fundamental characteristic of *all being*. The primary units of reality ("actual occasions" or "events") are understood to be *subjects* for themselves and as such, to include some degree of self-determination. Because to be is to have some power (perhaps only infinitesimal) of self-determination, there is freedom or creativity throughout the system.

Whitehead substitutes *the process of becoming* for the idea of substance. Subjectivity, then, is not a state but a process (hence the term, *process philosophy*). The process of becoming is a process of *feeling* the world; Whitehead's term is *prehension*. Feeling or prehending the world means entering into relationship with it. A subject does not exist before feeling, but emerges from feeling the world. Feelings are the direct connections between units of reality; they are the "food" on which subjectivity feeds and as sustenance, are incorporated into the becoming subject. The basic process of reality is the process of becoming a subject by becoming "internally related" to the world. Feminist process philosopher Catherine Keller notes, "*Relation, in other words, is more than a feminine or feminist preoccupation; it is the best metaphor for the nature of the universe.*"[16]

But how the becoming subject feels the given world and how the given world is incorporated into the becoming subject is not strictly determined. Relations, process thinkers explain, involve "in-fluence"; in the process of becoming, every actual occasion experiences the power of the past and the power of possibilities—not as determinative, but as influential—and shapes itself in response to these influences. The given world—which, for process theologians includes God—is "felt" by the becoming actuality and thus becomes constitutive of the arising subject. But again, though subjectivity arises in relation to the given world and though this relation is internal to the subject, there is always some degree of novelty and freedom at work in the emergence of subjectivity.

It is thus the case that as occasions of subjectivity arise, they are affected (influenced but not determined) by the power already at work in the universe. In perishing, they contribute to the welter of the past and become part of the influences inherited by the next becoming occasions.[17] As Whitehead writes, "It belongs to the nature of every 'being' that it is a potential for every 'becoming.'" Thus relational power is at the root of the dynamic of becoming: all beings have the capacity both to influence others and to be influenced

---

15. William E. Kaufman, *The Evolving God in Jewish Process Theology* (Lewiston, NY: Mellen, 1997); Lubarsky and Griffin, *Jewish Theology and Process Thought*.

16. Catherine Keller, "Postpatriarchal Postmodernity," in *Spirituality and Society: Postmodern Visions*, ed. David Ray Griffin (Albany: State University of New York Press, 1988) 75.

17. "The 'effects' of an actual entity are its interventions in concrescent processes other than its own. Any entity, thus intervening in processes transcending itself, is said to be functioning as an 'object.' It is the one general metaphysical character of all entities of all sorts, that they function as objects. It is this metaphysical character which constitutes the solidarity of the universe." Alfred North Whitehead, *Process and Reality: An Essay in Cosmology*, corrected edition, ed. David Ray Griffin and Donald W Sherburne (1929; reprint, New York: Free Press, 1978) 220.

by others.[18] In other words, every creature possesses two forms of creative power: the power of self-determination and the power of efficient causation. That this is so has important ramifications for the status of divine power.

A PROCESS THEODICY

In this metaphysical landscape of freedom and influence, the picture of divine power is significantly modified from that given in traditional theologies. God's power exists in a world of power and is, like all power, fundamentally relational. As with biblical, rabbinic, and kabbalistic theologies, process theology assumes the reality of human freedom and responsibility. It does so, however, without relying on the compromise of logic that characterizes classical Western religious thought, where divine omnipotence is upheld simultaneously with human freedom. The principle behind omnipotence is sustained: God is that being who influences *all* beings. God is omnipresent and omni-influential.

The process discussion of divine power takes place with full cognizance of the problem of evil. As Whitehead himself noted, "All simplifications of religious dogma are shipwrecked upon the rock of the problem of evil."[19] The process encounter with theodicy begins with the admission that genuine evil exists—that there are events without which the world would be better. And it affirms the two-fold power that is definitive of every creature. These set the parameters of the process reconception of divine power. In answer to the question, "How is the occurrence of any genuine evil compatible with a perfectly good creator *who could have unilaterally prevented all genuine evil while still making possible all the good?*" Process theism answers that because there is freedom and power throughout the created world, God does not act unilaterally.[20] Evil occurs because some degree of self-determination, that is, some degree of power, exists in beings who are inter-related with God, but not fully determined by God's will. It is the metaphysical consequence of the existence of free beings who are limited in (among other things) understanding, vision, energy, and sensitivity.

Moreover, as David Griffin has made clear, there is an evolutionary pattern that may be described as the "law of the variables of power and value" such that an increased capacity for feeling is related to an increased capacity to experience both good and evil and to contribute both positively and negatively to the experience of others. Such capacity is accompanied by a correlative increase in the power of self-determination, including the power to act contrary to God's direction.

> This doctrine means not only that God cannot occasionally interrupt the world's causal nexus. It also means that the divine purpose to bring about a world rich in value cannot—*metaphysically* cannot—be carried out without the risk of great evils. In this way, process philosophy is able to reconcile the facts of our world, as horrible as they often are, with belief in the

---

18. This is Bernard Loomer's definition of relational power, cited in Nancy Howell's *A Feminist Cosmology*, 116.

19. Alfred North Whitehead, *Religion in the Making* (1926; reprint, Cleveland: World, 1960) 74.

20. David Ray Griffin frames the question as cited in his book *Reenchantment without Supernaturalism: A Process Philosophy of Religion* (Ithaca, NY: Cornell University Press, 2001) 224–25.

wisdom and perfect goodness of this world's creator.[21]

This assessment of God's power resolves the classical problem of evil by revising the proposition that God is all-powerful and thus could single-handedly (so to speak) prevent evil events. Omnipotence is abandoned as an illogical concept in a system in which relationality is necessary rather than contingent. Omnipotence, process philosophers maintain, is both logically meaningless and theologically objectionable. A "monopoly theory of power," as Charles Hartshorne points out, is meaningless because power is by definition a relational term; divine power, existing in relationship with creaturely power, cannot be omnipotent.[22] God's power is "absolutely maximal, the greatest possible, but even the greatest power is still one power among others."[23] Hans Jonas, who formulated his theodicy in conversation with process philosophy, also objects, on the same philosophical grounds, to the notion of omnipotence.

> From the very concept of power, it follows that omnipotence is a self-contradictory, self-destructive, indeed, senseless concept... Absolute, total power means power not limited by anything, not even by the mere existence of something other than the possessor of that power... Absolute power then in its solitude, has no object on which to act. But as objectless power it is a powerless power, canceling itself out: "all" equals "zero" here. In order for it to act, there must be something else, and as soon as there is, the one is not all-powerful anymore, even though in any comparison its power may be superior by any degree you please to imagine. The existence of another object limits the power of the most powerful agent at the same time that it allows it to be an agent. In brief, power as such is a relational concept and requires relation... In short, it cannot be that all power is on the side of one agent only. Power must be divided so that there be any power at all.[24]

To this metaphysical paradox, Jonas adds his theological objections, arguing that "We can have divine omnipotence together with divine goodness only at the price of complete divine inscrutability." Jonas holds that the only Jewishly appropriate solution is to deny omnipotence, rather than divine goodness or intelligibility. A god who is hidden from human understanding, is a "profoundly un-Jewish conception," undercutting revelation and covenant.[25] Hence, with other process philosophers, Jonas rejects omnipotence.[26]

In rejecting omnipotence, process theologians do not thereby propose a powerless, passive, or hidden God. The second characteristic of a process theodicy involves the kind of power that God possesses and the way in which God

---

21. Ibid., 230.
22. Charles Hartshorne, *A Natural Theology for Our Time* (La Salle, IL: Open Court, 1967) 119.
23. Hartshorne, *Divine Relativity: A Social Conception of God*, 2nd ed. (New Haven: Yale University Press, 1964) 138.
24. Hans Jonas, "The Concept of God after Auschwitz," reprinted in Lubarsky and Griffin, *Jewish Philosophy and Process Thought*, 151–52.
25. Ibid., 152.
26. Among the few contemporary Jewish thinkers who have rejected divine omnipotence, most have done so under the influence of process philosophy. Such thinkers include Harold Schulweiss, William Kaufmann, Hans Jonas, Arthur A. Cohen, Levi Olan, and Milton Steinberg.

intervenes in the world. Process philosophy speaks of God's nature as dipolar, distinguishing between God's "primordial" nature, which is eternal and necessary, and God's "consequent" nature, which is contingent and responsive. In both cases, God is ever-present and ever-active in the world without violating creaturely freedom or the defining patterns of the natural world. God's power is understood as creative-redemptive power, operating as persuasive agency within each occasion and responding to the decisions of every occasion.

In the process *of concrescence* (Whitehead's term for *becoming),* every arising subject is influenced both by the past and by the possibilities inherent in the universe. Those possibilities are given in an ordered form to each occasion by God. In this way, God functions as "the organ of novelty" and the "lure for feeling," apart from which there could be neither novelty nor order in the world. This is what is termed the activity of God's "primordial nature" and it is one way in which God directly participates in the constitution of every subject. At every moment, God is present and efficacious, offering possibilities in line with God's goals of goodness and beauty. Because every creative act is by definition not fully determined by external agencies (else it would lack freedom and creativity), God's power cannot be coercive. God must work in tandem with other causal influences and with the element of self-determination that defines each occasion. Yet God is felt as an immanent power, responding to creaturely freedom with an influx of possibilities and thus actively working to shape the world.

In addition, process philosophers speak of God's consequent nature which is effected by the decisions made—at every moment—by those actualities in the process of concrescence. All that is decided, all that comes to be, finds everlasting effect in the immediacy of God's own life.[27] At every moment, the possibilities that God can offer the world are reintegrated in response to the actual decisions taking place within the world. Through God's integrative activity, all lives are remembered and continue to influence both God and the world. In this aspect of God's nature, God changes in response to the world.[28]

How, then, does God act in a world that is constituted by beings with some degree of self-determination, in which heightened sensitivity and complexity carry the possibility of both increased good and evil and in which God, therefore, is metaphysically constrained? "God's role," Whitehead writes, "is not the combat of productive force with productive force, of destructive force with destructive force. It lies in the patient operation of the overpowering rationality of his conceptual harmonization."[29] In a world in which all creatures have the two-fold powers of self-determination and efficient causation, God does not have either omnipotent or coercive power. But neither is God helpless. God has persuasive power over *all* things and, in fact, this kind of power *is* unlimited.[30] *Persuasion is power,* but it

27. Whitehead, *Process and Reality,* 346. "He [God] saves the world as its passes into the immediacy of his own life."

28. The distinction between God's primordial and consequent natures is spoken of by both Whitehead and Hartshorne as "di-polar" and affords a way of thinking of God as having both unchanging and responsive aspects.

29. Whitehead, *Process and Reality,* 346.

30. This very idea was insisted on by Rabbi Levi Olan in his essay "The Prophetic Faith in a

is power exercised in response to the integrity of other beings. Its manifestation is felt, but is not necessarily physically visible. For it is a kind of power that relies on the openness of individuals and acts internally. To speak of power in this way presumes a world that is not conceived of as mechanical, materialistic, or deterministic, that is, a world in which power can only be external and coercive. Rather, it is to think of the world as home to real subjectivity and freedom; in this kind of world, power is not control over but the capacity to influence the decisions of another. If human beings are in some way free and hence have some amount of power, then God works in a complicated world of relationships of power. And since process thinkers hold that it is not only human beings who have freedom and power, but that power and freedom are characteristics of the entire system of life, God is active in a world that is deeply complex. At every moment, God intervenes for good in the world, but at every moment God encounters the power that defines free and responsible creatures. Evil happens not because God allows it to happen, but because of the choices that are made by other free creatures who freely choose to ignore or oppose God's will.

Thus divine activity that is not coercive or omnipotent need not be equated with divine inactivity or powerlessness. Indeed, Buber's description of messianic activity—described as "hiddenness" but nonetheless clearly redemptive and creative—is expressive of the divine activity as it is framed in process metaphysics.

Hiddenness is the unannounced work that brings the Kingdom of God into the concrete forms which define the everyday, "hiding" the sacred within the profane world and thereby redeeming the world without unraveling it. Hiddenness is the means for continuity, for the continuity of creation—there is no break between redeemed and unredeemed time—where there is no saving knowledge, every act of the individual has bearing on the creative-redemptive process. The paradoxical nature of "hiddenness" is this: it is in concealment that the redemptive process reveals itself.[31]

Creative-redemptive power does not unravel, demolish, obliterate, or consume. It operates as persuasive agency, luring the world toward goodness and beauty and repairing the world as it fails to reach those goals.

CONCLUSION: A JEWISH FEMINIST PROCESS THEOLOGY AFTER THE HOLOCAUST

At the heart of Judaism is a divine-human partnership through which value and meaning become intimately known. The covenant is both a relationship of asymmetrical power in which God is in all ways understood as superior, and yet in which there exists a partnership. It is a relationship entered into by free subjects who regard each other as co-committed to an interpersonal relationship of trust, responsibility, and shared expectations. Within these parameters, what kind of power makes sense? Where there is both an extreme power differential and yet the

---

Secular Age," reprinted in *Jewish Theology and Process Thought* 30: 25–34, in which he wrote that "Power need not be coercive; it can be persuasive and unlimited."

31. Martin Buber, *The Origin and Meaning of Hasidism*, ed. and trans. Maurice Friedman (New York: Harper Torchbooks, 1966) 109.

requirement of mutuality, what kind of power is involved?

Clearly, coercive power violates covenantal mutuality. Though there is biblical affirmation of such power, there are important biblical, rabbinic, and kabbalistic renderings of divine power that point a different direction, toward the quiet, hidden work of non-violent responsiveness. When the rabbis of the post–Second Temple period reshaped Judaism, they did so in response to the failure of their military strength. They created a Judaism that could survive without political power and they remade their image of God within this new context. The God who is in exile with the Jewish People is a God who rejoices in a different kind of mastery: the mastery of texts, of *mitzvot,* and of prayer. They did not give up earlier conceptions of God's power as dominance, but that kind of power was deferred to a messianic future; in the present, imitation of God included, instead, the sustaining activities of study, prayer, and the doing of good deeds.

Post-Holocaust Jews face a situation akin to that of the rabbis who survived the destruction of 70 CE. Both process philosophy and feminist thought can contribute to that part of the rabbinic tradition which recognized the need for a reconstruction of divine power and human power, of the way God acts in the world and the way humans ought to act. What the rabbis came to understand—though they held this insight in tension with the tradition of dominating power—and what feminists and process thinkers have since affirmed—is that it is persuasive agency that empowers most fully. And the most powerful form of this kind of agency is love—love that encourages both the self-determination and the continuity of all beings. When God's power is conceived of as persuasive power, the language of love is given philosophical support. Bringing a process philosophical understanding of power and a feminist critique of patriarchal forms of power to bear on Jewish thought can lead to a more adequate way of imaging God's steadfast love in a post-Holocaust world.

Theological models of divine silence and invisibility continue to promote the very patterns of power that they mean to condemn. Eliezer Berkovitz and Irving Greenberg both oppose divine coercive omnipotence because it devalues human life. Yet divine silence in the form of passivity or hiddenness also devalues human life—as well as divine life—for God is denied significant participation in it. To exist and not be recognized, to have one's power denied or trivialized, to be called to suffer but to lack the ability to prevent suffering: these are characteristics that have unjustly marked women's lives. Women have risen up against these conditions now recognized as the outcome of degrading human relationships. Heeding women's experience, what is to be gained by a model of divine powerlessness that promotes the very corruptions women have rejected?

Theological models of powerlessness are built on a patriarchal understanding of power. Feminist critiques have exposed such an understanding of power to be inadequate. All too often, such power leads to abuse. In response, feminist thinkers have proposed a re-conception of power as relational, non-competitive, and ideally, non-coercive. The feminist critique of power is supported by a process metaphysics in which power characterizes all of life. Feminist alternatives to patriarchal power and process claims about the structure of reality have much to contribute to Jewish theologians who are searching for alternative ways to understand God's power and activity in the world. They offer ways to conceive of God as powerful without being coercive and as active in the world without overwhelming human freedom. In so doing, these alternatives offer an image of God that may in fact be deserving of *imitatio dei*.

Commentary

ARLETTE POLAND

THE POWER ASSOCIATED WITH the patriarchal deity is violent, interruptive, competitive, and coercive. According to Sandra B. Lubarsky, such dominating patriarchal notions of power lead to abuse and are inadequate for the realization of the covenantal relation on Judaism. The feminist project in this excerpt provides an eloquent criticism of patriarchal notions of power and is fully supported by "process metaphysics in which power characterizes all of life."[1] As a Jewish feminist theologian, Lubarsky describes the covenant between the people Israel and God as a mutual relation consisting of duties and responsibilities inherent to all sides of the relation.[2] In her chapter "Judaism and Process Thought: Between Naturalism and Supernaturalism," in the book she co-edited with David Ray Griffin,[3] Lubarsky points out that the dualism that results from ascribing omnipotence *and* an all-good nature to the deity is dissolved in the God of process thought largely because of the central position of relation. Ultimately, both process thought and Lubarsky agree that power is expressive of relation and therefore power is always contingent—never autonomous or absolute, not even the power of the deity.

Process explains that power and goodness are both embedded in and informed by relation. Both process theologians and Lubarsky affirm that power *must* be interdependent. In this way, mutual responsibility is part of creation and so part of the relation and the experience of and with the deity. God's power acts internally as God orders the possibilities for the occasion of becoming so it might (or might not) feel the possibilities in a similar way. Thus, just as for feminists, the key for process theologians is

---

1. Above, 190–91.

2. Some scholars argue that the covenant is voluntary. This argument seems to be accepted by Lubarsky by implication. However, biblical scholars such as Tammi Schneider, argue persuasively that the covenant is not a voluntary relation according to the Torah. It is a relation that is descriptive of the relation all Jews (whether born into or converted to the religion) automatically have with *YHVH* (God).

3. See Lubarsky and Griffin, eds., *Jewish Theology and Process Thought*, SUNY Series in Constructive Postmodern Thought (Albany: State University of New York Press 1996).

relation. In order to generate a non-patriarchal theology, argues Lubarsky, it is absolutely critical that feminists reconstruct divine omnipotence around the fact that relation is both fundamental and central for all existence.

The *Shoah* (Holocaust) is the perfect example to apply the matter of God's characteristics. Lubarsky correctly points out that Jewish theologians who address the *Shoah* fail to confront the matter of God's omnipotence. The central theme in the article presented here is that divine omnipotence, as articulated and expressed in patriarchal cultures is a mistake. Evil exists in the world we occupy because metaphysically-speaking creation involves risk since creation involves freedom. Process theology espouses a God/world relation that does not assuage the pain and reality of evil any more than it denies the truth of evil, but rather process theology places evil squarely in the midst of reality and alongside the deity.[4] So, when the theologian asks 'Where was God when the babies were burning?' Process theology can help the Jewish feminist answer "Right here, in the midst of it all."[5]

"Clearly, coercive power violates covenantal mutuality" states Lubarsky. Evil happens not because God allows it or because God is absent or hidden, or out of God's consideration for the freedom of the creatures. Evil happens simply and directly because of the choices that are made by the free creatures "who freely choose to ignore or oppose God's will." Regardless of the theodicy, the *Shoah* demands that not only Jewish theologians, but all of humanity answer how the absence of divine intervention can be considered an adequate response to any evil much less the evil perpetrated in the death camps. When God *has* to be omnipotent, Lubarsky points out, it would seem only two types of answers can be considered: either God is passive and therefore we can question if God is omnipotent after all, or God is omnipotent but chooses for various reasons to withhold that patriarchal notion of power.

The power of relation carries in it the potential for becoming a certain way into the future. The world thus is built out of power—relational power. In the end, Lubarsky brings Jewish feminist and process theologies together on the issue of divine omnipotence while using the extreme and real evil of the *Shoah* as her backdrop. A God who is actually hidden or absent from presence or understanding is a "profoundly un-Jewish conception" that undercuts both revelation and covenant in Judaism. This reprinting of a Jewish feminist's analysis that challenges divine omnipotence in such a relevant and realistic way is an excellent and logical beginning to the inevitable intersection of process and women's theologies in the future. Patriarchy must be dismantled and must be replaced by real life embodied experiences of evil such as there were in the *Shoah*. Evil is a risk in a creation where freedom is a metaphysical reality. But freedom cannot be privileged over the reality and centrality of

---

4. For more on process theology and theodicy see Marjorie Hewitt Suchocki *The End of Evil: Process Eschatology in Historical Context*, SUNY Series in Philosophy (Albany: State University of New York Press, 1988); or David Ray Griffin, *Evil Revisited: Responses and Reconsiderations* (Albany: State University of New York Press, 1991).

5. For more from Jewish feminist theology on the presence of the deity in the *Shoah*, see Melissa Raphael *The Female Face of God in Auschwitz: A Jewish Feminist Theology of the Holocaust*, Religion and Gender (London: Routledge, 2003).

connection and the dependence we have on each other.

STUDY QUESTIONS

1. What is the meaning of power for the feminist, the Jewish feminist, and the process theologian? How do they differ from or contribute to each other?

2. Should the patriarchal notion of power be challenged, replaced, dismantled, or what? What does Lubarsky suggest? What would process thought suggest?

3. How does the meaning of power in process theology help the meaning of power for the Jewish feminist theologian who has to deal with the covenant (as described herein)?

4. Does a process perspective assert that we cannot know God at all? Is it true from the Jewish feminist perspective? Why or why not?

15 Re-imaging Goddess/God

Carol P. Christ

Carol P. Christ is director of the Ariadne Institute for the Study of Myth and Ritual and formerly taught at Columbia University, Harvard Divinity School, Pomona College, San Jose State University, and California Institute of Integral Studies. Christ received the PhD from Yale University. Christ is a formative figure in feminist theology, whose leadership in the American Academy of Religion and whose classic anthology *Womanspirit Rising* (with Judith Plaskow) supported the early development of women's theological perspectives. Her research and writing span women's religious thought from ancient religions of the Goddess to contemporary feminist spirituality and theology. Christ engages process thought through the work of Charles Hartshorne. The excerpt is taken from *She Who Changes*, a 2003 book that re-imagines the divine as female.

Excerpt from *She Who Changes: Reimaging the Divine in the World*

RESTORING THE BODY AND THE WORLD

She changes everything She touches and everything She touches changes. The world is Her body. The world is in Her and She is in the world. She surrounds us like the air we breathe. She is as close to us as our own breath. She is energy, movement, life, and change. She is the ground of freedom, creativity, sympathy, understanding, and love. In Her we live, and move, and co-create our being. She is always there for each and every one of us, particles of atoms, cells, animals, and human animals. We are precious in Her sight. She understands and remembers us with unending sympathy. She inspires us to live creatively, joyfully, and in harmony with others in the web of life. Yet choice is ours. The world that is Her body is co-created. The choices of every individual particle of an atom, every individual cell, every individual animal, every individual human animal play a part. The adventure of life on planet earth and in the universe as a whole will be enhanced or diminished by the choices we make. She hears the cries of the world, sharing our sorrows with infinite compassion. In a still, small voice, She whispers the desire of Her heart: Life is meant to be enjoyed. She sets before us life and death. We can choose life. Change is. Touch is. Everything we touch can change.[1]

1. This description of She Who Changes is created in contrast to the picture of God as an Old White Man in chapter one. Echoes from the Bible,

This depiction of process philosophy's Goddess/God as She Who Changes contrasts sharply with the picture of God as an Old White Man with a long flowing beard discussed in chapter one. Process philosophy's understanding of the divine in the world challenges the assumptions of classical theism that are expressed in the traditional image of God. Whereas classical theism begins with a denial of the value of changing life, process philosophy affirms that change is inherent in every individual life in the universe at every moment and that change is the nature of the evolutionary process of life as a whole. Human beings were not created half way between animals and angels, as classical theism asserts. We evolved through a process of change within the web of life, sharing the capacity to feel and to feel the feelings of others and to exercise creative freedom with all other individuals. Goddess/God changes with the experiences of every individual in the changing world that is the divine body, while remaining unchangeable only in one respect: Goddess/God will always and everywhere relate to the world with creativity and love. Classical theism considered relationship to be a limitation and envisioned living alone or apart from others to be the most perfect state for both divinity and humanity. Process philosophy affirms touch or relationship as fundamental for all life, including divine life. In classical theism, divine power is unlimited. An omnipotent God is in control of the world; everything—even what appears to be evil—happens according to divine will and purpose. Process philosophy says that the power of Goddess/God is power with, not power over. The assertion of God's absolute and unlimited power creates the problem of evil: How could a good and loving God allow so much suffering to exist? Process philosophy answers that Goddess/God did not create suffering. The world is co-created by every individual in it. Death is part of life, but much of what we know as suffering is created by human beings. Goddess/God is with us in our suffering and inspires our efforts to lessen or transform it. Classical theism states that the goal of human life is to rise above the changing body and to share in the immortal life of God. Process philosophy asks us to enjoy finite and changing life that ends in death. The omnipotent God of classical theism is said to be the author of infallible revelation, given in the form of texts, teachings, traditions, or inspired individuals. Process philosophy counters that all human knowing is embodied and embedded in the world—and that it will always be fragmentary and in process. Classical theism asserts that an omniscient God already knows the fate of the universe. Process philosophy asks us to consider that the future of the universe is unknown even to Goddess/God. Though shaped by the past, the future will be created by the choices of a myriad of individual wills. This means that the outcome of human moral efforts to save or improve the world cannot be assured. The reason for hope is the open-ended creative process of life itself, which is supported and sustained by Goddess/God.

Process philosophy shares with feminist theology and thealogy a common interest in restoring the body and the world body, disparaged and denied in classical theism. What process philosophy

---

a Christian Sunday school hymn, the invocation to Kwan Yin, and the Reclaiming chant are intended.

has frequently failed to recognize is that restoring the body and the world body has enormous consequences for women. A feminist process paradigm will make feminist insight an integral part of process thinking. A feminist process paradigm will also ensure that process philosophers understand the body, the world body, and the divine body in physical terms and not simply as metaphysical concepts.

Feminist theologians have long recognized that women have been viewed as secondary or subordinate in dualistic anti-body traditions that follow Plato in making a sharp distinction between God and the unchanging soul on the one hand, and the changing body and nature on the other. In dualistic philosophies created by men, the rational soul of man is associated with the unchanging immortal realm of (a male) God, while woman is identified with the body, nature, and death. Feminists have called this way of thinking hierarchical dualism because one set of qualities—the unchanging, the rational, the soul, the male—is valued more highly than the other—the changing, the natural, the body, the female. In such traditions God must be imaged as male because maleness is associated with the unchangeable realm of soul and spirit. God cannot be imaged as female because femaleness is associated with the changing body, nature, and death.[2]

In light of this analysis, I asked a simple question at the end of the previous chapters of this book: Is the source of the theological mistakes of classical theism a rejection of embodied life that begins with rejection of the female body? In other words, are the six theological mistakes embedded in a way of thinking that is inherently anti-female? I suggest that the answer to this question is yes. The six theological mistakes are based in denial of the changing body and the changing world, which is rooted in a way of thinking that is inherently anti-female. "But," it might be objected, "anti-body thinking need not be anti-female. It only became so because men projected the body they despised onto women. After all," it might be added, "women are just as capable of rejecting the body as men. Look at the female saints who starved themselves to death. If women had created dualistic traditions, they might have been anti-male."[3] It is true that women have been enthusiastic supporters of anti-body traditions in the west and in the east. Still, it is not sheer coincidence that dualistic traditions have a particular antipathy toward the female body. Dualistic traditions reject not only the body but the whole physical world of which the body is a part. Inevitably they take a negative view of physical birth through a female body.

Indeed, many dualistic traditions contrast (inferior) physical birth to (superior) spiritual birth or "re-birth." Socrates called himself a midwife of the soul.

---

2. This is a commonplace in feminist theological analysis; see Mary Daly, *Beyond God the Father: Toward a Philosophy of Women's Liberation* (Boston: Beacon, 1973); Rosemary Radford Ruether, *Sexism and God-Talk: Toward a Feminist Theology*; Judith Plaskow, *Standing Again at Sinai: Judaism from a Feminist Perpsective* (San Francisco: Harper & Row, 1990); Naomi Goldenberg, *Returning Words to Flesh: Feminism, Psychoanalysis, and the Resurrection of the Body* (Boston: Beacon, 1990); and my *Laughter of Aphrodite: Reflections on a Journey to the Goddess* (San Francisco: HarperSanFrancisco, 1987), among many others.

3. Rita Gross in *Buddhism after Patriarchy* makes a similar argument. Few other feminists have advanced it, perhaps because most feminists are not interested in promoting or validating the ascetic world-view.

Circumcision rites claim male blood as more holy than the blood of birth. Baptism names water consecrated by men more powerful than the waters of birth. Enlightenment has been understood as release from the realm of birth and death. Dualistic anti-body philosophies originated in cultures in which more ancient traditions made a positive association between the body of the mother and the creative powers of Mother Earth or Goddess.[4] Dualistic traditions reject not only the female body through which we enter the physical world but the physical world itself, the earth that was known as the body of Goddess. If this is true, then we must recognize that dualistic traditions are not only inherently anti-female, but also matricidal.

But is calling dualistic traditions matricidal going too far? It could be argued that denying the body that gives us birth is not matricide or mother-murder but technically speaking mother-denial. However, the tradition of Platonic dualism arose in the ambience of the repeated performance of the *Orestia* of Aeschylus. In this trilogy, Orestes avenges the death of his father by killing his mother. At his trial the Goddess Athena justifies her vote in favor of the son who murdered his mother with the words, "No mother ever gave me birth."[5] There are good reasons for considering that rejection of the body of the mother is at heart matricide.

The mother who is murdered is not only the human mother, but also the physical world, the mother of all.

In challenging dualistic thinking, process philosophy pulled the rug out from under anti-female and matricidal habits of thought. Yet if process philosophy is implicitly feminist, then why did Whitehead and Hartshorne not state explicitly that process philosophy is a feminist philosophy? I think it is fair to say that this thought never occurred to either of them. Commenting on the history of science, Whitehead said, "There are some fundamental assumptions which adherents of all the variant systems within the epoch unconsciously presuppose. Such assumptions appear so obvious that people do not know what they are assuming because no other way of putting things has ever occurred to them."[6] I suggest that the idea that whole traditions of philosophical thinking had for centuries been systematically anti-female is an idea that simply did not occur to either Whitehead or Hartshorne.

What are we to make of this rather serious "oversight"[7] of these two great thinkers? The conclusion I would draw is that they were men of their own times, not ours. Whitehead and Hartshorne knew that some philosophers were male chauvinists,[8] but they assumed that

---

4. In classical Athens, the Eleusinian Mysteries dedicated to the Goddesses Demeter and Persephone were widely practiced. The Greeks recognized that these mysteries had an ancient origin; scholars have traced them back to early agricultural societies.

5. See Paul Roche, trans., *The Orestes Plays of Aeschylus* (New York: New American Library, 1962), *The Eumenides*, 190.

6. Alfred North Whitehead, *Science and the Modem World* (New York: The Free Press, 1967 (1925), 48.

7. An allusion to Charles Hartshorne's *Insights and Oversights of Great Thinkers: An Evaluation of Western Philosophy* (Albany: State University of New York Press, 1983).

8. See Hartshorne, *The Darkness and the Light: A Philosopher Reflects upon His Fortunate Career and Those Who Made It Possible* (Albany: State University of New York, 1990) 62–64.

philosophical systems were gender neutral because no other way of putting things ever occurred to them. That another way of putting things has occurred to us is testimony to the revolutionary power of the feminist movement of the last three decades of the twentieth century. Feminism has taught us to scrutinize all theories for explicit and implicit gender bias. A feminist process paradigm can help us to see that the theological mistakes of classical theism are disproportionately harmful to women because they are based in rejection of the female body through which we are born into the physical world

If the theological mistakes of classical theism—conceiving of divine power as unchanging and unsympathetic, omnipotent and omniscient, and the related views of infallible revelation and immortality—are not only inherently anti-female but also rooted in matricide, then spiritual feminists ought to avoid them at all costs. A feminist process paradigm can help us to recognize the importance of the alternatives to classical theism offered by process philosophy for our feminist efforts. In fact, many feminist theologians and thealogians, myself included, have been moving in the direction of affirming the process values of change, embodiment, relationship, sympathy (understanding, love, or compassion), creative freedom, enjoyment, and power with rather than power over. A feminist process paradigm can help us to recognize that these values are interconnected and thus require each other. It can also provide a fresh perspective from which to think about issues that have become controversial within feminist theologies and thealogies.

A feminist process paradigm can shed light on conflicts that have arisen in relation to attempts to reclaim the female body, the earth body, femaleness, and the feminine in feminist spirituality. Early on, spiritual feminists understood that affirming the changing body and especially the changing female body was a priority. At the first gathering of women theologians at Grailville in 1972, a widely reprinted retelling of the story of Adam and Eve entitled "The Coming of Lilith" challenged the symbolic association of the female body with sin and evil.[9] At about the same time, a group of women created a summer solstice ritual in which they formed a symbolic birth canal in order to birth each other into a circle of women. They raised power by placing their hands on each other's bellies. They marked each other's faces with menstrual blood saying: "This is the blood that promises renewal. This is the blood that promises sustenance. This is the blood that promises life."[10] In the ensuing years, Audre Lorde's groundbreaking essay "Uses of the Erotic: The Erotic as Power" was adopted as a kind of manifesto by Jewish, Christian, and Goddess feminists because it gave us permission to trust the feelings—including sexual feelings—of joy and pleasure that we experience in our bodies.[11] Women also began to create a wide variety of rituals to celebrate menarche, birth, and menopause.

9. See Judith Plaskow, "The Coming of Lilith," in *Womanspirit Rising: A Feminist Reader on Religion* (San Francisco: Harper & Row, 1979 [1989]) 198–209.

10. See Carol Christ, *Laughter of Aphrodite: Reflections on a Journey to the Goddess* (San Francisco: HarperSanFrancisco, 1987) 126.

11. See Judith Plaskow and Carol Christ, eds., *Weaving the Visions: New Patterns in Feminist Spirituality* (San Francisco: Harper & Row, 1989) 208–13. Carter Heyward, Rita Nakashima Brock, Judith Plaskow, and I are among those who have used Lorde's ideas in feminist work in religion.

The popularity of images of the naked female body of the Goddess in feminist art and ritual is testimony to women's hunger for symbols that express the creative and sacred powers of the female body.[12] This theme was picked up in the controversial Christian feminist prayer to Sophia that re-imagines *"women in your image: With warm nectar between our thighs."*[13] Though yoga is often said to be a method that leads to the transcendence of the body, feminist teachers and practitioners are more likely to understand yoga as a way of finding the spirit in the body and in the body as female.[14] Similarly feminists tend to view meditation not as a way to escape the world of "birth-and-death," but to learn to live more comfortably within it.[15] Like yoga, meditation can help us to become aware of the connections between body, mind, and spirit.

Much feminist work in religion has focused on relationship and interconnection, alleging that women's bodily experiences attune women to relationships, that women's way of knowing is through relationships, or that women have a special ability to sense the human connection to the earth and all of life. Many women have been drawn to Jungian thinking because it values aspects of life that have been traditionally called female or feminine, including the body, the unconscious, intuition, and relationship.[16] Some Christian feminists have begun to develop a more relational view of the world, or what they call a theology of "mutuality."[17] Many of them, along with Jewish and other feminist thinkers, have been inspired by Martin Buber's depiction of I-thou relationships with other people, with nature, and with God. Goddess feminists, ecofeminists, Asian feminists, and western women inspired by non-western religions speak of the web of relationships in which we are enmeshed as "the web of life" and they urge greater concern for nonhuman life.[18]

At the same time the meaning of the body, the female body, relationship, and interconnection have become highly contested questions within feminist thinking in religion. While many women have felt affirmed by images, rituals, and theories that celebrate the female body, relationship, and interconnection, others have found them limiting. Critics ask whether some feminists end up affirming conventional gender dichotomies, even if we do not intend to do so. Do rituals that celebrate menstruation, birth, and menopause

---

12. See Elinor Gadon, *The Once and Future Goddess* (San Francisco: HarperSanFrancisco, 1989); also see Meinrad Craighead, *The Mother's Songs: Images of God the Mother* (New York: Paulist, 1986), whose work has appealed to Christian, Jewish, and Goddess feminists.

13. See the Introduction.

14. Angela Farmer, *The Feminine Unfolding* (videotape) (Hohokus, New Jersey: Transit Media, 1999); also see Laura Cornell, *The Moon Salutation: Expression of the Feminine in Body, Psyche, Spirit* (Oakland, CA: Yogesh-wari Publications, 2000).

15. See Rita Gross, *Buddhism after Patriarchy*; and Miranda Shaw, *Passionate Enlightenment; Women in Tantric Buddhism* (Princeton: Princeton University Press, 1994).

16. See, for example, Christine Downing, *The Goddess* (New York: Crossroad, 1984); and Jean Shinoda Bolen, *Goddesses in Everywoman* (San Francisco: Harper & Row, 1984).

17. The use of this term is widespread; see, for example, Carter Heyward, *The Redemption of God: A Theology of Mutual Relation* (Washington DC: University Press of America, 1982).

18. The use of this term is also widespread; see, for example, eds. Irene Diamond and Gloria Feman Orenstein, *Reweaving the World: The Emergence of Eco-Feminism* (San Francisco: Sierra Club Books, 1990).

reinforce the idea that woman's primary role is motherhood and perhaps even that her place is in the home? Do images of the naked female body of the Goddess simply continue a long tradition of associating women with the body and nature, but not with the mind and freedom? What about the male body? What about women who do not have children? Women whose sexuality is directed to other women? Women who do not have partners? Women in abusive relationships?

Some academic feminists use the term "essentialism" (as in women are "essentially" embodied and relational) to characterize feminist standpoints that they feel lock women into one set of possible roles and behaviors while excluding others.[19] They point out that theories that assert a dichotomy between masculine and feminine or male and female characteristics or ways of being limit the possibilities of both women and men. Those who are uncomfortable with the emphasis on the female body, relationship, and interconnection in the thinking of other feminists have legitimate concerns. It is important to value the female mind as much as the female body. It is important to affirm that women are free and creative individuals. It is important to recognize that men as well as women are embodied. It is important to remember that relationships come in many varieties and that they can harm as well as nurture and heal. It is important that feminists not create new stereotypes that limit women's creativity and freedom.

A feminist process paradigm offers a perspective in which the concerns of both sides in what has become a sometimes acrimonious debate can be taken into account. In process philosophy, the importance of body, relationship, and connection to nature is affirmed, as in many feminist theologies and thealogies. Process philosophy also clearly understands that men as well as women are embodied, related, and interconnected in the web of life. The male body as well as the female body changes and dies. Men as well as women are internally related to others. Men as well as women are part of nature. Process philosophy offers a holistic understanding of the world in which change and embodiment and interdependence are affirmed for all individuals—women, men, animals, cells, the smallest particles of an atom, and Goddess/ God. Process philosophy also affirms that all individuals are free and creative. In such a world women and men can express creative freedom within our bodies, relationships, and connections to changing life. Process philosophy legitimates feminist re-imaginings of divine power through the lens of the female body and its connections to nature. Yet process philosophy reminds us that all bodies—male as well as female, nonhuman as well as human—are part of the divine body and thus can function as images of divinity.

There is no doubt that if compared to traditional stereotypes of masculinity and femininity, process philosophy's understanding of Goddess/God is more feminine than masculine. The divine sympathy, as Hartshorne said, has more in common with traditional understandings of a mother's love for her children than it does with traditional notions of

19. See Sheila Greeve Davaney, "The Limits of the Appeal to Women's Experience," in *Shaping New Vision: Gender and Values in American Culture*, eds. Clarissa W. Atkinson, Constance H. Buchanan, and Margaret Miles (Ann Arbor: University of Michigan Research Press, 1987) 31–49.

masculine power, including traditional notions of fatherhood. Like many feminist theologies and thealogies, process philosophy stresses what has been called the divine immanence—change, embodiment, relatedness, and interconnection.[20] Yet process philosophy also says that there also are ways in which Goddess/God is transcendent. It can thus help us to affirm the traditionally feminine attributes of embodiment and relatedness while not losing sight of human, nonhuman, and divine freedom and creativity, which have usually been thought of as masculine and transcendent.

While asserting that all individuals are embodied, related, and interconnected, process philosophy views all individuals as free and creative—from the smallest particle of an atom to Goddess/God. Thus for process philosophy there is no question of choosing mind over body or body over mind. Mind and body are one continuum. It is as true to say that all individuals are free and creative as it is to say that all individuals are embodied and related to others. In process philosophy all free and creative individuals are embodied, and all embodied individuals are related to other free and creative individuals. To imagine that freedom is somehow antithetical to relationship and embodiment (as many philosophies and many individuals, including some feminists, have done) is quite simply a mistake in thought. This does not mean that embodiment never limits the choices we have. All choices are limited choices. To wish it to be otherwise is also a mistake. Nor does it mean that individuals never experience conflicts between the responsibilities inherent in relationships and individual needs for free and creative expression. But there is no essential or necessary conflict between embodiment and relationship and interconnection on the one side and creative freedom on the other. Nor is there any need to state that women are more embodied, relational, and interconnected than men, for these qualities define all individuals. Process philosophy suggests that rather than arguing about who is right and who is wrong, feminists might join together in imagining a world in which embodiment, relationship, and creative freedom are understood to be components of all life in the universe.[21]

A feminist process paradigm sharply poses the question of the meaning of death in theologies and thealogies that affirm life in the body. Valerie Saiving's groundbreaking essay "The Human Situation: A Feminine View" launched the current wave of the feminist theology movement.[22] In a less well-known essay on feminism and process philosophy, Saiving prophesied: "The most basic assumption we have inherited from patriarchal culture, the one which feminists may find the most difficult to overcome, is that the enduring self is the true locus of value, and that the death of that self is the greatest adversary."[23] Saiving saw the dualism

---

20. See Starhawk, "Power, Authority, and Mystery: Ecofeminism and Earth-based Spirituality," in *Reweaving the World: The Emergence of Eco-Feminism*, ed. Irene Diamond and Gloria Feman Orenstein (San Francisco: Sierra Club Books, 1990) 73.

21. Keller's *From a Broken Web: Separatism, Sexism, and Self* (Boston: Beacon, 1986) discusses the relational self from a process standpoint.

22. Reprinted in *Womanspirit Rising,* 25–42.

23. Valerie C. Saiving, "Androgynous Life: A Feminist Appropriation of Process Thought," in *Feminism and Process Thought: The Harvard Divinity School/Claremont Center for Process Studies Symposium Papers,* ed. Sheila Greeve Davaney

of life and death as the source of all the other dualisms, including those between masculinity and femininity, rationality and emotionality, freedom and relationship. Though Saiving does not say so explicitly, this can be true only if the fear of death is a consequence of a rejection of life in the body, life that comes through the body of the mother. Saiving further suggests, following Whitehead, that the fear of death is related to the idea that the "enduring self" is the greatest value in life. If it is not, then what is? The answer is simple: the process of life itself. Valerie Saiving had already begun to suffer from disabling arthritis when she asked us if we could learn to include death within the process of life. Two decades later and apparently unaware of the way in which Saiving had anticipated her insight, Grace M. Jantzen suggested that western (male) philosophers and theologians have been obsessed with death and immortality because they ignored or despised "natality," birth and life.[24]

Perhaps because feminists have intuitively understood that concern with death and immortality begins with a rejection of birth, consideration of life after death has not been a focus in feminist work in religion. I have long suggested that Goddess religion teaches reverence for life that enables us to affirm finitude and death.[25] Rosemary Radford Ruether, writing from the perspective of an ecofeminist and cosmic understanding of Christianity states that this life rather than life after death should concern us.[26] Far more than Christianity, modern Judaism, including Jewish feminism, has focused on life in the body and this world rather than on the hope for life after death. However, as I noted earlier, some Goddess feminists and followers of non-western religions have found eastern theories of reincarnation attractive. Nor have all Christian and Jewish feminists concluded that the hope for life after death is inconsistent with affirming the body. Process philosophy asks us to consider whether belief in immortality or reincarnation is a legacy of dualistic thinking, east and west. Feminism sharpens the questions: Is the feminist intuition that life in the body and the world is to be affirmed and enjoyed compatible with belief in life after death? Do theories of re-birth and re-incarnation suggest that birth through a female body into a world that includes death simply isn't good enough? As the first and second generations of feminist theologians reach an age at which death is more present in our lives, perhaps we will reflect together on these questions.

Another area of controversy within feminist theologies and thealogies concerns the meaning of new symbols of Goddess/God as She. While spiritual feminists share a critique of the distant and judgmental God-out-there of traditional piety, we are not always clear about how to define the relation of Goddess/God to the world. Is God-She or Goddess immanent or transcendent? Should we call ourselves pantheists? Mystics? Polytheists? Monotheists? What do we mean by

---

(Lewiston, NY: Mellen, 1981), 28. The essay was presented as the Harvard University Dudelian Lecture in 1978.

24. Grace M. Jantzen, *Becoming Divine: Towards a Feminist Philosophy of Religion* (Bloomington: Indiana University Press, 1999).

25. See my *Laughter of Aphrodite*, 213–227.

26. See Rosemary Radford Ruether, *Gaia & God: An Ecofeminist Theology of Earth Healing* (San Francisco: HarperSanFrancsico, 1992) 251–53.

these terms? A feminist process paradigm can help us think about these questions as well. I believe that process philosophy's panentheism affirms the best insights of monotheism, mystical pantheism, and polytheism while avoiding the mistakes associated with traditional dualistic theism. Panentheism means that the world is "in" Goddess/God.[27] In process thought, the world is "in" Goddess/God because Goddess/God sympathetically feels the feelings of every creature. Insofar as the world is also understood to be the body of Goddess/God,[28] panentheism can also be said to mean that Goddess/God is "in" the world, is felt by and included in every creature. Panentheism differs from classical theism in not radically separating God from the world. Yet panentheism shares with monotheism "the intuition of unity," the sense that the divine power is a unifying principle in the world.[29] The divine power keeps the creative process of the universe from deteriorating into chaos. Panentheism shares with biblical and other religions the understanding that the divine power can be related to as Thou, that divine power is personal and cares about individuals and the world. Yet more clearly than biblical religion, panentheism asserts that divine power is always the power of persuasion, not coercion, power with, not power over. Because it understands the world to be the body of Goddess/God, panentheism agrees with mystical pantheism that the world is sacred. Though not asserting a multiplicity of divine powers, panentheism, like polytheism, is open to a wide range of images and symbols for divine power, as many as the individuals that make up the divine body.

"Panentheism" is not a word that is likely to slip easily into everyday language. Still, I suggest that feminists who have rejected the God-out-there of dualistic theism may find that panentheism expresses our new understanding of the divine in the world more clearly than theism, monotheism, pantheism, or polytheism. Theism is associated with dualism, radical separation, and power over. Monotheism carries the baggage of religious intolerance. Pantheism has difficulty asserting that individuals other than Goddess/God really exist. Polytheism denies that there is a unity underlying multiplicity. Panentheism affirms divine presence in a co-created world.

Panentheism also offers a new way of thinking about the question of how individuals are related to the whole, the question called "the problem of the one and the many." From traditional perspectives there are two options: either individuals are real, or all is one. Both of these options are problematic. To say that individuals are real takes account of our common sense understanding of individuality, difference, and freedom. Yet from most traditional perspectives, it leaves individuals separate from each other and from the divine ground and power. Against this view, monists have asserted that contrary to ordinary perception, all is one. Yet monism cannot explain individuality, difference, and creative freedom. Because it offers an understanding of the relationship of all individuals to each other and to the divine ground that does not obscure

---

27. As discussed in chapter two.

28. The idea that the world is the body of God is affirmed by Hartshorne but not Whitehead, as I have said.

29. Marcia Falk, "Notes on Composing New Blessings," in *Weaving the Visions*, 128.

individuality, difference, and creative freedom, process philosophy offers new way of thinking about an age-old question.

Panentheism is compatible with the intuitions of Goddess feminists and ecofeminists that the earth and its processes of birth, death, and regeneration are sacred. Similar views are found in the symbols of indigenous religions, for example in the images of Changing Woman of the Navajos and Oshun the Goddess of flowing waters of African and African American religions. Acceptance or affirmation of change in non-western religions such as Taoism or Buddhism is one reason that many feminists have turned to them. Christian ecofeminists imagine the world as the body of God.[30] Some Jewish feminists understand Shekhina as "She Who Dwells Within" (the changing world).[31] Yet feminists who affirm Goddess/God's relation to the changing world are often accused of romantically clinging to pre-modern ways of viewing the world that cannot be reconciled with science.

Process philosophy can help us to affirm ancient visions of the changing earth as sacred while expanding traditional understandings to include evolution. Ancient and traditional peoples imagined the starry heavens as a backdrop to life on earth. Yet we know that the earth is but one of the planets that circle our sun, which is one of millions of stars in the universe. It is unlikely that life occurs only on planet earth. While it was appropriate for ancient peoples to speak of earth as Goddess, it may be more appropriate for us to understand the world or the universe as the body of Goddess/God. A feminist process paradigm supports the feminist intuition that the earth body is sacred, while helping us to clarify our thinking and expand our vision. It also makes it clear that the desire to save the earth and its creatures is not misplaced romanticism.[32]

. . .

RE-IMAGINING SYMBOLS

In the introduction, I asked whether it is appropriate to use the titles Lady and Queen to refer to divine power as female. From a process perspective, these images, like the more common Lord and King of the Bible and traditional liturgies, reflect the model of power over. A feminist process paradigm can help us to understand why it is not enough simply to change the gender of images of domination. Because traditional and modern prayers that refer to Goddess or God-She as Lady or Queen do not express the process understanding of divine power as power with, further transformation of traditional imagery is necessary.

Marcia Falk's metaphor "Source of Life," suggesting a spring or a fountain, the waters that nourish life, is an attractive image of power with. The Source of Life may also call to mind the evolutionary process in which life began and for millions of years developed in the sea. However, Marcia Falk became dissatisfied with the image of the Source of Life, because for her it implied a separation between divine power and the world. In one of her later prayers, Falk writes, "The breath of my life will bless,"[33] without naming the

---

30. See Sallie McFague, *The Body of God: An Ecological Theology* (Minneapolis: Fortress, 1993).

31. See Lynn Gottlieb, *She Who Dwells Within: A Feminist Vision of a Renewed Judaism* (San Francisco: HarperSanFrancisco, 1995).

32. Sallie McFague uses process philosophy to make this point in *The Body of God*.

33. See the Introduction.

object of the blessing. In this prayer the world is alive with divinity. In Hebrew the phrase "breath of life" alludes to the divine spirit. Praying without separating ourselves and the world from the divine spirit is a powerful way of expressing the process understanding that the world is the body of divinity. Yet, from a process point of view, the combination of prayers to a divine power as Source of Life with others that invoke the breath of life is more complete than either would be alone.[34] In process philosophy the divine power is present in and not radically divorced from the world, but it is separate from other individuals in the sense that all individuals have a degree of creative freedom that is our own. For this reason, images naming divine power as separate from yet related to other individuals are appropriate. This separation is not absolute or radical, and it does not create the relation of dominant and dominated, because Goddess/God is internally related to every individual in the world. In feeling the feelings of every individual in a world that is the body of Goddess/God, the divine power is closer to us than we are to the cells of our own bodies. Thus, images in which there is no separation between the divine power and the world are also fitting. Insofar as none of the images that Falk chooses expresses the divine sympathy, the notion that Goddess/God cares about our lives and the fate of the world, from a process point of view Falk's images

need to be supplemented by more personal yet non-dominating imagery.

In the controversial prayer associated with the first Christian feminist Re-Imagining Conference, the divine power was invoked as "Sophia," a female name for the divine power that means "wisdom." Though "Sophia" might not have been a familiar name to all Christians, feminists had long been searching the Wisdom literature of the Bible and tradition for female images of God.[35] However, as this imagery also comes through patriarchal traditions, it too needs to be criticized and transformed.[36] The imagery that surfaced at the Re-Imagining Conference was a product of contemporary feminist creativity reshaping the resources of the past. From a process point of view, this activity is perfectly appropriate. For process philosophy, personal imagery is fitting because it expresses the divine sympathy for the world. Female imagery is also appropriate, because process philosophy rejects the dualistic understanding of transcendence as male and immanence as female. For process philosophy, the divine power can be imagined as having a body, for the world is the body of Goddess/God. The image of Sophia's body wet with milk and honey, reminding us of pleasures and

---

34. In other words, I agree with Falk's decision to keep both kinds of prayers in her prayer book, but not with her later argument that imagining the divine as an individual creates separation and therefore is inappropriate, nor with her assumption that personal language for divinity is not fitting.

35. This literature is widespread; see, for example, Susan Cady, Marian Ronan, and Hal Taussig, *Sophia: The Future of Feminist Spirituality* (San Francisco: Harper & Row, 1986); Maria Pilar Aquino and Elisabeth Schüssler Fiorenza, eds., *In the Power of Wisdom: Feminist Spiritualities of Struggle*, Concilium 2000/5(London: SCM, 2000) (also available in French, Spanish, Italian, German, and Dutch).

36. For a critique of the Sophia traditions, see Pamela J. Milne, "Voicing Embodied Evil: Gynophobic Images of Women in Post-Exilic Biblical and Intertestamental Text," *Feminist Theology* 30 (May 2002) 61–69.

sensations, exquisitely expresses the process understanding that the divine power wants us to enjoy life in our bodies.

The image of the Asian Buddhist Goddess Kwan Yin, already known to Asian and Asian American feminists and adopted by some Caucasian feminists, is another appropriate image for the divinity of process philosophy. Traditionally Kwan Yin is invoked in the chant "Namo Guan Shih Yin Pu-sa." This can be translated as "I call upon the bodhisattva who sees and hears the sufferings of the world."[37] Reverence for Kwan Yin comes from a strand of Buddhism that some would call theistic or perhaps panentheistic. From a process point of view, the image of Kwan Yin seeing and hearing the sufferings of the world beautifully evokes the process understanding of the divine power sympathetically feeling the feelings of the world. Kwan Yin is an important reminder that traditions other than European can be resources for images of the divine as female. Yet to the extent that the image of Kwan Yin suggests that the divine power shares our suffering but not our joy, her image needs to be supplemented by images such as that of Sophia giving birth or joyously making love. When we understand that life is meant to be enjoyed, we can also call on Kwan Yin to share our joy and to support our efforts to lessen suffering in the world.

Some Goddess feminists have found that the Hindu image of fierce Kali with her tongue sticking out, swords in her hands, and skulls on her belt, ready to battle the forces of evil, encourages western women to express anger about injustice and the restrictions of their lives. Contemporary Indian feminists have also used the image of Kali to promote feminist interests.[38] These women may have misunderstood or rejected some understandings of Kali found within traditional Hinduism.[39] However, the issue I wish to consider here is the creative use western women have made of the image of Kali in constructing feminist spiritual alternatives. If, as I have suggested, Goddess/God can express anger as part of a transformative process, then the image of angry Kali is a fully appropriate symbol of divinity. Her image may serve a useful purpose, as feminists insist that it does, of encouraging women to get in touch with repressed anger. Yet divine anger should never be imagined as expressing itself through violence, because violence is the method of power over. In contemporary India, militant Hindu women have invoked the Hindu Goddesses in support of aggressive Hindu fundamentalism and nationalism.[40] This calls attention to the need to creatively re-imagine images of the Goddess inherited from Indo-European warrior traditions. In India as well as

37. See Sandy Boucher, *Discovering Kwan Yin: Buddhist Goddess of Compassion* (Boston: Beacon, 1999) 107–8.

38. See Sharanda Sugirtharajah, "Hinduism and Feminism: Some Concerns," *Journal of Feminist Studies in Religion* 18.2 (2002) 103–4.

39. Rita Gross in a personal communication stated, "The severed head held by Kali is one's own, teaching us to accept our own limits and finitude. Until we can accept our mortality and finitude, we will never have peace or joy." Gross also said that I interpret the warrior aspect of Hindu Goddess imagery "too literally." While I agree with Gross that some aspects of Buddhist tradition do not take the warrior imagery literally, I am always "literal" when it comes to warrior images because I recognize their origin in warlike cultures and their potential to inspire violence and the notion that "God is on our side" when we go to war.

40. See Sugirtharajah, "Hinduism and Feminism," 104.

in Europe, the most ancient Goddess traditions were re-imagined when warrior tribes speaking Indo-European languages conquered traditional peoples.[41] As feminists continue the process of re-imagining Kali, her tongue—like that of her sister the ancient Greek Gorgon—would still be sticking out but the swords and trophies of battle would be removed. If, as some argue, the skulls on Kali's belt are not war trophies, but emblems of the prehistoric death Goddess, then they might be retained in a new (or older) context, not associated with the warrior's sword.

Kali also appeals to western feminists because her dark skin provides an inclusive alternative to the "whiteness" of God and of some of the Goddesses of European traditions. Insofar as traditional images of God are of an Old White Man, it is as important to reclaim Goddess/God as black or dark as it is to reclaim Goddess/God as female. Yet we should not identify dark-skinned Goddesses exclusively with qualities such as death and anger (as opposed to life and compassion), even when these qualities are understood positively. According to Marija Gimbutas, white was the color of death in Old European traditions, while black was the color of the fertile and transforming earth.[42] Re-imagining Kali in conjunction with other dark-skinned Goddesses such as the African water goddess Oshun, who represents fertility or creativity, sexuality, and love, provides a more complex image of the divine as female and dark-skinned.[43]

Feminists have also found the symbolism expressed in tarot cards, Goddess amulets, runes, and other forms of divination inspiring. Yet process philosophy asserts that there is no way of knowing the future until it actually is created by a multiplicity of wills. Then what is the meaning of divination? Perhaps it is this: whether we are asking about a love affair, a pregnancy, a job, the fate of a project, or the fate of the earth, no method of divination can tell us with certainty what will happen. On the other hand, the future will be a synthesis of things that already exist. Methods of divination can be understood as other than rational ways of getting a perspective on what already exists and as ways of imagining what we and others can create out of what already exists. There are people who are skilled in seeing possibilities in our lives that we may not see ourselves, or who are able to sense the desires of our hearts that we hide even from ourselves. Yet we must always take their advice with a grain of salt, for there is no one who can tell us what choices we will or should make, nor is there anyone who knows what choices others will make until they actually do make them.

Having discussed a number of important ways other feminists are re-imagining the divine in the world, I would now like to share some of the symbols I find meaningful in my life. I have discovered and shaped images, prayers, and rituals in many years of co-creative practice of feminist Goddess spirituality. The symbols I will discuss express the feminist process

---

41. Sanskrit is an Indo-European language. In *The Language of the Goddess* (San Francisco: Harper & Row, 1989), Marija Gimbutas documented the existence of pre-Indo-European Goddess traditions in Old Europe. Similar processes of transformation of pre-existing Goddess symbols by Indo-European warrior cultures occurred in Europe and India.

42. See *The Language of the Goddess*.

43. See Luisah Teish, *Jambalaya: The Natural Woman's Book of Personal Charms and Practical Rituals* (San Francisco: Harper & Row, 1985).

understanding of the divine in the world articulated in this book. These symbols have roots in a variety of traditions, and thus will be of interest to feminists practicing diverse spiritual paths. I know that we also need new images of the divine as male, but for me the need to discover and co-create healing images of the divine as female has been more pressing. I encourage others to continue to search for and co-create healing images of the divine as male.

An ancient and enduring expression of women's spiritual creativity is the creation of home altars.[44] Choosing items to place on a home altar and arranging them in a pleasing way is a literal expression of the process understanding that creating religious symbolism involves making a new synthesis of elements of the past. As they are not under the supervision of religious authorities, home altars are a way for women to express our own understandings of the sacred. Often items from different religious traditions are placed together in ways that blur boundaries. On the altar near me as I write, I set a terra cotta image of a seated snake Goddess from Neolithic Crete; a brass owl with blue protecting eyes and two brass owl babies; a porous gray volcanic stone with a red center shaped like a vagina from the island of Lesbos where I live; and a small plasticine statue of Saint Francis of Assisi. The Neolithic Goddess from Crete is the "mascot" of the Goddess pilgrimages to Crete for women that provide a spiritual grounding in my life. She sits proudly on ample buttocks and has thick, folded, snakelike arms and legs and a beaked face.[45] She symbolizes the creative powers of divinity as source and sustainer of the world that is the divine body. Owls are an image of the Bird Goddess, one of the most ancient symbols of the Goddess.[46] Animal imagery can be used for the Goddess when the world is understood to be the divine body. Birds have long been admired for their powers of flight. Owls hunt at night, reminding us that death is part of life and that gaining wisdom does not have to be imagined as only "en-lightenment," but can also be understood as learning to trust the darkness. The volcanic stone from my island suggests the explosive and transforming powers that lie within the earth, which is a part of the body of the Goddess. Red, the color of the blood of birth and menstruation, has long been associated with the Goddess; women's blood also has transformative power. An image of Saint Francis once stood in my grandmother's garden. Though his stigmata come from another age and an understanding of the divine in the world that I do not accept, the love of Saint Francis for the birds that sit on his arms shows that he intuitively understood himself to be a child of the earth. His image reminds me of the need to find new images of the divine in the world as male. My altar is on a wide window ledge. It is framed by terra cotta roofs, green plants and trees, the gray blue Aegean Sea, and the silhouette of the coast of Turkey. Just outside the window, blue and great tits, sparrows, chaffinches, and collared doves come to take seeds from the bird-feeders.

---

44. See Kay Turner, *Beautiful Necessity: The Art and Meaning of Women's Altars* (New York: Thames & Hudson, 1999).

45. There is a picture of this image in Carol Christ, *Rebirth of the Goddess* (New York: Routledge, 1998) 14.

46. See Marija Gimbutas, *The Language of the Goddess*.

I have images of the Goddess and of the earth as the image of the body of the Goddess in other places in my home. It is important for me to live in proximity to my neighbors (though I don't get along with all of them) and in contact with the beauty of the natural world (I am lucky enough to be able to do so). The small altar on my windowsill extends out to my balcony, across to my neighbor's homes and gardens, and beyond to the Aegean Sea and the coast of Turkey shaped by the same volcanic explosions as the island of Lesbos. In my imagination, my altar includes the whole universe that is the body of Goddess/God.

Following a suggestion made by Justine and Michael Toms of New Dimensions Radio, [47] I try to remember to pray on the first of every month, knowing that my prayer will connect with those of others who are praying on the same day. In my prayers, addressed to Goddess or Goddess/God, I begin with myself, giving thanks for life and love and asking for what 1 need. Though asking the divine power for help might be labeled "selfish" in some traditions, I have learned from Greek women who light candles in local churches that thanking the divine power and asking for help is one of the most fundamental of all religious gestures. It expresses a deep knowing that divine power is with us in the joys and sorrows, the desires and struggles of our daily lives.

A tyrant God might not have time to participate in my life or yours, but the sympathy of Goddess/God as understood in process philosophy is wide enough to include us all. After praying for myself, I enlarge the circle of my attention to include those closest to me, my cat and the dogs that sometimes share my home, neighbors, the plant and animal life in nearby gardens, and my closest friends and family. Then I name the island of Lesbos, its people, animals, plants, locks, and rivers, asking that the environment be preserved for all who live here. Gradually I expand the circle, naming others, asking that the hungry be fed, that those who are suffering find joy, that wars cease, and that human beings learn to live in harmony with all beings in the web of life on planet earth. When I am near a shrine church I often enter it and light candles, renewing my prayers for myself, for my friends, and for the world. Following Greek custom, I approach the icon of the Panagia (Mary), whose name means "She Who Is All Holy," look into her deep brown eyes, and kiss her image. Living in Greece I have learned that the Goddess never died: I can experience her presence in the images of the Panagia. Praying in Greek churches, I express my gratitude to Greek friends whose trust that divine help is "always there" has entered into my understanding of the divine sympathy.

---

47. New Dimensions is an independent producer of broadcast dialogues from a variety of traditions and cultures. Its goal is to deepen connections to self, family, community, the natural world, and the planet. See www.newdimensions.org.

Commentary

CONSTANCE WISE

In 1979 in *Womanspirit Rising: A Feminist Reader in Religion*, Carol P. Christ and her sister editor Judith Plaskow gathered twenty-four early works in feminist theology. In her own contribution to this volume, Christ provided the initial answer to "Why Women Need the Goddess." We need the Goddess so we can find and engage the "beauty, strength, and power of women." Christ and Plaskow marked the tenth anniversary of this first anthology by publishing a sequel—*Weaving the Visions*. In her essay, "Rethinking Theology and Nature," Christ introduces themes that will mark much of her later scholarship. One can hardly overemphasize the amazing impact of these two anthologies on later scholarship and on individual women's spiritual journeys. They led many of us out of the desert of patriarchy's demand for *hard* evidence into the *juicy* ovarian knowledge that arises from women's lived experience.

Carol P. Christ firmly believes that embodied experience provides the primary source of knowing about oneself, about the world, and about the divine. In *Diving Deep and Surfacing* (1980), she tests this belief by tracing women's experiences as portrayed in fiction, but her own life experiences soon become the source of the knowledge she wants to share. In *Laughter of Aphrodite* (1987), she traces her theological journey out of Christianity and into Goddess Spirituality. From this point on, she employs spiritual autobiography to some extent in all her works, always finding new ways of knowing and truth telling that arise from her own life. In *Rebirth of the Goddess: Finding Meaning in Feminist Spirituality* (1998), she takes this exploration to the level of explicit theology.

Even as she continued to explore feminist theology in these scholarly works, Christ emancipated her firm belief in the power of women's experience from the academy and took it to Greece, where in 1981 she began to lead women on tours of ancient Goddess sites. In 1993 she became the founding director of the Ariadne Institute for the Study of Myth and Ritual, which offers women spiritual pilgrimages to sacred locations in Greece.[1] Her work of leading women to explore embodied spiritual knowledge must be counted as significant a part of Christ's contribution to feminist theology as her scholarly writing.

In the excerpt included here, Christ continues many threads from her earlier scholarship—love of Nature, feminine images for the divine, and the power of women's experience. However, she weaves them through a new fabric—the philosophy of process thought. She turns

---

1. The website is www.goddessariadne.org/ariadne.htm.

to process thought because she believes it provides a good philosophical framework for Goddess Spirituality. She draws specifically on process thought as developed by Charles Hartshorne and shows that his views correspond to her own feminist assumptions. Like Christ, Hartshorne endorses women's equality, recognizes the significance of embodiment, considers the world to be fully relational, and sees humanity as embedded in nature. This fully relational natural world of which humans are a part comprises an ongoing process of change. Christ's goal is to weave these ideas into a "feminist process paradigm" to promote a more powerful understanding of women's selves, our world, and the divine.

Christ employs the term *Goddess/God* to designate a theistic understanding of the divine. That is, for her Goddess/God is a personal entity to whom she can relate through prayer and ritual. However, in laying out her understanding of this divine person, Christ explicitly avoids six theological mistakes Hartshorne has identified in classical thinking: that God is perfect and never changes, that in this perfect goodness God is unsympathetic to suffering, that God is all-powerful, that God is all-knowing, that the goal of human life is immortality after death, and that humans have access to infallible revelation through scripture.[2] Christ devotes several chapters to alternatives to these mistakes, each time adding a feminist critique to Hartshorne's reasoning.

In the chapter "Change Is," for example, she refutes the idea that God is a perfect being who never changes. "No," say both Christ and Hartshorne. Goddess/God participates in the ongoing process of change that constitutes reality. Moreover, rather than the sole source of creation *ex nihilo* that classical theology assumes God accomplishes, Goddess/God co-creates the world in cooperation with humans and all beings and participates fully in that world. This co-creative work results in a fully relational web of interconnected experiences. Each experience, from the interior life of the simplest atom to the work of Goddess/God, contributes to the ongoing process. The ever-present potential for change within this process allows all entities in the world, including humans and Goddess/God, to have freedom. Thus process thought overcomes the determinism that has often crept into Western theology. Moreover, this ever-changing reality consists of a unity of physical and mental events. By *physical events,* process thought means past events, the actual things that have happened to date; by *mental events,* it means the mental processing of past events by current entities. Thus process thought overcomes the God-world and mind-body splits that have long marked Western philosophy.

In accepting Hartshorne's reasoning here, Christ adds that if humans and Goddess/God are both mind-body unities, then bodies are important. If humans and Goddess/God can both introduce change, then both have creative freedom. Christ then raises an important point of feminist critique: The tendency to deny that humans have creative freedom, and the tendency to reject the body, might be linked to the secondary status Western

---

2. See Charles Hartshorne, *Omnipotence and Other Theological Mistakes* (Albany: SUNY Press, 1984).

philosophy has long accorded to both bodies and women.[3]

In her chapter "Touch Is," Christ explains the concept of divine sympathy. Rather than the perfect entity of unsympathetic goodness that classical theology assumes God to be, Goddess/God feels the experiences of the world and takes both pain and joy into divine reality. Even as humans know the world through our embodied experience, Goddess/God knows the world through divine embodiment. The world, however, is not perfect. Rather, the web of experiences is flawed, often because of human error. This excerpt offers Christ's vision of how a feminist process paradigm can help women participate in healing the web.

STUDY QUESTIONS

1. What does Christ mean by a "feminist process paradigm"? How would this new way of thinking promote healing of the web?

2. In *She Who Changes* (page 203), Christ lists the following characteristics of significant portions of feminist theology:

   - A focus on relationship and interconnection
   - The assertion that women's embodied experiences keep women attuned to relationships
   - The assertion that "women's way of knowing" is connected to relationships
   - The assertion that women possess a "special ability to sense human connection to the earth [or] all of life."

   She then raises the possibility that by strongly associating women with bodies, nature, and each other rather than with the world of ideas often associated with men, these characteristics of feminist theology take women back into the same essentialism imposed by patriarchy. How does Christ address this issue, and what do you think?

3. According to process thought, all entities, including humans, have some degree of freedom because we can introduce change into the patterns we inherit from the past. Part of the creative reshaping that Christ advocates is correcting the mistakes of classical theology. Is this move important to you? Why or why not?

4. Christ sees a feminist reshaping of the religious symbols we inherit as another way to exercise creative freedom. What new symbols does she suggest? What other new symbols do you suggest? Why is changing our symbols a powerful way to shape our reality?

5. Christ offers Marcia Falk's new wording for the Jewish Morning Blessing prayer, her own rewording of it, and her own new wording for the Doxology often sung in Christian worship. Could you use these new wordings in your own private or public ritual practice? Suggest new words for other these or other old standards. How do the words we use in ritual impact our understanding of ourselves, our world, and the divine?

---

3. Carol Christ, *She Who Changes: Re-imagining the Divine in the World* (New York: Palgrave Macmillan, 2003) 68.

16 African Traditional Religions and Womanism

MONICA A. COLEMAN

Monica A. Coleman is Associate Professor of Constructive Theology and African American Religions and Co-Director of The Center for Process Studies at Claremont School of Theology. She is also Associate Professor of Religion at Claremont Graduate University. She received degrees from Harvard University, Vanderbilt Divinity School and Claremont Graduate University. Her research interests include process theology, new movements in black and womanist theologies, African traditional religions (Yoruba-based traditions in the Americas), mental health and theology and religious pluralism. This excerpt is from chapter four of Making a Way Out of No Way: A Womanist Theology *(2008), where Coleman outlines a postmodern womanist soteriology based in Whiteheadian metaphysics.*

Excerpt from *Making a Way Out of No Way: A Womanist Theology*

SPIRIT POSSESSION

LEARNING FROM THE PAST also involves the active role that the ancestors play in our contemporary processes of becoming. A postmodern womanist theology seeks to affirm African traditional religions and their concepts about the ancestors. This affirmation extends the concept of immortality to include the activity of ancestors. I focus on the most complex activity of the ancestors in this world—spirit possession. In the act of spirit possession, ancestors convey their knowledge to the present generation and influence its future activity. Whitehead's metaphysics contains the framework for a philosophical understanding of spirit possession. I combine Whitehead's concept of objective immortality and Marjorie Suchocki's concept of subjective immortality to discuss the ways in which an ancestor can be fully present in God with knowledge and agency and then influence the present.

AFRICAN TRADITIONAL RELIGIONS AND CONSTRUCTIVE WOMANIST THEOLOGY

As African traditional religions came to the Americas in the memories of enslaved Africans, enslaved Africans helped to birth African American religions. Although sociologists and anthropologists continue to debate the degree to which African cultures influenced the birth of African American culture,[1] most scholars

1. Anthropologist Melville J. Herskovits, *The Myth of the Negro Past* (Boston: Beacon, 1958); and

agree that some type of transformation occurred as African traditional religions encountered other traditions. In his landmark book *Slave Religion,* Albert Raboteau describes African traditional religions in the Americas as living religions:

> It is important to realize, however, that in the Americas the religions of Africa have not been merely preserved as static "Africanisms" or as archaic "retentions." The fact is that they have continued to develop as living traditions putting down new roots in new soil, bearing new fruit as unique hybrids of American origin. African styles of worship, forms of ritual, systems of belief, and fundamental perspectives have remained vital on this side of the Atlantic, not because they were preserved in a "pure" orthodoxy but because they were transformed.[2]

In the Caribbean, where the French, Spanish, and Portuguese dominated the slave trade, African traditional religions syncretized with Catholicism. In the southeastern United States, enslaved Africans contended with the Protestant roots of British and American Christianity.

African traditional religions maintain an openness that allows them to adapt to the religious influence of other cultures. Although neighboring ethnic groups in Africa often have distinctly different traditional religions, it is not uncommon to see some of the same deities in two different religions—especially if there was an unusually friendly or hostile (enslavement) relationship between the two groups. Similarly, some Africans were exposed to Islam and Western Christianity prior to the Atlantic slave trade. Yet Raboteau also notes that Africans often mixed Islam and Christianity with traditional African beliefs, carrying verses of the Qur'an inside the amulets and charms of their traditional religions.[3] Nevertheless, Raboteau continues, most of the enslaved Africans held the traditional beliefs of their ethnic groups.

The missionary patterns of the Caribbean enslavers amplified the retention of African religions in the Caribbean. In British Jamaica, the Christianization of the slaves was a low priority: "The Church in the British slave colonies denied the Africans religious instruction for well over 200 years."[4] Among the French and Spanish colonies, African religions found similarities with the Catholic saints and thrived under the syncretic blending of the two religious systems: "The syncretism between Orisha [Worship] and Catholicism developed in part because of the multiplicity of saints who could be identified with Orisha deities."[5] Catholicism

---

sociologist E. Franklin Frazier, *The Negro Family in the United States* (Chicago: The University of Chicago Press, 1939) for the most famous discussants of this tension.

2. Albert J. Raboteau, *Slave Religion: The "Invisible Institution" in the Antebellum South* (New York: Oxford University Press, 1978) 4.

3. I use the term "syncretized," "creolized" and "blended" interchangeably to indicate the way that two or more religions and cultures encountered one another and created a new religion that bears the markers of its forebears. Indeed a new religion has come into being, but there are still strong commonalities with the "parent" religion. Within anthropology, these terms are hotly debated and connote the preferences of different emphases. Within the process of becoming described in the postmodern theological framework, these "new" religions are examples of the process of becoming on a larger cultural and religious scale.

4. Raboteau, *Slave Religion*, 5–7.

5. Leonard Barrett, "African Religion in the Americas: The Islands in Between" in *African*

was particularly, though unknowingly, predisposed to adaptation by African traditional religions. Catholicism's emphasis on ritual, belief in the saints, and the use of icons complemented the ways in which African traditional religions engaged their lesser deities.

Through both the triangular slave trade and contemporary reversionist attempts at recapturing traditional religions, the religion of the Yoruba people (of current-day Nigeria) has constituted a base for African-derived religious practices throughout the Caribbean, South America, and the United States. Although all these different manifestations of Yoruba-based religions share a similar cosmology and key religious concepts, they differ in ritual detail and linguistic referrals due to the different historical and religious contexts of the encounter between Yoruba religion and various New World situations. As Yoruba traditional religion travels through space, time, and circumstance, it syncretizes, or blends, with other religious and cultural traditions—most particularly Western Christianity and other African traditional religions.

Traditional Yoruba religion can be described as the worship of a supreme deity, *Olódùmarè/ Olórun*,[6] under various forces or deities, the *òrìṣà*. There is no adequate description for the *òrìṣà* outside of the Yoruba universe. They have been variously described as ministers of *Olódùmarè*, forces of nature, angelic forces, lower gods, and sub-deities. According to Yoruba lore, the *òrìṣà* are ancestors who did not return to earth because their *iwa* (human character or human consciousness) was so closely aligned with the character of *Olódùmarè*. While *Olódùmarè* is neither male nor female, nor embodied, the *òrìṣà* have genders, stories, and geographical and natural associations. The *òrìṣà* have their own characteristics, herbs, personalities, and devotees. Veneration of the *òrìṣà* is such an important part of Yoruba religion that the entire religion is often referred to as "*òrìṣà* worship." The telos of Yoruba religion is *iwà pele*. Yoruba religion identifies 401 *òrìṣà*, with five to ten *òrìṣà* having more importance and appearing more than the others. The wisdom and content of Yoruba is traditionally transmitted orally in the wisdom contained in myths, songs, and the *odu*, verses of wisdom and divination.

. . .

In the United States, African religious and cultural elements fared quite differently. There, the slave trade ended nearly a hundred years before it did in parts of the Caribbean. Thus, most slaves were American-born. In addition, there was a much lower ratio of slaves to masters in America, thereby increasing the contact between slave and enslaver. Tribal unity was not encouraged for fear of rebellion. Last, Protestantism's emphasis on the Bible and conversion experiences did not readily allow for the kind of religious and cultural blending found in the Caribbean. Although scholars have still found

---

Religions: A Symposium, ed. Newell S. Booth Jr. (New York: NOK Publishers, 1977) 193.

6. Many *òrìṣà* in Yoruba religion have multiple names although they signify the same force. This is partly attributable to the distribution of the religion throughout Yorubaland, and the Yoruba-based religions in the New World. This paper may refer to *Olódùmarè* / Olorun, Obatala/ Orìṣa-nla, Orunmila/ Ifà, Èṣù / Elegba/ Elegbara. This paper will also use the "ṣ" to indicate the sound of "sh." There is no consistency in scholarship (usually because of the capability of word processors and attempts to translate into English) so "*àṣẹ*" is also "ashe" and "*òrìṣà*" is also "orisha." Note *òrìṣà* is the same in the plural or singular usage.

"substantial instances of Africanisms in diet, dress, language, music, styles of labor, thought patterns and religious belief and practice" among African Americans, the appearance of African traditional religious elements was much more subtle.[7]

African religious elements appeared in the African American Christian and cultural practices of singing, dancing, spirit possession, and conjure.[8] Scholars have noted some similarities between traditional African religious practices and the Christian practices of baptism by immersion and ecstatic worship traditions such as the ring shout. It is, however, impossible to discern to what degree these practices were influenced by the African traditional religious heritage of the slaves or the evangelical Protestantism of the enslavers. Both traditions were mutually influential in the development of American Christianity. The uniquely African American development of spirituals and conjure beliefs are more easily identified with African traditional religious elements.[9] Still, these practices were syncretized with Protestantism, and were found most prominently among African American communities with a smaller degree of contact with European culture.[10]

When speaking of the presence of traditional Yoruba religion in the United States, one must also include contemporary reversionist attempts to reclaim cultural identity through an intentional revival of and return to ancient traditions. Practitioners will often refer to this system of belief and practices as "Ifa" or "Yoruba." In "African-Derived Religion in the African-American Community in the United States," Mary Cuthrell-Curry states that this manifestation of traditional Yoruba religion is much less obvious than in the Caribbean: "The dress of initiates and botanicas are the only two visible manifestations of the Yoruba Religion that a casual observer sees. The Religion (in most instances) does not have churches or buildings devoted to its practice."[11]

Although this Yoruba-derived traditional religion has been active in the United States since the 1960s, the Nation of Islam and the Christian fervor of the civil rights movement overshadowed it. Among native-born African Americans (and a smaller number of whites), this Yoruba religion is spread by conversion. African American practitioners of Yoruba religion are influenced in part by the Haitian and Cuban diaspora in the United States. For these African American practitioners, "conversion to the Yoruba Religion meant a rejection of Christianity and a searching for a religious perspective that would foster African-American identity."[12] Cuthrell-Curry estimates that there are probably Yoruba religious communities in every major city in the United States, while the most visible communities

---

7. Larry G. Murphy, ed., *Down by the Riverside: Readings in African American Religion* (New York: New York University Press, 2000).

8. Raboteau, *Slave Religion*, 55–92.

9. See Yvonne P. Chireau, *Black Magic: Religion and the African American Conjuring Tradition* (Berkeley: University of California Press, 2003).

10. See Margaret Washington Creel, *A Peculiar People: Slave Religion and Community Culture among the Gullahs* (New York: New York University Press, 1988).

11. Mary Cuthrell-Curry, "African-Derived Religion in the African-American Community in the United States," in *African Spirituality: Forms, Meanings and Expressions*, World Spirituality: An Encyclopedic History of the Religious Quest, ed. Jacob K. Olupona, no. 3 (New York: Crossroad, 2000) 450–51.

12. Ibid., 451.

are in Dade County, Florida, and New York City.¹³

Yoruba religion has also adapted to the American context. In some cases, adaptation is necessary because of geographical differences. For example, kola nuts do not grow in the United States, so Yoruba devotees in North America will use coconuts where kola nuts were traditionally employed. In other instances, African American practitioners have maintained preslave trade traditions that practitioners in Yorubaland have not. For example, in the United States, only men are allowed to serve as *babalawos,* priests who specialize in divination; in Nigeria, both men and women can be babalawos.¹⁴

In conclusion, blended forms of traditional Yoruba religion exist throughout the Americas. The religion has been further syncretized in the diaspora of those practitioners. All of these things contribute to both the uniqueness and diversity of black religions. African American religion must always contend with its African traditional religious heritage, whether it has been retained to greater or lesser degrees within the practice of Christianity or is practiced outside any association with Christianity.

Ancestors

The ancestors play a critical role in the practice of traditional African religions. Although traditional religions differ significantly, they share common themes: a communal conception of the divine that includes the worship of a high God through various spiritual powers or entities; the belief that the spirit lives on after death in the form, of spiritual knowledge; a belief in ancestors who should be honored, venerated, and consulted; the belief in divination—access to spiritual knowledge that will assist in solving problems in the world; the belief that offering food and animal sacrifices amplify prayers to the divine and the ancestors; belief in a neutral power—sometimes contained in herbs—that can be used for benevolent or malevolent purposes; and the belief that spirit possession and ritual song and dance are crucial forms of communication with the divine.¹⁵

The cosmology of traditional African religions does not fit into the Western philosophical and theological categories of monotheism and polytheism, mortal and immortal. African religions scholar Jacob K. Olupona describes four distinct types of deities in African religious systems.¹⁶ First, there is a Supreme Being who is identified as the creator of the universe. Second, there are "lesser deities" who are messengers of the Supreme Being. They serve as intermediaries between the Supreme Being and the created temporal world. These "lesser deities" are the direct objects of worship. Third, there are "culture heroes" who are "mythic founders of communities and villages who go through an apotheosis after their heroic sojourn on earth."¹⁷ Fourth, there are "ancestors," the deceased members of the

---

13. Ibid., 453–54.
14. Ibid., 458.
15. Gary Edwards and John Mason, *Black Gods: Orisa Studies in the New World* (Brooklyn: Yoruba Theological Archministry, 1985) 3–4.
16. Jacob K. Olupona, "To Praise and to Reprimand: Ancestors and Spirituality in African Society and Culture," in *Ancestors in Post-Contact Religion: Roots, Ruptures, and Modernity's Memory,* ed. Steven J. Friesen (Cambridge: Harvard University Press, 2001) 51.
17. Ibid.

lineage of the living.[18] Culture heroes are hard to classify because they seem to have some of the same characteristics of both the lesser deities in that "they are regarded as greater in importance and authority than the ancestors, whose sphere of influence is more or less limited to their lineage and their descendants."[19] In most African traditional religions, the Supreme Being is rather remote and rarely referenced outside of creation stories. It is the lesser deities and the culture heroes who have devotees; they perform activities such as spirit possession.

In African traditional religions, ancestors have a different role than the lesser deities and culture heroes. At death, one can become an ancestor; however, not all deceased persons are regarded as ancestors. In order to be an ancestor, one must have lived a morally exemplary life, lived to a very old age, died a "good death" (not by a disease such as smallpox or leprosy), and received a proper burial by one's family. There is a strong relationship between the ancestors and members of their lineage, as the ancestors' living family members must consciously remember them and honor them through storytelling and the building of shrines and altars. These ancestors are usually honored in the way previously described. This honoring of the ancestors is often referred to as "ancestor veneration" or "ancestor worship."[20]

This focus on the ancestors causes many observers to interpret the activity as "worship." Postmodern womanist theology notes that ancestors are "kept alive" in the present in these activities, which are a kind of rememory.

Ancestors appear to be like humans in that one often assumes that they do the same things in the spiritual realm that they did while living in mortal bodies: "Like humans, they drink, eat and excrete."[21] Yet they are unlike humans in that the ancestors have a moral responsibility to the living. They serve to remind the living to live according to the norms of society, and acting against these norms is said to "anger the ancestors." Olupona describes this quality of the ancestors as significantly different from humanity: "In order to function [as guardians of morality], the ancestors are freed of the human weaknesses and conditions of pettiness, particularly common among living lineage members. They are, therefore, eminently qualified to act as the guardians of social and moral order in the world."[22] Thus, ancestors are not simply human beings who maintain activity after death. "Through the process of death, ancestors undergo a change in their ontological status that makes them into supernatural

---

18. I use "ancestors" as I describe the term presented by Olupona. This reflects the way the term is used within African traditional religions. This "ancestor" will be distinguished from my use of the term, ancestor.

19. Ibid.

20. Again, Carol P. Christ has a different way of thinking of ancestor veneration in keeping with the previously noted understanding of place and spirit. She writes, "Venerating the ancestors is not simply about connection to human forebears, but also about their connection (and our own) to place. Venerating the ancestors is a way of expanding the boundaries of our skins, horizontally through time, and vertically into the earth. When we feel ourselves connected to places, we are more likely to want to preserve them." See Carol P. Christ, "We are Nature: Environmental Ethics in a Different Key," (paper presented at the Sixth International Whitehead Conference, Salzburg, Austria, 5 July 2006).

21. Olupona, "To Praise and to Reprimand," 50.

22. Ibid., 57.

entities."[23] Ancestors are transformed in the afterlife; they have a divine quality to them. In summary, African traditional religions affirm that human beings can live on after death. The ancestors, along with lesser deities and culture heroes, have special knowledge that can be accessed by the living through rituals of remembrance, rites of divination, or spirit possession.

I use the term *ancestor* as a philosophical term to refer to a spiritual force or soul that is disembodied, at times because of the death of the mortal body, as in the case of the ancestors as they are described in the context of African traditional religions. This term also refers to the lesser deities and culture heroes who are more properly objects of worship and have a larger role in African traditional religions. I acknowledge the differences between lesser deities, culture heroes, and ancestors that are maintained in African traditional religions. One would not consider most òrìṣà as having once been mortal, and the ancestors do not "possess" devotees. However, I also want to illustrate some of their similarities. There are culture heroes that seem to be regarded as òrìṣà. For example, among the Yoruba, Ṣango is the legendary king of the village of Oyo; yet his "death" was a disappearance into the ground, and he is now considered an òrìṣà by Yoruba devotees in both Africa and the Western hemisphere.

Grouping òrìṣà, culture heroes, and ancestors together stresses the ways that they are similar kinds of beings. Olupona seeks to challenge the idea that ancestors are elders who are ontologically different from the supernatural lesser deities (òrìṣà) and spirits. He acknowledges that some understandings of African religions draw a clear line between the sacred and the profane, but he argues that this is not the case in the African setting.[24] My confluence of terms is not merely convenient and philosophical; it is also illustrative of the similarities between distinct forces and the fluidity between the spiritual world and the world in which we live. My terminology is also reflective of the kind of syncretism that has occurred as African traditional religions have been adapted and practiced in the Americas. This is yet another reason why the practice of African traditional religions appears to many as ancestor worship. The close relationship between the "ancestors" and the "supernatural" or "divine" easily conflates whether the object of worship is simply the memory of one who has died or one who is divine. The following discussion of spirit possession will offer an explanation of how the ancestors and God are connected, and why it can be so difficult to distinguish the two.

Spirit Possession

In African traditional religions, spirit possession is an important resource for the interaction between the ancestors and the present generation.[25] Social anthropologist I. M. Lewis defines spirit possession as a "mystical exaltation in which [one's] whole being seems to fuse in a glorious communion with the divinity."[26] Carl

---

23. Ibid., 58.

24. Ibid., 60–61.

25. The concept of spirit possession is widely used by ethnographers and anthropologists to refer to a religious practice that is common to the world's indigenous religions, and sometimes found in Western religious practices as well—most notably those influenced by Christian holiness and Pentecostal traditions.

26. I. M. Lewis, *Ecstatic Religion: A Study of*

Becker defines spirit possession as "the phenomenon in which persons suddenly and inexplicably lose their normal set of memories, mental dispositions, and skills, and exhibit entirely new and different sets of memories, dispositions, and skills."[27] Spirit possession leads to such phenomena as speaking in tongues, the transmission of messages from the dead, and other mystical gifts. Spirit possession occurs when an ancestor's spirit strongly influences the living person in order to communicate to and through this person, displacing his or her normal sense of consciousness.

My concept of ancestral immortality accounts for the process by which the human past can access and fill the present in such a way as to produce the experience of spirit possession. A metaphysical concept of spirit possession must allow for (1) the possibility of life after death and the existence of the ancestors, (2) action and perception on the part of those ancestors, (3) a way for those ancestors to "return to" the present world, and (4) a way for the present to access those ancestors and conform to their influence.

POSTMODERN THEOLOGICAL FRAMEWORK

The concept of the ancestors rests on a general concept of immortality. Whitehead's concept of immortality explains that what has died to the world is indeed accessible to the present. What has died to the world is present and alive in God and the world, but only objectively. That means that the world and God have access to the fact of what has happened but cannot feel the past in its experience of itself. God and the world can sympathize with what has happened in the world, but they don't know us as we feel within ourselves. The present can feel the past with a high level of sympathy, but the present cannot feel the past completely. Likewise, God can sympathize with the world, but we cannot be known as we knew ourselves. No one, not even God, can feel us from the inside out. Neither God nor those in the world can feel the past "subjectively."

A traditional African religious understanding of spirit possession believes that the living have access to more than just the fact of the ancestors' existence. The living must also be able to access the experience of the ancestors. This necessitates a kind of subjective immortality.

Marjorie Suchocki develops a concept of subjective immortality using Whitehead's metaphysics.[28] She argues that in the process of becoming, there is a moment between when we become something new and when we cease being the old person where we can "enjoy" ourselves. By "enjoy," I mean that we can have a sense of who we are and offer that self to the world and to God. If there are feelings

---

Shamanism and Spirit Possession, 3rd ed. (1971; reprinted, New York: Routledge, 2003) 15.

27. Carl B. Becker, *Paranormal Experience and Survival of Death* (Albany: State University of New York Press, 1993) 11, quoted in David Ray Griffin, *Parapsychology, Philosophy and Spirituality: A Postmodern Explanation* (Albany: State University of New York Press, 1997) 169.

28. See Marjorie Suchocki, *The End of Evil: Process Eschatology in Historical Context* (Albany: State University of New York Press, 1988) for a full discussion of this concept. I've omitted many details of her description in the interest of using more accessible language than the discipline-specific language of process theology. I've tried to retain the spirit of her argument, highlighting those aspects that contribute to the concept of ancestral immortality outlined here.

and experiences of self in this intermediate or transitory place, then those feelings and experiences are available to those we influence. Our feelings and experiences are only partially available to the rest of the world. The world can never know us as we know ourselves. But our feelings and experiences are fully available to God. God feels us, knows us, takes us into God's self. And God does not just know us by the fact of who we were and who we are, but by how we experience ourselves. That is, God knows us from the inside out. Thus, God can feel our feelings. God does really suffer with us and rejoice with us.

While there is a distinction between having access to what happened in the past and having access to how those in the past felt, it is not as big a difference as it may originally appear to be. The concept of "subjective immortality" enlarges the scope of how we feel the influence of the past and how God feels and incorporates the world into God's self. Suchocki describes subjective immortality as "a difference of degree rather than kind."[29] Subjective immortality is significant inasmuch as it is important to most of us that, even while others in the world cannot completely know us, God should be able to know and feel us both in terms of what has happened to us and in terms of how we feel.

We can enjoy ourselves or "experience" ourselves even as we are becoming something new. This enjoyment continues when we die to the world and continue on in God. Because we—our spirits, our souls, now the ancestors—retain experience within God, the ancestors experience the world as God experiences it. Thus, within God, the ancestors can (1) experience themselves as themselves, (2) experience themselves in God, and (3) experience the way that God relates them to God's vision. The ancestors have access to what is happening in the world because God is taking in the events of the world into God's self. Here, there is a genuine life after death—life in God. For Suchocki, this is the kingdom or community of heaven. In our context, this is the ancestral realm where ancestors commune with one another and with God while "looking in" on the activity of the world. That is why we say that the ancestors have access to more knowledge than the living. We only know our part of the world, what is happening within our corner of the world. The ancestors, now a part of God, have access to the entire world. Thus, we are broader in death and in God than we are in life.

POSTMODERN WOMANIST THEOLOGY

The possibilities that we consider when we make decisions come from God. God orders these possibilities, calling us to choose those options that lead to a vision of the common good. This movement of God is shaped by what happens in the world and how God relates that to God's vision. Now that we consider the ancestors to be a part of God and think of them as having knowledge and experience as they participate in God, we can see that they influence what God offers to the world. As God integrates all these inputs with God's vision, the ancestors are available to those of us in the land of the living—through God. They are available not just in the fact of who they were, the fact that they

---

29. Ibid., 96

existed, but at least in part in their knowledge and experience. Thus, as we in the land of the living are influenced by God, we can also feel or incorporate the ancestors—with their expanded knowledge—into ourselves. For this reason, African traditional religions portray ancestors as uniquely connected to the divine. [Karen] Baker-Fletcher affirms this divine quality of the ancestors: "[Ancestors] are considered part of present, past, and future reality [or 'possibility']."[30] The concept of ancestral immortality acknowledges that one of the ways that the world experiences the past is in the call from God. We have access to the ancestors in God's calling to the world.

In what I have described in terms of spirit possession and African traditional religions, the agency of spirit possession belongs to those of us in the present, in the land of the living. Whether or not an ancestor's spirit "possesses" an individual depends on how we take in the influence from God. In this sense, spirit possession is more aptly described thusly: When a human being dies, she becomes an ancestor. Inside God, this ancestor has actuality, experience (objectivity and subjectivity), and a broader knowledge of the world than she did when she died. Here, the ancestor can be said to "commune" with other ancestors. Hence, the consequent nature of God could rightly be referred to as an "ancestral realm" or "spiritual realm." Since the events (and now feelings) of the world are evaluated within God's nature according to their value and the best that can be found and then related to the possibilities available to the world, the ancestors are present in God's calling to the world. When we embrace the new possibilities offered to us in God's calling, we may be "possessed" with a spirit of an ancestor.

There are still questions: Does God passively contain the ancestors in God's offering of possibilities to the world, or does the ancestor have knowledge *and* agency as it is available to the living? Does the ancestor know that he or she is available to the present world? Does the ancestor want to be incorporated into the living? And if so, for what purpose?

There is still a problem in what I have described. In the concept of God I have outlined, God is constantly integrating the world with what's possible and the divine vision. When the ancestors are present in God, they are being integrated and woven into the mix. So, when the ancestors are presented to the world through the movement of God, they are not presented in their individual forms. Rather, they are "swirled together" with all these possibilities. Still, we are not overcome by all of this. How is this possible?

As we are influenced by the past and what is possible, we are pretty selective. We aren't even aware of how selective we are. It is "preconscious." Some people may be predisposed to selecting particular ancestors. For example, being born into a particular lineage may predispose one—consciously or not—to selecting a particular ancestor. Perhaps we know that our ancestors focused on one particular òrìṣà, and we choose to honor that same ancestor. Or perhaps we aren't even aware of this, but we seem to be drawn to particular colors and idiosyncrasies

---

30. Karen Baker-Fletcher and Garth Kasimu Baker-Fletcher, *My Sister, My Brother: Womanist and Xodus God-Talk*, Bishop Henry McNeal Turner/Sojourner Truth Series in Black Religion 12 (1997; reprint, Eugene, OR: Wipf & Stock, 2002) 91.

and personalities, and we later learn that an ancestor honored the òrìṣà with those qualities. Likewise, practices that are said to "induce possession" such as participating in certain rituals or the beating of certain rhythms also influence the selecting of particular ancestors. Thus, one might say that there are factors, conscious and preconscious, that can be said to structure or influence an individual's process of how she incorporates certain ancestors.

Spirit possession can be described in this way: When a human being (the body) dies, the spirit lives on. This disembodied spirit is an ancestor. As she participates in God, this ancestor spirit can still know what is happening in the world. Here, she is also woven together with all the other aspects that influence God. This is the expanded knowledge of the ancestor. As this ancestor is related to God's vision and incorporated into what God will offer to the world, she maintains her knowledge and agency, while her purposes align with those of God. This ancestor is now included (along with many other possibilities available to the living) in the movement of God in the world. Those of us in the land of the living never lose our ability to make our own decisions. For possession to occur, an individual must select and conform to the influence of the ancestor. The individual can always reject the lure of the ancestor as it is contained in the influence from God. Yet the ancestor may even be felt and incorporated when the individual is particularly receptive to influence, for example, during sleep. Thus, we may say the ancestor "came to me in a dream." When the individual selects and conforms to the influence of this ancestor, the spirit "possesses" the receptive individual.

Many African traditional religions acknowledge this kind of activity. Thus, devotees may engage in meditations, altar construction, worship, and so on in order to position themselves to "hear the voices of the ancestors." Likewise, people will also participate in sweat lodges, festivals, masquerades, drumming, dancing, and other "rituals of remembrance" in order to draw the ancestors, or a particular ancestor, to influence the present. We may beat out a distinct rhythm or display certain objects, believing that the ancestor can perceive these actions and that they will get the ancestors' attention. The living want to receive some type of communion with the ancestor.

Metaphysically, of course, these acts really influence the ways we incorporate the variety of inputs that are available to us. Similarly, the ancestor may "cause" an individual to dance in a specific manner. The individual may recall a dream with the imagery or names of the ancestors. As the individual dances a particular dance or exhibits certain behavior, the presence of that ancestor is acknowledged. The influence of the ancestor is known in its specificity. Even though the ancestors are said to "come to" the living, the living individual "calls" and "selects" the ancestors from the multiplicity of available possibilities in God's offer to the world.

Final questions remain: Why does an ancestor influence the world? For what purpose does an ancestor "come" to the present? A full concept of spirit possession states that spirit possession is often the result of an ancestor asserting herself into the temporal world. That is, the ancestor herself desires to possess the present occasion. In *Varieties of African American Religious Experience*, Anthony

B. Pinn refers to spirit possession in Haitian Vodun as a way in which the ancestors "manifest and provide information for various persons gathered, reveal their flaws and suggest alterations in behavior or attitude."[31] Pinn's description attributes activity and purpose to the ancestors. Likewise, Baker-Fletcher believes that some ancestors have particular reasons for wanting to influence the temporal world. From her reading of *Beloved*, she concludes that disrememberment brings "angry haunting by the ancestors."[32] She believes that the people who have died unjustly seem to be more insistent about being recognized in the present. Baker-Fletcher asserts that some ancestors act powerfully because they want the present world to acknowledge them, know something, and/or do something on their behalf.

African traditional religions express the ancestors' influence in the world as an ancestor who "wants to come back" to the present. The ancestor may have unfinished business, wisdom to convey, steps to dance, or stories to tell that will help the present generation choose the best path in their current decision-making process. That is, there appears to be some kind of purpose in the act of spirit possession.

Traditional African religions suggest that there can be a normative motivation for spirit possession. African traditional religions often describe the ancestors as guiding individuals into right relationship with the sacred and each other. For example, in traditional Yoruba religion, the ancestors are there to guide the believer into the development of good character, or *ìwà pèlé*. *Ìwà pèlé* is achieved by consistent righteous actions through complex processes of divination with a priest and possession by the ancestral spirits.[33] Those pursuing *ìwà pèlé* ascribe to high moral character, maintain composure in all situations, have unblemished reputations, conduct philanthropic deeds, and practice internal and external cleanliness. In other words, the ancestors want to help the present generation to be the best that it can be. They want their knowledge and experiences to be used for the achievement of creative transformation. Through spirit possession, the ancestors strive to guide the present generation toward creative transformation. This is the purpose of possession. In this philosophical system, can an ancestor have a hope or a longing for how the ancestor might be incorporated by the present? Both Whitehead and Suchocki suggest a move in this direction, but they don't go all the way.[34] Whitehead believes that, in the process of becoming, we have hopes for how we will be in the next moment. Whitehead acknowledges that those of us in the present can influence our futures. What we contribute to the world as we become our own thing includes a thrust for our future: "[T]he future has *objective* reality in the present, but no *formal* actuality. For it is inherent in the constitution of the immediate, present actuality that a future will supersede it . . . Thus each [aspect of the world] . . . experiences a future which must

---

31. Anthony B. Pinn, *Varieties of African American Religious Experience* (Minneapolis: Fortress, 1998) 33.

32. Baker-Fletcher and Baker-Fletcher, *My Sister, My Brother*, 156.

33. See Awo Fá'lokun Fatunmbi, *Ìwa-pèlé: IFA QUEST, The Search for the Source of Santería and Lucumí* (Bronx: Original Publications, 1991).

34. Suchocki does have an active subjective immortality in God, but not in the world.

be actual, although the completed actualities of that future are undetermined."[35] In other words, the details are undetermined, but we do consider the future. Our hopes for the future are implied, and therefore in some way present, in what we have done.

Suchocki refers to a human being's vision for the future as *imagination*. When we make decisions about what we are going to do now, we have a sense of our future: "Through imagination, one transcends one's present circumstances and envisions a future . . . Through this vision of the future, the self participates in the transformation of the present; . . . [Transcendence through imagination calls upon the novelty of that which may yet be, the future."[36] We often evaluate how we will impact the future. Whitehead and Suchocki agree that as we make decisions and continue on in life, we can and often do consider how we may impact the future. I believe that this is also true of the ancestors. Because the ancestors are related to God's vision for the world, they hope or imagine that their impact in the world will be in alignment with the purposes of God. Like God, the ancestor aims at the ideals of truth, beauty, art, adventure, peace, and justice. That is, ancestors also aim at creative transformation. As the ancestor is incorporated by those of us in the world, his or her knowledge and experience are also guiding the world toward this vision of creative transformation. The power of the ancestors is available to the world through God's calling.

Although the ancestors want to provide information to the living to guide us toward a vision of the common good or, as in the earlier example, *ìwà pèlé*, how and whether or not this information is accessed depends on the agency of the living. The ancestors are not coercive. The ability to incorporate the ancestor lies within the living individual, and the individual has true freedom and agency in determining how and in what direction she will become. Thus, the knowledge and agency of the ancestor, while purposive and directed toward God's vision, can be used and transformed by an individual creatively *or* destructively.

In a postmodern theological framework, we are always partly self-determining, and we may or may not become in accordance with God's vision for us. David Ray Griffin affirms such a possibility when he writes, "[T]he soul's power can be exerted directly on actualities beyond one's own body, both 'physical' things and other souls. This power can, in relation to living matter, either promote or discourage growth, either bless or curse."[37] Likewise, African traditional religions continually affirm that the power that comes from or through the divine—whether we are referring to the ancestors, herbal knowledge, or a force such as *àṣẹ*—is morally neutral. Evil, "demon-possession," or "witchcraft" are results of its manipulation by those with evil intentions and destructive purposes. Likewise, *ìwà pèlé*, to use that earlier example, comes from those who are intentionally "seeking blessings" or who purposively

35. Alfred North Whitehead, *Process and Reality: An Essay in Cosmology*, Corrected Edition, eds. David Ray Griffin and Donald W. Sherburne (New York: Free Press, 1978) 215.

36. Marjorie Hewitt Suchocki, *The Fall to Violence: Original Sin in Relational Theology* (New York: Continuum, 1994) 41.

37. David Ray Griffin, *Parapsychology, Philosophy and Spirituality: A Postmodern Explanation* (Albany: State University of New York Press, 1997) 273.

try to become in such a way as to promote the vision of God. A postmodern womanist theology encourages us to use our access to the knowledge and experiences of the ancestors for creative transformation.

This understanding of spirit possession may be applicable outside of African traditional religious experiences. For example, charismatic Christians may find some resonance with this concept. The Gospel of John describes the Holy Spirit as the ancestral spirit of Jesus. Jesus speaks to the disciples and tells them, "Nevertheless I tell you the truth: it is to your advantage that I go away, for if I do not go away, the Comforter will not come to you; but if I go, I will send him to you" (John 16:7). In the way that I have used the term *ancestor*, the Holy Spirit can be understood as an ancestor. Thus, a postmodern theology can also explain what some Christians call "getting happy," "feeling the spirit," "speaking in tongues," and/or "holy dancing." It can also account for what some Christian women in the South Carolina low country call "tulking to de dead," an "ongoing exchange between the living and the dead—prevalent in their song traditions, worship services, and daily activities of church work, storytelling and sweetgrass basketry."[38] This theology both explains those experiences as valid within a contemporary worldview and affirms them as healthy.

---

38. LeRhonda S. Manigault, "Listening to the Dead Speak: Gullah/Geechee Women and the Ethnographic Imagination," (paper presented at the Workshop on Race and Religion: Thought, Practice and Meaning, University of Chicago, Chicago, IL, 30 October 2007). See LeRhonda S. Manigault, "'Ah Tulk to de Dead All de Time': An Investigation of Gullah Culture through Womanist Ethnography" (PhD diss., Emory University, 2007).

CONCLUSION

A postmodern womanist theology believes that the past is a critical dimension in "making a way out of no way." This theology asserts that "those who have died have never left." The past shapes who and how we are in the world. We are encouraged to remember the past and to do so in the context of community. We are working toward wholeness when we remember the past, lift up the most creative and life-giving activities, and carry those activities on into our current forms of becoming. A postmodern womanist theology also acknowledges the ancestors' constructive role in the process of salvation. The ancestors can creatively transform us as they teach and heal us—helping us to be the best individuals and communities that we can be. The ancestors can also assist us as we transform the world. When the ancestors guide us toward creative transformation, they not only represent the vision of God but also become part of the transformed community itself.

The processes of rememory and spirit possession can produce destructive or creative effects within the world. Remembering and embracing the past does not always help us to move creatively into the future. A postmodern womanist theology insists that we *learn* from the past and then use what we have learned, what we have experienced, toward God's ideals of truth, beauty, adventure, art, peace, justice, and quality of life. Creative transformation remains the process, goal, and measure for "making a way out of no way."

There is an ethical imperative in postmodern womanist theology and its understanding of how we learn from the past. It insists that contemporary humans remember the past. Honoring, embracing, and repeating the creative dimensions of the past allow human beings to transform the temporal world creatively with the unique knowledge of the past. We must, therefore, be about the business of re-memory. We should pour libations, light candles, tell stories, and pursue ideals. We should try to attune ourselves to the activity of the ancestors, pay attention to our dreams and visions, and allow ourselves to be possessed. We should be open to the lessons from the ancestors that creatively transform us to creatively transform the world. We increase our consciousness of the past and our own resources for attaining health, wholeness, and quality of life when we regularly and ritually acknowledge the past and conform according to God's calling. Thus, we open ourselves to "being possessed by the spirits of the ancestors." We can, as suggested in the introduction remember the ancestors and dance ourselves and our communities in wholeness. Metaphysically, we discipline our own souls and can selectively incorporate particular ancestors and use their knowledge and agency to augment our own ability to creatively transform the world.

Commentary

Carolyn Roncolato

Monica A. Coleman's book *Making a Way Out of No Way: A Womanist Theology* is a groundbreaking work of imaginative and provocative constructive theology. Elaborating on the themes of her earlier writings, in this text she proposes a postmodern womanist theology. The excerpt presented in this collection is an example of her creative and rigorous academic endeavor to hold in conversation postmodern process theology and womanism.

Coleman's work is important to the fields of process thought and womanist and feminist theology for a number of reasons. There are four contributions of Coleman's work that I find particularly important. First, a substantial amount of work has been done on the conversation between (white) feminist theology and process thought. Coleman is among the first to outline such a conversation between womanist theology and process thought. In so doing, she reveals that womanism has a critically different stake in process thought than white feminism. Furthermore, process theology has unique things to gain from dialogue with womanism that it has not gained from conversations with white feminist theology.

Second, Coleman is concerned with the lived-out realities of postmodern philosophical theory and uses experience as a primary source for her academic project. Coleman opens *Making a Way out of No Way* with the story of a domestic violence survivor, Lisa, who is a part of a support group at a domestic violence program where Coleman once worked. On this particular day, Lisa's boyfriend had torn her hair out after beating her. The group of women gathered sits with Lisa, listens to her story, and braids her hair back together. Coleman writes, "I needed something to say to Lisa . . . I wanted to affirm that braiding patchwork hair was more than an act of compassion, that it might indeed be an act of salvation. I wanted to connect the specificity of her story with a worldview that acknowledges the reality of evil and loss and finds opportunities for life in each moment without either waiting on God to make it happen or making Lisa do it all herself. I needed a postmodern womanist theology."[1]

By beginning with this story, Coleman declares that this is a valid starting place for theology and that any valid theology must be accountable to victims who are silenced and communities who are disenfranchised. With this opening story, Coleman reminds the reader that theology is not merely a theoretical project but is rather a matter of survival, a matter of life and death. Coleman's project is born of experience, born of presence to black women's realities, and born of the need to do accountable and sustainable theology.

Third, in bringing together womanist and process theologies, Coleman allows each thought system to speak to the other. Each theological system offers the other new tools and new insights. Coleman uses womanism to call process theology out of the dangerous trap of remaining solely in the realm of philosophical theory. She notes that process theology "is often accused of an overreliance on philosophy and theory, with insufficient grounding in the concrete experiences of people . . . yet process theology contains the requisite elements for using a variety of sources in its commitment to experience."[2] Coleman calls forth these tools, taking seriously the call to look at human experience for clues to theology. She liberates process thought from its hegemonic roots and tendencies by demonstrating the ways it can be a liberating agent of transformation for black women. On the other hand, she demonstrates how the metaphysics of process theology can both open womanism up to new possibilities and provide support for some of its foundational claims. Coleman is not providing a theoretical and philosophical framework to black women's experience in order to give them validity, nor is she concerned with giving experiential proof to process theology. Rather, Coleman's work celebrates the ways the tension and dialogue between the two areas of thought can birth new and liberating ideas.

Finally, Coleman uses the metaphysical concepts of process thought to argue for a de-centering of Christ in womanist theology. This call distinguishes her from

---

1. Monica A. Coleman, *Making a Way Out of No Way* (Minneapolis: Fortress, 2008) 3.

2. Monica A. Coleman, "An Exchange of Gifts," in *Handbook of Process Theology*, ed. Jay McDaniel and Donna Bowman (St Louis: Chalice, 2006) 70.

many other womanist theologians. She proposes that the traditional womanist idea of "making a way out of no way" be understood in terms of process theology's concept of creative transformation. Coleman writes, "If Christ is removed from the center of black theologies, new images will emerge ... 'Making a way out of no way' as creative transformation gives an indigenous metaphor for both Christian and non-Christian womanist theologies in pluralistic dialogue."[3] As we see in the included chapter, Coleman is particularly concerned with making room within womanist theology for African traditional religions. She claims that African American religion must always deal with its African religious heritage, whether or not this heritage fits within Christianity. Process theology provides tools to make room in womanism for the pluralism that is a real part of black women's lives.

At the intersection of these three traditions—process, womanist, and African traditional religion—Coleman locates new liberating potentialities. Her work births ideas that are important for both academic theology and the lived out reality of communities. Her discussion of the past in the included chapter, is a good example of what can happen when all of these traditions speak to each other. The intersection of these three theological systems acknowledges the perpetual power of past, the necessity of dealing with it as individuals and communities, and the importance of being present to our ancestors. Coleman suggests that when we remember, grieve, and celebrate the past, it can be the creative fuel for the present and future projects of liberation.

Coleman's work asserts that these theological ideas are not merely thoughts or academic dialogues. They are rituals, songs and stories, and lived out tradition. They are not merely for the thinking, but for the living: "We should pour libations, light candles, tell stories, and pursue ideals. We should try to attune ourselves to the activity of the ancestors, pay attention to our dreams and visions, and allow ourselves to be possessed."[4] Coleman calls for imagination in the production of theology. She declares that attention must be paid to experience, to the tears of the victims who weep, and to the utopic narratives of black women's redemptive imaginations. Her work demonstrates the creative and profound imaginings possible when we open our theological purview and engage in creative dialogue. Performing the very thing she proposes, Coleman upholds those who have come before her, the womanists, feminists, and process theologians who have founded and formed their fields. With the help of these ancestors she creatively transforms that which they have given into new possibilities and new life.

The themes of Coleman's book lay the groundwork for future feminist, womanist, and process theologies. Her work is foundational to a new wave of womanist thought in which the true multiplicity of women's experience is taken seriously. Coleman's incorporation of African traditional religions and in particular her understanding of spirit possession opens up both womanist and process theology to the possibilities of divine multiplicity. With images of ancestral immortality, Coleman demonstrates ways to move

3. Ibid., 170.

4. Coleman, *Making a Way Out of No Way*, 122.

beyond a strictly monotheistic divinity allowing for more pluralistic understandings of the divine. This metaphysical interpretation shows ways in which process thought can provide means for true theological pluralism. This book suggests that the future of womanist and process theologies lies in uncovering and validating the multiplicities of our experiences, our traditions, and our theology.

STUDY QUESTIONS

1. In what ways is Coleman's understanding of the power of the past rooted in process theology, and in what ways is it womanist?

2. What makes Coleman's womanist approach to process thought different from the approaches of white feminist theology?

3. In what ways does Coleman rely upon traditional womanist claims and traditions? In what ways does she diverge?

4. Why is the issue of spirit possession important for Coleman?

5. According to Coleman, what is the difference between objective and subjective immortality, and how does this difference matter for ancestor worship?

Contributors

KATHLYN A. BREAZEALE is Associate Professor of Religion at Pacific Lutheran University in Contemporary Theology, focusing on feminist and womanist theologies. She is the author of *Mutual Empowerment: A Theology of Marriage, Intimacy, and Redemption* (Fortress, 2008) and several articles dealing with issues of sexuality and marriage from a feminist process theological perspective. Other areas of research and publication include the intersection of feminist theology, the arts, and social justice; religion and public life; and feminist pedagogy. Her current projects include developing a pedagogy for using film, art, service learning and bioregional perspectives in teaching liberation theologies, and an ecofeminist theological analysis of how women and men who are considered "closer to nature" are denigrated, particularly the Sámi people of Scandinavia and the Spiritual and Shouter Baptists of Trinidad and Tobago. Kathi also expresses her theological and pedagogical interests in her work as a liturgical dancer.

MONICA A. COLEMAN is Associate Professor of Constructive Theology and African American Religions and Co-Director of The Center for Process Studies at Claremont School of Theology. She is also Associate Professor of Religion at Claremont Graduate University. She received degrees from Harvard University, Vanderbilt Divinity School and Claremont Graduate University. Her research interests include process theology, black and womanist theologies, African traditional religions, mental health and theology and religious pluralism. She is the author of *The Dinah Project: a Handbook for Congregational Response to Sexual Violence* and *Making a Way Out of No Way: A Womanist Theology*.

NANCY R. HOWELL is Professor of Theology and Philosophy of Religion at Saint Paul School of Theology and Adjunct Professor of Bioethics at Kansas City University of Medicine and Biosciences. Her ecofeminist research is indebted to process theology and liberation theologies and is inspired by chimpanzees and bonobos. Her master's thesis and her Claremont Graduate School dissertation on Whitehead and feminism birthed a life-long commitment to justice for women and nature. Her process relational theology is concerned with the relationship of science and religion, which Howell deconstructs and reconstructs in terms of social location. She is author of *A Feminist Cosmology: Ecology, Solidarity, and Metaphysics* and associate editor of the *Encyclopedia of Science and Religion*.

KRISTA E. HUGHES is Assistant Professor of Theological Studies at Hanover College (Hanover, Indiana). A constructive theologian, she works at the intersection of feminist and process theologies, history of doctrine, and continental philosophy. She is author of several essays and book reviews, including "Intimate Mysteries: A Sensible Apophatics of Love" and "In the Flesh: A Feminist Vision of Hope." She is currently working on a book manuscript tentatively entitled *Dance of Grace: A Feminist Theology of the Gift*, which explores questions of agency, gift, corporeality, and aesthetics in the movement of grace.

KIRSTEN A. S. MEBUST is Visiting Professor of Theology at Augustana College, Sioux Falls, South Dakota, a college of the Evangelical Lutheran Church in America. She is a PhD candidate at Claremont Graduate University in the Philosophy of Religion and Theology program, completing a dissertation in imagination as *imago Dei*. She studied with Sallie McFague at Vanderbilt University in 2000. She received her Master of Divinity from Luther Theological Seminary in Saint Paul, Minnesota, in 1999. Her home is in Minneapolis, where she is a member of University Lutheran Church of Hope, daughter of Duane and Marcheta Scribner, married to Bruce Mebust, and mother of Solveig and Anna Mebust.

ANN M. PEDERSON is a Professor of Religion at Augustana College in Sioux Falls, South Dakota. She served as Interim Campus Pastor during 2009–2010. She is also on the Section of Ethics and Humanities at the Sanford School of Medicine. Her primary academic interests are Lutheran constructive theology, the relationship between religion and medicine, and feminist theology. She earned her BA from Montana State University in music, her MA in Religious Studies from United Theological Seminary (Twin Cities, MN), and an MDiv, ThM, and PhD from the Lutheran School of Theology at Chicago. She has authored three books and many articles for such journals as *Zygon*, *Dialog*, *Word and World*, *Currents in Theology and Mission*.

ARLETTE POLAND teaches religious studies at California State University at San Bernardino, the University of Redlands and College of the Desert in Palm Desert. After receiving degrees from The University of California at Berkeley and San Francisco Law School and practicing law, Poland returned to school where she received the MA from Claremont School of Theology and the PhD in Philosophy of Religion from Claremont Graduate University. She teaches in the fields of World Religions, History of Buddhism, Science and Religion and Women's Studies in Religion. Her research places the thought of Alfred North Whitehead in conversation with Rabbi Abraham Heschel; and Jewish, feminist and process theologies in conversation with Buddhism.

CARYN D. RISWOLD is Associate Professor of Religion and Chair of Gender and Women's Studies at Illinois College in Jacksonville, Illinois. A native of South Dakota, she earned a BA from Augustana College (SD), an MA from the Claremont School of Theology, and the ThM and PhD from the Lutheran School of Theology at Chicago. Her most recent book is *Feminism and Christianity: Questions and Answers in the Third Wave* (Cascade Books, 2009). She is also the author of *Two Reformers: Martin Luther and Mary Daly as*

Political Theologians (2007), *Coram Deo: Human Life in the Vision of God* (2006), and several articles in journals like *Dialog*, *Political Theology*, and *The Lutheran*.

CAROLYN RONCOLATO is a PhD student at Chicago Theological Seminary where she is working on the intersection of feminist theology and process thought. Carolyn's academic work has focused on the relationship of intimate violence against women to theology. Carolyn received her Master of Arts degree from Chicago Theological Seminary and her Bachelor of Arts degree from Allegheny College in Meadville, Pennsylvania.

HELENE TALLON RUSSELL is Associate Professor of Theology at Christian Theological Seminary. She earned a PhD at Claremont Graduate University, studying under Marjorie Suchocki and serves on the board of Process and Faith. She is the author of *Irigaray and Kierkegaard: Multiplicity, Relationality and Difference* (Mercer University Press 2009). She has also written articles on connections between process thought and Kierkegaard. Her next research project includes exploring an interface between Luce Irigaray and process feminist theology. She is actively engaged in All Saints Episcopal Church in Indianapolis and lives with her Sun Conure, Tangelo.

JEANYNE B. SLETTOM is Adjunct Professor of Theology at Claremont School of Theology and United Theological Seminary of the Twin Cities. She received the PhD in Religion from Claremont Graduate University. She is the director of Process & Faith, a faculty center of the school of theology, and editor of the organization's journal, *Creative Transformation*.

She is the co-editor of *The Process Perspective: Frequently Asked Questions of Process Theology* (Chalice, 1993) and its sequel, *The Process Perspective II* (Chalice, 2011). She is also the managing editor of *Process Studies*, the journal of the Center for Process Studies, and she writes liturgies.

NICHOLE TORBITZKY graduated from Pittsburgh Theological Seminary in 2000, where she earned her master's degree in Divinity. She was ordained by the United Church of Christ and began serving the First Reformed United Church of Christ in Vandergrift, Pennsylvania that same year. Torbitzky is currently a PhD Candidate in Philosophy of Religion and Theology at Claremont Graduate University. She is working with Roland Faber and Susan Nelson on her dissertation in process atonement theory. Early in 2005, she accepted a call as Associate Pastor at First Christian Church of Ontario, California.

MARIT A. TRELSTAD is Associate Professor of Constructive Theology at Pacific Lutheran University. She is editor of and contributor to *Cross Examinations: Readings on the Meaning of the Cross Today* (Fortress, 2006). In the past three years, she worked as a feminist theologian on the Evangelical Lutheran Church in America's Task Force on Human Sexuality, which constructed a social statement for the church. Recently, she has worked alongside feminist, womanist, mujerista and Asian feminist theologians on a book entitled *Transforming Lutheran Theologies*. Her theological focus has been primarily on soteriology, Christology, theological anthropology and pedagogy from a process, feminist perspective. She has presented several papers at the American

Academy of Religion with recent papers developing the covenantal ontology that is the focal point of her own constructive theology.

CONSTANCE WISE has been a practicing Feminist Wiccan for thirty years and co-founded two Feminist Wiccan covens in Denver. She earned the doctorate in Theology and Religious Studies from the Joint PhD Program of Iliff School of Theology and the University of Denver. She teaches religious studies, women's studies, and philosophy at the University of Colorado at Denver and Metropolitan State College of Denver. She is the author of *Hidden Circles in the Web: Feminist Wicca, Occult Knowledge, and Process Thought* (2008). Her primary scholarly interest is promoting positive acceptance of religious pluralism; for her next project she will explore process thought as a possible philosophical foundation for understanding the worship of different deities among the diverse religions in the United States, a phenomenon she calls "America's polytheism."

Chapter Sources

Chapter 4

Valerie Saiving. "Androgynous Life." In *Feminism and Process Thought: The Harvard Divinity School/Claremont Center for Process Studies Symposium Papers*, edited by Sheila Greeve Davaney, 11–31. Symposium Series 6. Lewiston, NY: Mellen, 1981.

Chapter 5

Marjorie Hewitt Suchocki. *God, Christ, Church: A Practical Guide to Process Theology*, 2–5, 49–61. New and revised ed. New York: Crossroad, 1989.

Chapter 6

Rosemary Radford Ruether. *Sexism and God-Talk: Toward a Feminist Theology*, 68–71. Boston: Beacon, 1993.

———. *Gaia and God: an Ecofeminist Theology of Earth Healing*, 240–53. San Francisco: HarperSanFrancisco, 1992.

Chapter 7

Susan L. (Dunfee) Nelson. "The Sin of Hiding: A Feminist Critique of Reinhold Niebuhr's Account of the Sin of Pride." *Soundings: An International Journal* 65 (1982) 316–26.

Chapter 8

Catherine Keller. *From a Broken Web: Separation, Sexism, and Self*, 7–15, 26–27, 248–52. Boston: Beacon, 1986.

Chapter 9

Rita Nakashima Brock. *Journeys by Heart: A Christology of Erotic Power*, 39–47. New York: Crossroad, 1988. Reprinted, Eugene, OR: Wipf & Stock, 2008.

Chapter 10

Sallie McFague. *The Body of God: An Ecological Theology*, 52–55, 141–50. Minneapolis: Fortress, 1993.

Chapter 11

Karen Baker-Fletcher. *Dancing with God: The Trinity from a Womanist Perspective*, 149–52, 153–57, 159–64, 165–69. St. Louis: Chalice, 2006.

Chapter 12

Nancy R. Howell. "The Importance of Being Chimpanzee." *Theology and Science* 1 (2003) 179–91.

Chapter 13

Ann M. Pederson, *God, Creation and All That Jazz: A Process of Composition and Improvisation*, 33–53. St. Louis: Chalice, 2000.

Chapter 14

Sandra B. Lubarsky. "Reconstructing Divine Power: Post-Holocaust, Feminism and Process Philosophy." In *Women and Gender in Jewish Philosophy*, edited by Hava Tirosh-Samuelson, 289–91, 299–311. Bloomington: Indiana University Press, 2004.

Chapter 15

Carol P. Christ. *She Who Changes: Re-Imagining the Divine in the World*, 197–210, 230–36. New York: Palgrave Macmillan, 2003.

Chapter 16

Monica A. Coleman. *Making a Way Out of No Way: A Womanist Theology*, 107–9, 111–23. Minneapolis: Fortress, 2008.

Bibliography

A general source for students or others seeking definitions of technical terms in process thought:

Cobb, John B., Jr. *Whitehead Word Book: A Glossary with Alphabetical Index to Technical Terms in "Process and Reality."* Claremont, CA: P & F, 2008. Available in print at www.processandfaith.org/ or online at http://www.processandfaith.org/publications/WordBookWeb.pdf.

Anderson, Bonnie S., and Judith P. Zissner. *A History of Their Own: Women in Europe from Prehistory to the Present.* 2 vols. New York: Harper & Row, 1988.

Arakawa, Dianne E. "Feminist Theology and Process Thought: Their Relationship." *Unitarian Universalist Christian* 37.3-4 (1982) 11-20.

Armstrong, Susan. "A Feminist Reading of Hegel and Kierkegaard." In *Hegel, History, and Interpretation*, edited by Shaun Gallagher, 227-41. SUNY Series in Hegelian Studies. Albany: State University of New York Press, 1997.

———. "Nonhuman Experience: A Whiteheadian Analysis." *Process Studies* 18 (1989) 1-18.

Armstrong, Susan, and Gael Hodgkins. Review of *The Wounded Woman: Healing the Father-Daughter Relationship*, by Linda Schierse Leonard. *Humboldt Journal of Social Relations* 10 (1983) 258-60.

Baker-Fletcher, Karen. "Afro-American Thoughts on God in Creation." *Earth Letter* (Spring 2007) 5-6.

———. *Dancing with God: The Trinity from a Womanist Perspective.* St. Louis: Chalice, 2006.

———. "Dust and Spirit." In *Strike Terror No More: Theology, Ethics, and the New War*, edited by Jon L. Berquist, 280-86. St. Louis: Chalice, 2002.

———. "Passing on the Spark: A Womanist Perspective on Theology and Culture." In *Changing Conversations: Religious Reflection & Cultural Analysis*, edited by Dwight N. Hopkins and Sheila Greeve Davaney, 145-62. New York: Routledge, 1996.

———. *Sisters of Dust, Sisters of Spirit: Womanist Wordings on God and Creation.* Minneapolis: Fortress, 1998.

———. "Something or Nothing: An Eco-Womanist Essay on God, Creation and Indispensbility." In *This Sacred Earth: Religion, Nature, Environment*, edited by Roger S. Gottlieb, 428-37. 2nd ed. New York: Routledge, 2004.

———. "Whiteheadian Metaphysics as a Resource for Womanist Theology." In *Process Thought and East Asian Culture: Process Theology*, 79-94. Conference monograph, Seoul, South Korea, 2004.

———. "A Womanist Journey." In *Deeper Shades of Purple: Womanism in Religion and Society*, edited by Stacy M. Floyd-Thomas, 158-75. Religion, Race, and Ethnicity. New York: New York University Press, 2006.

———. "Why Womanist Theology? Process Relational Reflections." Keynote lecture given at *Process Thought and East Asian Culture*, 87-109. Conference monograph. Seoul, South Korea, 2004.

Baker-Fletcher, Karen, and Garth Kasimu Baker-Fletcher. *My Sister, My Brother: Womanist and Xodus God Talk.* 1997. Reprinted, Eugene, OR: Wipf & Stock, 2002.

Beardslee, William A. "Ethics and Hermeneutics." Unpublished.

———. "Reply to Nancy Howell." Unpublished.

Berg, Christian. "Review of *A Feminist Cosmology: Ecology, Solidarity, and Metaphysics*, by Nancy R. Howell." *Process Studies* 31 (2002) 161-64.

Birke, Lynda et al. "Animal Performances: An Exploration of Intersections between Feminist Science Studies and Studies of Human/Animal Relationships." *Feminist Theory* 5 (2004) 167-83.

Bibliography

Bracken, Joseph A., and Marjorie Hewitt Suchocki, editors. *Trinity in Process: A Relational Theology of God*. New York: Continuum, 1997.

Breazeale, Kathlyn A. "Don't Blame It on the Seeds: Toward a Feminist Process Understanding of Anthropology, Sin, and Sexuality." *Process Studies* 22.2 (1993) 71–73.

———. "Dualism without Domination: A Reinterpretation of Dualism for Ecofeminist Theory." In *Constructing a Relational Cosmology*, edited by Paul O. Ingram, 54–68. Princeton Theological Monograph Series 62. Eugene, OR: Pickwick, 2006.

———. "Marriage after Patriarchy?" *Creative Transformation* 8.3 (1999) 6–9.

———. "Marriage after Patriarchy?: Partner Relationships and Public Religion." In *Religion in a Pluralistic Age: Proceedings of the Third International Conference on Philosophical Theology*, edited by Donald A. Crosby and Charley D. Hardwick, 71–81. American Liberal Religious Thought. New York: Lang, 2001.

———. *Mutual Empowerment: A Theology of Marriage, Intimacy, and Redemption*. Minneapolis: Fortress, 2008.

———. "Process Perspectives on Sexuality, Love, and Marriage." In *Handbook of Process Theology*, edited by Jay McDaniel and Donna Bowman, 120–35. St. Louis: Chalice, 2006.

———. "Toward a Process Theology of Partnership: Redemption through Intimacy and Mutual Empowerment." Center for Process Studies Seminar, Claremont, CA, 16 July 2003. Unpublished.

Breazeale, Kathlyn A., and William A. Beardslee, "Teenage Sexuality and Spirituality: Can These Two Become One?" In *Now What's a Christian to Do?*, edited by David P. Polk, 45–72. St. Louis: Chalice, 1994.

Briggs, Sheila. "A History of Our Own: What Would a Feminist History of Theology Look Like?" In *Horizons in Feminist Theology*, edited by Rebecca S. Chopp and Sheila Greeve Davaney, 165–78. Minneapolis: Fortress, 1997.

———. "Imagining Post-Patriarchy." Unpublished.

———. "Sexual Justice and the Righteousness of God" In *Sex and God: Some Varieties of Women's Religious Experience*, edited by Linda Hurcombe, 251–77. New York: Routledge & Kegan Paul, 1987.

———. *Toward a Theology of Eros*. Transdisciplinary Theological Colloquia. New York: Fordham University Press, 2006.

Brock, Rita Nakashima. "Artemis vs. Christ: Problems in Christology and Their Relation to Feminism." Unpublished.

———. "Beyond Jesus the Christ: A Christology of Erotic Power." Unpublished.

———. "The Emptiness of Power and the Power of Emptiness: Feminism and Buddhism on the Ontology of Power." Unpublished.

———. "A Feminist Consciousness Looks at Christology." *Encounter* 41 (1980) 319–31.

———. "The Feminist Redemption of Christ." In *Christian Feminism: Visions of a New Humanity*, edited by Judith L. Weidman, 55–74. San Francisco: Harper & Row, 1984.

———. *Journeys by Heart: A Christology of Erotic Power*. New York: Crossroad, 1988. Reprinted, Eugene, OR: Wipf & Stock, 2008.

———. "Power, Peace, and the Possibility of Survival." In *God and Global Justice: Religion and Poverty in an Unequal World*, edited by Frederick Ferré and Rita H. Mataragnon, 17–35 New York: Paragon, 1985.

———. "Reconstituting the World: Feminist and Process/Relational Visions of Freedom." Unpublished.

———. Review of *Feminism and Process Thought*, edited by Sheila Greeve Davaney. *Process Studies* 12 (1982) 46–50.

———. Review of *God's Power: Traditional Understanding and Contemporary Challenges*, by Anna Case-Winters. *Process Studies* 22 (1993) 58–60.

———. "Transcendence, Love, and Agency: A Feminist Critique of Power." Paper presented at the American Academy of Religion, 23–26 November 1985. Unpublished.

———. "Unholy Goodness and the Feminist Redemption of Christ." Unpublished.

———. "What Shall We Do between the Times?" 1993. Unpublished.

———. "Pacific, Asian, and North American Asian Feminist Theologies." In *Feminist Theologies: Legacy and Prospect*, edited by Rosemary Radford Ruether, 45–54. Minneapolis: Fortress, 2007.

Brock, Rita Nakashima, and Rebecca Ann Parker. *Saving Paradise: How Christianity Traded Love of This World for Crucifixion and Empire*. Boston: Beacon, 2008.

Bromell, David J. "Sallie McFague's 'Metaphorical Theology.'" *Journal of the American Academy of Religion* 61 (1993) 485–503.

Brooten, Bernadette. "Violence against Women in Rabbinic Literature." Unpublished.

Brown, B. Susan. "Of Starfish and Throwers of Stars: Wholeness and Relation." Unpublished.

Bucher, Christina. "A Response to Bernadette Brooten's Paper." Unpublished.

Cady, Linell E. "Identity, Feminist Theory, and Theology: An Emerging Historicist Alternative." In *Horizons in Feminist Theology*, edited by Sheila Greeve Davaney and Rebecca Chopp, 17–31. Minneapolis: Fortress, 1997.

———. "Relational Love: A Feminist Theological Exploration." In *Embodied Love: Sensuality and Relationship as Feminist Values*, edited Paula Cooey et al., 135–49. New York: Harper & Row, 1987.

———. *Religion, Theology, and American Public Life*. SUNY Series in Religious Studies. New York: State University of New York Press, 1993.

———. "Theories of Religion in Feminist Theologies." *American Journal of Theology and Philosophy* 13 (1992) 183–93.

Carr, Anne E. "Providence, Power and the Holy Spirit." *Horizons* 29 (2002) 80–93.

Casanova, Judith Boice et al. *What about Abortion?* Process Perspectives on Hard Issues Series. Claremont: Process and Faith, 1990.

Case-Winters, Anna. *God's Power: Traditional Understandings and Contemporary Challenges*. Louisville: Westminster John Knox, 1990.

———. "God's Power." PhD diss., Vanderbilt University, 1990.

———. *Reconstructing a Christian Theology of Nature: Down to Earth*. Ashgate Science and Religion Series. Hampshire, UK: Ashgate, 2007.

Chiaramonte, Lee. "A Harrisonian Ontology of the Stone Butch as Process Relational *Imago Dei*." *Theology & Sexuality* 11 (1999) 75-90.

Chopp, Rebecca. "Feminism's Theological Pragmatics: A Social Naturalism of Women's Experience." *Journal of Religion* 67 (1987) 239–56.

Chopp, Rebecca S., and Sheila Greeve Davaney, editors. *Horizons in Feminist Theology: Identity, Traditions, and Norms*. Minneapolis: Fortress, 1997.

Christ, Carol P. "The Challenge of the Prehistoric Goddesses: Rethinking Theology and Nature." Unpublished.

———. "Feminist Re-imaginings of the Divine and Hartshorne's God: One and the Same?" *Feminist Theology* 11 (2002) 99–115.

———. "Feminist Revisionings of Divine Power and Hartshorne's God." Unpublished.

———. "In the Wake of Matricide: A Feminist Process Paradigm." Paper presented at Center for Process Studies Seminar, Claremont, CA, 19 November 2002.

———. "The Last Dualism: Life and Death in Goddess Feminist Thealogy." Unpublished.

———. "The Meaning of the Goddess." In *Rebirth of the Goddess: Finding Meaning in Feminist Spirituality*, 89–112. Reading, MA: Addison-Wesley, 1997.

———. "Rebirth of the Goddess." Unpublished.

———. *Rebirth of the Goddess: Finding Meaning in Feminist Spirituality*. Reading, MA: Addison-Wesley, 1997.

———. "Re-imagining the Divine in the World as She Who Changes." *O Imaginário Feminino da Divindade* 11 (2005) 29–39.

———. "Rethinking Theology and Nature" In *Weaving the Visions: New Patterns in Feminist Spirituality*, edited by Judith Plaskow and Carol P. Christ, 314–25. San Francisco: Harper & Row, 1989.

———. "Review of *Constructing a Relational Cosmology*, edited by Paul O. Ingram." *Process Studies* 36 (2007) 137–40.

———. *She Who Changes: Re-Imagining the Divine in the World*. New York: Palgrave/St. Martin's, 2003.

———. "Theological and Political Implications of Re-imagining the Divine as Female." *Political Theology* 8 (2007) 157–70.

Christ, Carol P., and Kathryn Rountree. "Humanity and the Web of Life." *Environmental Ethics* 28 (2006) 185–200.

Clements, Heather Ann. "Eating God: Beyond a Cannibalizing Christianity." *Process Studies* 22 (1993) 93–106.

———. "A Process of Survival: A Feminist Theodicy of Sexual Abuse." *Creative Transformation* 3.1 (1993) 3–4.

———. "The Redemption and Sanctification of Human Gender and Sexuality: A Constructive Wesleyan Proposal." *Wesleyan Theological Journal* 41 (2006) 200–226.

Cobb, John B., Jr. "Buddhism, Whitehead, and the Feminist-Ecological Religion." Unpublished.

———. "Feminism and Process Thought: A Two-Way Relationship." *Feminism and Process Thought: The Harvard Divinity School/Claremont School of Theology Symposium Papers*, edited by Sheila Greeve Davaney, 32–61. Symposium Series 6. New York: Mellen, 1981.

———. "God and Feminism." In *Talking about God: Doing Theology in the Context of Modern*

Pluralism, edited by John B. Cobb Jr., and David Tracy, 75–91. New York: Seabury, 1983.

———. "God the Father Almighty." In *Christian Theology: A Case Method Approach*, edited by Robert A. Evans and Thomas D. Parker, 66–69. Harper Forum Book. New York: Harper & Row, 1976.

———. "The Influence of Feminist Theory on My Theological Work." *Journal of Feminist Studies in Religion* 7 (1991) 107–10.

———. "Justice and Birth Control." *Zion's Herald* (July/August 2005) 13–14, 43.

———. "On Being a Thinking Christian." *The Monkawa Vision* 5:3 (August 1994) 1–2.

———. "Postscript: The Trinity and Sexist Language." In *Christ in a Pluralistic Age*, by John B. Cobb, Jr., 259–64. Philadelphia: Westminster, 1975.

———. "Response to Sallie McFague." Unpublished.

———. "Review of *Models of God: Theology for an Ecological, Nuclear Age*, by Sallie McFague." *Religious Studies Review* 16 (1990) 40–42.

Cobb, John B., Jr., and Charles Birch. "A Just and Sustainable Role for Women." In *The Liberation of Life*, 309–17. Cambridge: Cambridge University Press, 1981.

Cobb, John B., Jr., and David Ray Griffin. "The Church and Women's Liberation." In *Process Theology: An Introductory Exposition*. Philadelphia: Westminster, 1976.

Coleman, Monica A. "Attention to the Ancestors: Black Theology, African Traditional Religions, and a Process Metaphysic." Paper presented at the American Academy of Religion annual meeting, Philadelphia, 21 November 2005.

———. *The Dinah Project: A Handbook for Congregational Response to Sexual Violence*. Cleveland: Pilgrim, 2004.

———. "An Exchange of Gifts: Process and Womanist Theologies." In *Handbook of Process Theology*, edited by Jay McDaniel and Donna Bowman, 160–76. St. Louis: Chalice, 2006.

———. "From Models of God to a Model of Gods: How Whiteheadian Metaphysics Facilitates Western Language Discussion of Divine Multiplicity." *Philosophia* 35 (2007) 329–40.

———. "Life after Death and Religious Pluralism: Three Process Feminist Approaches." The Future of Process Thought." Paper presented at the annual meeting of the Highlands Institute for American Religious and Philosophical Thought (HIARPT). Highlands, NC, 17 June 2009.

———. *Making a Way out of No Way: A Womanist Theology*. Innovations. Minneapolis: Fortress, 2008.

———. "Must I Be Womanist?" *Journal of Feminist Studies in Religion* 22 (2006) 85–96.

———. "Process Thought and Womanist Theology: Black Women's Science Fiction as a Resource for Process Theology." Paper presented at the Center for Process Studies Seminar. Claremont, CA, 29 April 2003.

———. "Walking in the Whirlwind: A Whiteheadian-Womanist Soteriology." PhD diss., Claremont Graduate University, 2004.

———. "'The Work of Your Own Hands': Doing Black Women's Hair as Religious Language in Gloria Naylor's *Mama Day*." *Soundings: An Interdisciplinary Journal* 85 (2003) 121–39.

———. "The World at Its Best: A Process Construction of a Wesleyan Understanding of Entire Sanctification." *Wesleyan Theological Journal* 37 (2002) 130–52.

———. "You Gotta Believe: The Future of Process Theology—In and Outside of the Academy." Paper presented at the American Theological Society Midwest Division Meeting, McCormick Theological Seminary, Chicago, IL, 27 October 2006.

Cooey, Paula M. "Review of *Gaia & God*, by Rosemary Radford Reuther." *Journal of the American Academy of Religion* 63 (1995) 169–70.

Cooey, Paula M., et al., editors. *After Patriarchy: Feminist Transformations of World Religions*. Faith Meets Faith Series. Maryknoll, NY: Orbis, 1991.

Cooper, Burton. "Metaphysics, Christianity and Sexism: An Essay in Philosophical Theology." *Religious Studies* 16 (1980) 179–93.

Daly, Mary. *Beyond God the Father: Toward a Philosophy of Women's Liberation*. Boston: Beacon, 1973.

———. *The Church and the Second Sex*. Boston: Beacon, 1968.

———. "The Courage to Leave: A Response to John Cobb's Theology." In *John Cobb: Theology in Process*, edited by David Ray Griffin and Thomas J. J. Altizer, 84–98. Philadelphia: Westminster, 1977.

Davaney, Sheila Greeve. "Culture, Power, and the Quest for a Just Order." Unpublished.

———. *Divine Power: A Study of Karl Barth and Charles Hartshorne*. Philadelphia: Fortress, 1986.

———, editor. *Feminism and Process Thought: The Harvard Divinity School/Claremont Center for*

Process Studies Symposium. Symposium Series 6. New York: Mellen, 1981.

———. "Feminism, Process Thought and the Wesleyan Tradition." In *Wesleyan Theology Today*, edited by Theodore Runyon, 1–13. Nashville: Kingswood, 1985.

———. "God, Power, and the Struggle for Liberation: A Feminist Contribution." In *Charles Hartshorne's Concept of God*, edited by Santiago Sia, 57–75. Studies in Philosophy and Religion 12. Dordrecht: Kluwer, 1990.

———. "Journey from the Heartland." Unpublished.

———. "Process Thought." In *An A to Z of Feminist Theology*, edited by Lisa Isherwood and Dorothea McEwan, 189–92. Sheffield, UK: Sheffield Academic, 1996.

Doak, Mary. "Feminism, Pragmatism, and Utopia: A Catholic Theological Response." *American Journal of Theology and Philosophy* 24 (2003) 22–39.

Dombrowski, Daniel A., and Robert Deltete. *A Brief, Liberal, Catholic Defense of Abortion.* Urbana: University of Illinois Press, 2000.

Dunfee, Sue. "The Sin of Hiding: A Feminist Critique of Reinhold Niebuhr's Account of the Sin of Pride." *Soundings* 65 (1982) 316–27.

Eaton, Heather. *Introducing Ecofeminist Theologies.* Introductions in Feminist Theology 12. London: T. & T. Clark, 2005.

Estebanez, Emilio G. Review of *Der Ich-Wahn*, by Catherine Keller. *Estudios Filosóficos* 42 (1993) 208–9.

Famisaran, Trisha. "Chung Hyun Kyung: What Women Want in the Islamic Worlds." *Process Perspectives: Newsmagazine of the Center for Process Studies* 30 (2008) 12.

Farmer, Ronald L. "Women Who Followed Jesus: Reflections on Luke 8:1–3 and John 19:25b–27." *Creative Transformation* 13.2 (2004) 12–13.

Frankenberry, Nancy. "Classical Theism, Panentheism, and Pantheism: On the Relation between God Construction and Gender Construction." *Zygon* 28 (1993) 29–45.

———. "Philosophy of Religion: Philosophy of Religion in Different Voices." In *Philosophy in a Feminist Voice: Critiques and Reconstructions*, edited by Janet A. Kourany, 173–203. Princeton: Princeton University Press, 1998.

———. "Pragmatists, Predatory Males, and Tough Broads." *American Journal of Theology and Philosophy* 24 (2003) 40–52.

Frost, Edward A. "Toward a Theology of Relationship." In *Resources for Study and Worship*, edited by F. Forrester Church, 6–18. What Unitarian Univeralists Believe: Living Principles for a Living Faith. Boston: Unitarian Universalist Denominational Grants Panel, 1987.

Fulkerson, Mary McClintock. *Changing the Subject: Women's Discourses and Feminist Theology.* Minneapolis: Fortress, 1994.

Gelpi, Donald L. "A Peircean Approach to Trinity as Community: A Response to Some Responses." *Horizons* 27 (2000) 114–30.

Goodman, Amy, and Ellie Smeal. "This Is What a Feminist Looks Like." Online: *Democracy Now*, http://www.democracynow.org/2009/1/27/ms_magazine_on_barack_obama_this/.

Grant, Colin. "Feminist Theology Is Middle Class." *Encounter* 45 (1984) 393–402.

Grant, Jacquelyn. "The Sin of Servanthood." In *A Troubling in My Soul: Womanist Perspectives on Evil and Suffering.* Edited by Emilie M. Townes. Maryknoll, NY: Orbis, 1993.

Grau, Marion. "Caribou and Carbon Colonialism: Toward a Theology of Arctic Place." In *Ecospirit: Religions and Philosophies for the Earth*, edited by Laurel Kerns and Catherine Keller, 433–53. New York: Fordham University Press, 2007.

———. "Divine Commerce—A Post-Colonial Christology for Times of Neo-Colonial Empire." In *Postcolonial Theologies: Divinity and Empire*, edited by Catherine Keller et al., 164–84. St. Louis: Chalice, 2004.

———. *Of Divine Economy: Refinancing Redemption.* New York: T. & T. Clark, 2004.

Griffin, David R. "The World as God's Body: A Response to Sallie McFague's Postmodern Metaphorical Theology." Unpublished.

Gu, Linyu. "Process and Shin No Jiko ('True Self'): A Critique of Feminist Interpretation of 'Self-Emptying.'" *Journal of Chinese Philosophy* 27 (2000) 201–14.

Guenther-Gleason, Patricia Ellen. *On Schleiermacher and Gender Politics.* Harvard Theological Studies 43. Harrisburg, PA: Trinity, 1997.

Harrison, Beverly Wildung. Review of *Feminism and Process Thought: The Harvard Divinity School/Claremont Center for Process Studies Symposium Papers*, edited by Sheila Greeve Davaney. *Signs* 7 (1982) 704–10.

Haraway, Donna. "The Search for Organizing Relations: An Organismic Paradigm in 20th-

Bibliography

Century Developmental Biology." PhD diss., Yale University, 1972.

Hart, Richard E. "Susanne K. Langer, 1895–1985." In *The Blackwell Guide to American Philosophy*, edited by Armen T. Marsoobian and John Ryder, 239–46. Blackwell Philosophy Guides 16. Malden, MA: Blackwell, 2004.

Hartshorne, Charles. "Male Bias in Theology." In *Omnipotence and Other Theological Mistakes*, 56–57. Albany: State University of New York Press, 1984.

Heyward, Isabel Carter. *The Redemption of God: A Theology of Mutual Relation*. Washington, DC: University Press of America, 1982.

———. "An Unfinished Symphony of Liberation: The Radicalization of Christian Feminism among White U.S. Women: A Review Essay." *Journal of Feminist Studies in Religion* 1 (1985) 99–118.

Heyward, Linda. Review of *Gaia and God: An Ecofeminist Theology of Earth Healing*, by Rosemary Radford Ruether. *Earthlight* 20 (Spring 1993) 17.

Hoeft, Jeanne M. *Agency, Culture, and Human Personhood: Pastoral Theology and Intimate Partner Violence*. Princeton Theological Monograph Series 97. Eugene, OR: Pickwick Publications, 2009.

———. "Toward a Pastoral Theology of Resistance to Violence." *Journal of Pastoral Theology* 16 (2006) 35–52.

Holmes, Barbara. "Exposing the Hustle, Reclaiming the Flow: Film and the Lure of Processive Liberation Theologies. Paper presented at the American Academy of Religion annual meeting. Philadelphia, 21 November 2005.

Hough-Trapp, Andrea. "The Process God as Pregnant Mother." Unpublished.

Howell, Nancy R. "Abortion and Religion." In *New Essays on Abortion and Bioethics*, edited by Rem B. Edwards, 125–49. Advances in Bioethics 2. Greenwich, CT: Jai, 1997.

———. "Beyond *A Feminist Cosmology*." In *Constructing a Relational Cosmology*, edited by Paul O. Ingram, 104–16. Princeton Theological Monograph Series 62. Eugene, OR: Pickwick Publications, 2006.

———. "Challenging the Hierarchical Mind." *Prism* 8.1–2 (1995) 12–14.

———. "Co-Creation, Co-Redemption, and Genetics." *American Journal of Theology and Philosophy* 20 (1999) 147–63.

———. "Domestic Violence Resources for the Classroom." *Newsletter of the Women's Caucus: Religious Studies* 4.2 (1995) 6–7.

———. "Ecofeminism: What One Needs to Know." The Teachers' File. *Zygon: Journal of Religion and Science* 32 (1997) 231–41.

———. "Ecofeminist Thinking and Living with Antihierarchicalism." Unpublished.

———. "Embodied Transcendence: Bonobos and Humans in Community." *Zygon: Journal of Religion and Science* 44 (2009) 601–12.

———, guest editor. "Feminism and Process Thought." Special issue, *Process Studies* 22.2 (1993).

———. "Feminism and Process Thought." *Process Studies* 22.2 (1993) 69–70.

———. "A Feminist Appreciation of Loomer's Relational Vision." Unpublished.

———. *A Feminist Cosmology: Ecology, Solidarity, and Metaphysics*. Amherst, NY: Humanity, 2000.

———. "Feminist Liberation Theology and Whiteheadian Process Theology." MTh thesis, Southeastern Baptist Theological Seminary, 1984.

———. "A Feminist Theory of Relations Based upon the Philosophy of Alfred North Whitehead." PhD diss., Claremont Graduate School, 1991.

———. "Generosity and Power: When It Is More Blessed to Receive." *Creative Transformation* 4.3 (1995) 6–10.

———. "A God Adequate for Primate Culture." *Journal of Religion and Society* 3 (2001) Online: http://moses.creighton.edu/JRS/2001/2001-4.html/.

———. "Implications of Science for Religious Life." *American Journal of Theology and Philosophy* 27 (2006) 154–72.

———. "The Importance of Being Chimpanzee." *Theology and Science* 1 (2003) 179–91.

———. "The Importance of Difference in Science-Religion Course Pedagogy." In *Research in the Humanities, Sciences through Buddhist Life Perspectives*, Center for Humanities, Science and Religion, 2002–2006, edited by Ryusei Takeda, 201–15. Kyoto, Japan: Ryukoku University, 2007.

———. "In Response to David L. Wheeler." In *Searching for an Adequate God: A Dialogue between Process and Free Will Theists*, edited by John B. Cobb Jr. and Clark H. Pinnock, 149–54. Grand Rapids: Eerdmans, 2000.

———. "Living in the Matrix: A Whiteheadian Ecofeminist Reflection on Hierarchy." In *Research in the Humanities, Sciences through Buddhist Life Perspectives*, Center for Humanities, Science and Religion, 2002–2006, edited by Ryusei Takeda, 217–41. Kyoto, Japan: Ryukoku University, 2007.

———. "Openness and Process Theism: Respecting the Integrity of Two Views." In *Searching for an Adequate God: A Dialogue between Process and Free Will Theists*, edited by John B. Cobb Jr. and Clark H. Pinnock, 53–79. Grand Rapids: Eerdmans, 2000.

———. "The Paradox of Power: An Ecofeminist Reflection upon Diversity and Value." In *Religious Experience and Ecological Responsibility*, edited by Donald Crosby and Charley D. Hardwick, 207–24. American Liberal Religious Thought 3. New York: Lang, 1996.

———. "The Promise of a Process Feminist Theory of Relations." *Process Studies* 17.2 (1988) 78–87.

———. "The Promise of Buddhist-Christian Dialogue on Science and Religion: Continuing Dialogue on Ecology." In *Buddhism and Science: Buddhism and Environmental Bioethics: Buddhist-Christian Dialogue*, Center for Humanities, Science and Religion, 2002–2006, edited by Ryusei Takeda, 35–45. Kyoto, Japan: Ryukoku University, 2007.

———. "Radical Relatedness and Feminist Separatism." In *Que(e)rying Religion: A Critical Anthology*, edited by Susan E. Henking and Gary D. Comstock, 171–77. New York: Continuum, 1997.

———. "Radical Relatedness and Feminist Separatism." *Process Studies* 18.2 (1989) 118–26.

———. "Relations between *Homo Sapiens* and Other Animals: Scientific and Religious Arguments." In *The Oxford Handbook of Religion and Science*, edited by Philip Clayton and Zachary Simpson, 945–61. Oxford Handbooks. Oxford: Oxford University Press, 2006.

———. "Science, Religion, and Women." In *The Encyclopedia of Women and World Religion*, edited by Serinity Young et al., 2:873–75. 2 vols. New York: Macmillan, 1999.

———. "Theism." In *The Encyclopedia of Women and World Religion*, edited by Serinity Young, 2:970–71. New York: Macmillan Reference USA, 1999.

———. "A Theologian Coming to Voice." *Dialog: A Journal of Theology* 37 (1998) 231–41.

———. "Uniqueness in Context." *Zygon: Journal of Religion and Science* 42 (2008) 493–503.

———. "Uniqueness in Context." *American Journal of Theology and Philosophy* 28 (2007) 364–77.

———. "A Whiteheadian Case for Diversity in Science and Religion." *CTNS Bulletin: The Center for Theology and the Natural Sciences* 19.4 (1999) 3–10.

Huffaker, Lucinda Stark. *Creative Dwelling: Empathy and Clarity in God and Self.* American Academy of Religion Academy Series 98. Atlanta: Scholars, 1998.

———. "Feminist Theology in Process Perspective." In *Handbook of Process Theology*, edited by Jay McDaniel and Donna Bowman, 177–87. St. Louis: Chalice, 2006.

Hunt, Mary E. Review of The *Coming of Lilith: Essays on Feminism, Judaism, and Sexual Ethics*, by Judith Plaskow. *Journal of the American Academy of Religion* 74 (2006) 998–1001.

Ingram, Paul O., editor. *Constructing a Relational Cosmology*. Princeton Theological Monograph Series 62. Eugene, OR: Pickwick Publications, 2006.

Jantzen, Grace M. "A God according to Our Own Gender." In *Becoming Divine: Towards a Feminist Philosophy of Religion*. Bloomington: Indiana University Press, 1999.

Joh, Wonhee Anne. *The Heart of the Cross: A Postcolonial Christology*, Louisville: Westminster John Knox, 2006.

———. "Korean American Feminist Hybrid Prehensions: Feminist Relationality, Postcolonial Difference, and the Power of Jeong." Paper presented at the fifth International Whitehead Conference, Seoul, Korea, 27 May 2004. Unpublished.

Keady, Richard E. "Post-Patriarchal Process-Feminist Dialogue: Death's Contributions to the Creative Advance." Unpublished.

———. "Theology and Sexuality: The Classification of Theistic Doctrines and the Sexual Experience of God." Unpublished.

Keiller, Barbara Booth. "Discovering Yoni Energy: Lifting the Veils of Religious Syncretism." Unpublished.

Keller, Catherine. "Afterword." In *Through the Earth Darkly: Female Spirituality in Comparative Perspective*, edited by Jordan Paper, 267–69. New York: Continuum, 1997.

Bibliography

———. *Apocalypse Now and Then: A Feminist Guide to the End of the World.* Boston: Beacon Press, 1996.

———. "Burning Tongues: A Feminist Trinitarian Epistemology." In *Introduction to Christian Theology: Contemporary North American Perspectives*, edited by Roger A. Badham, 225–36. Louisville: Westminster John Knox, 1998.

———. "Christianity." In *A Companion to Feminist Philosophy*, edited by Alison M. Jaggar and Iris Marion Young, 225–35. Blackwell Companions to Philosophy 13. Malden, MA: Blackwell, 1998.

———. "Delores Williams: Survival, Surrogacy, Sisterhood, Spirit." *Union Seminary Quarterly Review* 58 (2004) 84–94.

———. "Eschatology." In *Dictionary of Feminist Theologies*, edited by Letty M. Russell and J. Shannon Clarkson, 86–87. Louisville: Westminster John Knox, 1996.

———. *Face of the Deep: A Theology of Becoming.* London: Routledge, 2003.

———. "Feminism and the Ethic of Inseparability." In *Women's Consciousness, Women's Conscience: A Reader in Feminist Ethics*, edited by Barbara Adolsen et al., 251–63. Minneapolis: Winston, 1985.

———. "The Flesh of God: A Metaphor in the Wild." In *Theology That Matters: Ecology, Economy, and God*, edited by Darby Kathleen Ray, 91–107. Minneapolis: Fortress, 2006.

———. *From a Broken Web: Separation, Sexism, and Self.* Boston: Beacon, 1986.

———. "From Top to Bottom: The Holy Ghost and Gospel of Lynda Hart." Special issue, *Women & Performance: A Journal of Feminist Theory* (Lynda Myoun Hart Memorial Issue) 13 (2002) 147–58.

———. *God and Power: Counter-Apocalyptic Journeys.* Minneapolis: Fortress, 2005.

———. "Goddess, Ear, and Metaphor: On the Journey of Nelle Morton." *Journal of Feminist Studies in Religion* 4 (1989) 51–67.

———. "Is that All? Gift and Reciprocity in Milbank's *Being Reconciled*." In *Interpreting the Postmodern: Responses to "Radical Orthodoxy,"* edited by Rosemary Radford Ruether and Marion Grau, 18–35. New York: T. & T. Clark, 2006.

———. "The Jesus of History and the Feminism of Theology." In *Jesus and Faith: A Conversation on the Work of John Dominic Crossan*, edited by Jeffrey Carlson and Robert A. Ludwig, 71–82. Maryknoll, NY: Orbis, 1994.

———. "The Lost Chaos of Creation." *The Living Pulpit* 9.2 (2000) 4–5.

———. "The Lost Chaos of Creation." *Creative Transformation* 12.1 (2003) 2–6.

———. "Mary Daly." In *A New Handbook of Christian Theologians*, edited by Donald W. Musser and Joseph L. Price, 127–34. Nashville: Abingdon, 1996.

———. "Moaning Doves." *Theo Spirit: Newsletter of the Drew University Theological School* 4.1 (2005) 9–11.

———. "More on Feminism, Self-Sacrifice, and Time; or, Too Many Words for Emptiness." *Buddhist-Christian Studies* 13 (1993) 211–19.

———. "The Mystery of the Insoluble Evil: Violence and Eschatology in Marjorie Suchocki." In *World without End: Christian Eschatology from a Process Perspective*, edited by Joseph Bracken, 46–71. Grand Rapids: Eerdmans, 2005.

———. "Nelle Morton: 'Hearing to Speech.'" Special issue, *The Christian Century*, "In Praise of Teachers," 7–14 February 1990, 127.

———. "Of Swallowed, Walled and Wordless Women." *Soundings* 65 (1982) 328–39.

———. *On the Mystery: Discerning Divinity in Process.* Minneapolis: Fortress, 2008.

———. "Piling Together & Hopefully Saving: Eschatology as a Feminist Problem." *The Eden Journal* 1.2 (1992) 10–20.

———. "Pneumatic Nudges: The Theology of Moltmann, Feminism, and the Future." In *The Future of Theology: Essays in Honor of Jürgen Moltmann*, edited by Miroslav Volf, et al., 142–53. Grand Rapids: Eerdmans, 1996.

———. "Postmodern 'Nature,' Feminism and Community." In *Theology for Earth Community: A Field Guide*, edited by Dieter T. Hessel, 93–102. Maryknoll, NY: Orbis, 1996.

———. "The Place of Multiple Meanings: The Dragon Daughter Rides Today." *Journal of Chinese Philosophy* 32 (2005) 281–96.

———. "Roundtable Discussion: Feminist Reflections on Separation and Unity in Jewish Theology." *Journal of Feminist Studies in Religion* 2 (1986) 118–21.

———. "Salvation Flows: Eschatology for a Feminist Wesleyanism." *Quarterly Review* 23 (2003) 412–24.

———. "Scoop Up the Water and the Moon Is in your Hands: On Feminist Theology and Dynamic Self-Emptying." In *The Emptying God: A Buddhist-Jewish-Christian Conversation*, edited by John B. Cobb Jr. and

Christopher Ives, 102–15. Faith Meets Faith Series. Maryknoll, NY: Orbis, 1990.

———. "Seeking and Sucking: On Relation and Essence in Feminist Theology." In *Horizons in Feminist Theology: Identity, Tradition, and Norms*, edited by Rebecca S. Chopp and Sheila Greeve Davaney, 54–78. Minneapolis: Fortress, 1997.

———. "Separation, Sexism and Spirit." In *Spirit-Centered Wholeness beyond the Psychology of Self*, edited by H. Newton Malony et al., 61–78. Studies in the Psychology of Religion 2. Lewiston, NY: Mellen, 1988.

———. "She Talks Too Much: Magdalene Meditations." In *Toward a Theology of Eros: Transfiguring Passion at the Limits of Discipline*, edited by Virginia Burrus and Catherine Keller, 234–54. Transdisciplinary Theological Colloquia. New York: Fordham University Press, 2006.

———. "Talk about the Weather: The Greening of Eschatology." In *Ecofeminism and the Sacred*, edited by Carol J. Adams, 30–49. New York: Continuum, 1993.

———. "'To Illuminate Your Trace': Self in the Late Modern Feminist Theology." *Listening* 25 (1990) 211–24.

———. "Toward a Postpatriarchal Postmodernity." In *Spirituality and Society: Postmodern Visions*, edited by David Ray Griffin, 63–80. SUNY Series in Constructive Postmodern Thought. Albany: State University of New York Press, 1988.

———. "Toward an Emancipatory Wisdom." In *Theology and the University: Essays in Honor of John B. Cobb, Jr.*, edited by David Ray Griffin and Joseph C. Hough, Jr., 125–47. Albany: State University of New York Press, 1991.

———. "Where I Trace Your Body: Love in Process." *Creative Transformation* 8.3 (1999) 17–23.

———. "Wholeness and the King's Men." *Anima* 11 (1985) 84–95.

———. "Why Apocalypse, Now?" *Theology Today* 49 (1992) 189–95.

———. "Why Apocalypse Now?" In *Images of the End & Christian Theology*, edited by Roger Williamson, 15–28. Uppsala, Sweden: Life & Peace Institute, 1990.

———. "Women against Wasting the World: Notes on Eschatology and Ecology." In *Reweaving the World: The Emergence of Ecofeminism*, edited by Irene Diamond and Gloria Feman Orenstein, 249–63. San Francisco: Sierra Club Books, 1990

———. "Warriors, Women, and the Nuclear Complex: Toward a Postnuclear Postmodernity." In *Sacred Interconnections: Postmodern Spirituality, Political Economy, and Art*, edited by David Ray Griffin, 63–82. SUNY Series in Constructive Postmodern Thought. Albany: State University of New York Press, 1990.

Keller, Catherine, and Anne Daniell, editors. *Process and Difference: Between Cosmological and Poststructuralist Postmodernisms*. SUNY Series in Constructive Postmodern Thought. Albany: State University of New York Press, 2002.

Keller, Catherine, and Virginia Burrus, editors *Toward a Theology of Eros: Transfiguring Passion at the Limits of Discipline*. Transdisciplinary Theological Colloquia. New York: Fordham University Press, 2006.

Keller, Catherine, and Laurel Kearns, editors. *Ecospirit: Theologies and Philosophies for the Earth*. Transdisciplianry Theological Colloquia. New York: Fordham University Press, 2007.

Krafte-Jacobs, Lori. "The 'Essence' of Judaism: A Process-Relational Critique." In *Jewish Theology and Process Thought*, edited by Sandra B. Lubarsky and David Ray Griffin, 75–87. SUNY Series in Constructive Postmodern Thought. Albany: State University of New York Press, 1996.

Lambert, Jean. "Becoming Human: A Contextual Approach to Decisions about Pregnancy and Abortion." In *Feminism and Process Thought: The Harvard Divinity School/Claremont Center for Process Studies Symposium Papers*, edited by Sheila Greeve Davaney, 106–37. Symposium Series 6. New York: Mellen, 1981.

———. Review of *Our Right to Choose*, by Beverly Wildung Harrison. *Journal of Religion* 66 (1986) 90–91.

———. "Toward a Wesleyan-Feminist Christology: Can a Disembodied Christ Help Anybody?" In *Wesleyan Theology Today*, edited by Theodore Runyun, 170–79. Nashville: Kingswood, 1985.

Lancaster, Sarah Heaner. "God and the Socially Located Subject: A Process Framework for Poststructural Feminism." *Faith and Philosophy: Journal of the Society of Christian Philosophers* 19 (2002) 195–213.

Bibliography

Leclerc, Diane. "Gendered Sin? Gendered Holiness? Historical Considerations and Homiletical Implications." *Wesleyan Theological Journal* 39 (2004) 54–73.

Livezey, Lois Gehr. "Human Rights and Gender Justice: The Case of Domestic Violence." *Process Studies* 33 (2004) 199–222.

———. "Human Rights and Social Ethics." Unpublished.

———. "Women, Power, and Politics: Feminist Theology in Process Perspective." *Process Studies* 17.2 (1988) 67–77.

Lorenzen, Lynne Faber. *The College Student's Introduction to the Trinity*. Collegeville, MN: Liturgical, 1999.

Lubrasky, Sandra B. "Beauty, Feminism, and Jewish Theology." *Creative Transformation* 14.2 (2005) 2–6.

———. "Covenant and Responsible Creativity: Toward a Jewish Process Theology." In *Handbook of Process Theology*, edited by Jay McDaniel and Donna Bowman, 274–85. St. Louis: Chalice, 2006.

———. "Having a Child: Jewish Faith in the Process of Redemption." Paper presented at Process Theology and Jewish Theology, Hebrew Union College, New York City, 13–15 April 1986. Unpublished.

Lubrasky, Sandra B., and David Ray Griffin, editors. *Jewish Theology and Process Thought*. SUNY Series in Constructive Postmodern Thought. Albany: State University of New York Press, 1996.

MacNevin, Sandra A. Surette. "Mary Daly's Radical Feminist Ontology: A Whiteheadian Feminist Critique." MA critique, Claremont Graduate School, 1986.

Man, Eva Kit Wah. "The View of Nature in Eco-feminism and Chinese Philosophy." *The International Journal for Field-Being* 1 (2001). Online: http://iifb.org/journal/Vol_1/PartsI/V1P1-No10_Man_1179607914091.pdf.

Masson, Robert. "Analogy and Metaphoric Process." *Theological Studies* 62 (2001) 571–96.

McAfee, Noelle Claire. "Resisting Essence: Kristeva's Process Philosophy." *Philosophy Today* 44 supp. (2000) 77–83.

McDaniel, Jay. "Christianity in Process: The Challenge and Promise of Feminist Theology." Unpublished.

———. "Feminism, Buddhism, and Physics: Three Catalysts for a New Christianity." Unpublished.

———. "A Postpatriarchal Christianity." In *Of God and Pelicans: A Theology of Reverence for Life*. Louisville: Westminster John Knox, 1989.

———. "Self-Affirmation and Ego-Transcendence: The Encounter of Christianity with Feminism and Buddhism." *Buddhist-Christian Studies* 7 (1987) 215–32.

———. "Six Characteristics of Postpatriarchal Christianity." *Zygon: Journal of Religion and Science* 25 (1990) 187–217.

———. "Six Characteristics of Postpatriarchal Christianity." In *Readings in Ecology and Feminist Theology*, edited by Mary Heather Mackinnon and Moni McIntyre, 299–326. Kansas City: Sheed & Ward, 1995.

McDaniel, Jay, and Donna Bowman, editors. *Handbook of Process Theology*. St. Louis: Chalice, 2006.

McEwan, Dorothea. "Alienation." In *An A to Z of Feminist Theology*, edited by Lisa Isherwood and Dorothea McEwan, 5. Sheffield, UK: Sheffield Academic, 1996.

———. Review of *Models of God: Theology for an Ecological, Nuclear Age*, by Sallie McFague. *Religious Studies Review* 16 (1990) 36–40.

———. "Social Theories of Knowledge: Liberationist Appropriation and Feminist Rejoinder." Unpublished.

McFague, Sallie. *The Body of God: An Ecological Theology*. Minneapolis: Fortress, 1993.

———. *Life Abundant: Rethinking Theology and Economy for a Planet in Peril*. Minneapolis: Fortress, 2000.

———. *Metaphorical Theology: Models of God in Religious Language*. Philadelphia: Fortress, 1982.

———. "Models of God for an Ecological, Evolutionary Era: God as Mother of the Universe." In *Physics, Philosophy, and Theology: A Common Quest for Understanding*, edited by Robert J. Russell et al., 249–72. Vatican City: Vatican Observatory, 1988.

———. *Models of God: Theology for an Ecological, Nuclear Age*. Philadelphia: Fortress, 1987.

———. *A New Climate for Theology: God, the World, and Global Warming*. Minneapolis: Fortress, 2008.

———. *Speaking in Parables: A Study in Metaphor and Theology*. Philadelphia: Fortress, 1975.

———. *Super, Natural Christians: How We Should Love Nature*. Minneapolis: Fortress, 1997.

———. "The World as God's Body." *The Christian Century* 105 (20–27 July 1988) 671–73.

———. "An Earthly Theological Agenda." In *Ecofeminism and the Sacred*, edited by Carol J. Adams, 84–98. New York: Continuum, 1993.

McTernan, Vaughan. "Openings for Feminist Theorists and Theologians to Talk of the Divine: A Response to Zandra Wagoner." *American Journal of Theology and Philosophy* 28 (2007) 271–77.

———. "Performing God: God, Organicism, and Postmodernism." *American Journal of Theology and Philosophy* 23 (2002) 236–51.

Mebust, Kirsten. "*Religion in the Making* and Alfred North Whitehead," *Creative Transformation* 18.1 (2009) 15–20.

Mesle, Barbara Hiles, and C. Robert Mesle. "'Tangled, Muddy, Painful, and Perplexed': Pragmatism, Feminism, and Life." *American Journal of Theology and Philosophy* 24 (2003) 80–99.

Mooney, Regina. Response to Catherine Keller, "Gender, Justice and Generosity." Unpublished.

Moore, Mary Elizabeth Mollino. *Covenant & Call: Mission of the Future Church*. Equipping the Future Church 1. Nashville: Discipleship Resources, 2000.

———. "Critiquing Codependence Theory and Reimaging Psychotherapy: A Process-Relational Exploration." *Process Studies* 29.1 (2000) 103–23.

———. "Discovering Builder-God and Wisdom-Woman." *Creative Transformation* 12.1 (2003) 14–15.

———. "Feminist Practical Theology and the Future of the Church." In *Pastoral-Theologische Informationen: The Struggles over the Future of the Church*, edited by Harmut Heidenreich and Reinhard Schmidt-Rost, 189–209. Mainz: Pastoraltheologische Informationen, 1995.

———. "Feminist Theology and Education." In *Theological Approaches to Christian Education*, edited by Jack L. Seymour and Donald E. Miller, 63–80. Nashville: Abingdon, 1990.

———. "Imagine Peace: Knowing the Real, Imagining the Impossible." In *Handbook of Process Theology*, edited by Jay McDaniel and Donna Bowman. 201–16. St. Louis: Chalice, 2006.

———. *In the Beginning and in the Middle*. Claremont, CA: Moore Multicultural Resource and Research Center, 1997.

———. "Inclusive Language and Power: A Response to Letty Russell." *Religious Education* 80 (1985) 603–14.

———. *Ministering with the Earth*. St. Louis: Chalice, 1998.

———. "One Spirit—Many Stories: Contemporary Laywomen Share Their Vocational Visions." In *Spirituality and Social Responsibility: Vocational Vision of Women in the United Methodist Tradition*, edited by Rosemary Skinner Keller, 265–88. Nashville: Abingdon, 1993.

———. *Teaching from the Heart: Theology and Educational Method*. Minneapolis: Fortress, 1991.

———. "The Unity of the Sacred and the Public: Possibilities from Feminist Theology." In *Theological Perspectives on Christian Formation: A Reader on Theology and Christian Education*, edited by Jeff Astley et al., 264–89, 329. Grand Rapids: Eerdmans, 1996.

———. "Wisdom, Sophia, and the Fear of Knowing." *Religious Education* 92 (1997) 227–43.

———. "Women and Men in the Social Order." In *Religious Education as Social Transformation*, edited by Allen J. Moore, 66–91. Birmingham, AL: Religious Education Press, 1989.

Moore, Mary Elizabeth Mollino, and Yolanda Y. Smith. "Olivia Pearl Stokes: A Living Testimony of Faith." In *Faith of Our Foremothers: Women Changing Religious Education*, edited by Barbara Anne Keely, 100–120. Louisville: Westminster John Knox, 1997.

Morgan, Kathryn Pauly. "Desperately Seeking Evelyn, or, Alternatively, Exploring Pedagogies of the Personal in Alfred North Whitehead and Feminist Theory." *Philosophy of Education* (2001) 369–77.

Nelson, Julie A. "Breaking the Dynamic of Control: A Feminist Approach to Economic Ethics." Unpublished.

———. "Clocks, Creation and Clarity: Insights on Ethics and Economics from a Feminist Perspective." *Ethical Theory and Moral Practice* 7 (2004) 381–98.

———. "Confronting the Science/Value Split: Notes on Feminist Economics, Institutionalism, Pragmatism, and Process Thought." *Cambridge Journal of Economics* 27 (2003) 49–64.

———. "Once More, With Feeling: Feminist/Process Economics Meets Critical Realism." Unpublished.

———. "Value as Relationality: Feminist, Pragmatist, and Process Thought Meet Economics." *Journal of Speculative Philosophy* 15 (2001) 137–51.

Bibliography

Nelson, Susan. *Beyond Servanthood: Christianity and the Liberation of Women*. Lanham, MD: University Press of America, 1989.

———. *Healing the Broken Heart: Sin, Alienation, and the Gift of Grace*. St. Louis: Chalice Press, 1997.

———. "Sin and the Possibility of Social Transformation: Reinhold Niebuhr's Doctrine of Sin and Self-Sacrifice Revisited." Unpublished.

———. "The Sin of Hiding: A Feminist Critique of Reinhold Niebuhr's Account of the Sin of Pride." *Soundings* 65 (1982) 316–27.

———. "Women in Ministry: Estrangement from Ourselves." *Quarterly Review* 9 (1989) 52–74.

Nietzsche, Friedrich. *The Portable Nietzsche*. Selected and translated, with an introduction and notes by Walter Kaufmann. The Viking Portable Library. New York: Viking, 1954.

O'Conner, June. "A Christian Feminist Concept of God." Unpublished.

———. "Response to *Models of God for an Ecological Nuclear Age: The World as the Body of God*, by Sallie McFague." Unpublished.

———. "Sensuality, Spirituality, Sacramentality." *Union Seminary Quarterly Review* 40 (1985) 57–70.

Ogden, Schubert. "Is the Gospel Message Liberating for Women?" *Perkins School of Theology Journal* 38.3 (1985) 19–21.

Peacocke, Arthur R., and Ann Pederson. *The Music of Creation*. Theology and the Sciences. Minneapolis: Fortress, 2005.

Pederson, Ann Milliken. "All God's Critters: Feminist Theology and Darwin." *Word and World* 29.1 (2009) 47–55.

———. "The Centrality of Incarnation," *Zygon: Journal of Religion and Science* 43 (2008) 57–65

———. "Feminist Cosmology." In *Encyclopedia of Science and Religion*, edited by J. Wentzel Vrede van Huyssteen et al., 326–27. New York: Macmillan, 2003.

———. "Feminist Perspectives in Theology and Medicine." In *The Oxford Handbook of Religion and Science*, edited by Philip Clayton and Zachary Simpson, 836–49. Oxford Handbooks. Oxford: Oxford University Press, 2006.

———. "Feminist Theology." In *Encyclopedia of Science and Religion*, edited by J. Wentzel Vrede van Huyssteen et al., 327–29. New York: Macmillan, 2003.

———. *God, Creation, and All That Jazz: A Process of Composition and Improvisation*. St. Louis: Chalice, 2001.

———. "Instability and Dissonance: Provocations from Sandra Harding." *Zygon: Journal of Religion and Science* 30 (1995) 369–82.

———. "Two Reformers: Luther and Pilates." *Currents in Theology and Mission* 36 (2009) 287–90.

———. "South Dakota and Abortion: A Local Story of How Religion, Medical Science, and Culture Meet." *Zygon: Journal of Religion and Science* 42.1 (2007) 123–32

———. *Where in the World is God? Variations on a Theme*. St. Louis: Chalice, 1998.

Pederson, Ann Milliken, and William Watson. "Abortion." In *Encyclopedia of Science and Religion*, edited by J. Wentzel Vrede van Huyssteen et al., 1:1–4. 2 vols. New York: Macmillan, 2002.

Plaskow, Judith. *Sex, Sin and Grace: Women's Experience and the Theologies of Reinhold Niebuhr and Paul Tillich*. Washington, DC: University Press of America, 1980.

———. *Standing Again at Sinai*. San Fran-cisco: Harper & Row, 1990.

Poling, James N. *Deliver Us from Evil: Resisting Racial and Gender Oppression*. Minneapolis: Fortress, 1996.

———. "God, Sex and Power." *Theology and Sexuality* 11.2 (2005) 55–70.

Porter, Jean. "The Feminization of God: Second Thoughts on the Ethical Implications of Process Theology." Unpublished.

Riswold, Caryn. *Coram Deo: Human Life in the Vision of God*. Princeton Theological Monograph Series 58. Eugene, OR: Pickwick Publications, 2006.

———. "*Coram Mundo*: A Lutheran Feminist Anthropology of Hope" *Dialog: A Journal of Theology* 48.2 (2009) 132–39.

———. "*Imago Dei* and *Coram Mundo*: Theological Anthropology for Human Life Today, or The World Is the Woman." *Journal of Lutheran Ethics* 8 (2008). Online: http://www.elca.org/What-We-Believe/Social-Issues/Journal-of-Lutheran-Ethics/Issues/January-2008/Imago-Dei-and-Coram-Mundo-Theological-Anthropology-for-Human-Life-Today-or-The-World-is-The-Woman.aspx.

Rivera, Mayra. "Ethical Desires: Toward a Theology of Relational Transcendence." In *Toward a Theology of Eros: Transfiguring Passion at the Limits of Discipline*, edited by Virginia

Burrus and Catherine Keller, 255–70. Transdisciplinary Theological Colloquia. New York: Fordham University Press, 2006.

———. "God at the Crossroads: A Postcolonial Reading of Sophia." In *The Postcolonial Biblical Reader*, edited by R. S. Sugirtharajah, 238–54. Oxford: Blackwell, 2006.

——— et al., editors. *Postcolonial Theologies: Divinity and Empire*. St. Louis: Chalice, 2004.

———."Radical Transcendence: A Latina Postcolonial Reading of Divine Otherness." In *Interpreting the Postmodern: Responses to "Radical Orthodoxy,"* edited by Rosemary Radford Ruether and Marion Grau, 119–40. New York: T. & T. Clark, 2006.

———. *The Touch of Transcendence: A Postcolonial Theology of God*. Louisville: Westminster John Knox, 2007.

Ross, Mary Ellen. "Feminism and the Problem of Moral Character." *Journal of Feminist Studies in Religion* 5.2 (1989) 47–64.

Ross, Susan A. "Women, Beauty, and Justice: Moving beyond von Balthasar." *Journal of the Society of Christian Ethics* 25 (2005) 79–98.

Ruether, Rosemary Radford. "Christianity and the Family: Ancient Challenge, Modern Crisis." Lecture given at St. Jerome's Centre for Catholic Experience, St. Jerome's University, Waterloo, Ontario, 9 March 2001.

———. "Ecofeminism: First and Third World Women." *American Journal of Theology and Philosophy* 18 (1997) 33–45.

———. *Gaia & God: An Ecofeminist Theology of Earth Healing*. San Francisco: HarperSanFrancisco, 1992.

———. *Sexism and God-Talk: Toward A Feminist Theology*. Boston: Beacon, 1983.

Ruether, Rosemary Radford, and Marion Grau, editors. *Interpreting the Postmodern: Responses to "Radical Orthodoxy."* New York: T. & T. Clark, 2006.

Russell, Helene T. "Process Theology and the Lectionary: Sermons and Sermon Themes on the Lectionary Readings from the Perspective of Process Theology." Center for Process and Faith, Claremont, CA, 2005. Online: http://www.processandfaith.org/.

———. "We are One, but We Are Not the Same: Diversity and Unity." *Encounter* 67 (2006) 75–80.

———. "Women and Ministry." *Encounter* 65 (2004) 1–8.

Saiving, Valerie. "Androgynous Life: A Feminist Appropriation of Process Thought." In *Feminism and Process Thought: The Harvard Divinity School/Claremont Center for Process Studies Symposium Papers*, edited by Sheila Greeve Davaney, 11–31. Symposium Series 6. New York: Mellen, 1981.

———. "The Human Situation: A Feminine View." In *Womanspirit Rising: A Feminist Reader in Religion*, edited by Carol P. Christ and Judith Plaskow, 25–42. San Francisco: Harper & Row, 1979.

———. "The Human Situation: A Feminine View." In *Creation and Humanity: The Sources of Christian Theology*, edited by Ian A. McFarland, 289–303. The Sources of Christian Theology. Louisville: Westminster John Knox, 2009.

———. "Our Bodies/Our Selves: Reflections on Sickness, Aging and Death." Unpublished.

Schofield, Chuck. "Responses to Globalization from an Ethic of Interdependence: How Normative Ethics Derivable from the Relational Worldviews of Process and Feminist Theologies Can Help America Respond to Globalization." MA thesis, Claremont School of Theology, 2007.

Schroeder, Susan G. "Woman . . . You Are Free!" *Creative Transformation* 4.1 (1994) 9–12.

Schwarz, Hans. "Evil in Contemporary Theological Discussion." In *Evil: A Historical and Theological Perspective*, 163–98. Translated by Mark Worthing. Minneapolis: Fortress, 1995.

Soelle, Dorothee, and Shirley A. Cloyes. *To Work and to Love: A Theology of Creation*. Philadelphia: Fortress, 1984.

Stupar, Lisa. "Implications of Bracken's Process Model of the Trinity for Contemporary Feminist Theology." *Horizons* 27 (2000) 256–75.

Suchocki, Marjorie Hewitt. "Anxiety and Trust in the Feminist Experience." *Journal of Religion* 60 (1980) 459–71.

———. "The Birth of Death." *The Christian Century* 102.7 (27 February 1985) 229–30.

———. "The Challenge of Mary Daly." *Encounter* 41 (1980) 307–17.

———. "Civil Religion and the Women's Movement." Unpublished.

———. "Coming Home: Wesley, Whitehead, and Women." *The Drew Gateway* 57.3 (1987) 31–43.

———. "Earthsong, Godsong: Women's Spirituality." *Theology Today* 45 (1989) 392–402.

———. *The End of Evil: Process Eschatology in a Historical Context*. SUNY Series in

Bibliography

Philosophy. Albany: State University of New York Press, 1988.

———. *The Fall to Violence: Original Sin in Relational Theology.* New York: Continuum.

———. *God, Christ, Church: A Practical Guide to Process Theology.* New rev. ed. New York: Crossroad, 1989.

———. "God for Us." PhD diss., Claremont Graduate School, 1974.

———. "God, Sexism, and Transformation." In *Reconstructing Christian Theology,* edited by Rebecca Chopp and Mark Lewis Taylor, 25–48. Minneapolis: Fortress, 1994.

———. "Holiness: An Ecclesiology of Renewal." Unpublished.

———. "The Idea of God in Feminist Philosophy." *Hypatia* 9.4 (1994) 57–68.

———. *In God's Presence: Theological Reflections on Prayer.* St. Louis: Chalice, 1996.

———. "In Search of Justice: Religious Pluralism from a Feminist Perspective." In *The Myth of Christian Uniqueness: Toward a Pluralistic Theology of Religions,* edited by John Hick and Paul F. Knitter, 149–60. Maryknoll, NY: Orbis, 1987.

———. "Openness and Mutuality in Process Thought and Feminist Action." In *Feminism and Process Thought: The Harvard Divinity School/Claremont Center for Process Studies Symposium Papers,* edited by Sheila Greeve Davaney, 62–82. Symposium Series 6. New York: Mellen, 1981.

———. "Review of *Apocalypse Now and Then: A Feminist Guide to the End of the World,* by Catherine Keller." *Process Studies* 29 (2000) 179–83.

———. "A Servant Office: The Ordination of Women." *Religion in Life* 47 (1978) 197–210.

———, et al., editors. *Sunde: Eine universtandlich Gewordenes.* Heidelberg: Neukirchener, 1997.

———. "Theological Foundations for Ethnic and Gender Diversity in Faculties or Excellence and the Motley Crew." *Theological Education* 26.2 (1990) 35–50.

———. "The Unmale God: Reconsidering the Trinity." Unpublished.

———. "Utopia, Dystopia: The Pragmatic Value of Vision." *American Journal of Theology and Philosophy* 24 (2003) 53–60.

———. "Weaving the World." *Process Studies* 14.2 (1985) 76–86.

———. *The Whispered Word: A Theology of Preaching.* St. Louis: Chalice, 1999.

Sullivan, Shannon. "Intersections between Pragmatist and Continental Feminism." In *The Stanford Encyclopedia of Philosophy,* edited by Edward N. Zalta. 2004. Online: http://plato.stanford.edu/archives/fall2004/entries/femapproach-prag-cont/.

Thandeka. "The Self between Feminist Theory and Theology." In *Horizons in Feminist Theology: Identity, Tradition, and Norms,* edited by Rebecca S. Chopp and Sheila Greeve Davaney, 79–98. Minneapolis: Fortress, 1997.

Thie, Marilyn. "Dethroning the Patriarchal God: A Whiteheadian Analysis." Unpublished.

———. "Feminist Concerns and Whitehead's Theory of Perception." *Process Studies* 8 (1978) 186–91.

———. "A Whiteheadian Method for Feminist Theology." Unpublished.

Todd, Douglas. "Deciding 'Magic' Moment of Personhood." *Vancouver Sun,* 8 December 1990: D15.

Tomm, Winnie. *Bodied Mindfulness: Women's Spirits, Bodies, and Places.* Waterloo, ON: Wilfrid Laurier University Press, 1995.

———. "Embodied Spiritual Consciousness: Beyond Psychology." *Feminist Theology* 10.30 (2002) 8–29.

———. "A Religious Philosophy of Self." In *Gender, Genre and Religion: Feminist Reflections,* edited by Morny Joy and Eva K. Neumaier-Dagyay, 239–55. Waterloo, Ontario : Wilfrid Laurier University Press, 1995.

Trelsted, Marit. "All is Not Lost: Solidarity and the Particularity of Love." In *Constructing a Relational Cosmology,* edited by Paul Ingram, 17–36. Princeton Theological Monograph Series 62. Eugene, OR: Pickwick Publications, 2006.

———, editor. *Cross Examinations: Readings on the Meaning of the Cross Today.* Minneapolis: Fortress, 2006.

———. "Defining the Self in a Relational Philosophical Theology." PhD diss., Claremont Graduate University, 2000.

———. "The Ethics of Effective Teaching: Challenges from the Religious Right and Critical Pedagogy." *Teaching Theology and Religion* 11.4 (2008) 191–202.

———. "Lavish Love: A Covenantal Ontology." In *Cross Examinations: Readings on the Meaning of the Cross Today.* Minneapolis: Fortress, 2006.

———. "Relationality Plus Individuality: The Value of Creative Self Agency." *Dialog: A Journal of Theology* 38.3 (1999) 193–98.

———. "The Way of Salvation in Luther's Theology: A Feminist Evaluation." *Dialog: A Journal of Theology* 45.3 (2006) 236–45.

———, and Christian Batalden Scharen. "Remembering Re-Imagining." *Dialog: A Journal of Theology* 33.3 (1994) 230–32.

Ulshöfer, Gotlind. "A Whiteheadian Business Ethics and the Western Hemisphere." *Journal of Business Ethics* 23 (2000) 67–71.

Viney, Donald W. "Taking Feminism Seriously in the Philosophy of Religion." Unpublished.

Voskuil, Duane. "Review of *She Who Changes: Re-Imagining the Divine in the World*, by Carol P. Christ." *Process Studies* 33 (2004) 341–43.

Walker, Corey D. B. "Review of *Face of the Deep: A Theology of Becoming* by Catherine Keller. *Journal of the American Academy of Religion* 75 (2007) 733–36.

Wang, Zhihe. "What Can Whitehead's Philosophy Contribute to Feminism?" *Process Studies* 31 (2002) 125–37.

Washbourn, Penelope. *Becoming Woman: The Quest for Wholeness in Female Experience*. New York: Harper & Row, 1979.

———. "The Change of Life." In *Sexuality and the Sacred: Sources for Theological Reflection*, edited by James B. Nelson and Sandra P. Longfellow, 288–96. Louisville: Westminster John Knox, 1994.

———. "The Dynamics of Female Experience: Process Models and Human Values." In *Feminism and Process Thought: The Harvard Divinity School/Claremont Center for Process Studies Symposium Papers*, edited by Sheila Greeve Davaney, 83–105. Symposium Series 6. New York: Mellen, 1981.

———. *Fasen in Het leven de Vrouw*. Ontwikkelingen in de Jungiaanse psychologie.. Rotterdam: Leminscat, 1985.

———. "Process Thought and a Theology of Sexuality." In *God, Sex, and the Social Project: The Glassboro Papers on Religion and Sexuality*, edited by James H. Grace, 21–37. Symposium Series 2. New York: Mellen, 1978.

———, compiler. *Seasons of Woman: Song, Poetry, Prayer, Myth, and Story*. New York: Harper & Row, 1979.

Watkins, June. "Arabinda Basu: A Hindu Process Thinker." *Process Perspectives* 22.1 (1999) 13.

———. "Earthism vs. Economism: The Theology of John Cobb." *Process Perspectives* 22.3 (2000) 12.

———. "Faith, Wealth, and Community Leadership." *Process Perspectives* 21.2 (1998) 10.

Weeden, Theodore. "Mary: A Protestant Perspective." Unpublished.

Whitehead, Alfred North. "Liberty and the Enfranchisement of Women." *Process Studies* 7 (1977) 37–39.

———. *Process and Reality: An Essay in Cosmology*. Edited by David Ray Griffin and Donald W. Sherburne. Corrected edition. Gifford Lectures 1927–1928. New York: Free Press, 1978.

Williams, Daniel Day. "Justice between Men and Women" (section of ch. 12). In *The Spirit and the Forms of Love*, 241. New York: Harper & Row, 1968.

Williams, Delores. "A Womanist Perspective on Sin." In *A Troubling in My Soul: Womanist Perspectives on Evil and Suffering*. Edited by Emilie M. Townes. Maryknoll, NY: Orbis, 1993.

Wise, Constance. "An Alternative to Gender Essentialism Based on Process Thought." *Process Studies* 34 (2005) 279–96.

———. *Hidden Circles in the Web: Feminist Wicca, Occult Knowledge, and Process Thought*. The Pagan Studies Series. Lanham, MD: AltaMira, 2008.

———. "Power in the Sacred Circle: A Metaphysics for Feminist Wicca Based on Process Thought." PhD diss., Iliff School of Theology, 2003.

———. "A Process Epistemology for Wiccan Occult Knowledge." *The Pomegranate: International Journal of Pagan Studies* 6 (2004) 119–211.

The Women's Movement for Justice and Peace. "The Cry of Zairian Women: We Want Peace!" Letter dated 7 November 1996. Unpublished.

Young, Katherine K. "Having Your Cake and Eating It Too: Feminism and Religion." *Journal of the American Academy of Religion* 67 (1999) 167–98.

Young, Pamela Dickey. *Christ in a Post-Christian World: How Can We Believe in Jesus Christ When Those around Us Believe Differently—Or Not at All?* Minneapolis: Fortress, 1995.

———. *Feminist Theology/Christian Theology: In Search of Method*. Eugene, OR: Wipf & Stock, 2000.

———. *Re-creating the Church: Communities of Eros*. Harrisburg: Trinity, 2000.

———. "The Resurrection of Whose Body? A Feminist Look at the Question of Transcendence." *Feminist Theology* 30 (2002) 44–51.

Index

abstraction, 21, 58, 61, 106
actual occasion, 14, 33, 38–40, 51, 54, 66, 185; absolute minimum, 67; actual entities, 14, 37–38, 131; actual worlds, 15, 17, 39; drops of experience, 14, 94; finite occasion, 53–55; fundamental actualities, 41–42; *see also* process philosophy
African American, xv, 4, 8, 10, 24, 84, 114, 127, 138–39, 141–43, 163, 204, 213, 216–17, 223–24, 229; diaspora, 216–17; *see also* feminism: black, womanism
ancestors, 141, 146, 152, 213, 215, 217–27, 229, 230
androgyny, 32–37, 40–45, 86; *see also* misogyny
animals, xiv, 4, 14, 18, 27, 42, 64–65, 68–70, 73, 117–18, 130, 145–46, 149–59, 172, 194–95, 200, 209, 217; morality, 145, 150–54, 218; *see also* bonobos, chimpanzees, God: image of, primates, uniqueness
anthropocentrism, 21, 126; *see also* cosmocentrism
Arachnean spirituality, 95–97, 99
Aristotle, 12, 47, 58
Asian American, 112, 206
Augustine, 47, 58, 75, 135–36, 155

Baker, Vanessa, 127, 129, 138–39
Baker-Fletcher, Karen, xv, 127, 142–44, 222, 224; *see also* womanism
Bateson, Mary Catherine, 160–63, 165–66, 168, 169, 176
becoming, 14–17, 38–39, 51, 53–55, 77, 80, 93, 99, 130–31, 158, 185, 191, 213–14, 220, 224, 226; *see also* substance, process philosophy
bonobos, 146–47, 153; *see also* animals, primates
breath of life, 118, 122, 205

Brock, Rita Nakashima, xv, 11, 23, 27, 101, 110–12, 198
Buddhism, 11, 19, 196, 199, 204, 206

chimpanzees, 145–158; *see also* animals, primates, uniqueness
Christ, Carol P., xv, 5, 11, 89, 95–96, 122, 194, 198, 208, 210, 212, 218
Christianity, 3, 11, 19, 48, 60, 62, 71, 74–75, 104, 110–12, 121, 123–24, 129, 142, 144, 155, 167–70, 179, 202, 210, 214–17, 229; Christian theology, xiii, 13, 63, 74–75, 98, 111, 122–23, 158–60, 176; Christology, 10, 62, 101, 110–11, 139, 168–71; *see also* Jesus
Claremont: Graduate School, 46, 60, 74, 85, 101, 145, 178, 213; School of Theology, 13, 46, 74, 142, 213; *see also* Cobb, John B., Jr.
Cobb, John B., Jr., xiv–xv, 66, 72, 111, 142–43, 168–72; biography of, xiv–xv, 13–14; *see also* Hartshorne, Charles, process philosophy
co-creation, 103, 106–7, 110, 160, 173, 176, 194–95, 208, 211; created co-creator, 172–76; *see also* Hefner, Philip
Coleman, Monica, xv–xvi, xviii, 4, 131–32, 213, 227–30; *see also* womanism
communication, 7, 46, 94, 117, 146, 148, 153–54, 206, 217
concrescence, 15, 38–40, 42, 44, 51–55, 167, 185, 188; *see also* creativity, process philosophy
constructive theology, 24, 72, 74, 85, 127, 160, 227
cosmocentrism, 118; *see also* anthropocentrism
creation, xvii, 10, 16–18, 25–26, 34, 38–39, 41, 46, 56, 61–63, 71–72, 91, 99, 115, 117–18, 120–25, 129–30, 132, 134–35,

253

Index

creation (*cont.*)
141–42, 158, 160, 165–70, 172–77, 189, 191–92, 208, 211, 218; *creatio continua*, 173; *creatio ex nihilo*, 173; *see also* ecofeminism

creativity, 16, 24, 53–55, 66, 70, 72, 80–81, 83, 94, 101–2, 106, 112, 130–32, 135, 138, 161–73, 175–77, 185, 188, 194, 195, 200–201, 205, 207–8; concrescent, 53–55; transitional, 53, 55; *see also* process philosophy

Csikszentmihalyi, Mihaly, 163–66, 177

culture: definition, 147; oral, 106–7; *see also* De Waal, Frans

Daly, Mary, xiii–xiv, 5, 11, 20, 25, 32, 114, 196

Darwin, Charles, 47–48, 146, 155–56

Davaney, Sheila Greeve, xiv, 22, 31, 44, 200–201

de Beauvoir, Simone, xiii, 34, 85, 90–91

de Waal, Frans, 147–48, 150–54, 156–57, 159; *see also* culture

death, 18, 35, 40–41, 45, 54, 61, 63, 68, 79, 103, 112, 118, 121–22, 128–31, 137–40, 167, 169–71, 173, 178, 192, 194–97, 199, 201–2, 204, 207, 208, 211, 217–21, 228; *see also* dualism

dipolarity: of God, 18, 27, 66, 71, 75, 77, 188; of humanity, 76; *see also* process philosophy

dualism, 21, 25–26, 35, 40–41, 60–61, 63, 88, 152, 183, 191, 196–97, 201, 203; creator/creature, 25; life/death, 35, 40–41, 68, 129, 194, 202, 228; mind/body, 107, 118–19; nature/culture, 152

Dunfee, Sue, 9, 89

ecofeminism, 26, 60, 62, 66, 71–73, 115, 117, 145, 201–2; theology of, 26, 60, 62, 66, 71–73, 202

embodiment, 7, 27, 32, 37, 90, 96, 100, 103, 107, 110, 112–20, 123–26, 129, 176, 192, 195–96, 200–201, 210, 212, 215; differences, 114; fear of body, 196–197; and love, 27, 110; *see also* dualism

epistemology, 113, 115, 126, 162; attention, 115; feminist, 113, 115, 126

Eros, 16, 27, 96, 97, 102–3, 107, 108, 111; *see also* power: erotic

eschatology, 58, 66, 192, 220; *see also* Christianity

essentialism, 21, 23, 89, 114, 200, 212

evil, problem of, 18, 177, 186–87; *see also* process theology: theodicy of

experience: as a theological source, 5–6, 8, 21, 23, 43, 49, 108, 123, 221, 228; in feminism, 7, 43, 58; as personal, 5, 7

feeling, 15, 17, 24, 38, 49, 51, 54–55, 87, 92, 94, 97, 104, 106–7, 130–31, 151, 166, 185–88, 205–6, 226; *see also* concrescence

femininity, xiii, 5, 9, 11, 21, 25, 26, 31, 34, 43, 63, 74, 80–81, 89–91, 98, 165, 180, 183, 185, 198–202, 210

feminism: black, 20, 24; consciousness, 5, 22, 32; Jewish, 7, 178, 181, 191–93, 202, 204

God: and the world, xvii, 15, 56, 116–21, 123–24, 135, 167–68, 171, 188, 220; as Goddess/God, 195, 200–205, 207, 209, 211–12; as Patriarch, 10, 61, 181, 192; consequent nature, 17, 57, 131, 188; creation and, 10, 18; image of, 154–55, 184, 190–91, 195; initial aim of, 17, 39, 52, 54–59, 66, 135; as Mother, 116, 199; primordial nature, 17–18, 53, 57, 62, 66, 71, 99, 188; self-limitation, 179; subjective presence, 59; *see also* dipolarity, process theology, process philosophy

Goddess/goddess: as God, 11, 60–63, 66, 93, 95–96, 194–212; traditional forms, xv, 19, 28, 207

grace, 83, 93, 95, 108–9, 131, 133, 135–42, 144, 167–68, 170, 174, 176

Greenberg, Irving, 179–80, 182–83, 190

Griffin, David Ray, 14–15, 66, 72, 103–4, 107–8, 184–87, 191–92, 220, 225; *see also* process philosophy

Hartshorne, Charles, xiii, xv, 13, 17, 20–21, 27, 28, 42, 101, 107, 111, 125, 131, 184, 187–88, 194, 197, 200, 203, 211; biography, 13; Whitehead and, 21, 27–28, 111, 188, 197; *see also* omnipotence, process philosophy, process theology

heaven, 18, 91, 130–32, 135, 144, 221; *see also* hell
Hefner, Philip, 158, 173–76; *see also* co-creation
hell, 131–33, 144; *see also* heaven
Hinduism, 206; image of Kali, 206, 207
Holocaust, *see* Shoah
Howell, Nancy R., xv–xvi, xviii, 145, 154, 157–59, 181, 186

immortality, 53–54, 72–73, 88, 130–31, 198, 202, 211, 213, 220–22, 224, 229–30
improvisation, 160–64, 176–77; *see also* jazz
interdependence, xv, xvii, 18, 92, 179, 181, 200

Janeway, Elizabeth, 104–5, 107–9
jazz, 160–61, 163–65, 167–69, 172, 176; *see also* improvisation
Jesus, 48, 57, 62–63, 77, 111–12, 117, 121–24, 127–29, 134, 137–43, 169–72, 174, 176, 226; *see also* Christianity, God, Mary
Jonas, Hans, 184, 187
Judaism, 3, 11, 19, 28, 179–80, 182–83, 189–92, 196, 202, 204; *see also* feminism: Jewish; Shoah

Keller, Catherine, xiv–xv, 44–45, 72, 85, 98–100, 119, 183, 185, 201

mujerista theology (Latin American women), 4, 20, 83, 144
Lubarsky, Sandra B., xv, 11, 178, 184–85, 187, 191–93

Mary (Mother of Jesus), 127, 129, 139
McFague, Sallie, xv, 27, 113, 115, 117, 125–26, 204; *see also* ecofeminism
misogyny, 4, 22, 79; *see also* androgyny
Montuori, Alfonso, 162–63, 165, 176

natural theology, 19, 83, 120–21; *see also* theology of nature
Nelson, Susan L., xv, 9, 13, 74, 82–84, 108
Niebuhr, Reinhold, xiii, 9–10, 74–80, 82–83, 89; *see also* sin: of pride

omnipotence, 13, 27–28, 107, 110, 179–82, 186–87, 190–92, 211; *see also* Hartshorne, Charles

organic model of the world, xv, 113, 115–16, 119, 123
organism, philosophy of, 12–14, 184

panentheism, xv, 17, 119, 123–24, 203–4, 206; *see also* process theology
pantheism, 96, 123, 203
Pederson, Ann M., xv, 160, 175–77
personhood, 27, 61, 69, 81, 154; of chimpanzee, 154; *see also* God: image of
physics, 67; quantum mechanics, xiii, 58, 63; subatomic, 12, 63, 66–68, 71, 73
Plaskow, Judith, 5, 7, 9, 11, 82, 89, 96, 122, 181–82, 194, 196, 198, 210
Plato, 12, 47, 54, 155, 196
postmodernism: science and, 116; womanism and, 213, 227–28
power: coercive, 28; domination, 40, 179, 180, 182–83, 190; erotic, 101–103, 106–7, 110–12; forms of, 182; persuasive, 17, 167, 180, 184, 188, 190, 203; relational, 28, 112, 185–86, 192; *see also* God
praxis, xviii, 21, 24, 26–27
prehension, 15, 54, 56, 185; *see also* process philosophy
primates, 145–47, 149, 152–54, 156, 158; language, 149; *see also* animals, bonobos, chimpanzees
Process Studies, xiv, 14, 22, 44, 46, 170, 201, 213
process philosophy, xiv–xv, xviii, 5, 12–14, 17, 19, 21–28, 31–32, 42–46, 58, 99, 105, 107, 143–44, 157, 179–80, 184, 187, 191–212, 227–28, 230; becoming, 14–17, 38–39, 51, 53–55, 77, 80, 93, 99, 130–31, 158, 185, 191, 213–14, 220, 224, 226; future, 16, 130, 222; metaphysics, 13–14, 16, 23, 27, 43, 136, 144, 189–90; subjective aim, 39; substance as being, 25, 36, 43, 46, 70, 85, 87, 95, 98, 136, 176, 185; *see also* Hartshorne, Charles; Whitehead, Alfred North
process theology, xiii–xviii, 3, 13–14, 17–28, 44, 48, 58, 60, 62, 66, 71, 82–83, 111, 115, 119, 124, 129, 142, 144–45, 167, 186, 192–93, 213, 220, 227–30; relationality, xiii, xv, 21, 25, 27, 43, 45, 48, 50–53, 55–56, 58, 67, 180–83, 187; rhythm of, 40–41; theodicy of, 177, 180, 186–87, 192

255

Index

process-relational theology, *see* process theology
Protestant theology, 82, 128–29, 142, 214

Raboteau, Albert, 214, 216
reflective consciousness, 68, 71–73
resurrection, 128, 130–31, 133–34, 141, 144
Ruether, Rosemary Radford, xiv, 8, 60, 63, 71–73, 181, 196, 202; *see also* ecofeminism
Russell, Helene Tallon, xv–xvi, xviii, 12

Saiving, Valerie, xiii–xiv, 5, 9, 22, 31, 43–45, 82, 89, 201–2
salvation, xiii, 64, 110–12, 131, 143, 154, 169–71, 226, 228; *see also* Christianity
science, theological dialogue with, 22, 27, 204
sexuality, 4, 102, 159, 200, 207; sexual orientation, 4, 26
Shoah (Holocaust), 121, 138, 178–80, 182, 190, 192; theologies of, 28, 178–80, 182, 190; *see also* feminism: Jewish, process theology: theodicy of
sin, 74, 82; chimpanzee, 154; of hiding, 9, 74–81, 83–84, 89; of pride, 9, 74–82, 89; relational view, 83
Soelle, Dorothee, 25, 166–68
Sophia, 199, 205–6
soteriology, 58, 111, 131, 213; redemption, 63, 75, 112, 122, 131–32, 135, 144, 169, 174–75; *see also* Christianity
soul, 26, 55–56, 79, 87, 93, 108, 118, 139, 154–55, 172, 196, 219, 225
spirit theology, 117, 120, 126
Stanford, Craig, 146–51, 153, 156
Suchocki, Marjorie Hewitt, xiv–xvi, xviii, 10, 44, 46, 51, 58–59, 66, 130–33, 142–44, 192, 213, 220–21, 224–25

Teilhard de Chardin, Pierre, 62, 64–66, 71, 115
thealogy, as opposed to theology, 11, 20, 26, 62, 195, 198, 200–202
theological anthropology, 72, 157–58
theology of nature, 62, 120–21; *see also* natural theology
third way, 99–100
transformation: creative, 18, 27, 83, 132, 136, 168–72, 177, 224–26, 229; mutual, 58, 109; *see also* creativity
transmutation, 53, 110
Trinity, 127, 131, 134–37, 141–42, 144

uniqueness: chimpanzee, 157–58; human, 145–46, 152–53, 156–59; *see also* God: image of

Western thought, xiii, 6, 12–13, 35, 40, 65, 85–86, 98, 105, 112–14, 116, 125, 155–56, 167–68, 183, 186, 197, 211, 214–15, 217, 219; objectivity of, 34, 54–55, 105, 113, 153, 222
Whitehead, Alfred North, xiii–xiv, 12–16, 20–21, 23–28, 31–33, 37–48, 53–55, 58–59, 62, 66, 71–72, 99, 101, 108, 111, 125, 131, 158, 165–68, 171–72, 175–76, 184–86, 188, 197, 202, 203, 213, 218, 220, 224–25; and Hartshorne, 21, 111, 188, 197; cosmology of, 25, 28; determinateness of, 53–54; *see also* process philosophy
Wieman, Henry Nelson, 13, 108–109
womanism, xv, 4, 10, 20–21, 23–24, 44–45, 83, 127, 129–31, 139, 142–44, 213, 218, 222, 226–30; *see also* African American, feminism: black

[Editors' Note: The editors acknowledge with great appreciation the work of John Slattery in preparing the index.]

www.ingramcontent.com/pod-product-compliance
Lightning Source LLC
Chambersburg PA
CBHW080546230426
43663CB00015B/2729